WORKBOOK
for the seventh edition of
An Introduction to Positive Economics

WORKBOOK

for the seventh edition of
An Introduction to Positive Economics

Richard G. Lipsey, David Forrest
and Wendy Olsen

WEIDENFELD AND NICOLSON LONDON

© 1989 Richard G. Lipsey, David Forrest and Wendy Olsen

First published 1967
Revised edition 1971
Reprinted 1972
Reprinted 1974
Revised edition 1975
Revised edition 1979
Reprinted 1982
Revised edition 1983
Revised edition 1989

All rights reserved. No part of this publication may be reproduced, stored in a retrieval system, or transmitted, in any form or by any means, electronic, mechanical, photocopying, recording or otherwise without the prior permission of the copyright owners.

Weidenfeld and Nicolson
91 Clapham High St London SW4

ISBN 0 297 79558 9

Text set in 11/13 pt Compugraphic Baskerville,
printed and bound in Great Britain at The Bath Press, Avon

Contents

	Instructions for Use	vi
1	Economic Issues	1
2	Economics as a Social Science	6
3	The Tools of Economics	9
4	Basic Economic Concepts	15
5	Demand, Supply and Price	17
6	Elasticity and Consumers' Surplus	24
7	Applications of Price Theory	32
8	Indifference-Preference Theory	38
9	Uncertainty, Risk and Other Issues	52
10	The Firm, Production and Cost	54
11	Costs and Output	57
12	Perfect Competition	65
13	Monopoly	72
14	Imperfect Competition	80
15	Applications	88
16	Criticisms and Tests	96
17	Factor Incomes in Competitive Markets	98
18	The Income of Labour	109
19	The Income of Capital	112
20	Criticisms and Tests	117
21	The Gains From Trade	119
22	Barriers to Trade	124
23	The Case for the Free Market	127
24	The Case for Government Intervention	131
25	Aims and Objectives of Government Policy	135
26	Macroeconomic Concepts and Variables	137
27	National Income in a Two-Sector Model	143
28	The Consumption Function	151
29	National Income in More Elaborate Models	158
30	Money and the Price Level	167
31	Monetary Equilibrium	174
32	The *IS-LM* Model	182
33	The Aggregate Demand, Aggregate Supply Model	191
34	Inflation	197
35	Employment and Unemployment	204
36	Fluctuations and Growth	209
37	Demand Management 1: Fiscal Policy	218
38	Demand Management 2: Monetary Policy	232
39	Exchange Rates	243
40	Macroeconomic Policy in an Open Economy	247
41	Growth in Less Developed Countries	253
42	Macroeconomic Controversies	255
	Answers	257

Instructions for Use

There is a chapter in the *Workbook* for every chapter in *Positive Economics*. The chapters in the *Workbook* fall into two categories: first, those accompanying analytic chapters of the textbook and, second, those accompanying discursive chapters. The former are in the great majority, and have two sections:

(1) The study guide and questions to be answered in the text;
(2) Questions for essay or class discussion.

The latter have only section (2).

HOW TO ANSWER THE QUESTIONS

Where alternative answers are printed in the text, e.g. raise/lower/indeterminate or T/F (True/False), you should circle the answer you consider correct. Longer multiple-choice questions use letters, rather than numbers, to mark the alternative answers. Again, you should circle the letter of the answer or answers you consider correct. For questions which require a written answer, space appropriate to the length of the correct answer is left in the text.

For the benefit primarily of the student working alone, some parts of the *Workbook* are written in a programmed form, and the student is asked to check each answer after attempting the question. These sections can also be used for class work, in which case some of the instructions, for example 'If you answered Q9 wrongly, re-read pp. 306–11,' can be ignored or replaced by explanation from the class tutor.

Where reference is made in the text to e.g. 'table 3.3' or 'page 87', unless it is stated otherwise the reference is to R. G. Lipsey, *An Introduction to Positive Economics*, seventh edition.

In the graphical questions, if your answer is not exactly the same as the answer given, but is very near, you should first check that the discrepancy does not arise from slight inaccuracy in reading the graph, which is not an important mistake.

CHAPTER 1
Economic Issues

THE SOURCE OF ECONOMIC PROBLEMS

Q1 Scarcity has been termed the basic economic problem. How would you define it?

Scarcity implies the need to make choices between alternative commodities or sets of commodities.

Q2 What is the economist's term for the cost of obtaining one commodity measured in terms of the quantity of other commodities that could have been obtained instead?

Q3 (1) What are the three main divisions into which we classify the resources available for producing different commodities?

(2) Sometimes a fourth category is distinguished. What is it? ⎯⎯⎯⎯⎯⎯⎯⎯

(3) What are these three or four kinds of resources called collectively?

Q4 Lipsey lists seven general questions that confront all societies, capitalist or otherwise. Four of these are questions posed by *microeconomics*. Complete the list of microeconomic problems:

(1) What commodities are being produced and in what quantities?

(2) ⎯⎯⎯⎯⎯⎯⎯⎯⎯⎯⎯⎯⎯⎯⎯⎯⎯⎯⎯⎯⎯⎯⎯⎯⎯⎯⎯

(3) ⎯⎯⎯⎯⎯⎯⎯⎯⎯⎯⎯⎯⎯⎯⎯⎯⎯⎯⎯⎯⎯⎯⎯⎯⎯⎯⎯

(4) How efficient is the society's production and distribution?

Q5 (1) Of the remaining three questions, which one is raised by the possibility that the economy is operating *inside* its production possibility boundary?

(2) What other possibility could explain an economy operating inside its boundary?

Q6 Why is the production possibility boundary drawn downward-sloping?

1

Q7 Refer to Fig. 1, which is a production possibility graph. The economy depicted produces guns and butter: in popular discussion, the choice between these two goods is often used as a way of symbolizing the more realistic dilemma of having to choose between a whole range of military goods on the one hand and a whole range of civilian goods on the other.

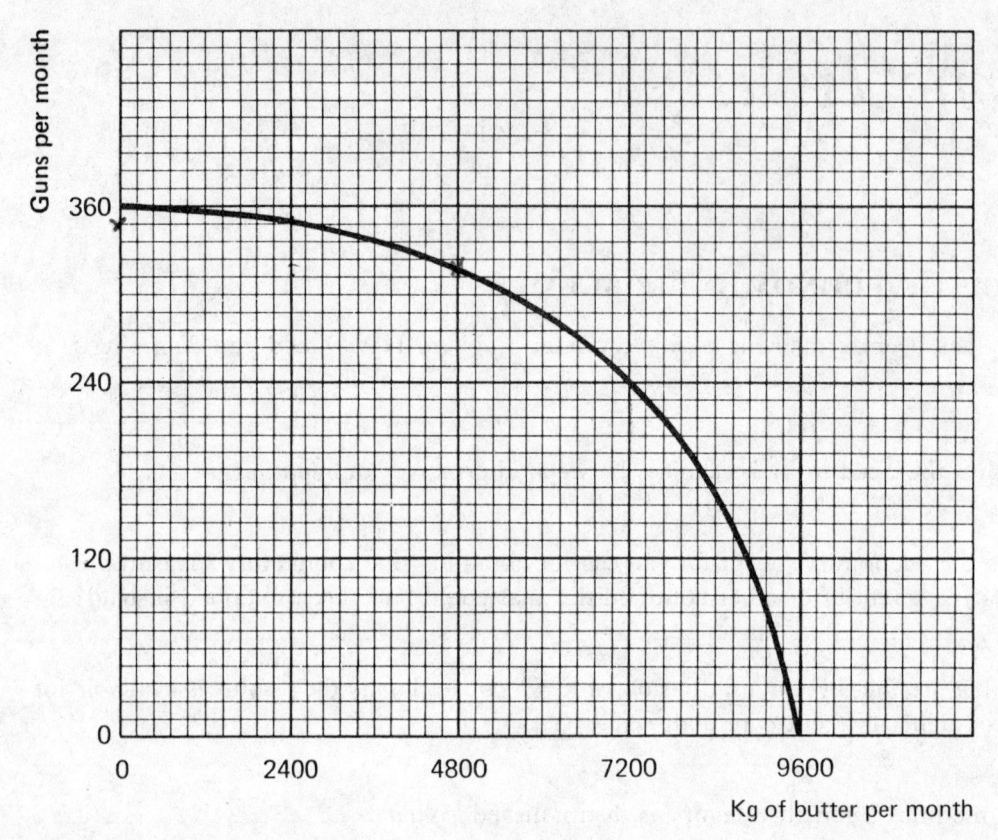

Fig. 1

(1) If 240 guns per month are produced, what is the maximum amount of butter per month that can be produced? _____

(2) If something happens to cause unemployment in this society (where none existed before), what shift would occur in the curve?
_____

(3) How many extra guns per month can we get if we drop from consuming 4,800 kg of butter per month to 2,400 kg of butter per month? _____

(4) What is the *opportunity cost* of the extra guns in (3)? _____

MARKET ECONOMIES

Economics began when society started to organize in the way described by Lipsey on pp. 8–9.

Q8 The following paragraph is a précis of an article in a Sunday colour supplement. Which of the economic concepts listed below are applicable to the community described?

'An ecological community has been started on a Welsh farm by some people who are dissatisfied with many elements of modern economic life. The girls look after the hens and cattle, the men do the heavy work in the fields. They make their own clothes, in part from leather from their own cattle tanned in the nearby town, in a tannery owned by a friend who accepts poultry in payment. The same method is used to pay the thatcher whose skill is sometimes required – other building jobs they can all manage. It's a hard life, but they all say that they enjoy it, although, especially in the spring, they would like more spare time for leisure.'

(a) Surplus and specialization ☐
(b) Money ☐
(c) Factor services ☐
(d) Division of labour ☐
(e) Scarcity ☐

There are three essential concepts introduced in this section:

(1) Consumer
(2) Producer
(3) Market mechanism

The market mechanism is the means by which the behaviour of consumers and producers interacts to determine what is produced, and how it is allocated. This it does by establishing a price for each commodity. Consumers are people who demand goods, producers those who supply them – that consumers are pretty well always producers and vice versa, presents no difficulties here (it will later); we merely choose to separate these two functions for the purpose of our analysis. This sort of abstraction is a part of all theory-building.

A CHANGE IN DEMAND

(Remember, we assume that all factors affecting demand, other than the one in question, remain constant.)

Q9 In 1988, Americans received advice that the consumption of oats (such as in porridge) improved health by lowering cholesterol levels. Porridge suddenly became more popular than it had been relative to wheat-based breakfast cereals. Which of the following would you expect to observe once the market mechanism had reacted to this change?

(a) A higher price of porridge ☐
(b) A lower price of porridge ☐
(c) Higher production of porridge ☐
(d) Lower production of porridge ☐
(e) Higher prices for other breakfast cereals ☐
(f) Lower prices for other breakfast cereals ☐
(g) Higher production of other breakfast cereals ☐
(h) Lower production of other breakfast cereals ☐

A CHANGE IN SUPPLY

Q 10 The cost of producing electricity rises because environmentalists have nuclear power stations closed down. What would you expect to observe once the market mechanism had reacted to this change?

(a) A fall in gas prices ☐
(b) A rise in gas prices ☐
(c) A fall in electricity prices ☐
(d) A rise in electricity prices ☐

In which direction would you expect monthly production to change?

For Electricity: up/down/no change
For gas: up/down/no change

Q 11 Now consider the markets for (i.e. the demand for and supply of) cricket bats and tennis racquets. Assume that many people play both games. Give explanations for the following events, or say why you cannot.

(1) More people prefer tennis this summer, and the price of tennis racquets has gone up.

_____
_____

(2) There are fewer people who now have the patience to make cricket bats, and more tennis is being played this summer.

_____
_____

(3) Cat-gut has become more expensive, so more cricket bats will be sold this summer.

_____
_____

(4) The changes described in (3) will bring about an increase in the supply of cricket bats, so to prevent surpluses accumulating the price will have to fall. So cricket bats will become cheaper, tennis racquets more expensive.

_____

Now check your answers.

If you got (2) or (3) wrong, remember that the initial change in each question will cause the price to change and this change in price will induce further reaction on the part of consumers and producers.

If you got (4) wrong, remember that an increased supply of a commodity may be *caused* by an increase in demand and therefore price, or *may cause* a decrease in price in order to avoid unsold stocks – but not both!

Q 12 A decrease in the price of a good, accompanied by a larger sale of that good, might mean:

(a) Demand has increased, so people have bought more.
(b) Supply has increased, so the price has had to drop.
(c) An increase in demand has caused an increase in supply and a subsequent drop in price.

Check your answer. It is essential that you should understand this, and if you are still worried you ought to re-read Lipsey Chapter 1 from the heading 'How Market Economies Work' to the end.

Remember, an increase in the quantity sold may be caused by a rise in demand, in which case prices will rise as well. Equally, it may be caused by an increase in the quantity producers wish to sell at each price, without there being any change in consumers' tastes, in which case prices must fall.

QUESTIONS FOR DISCUSSION

1 Why might a government which comes to power at a time of unemployment find greater political acceptance for an increase in military expenditure than one which comes to power at a time when all the resources of society are fully employed?

2 Suppose you go to university or polytechnic to study economics. Carefully assess what is the *opportunity cost* to you of that choice. How would the opportunity cost change if students were given repayable loans rather than unconditional grants?

3 The downward-sloping production possibility boundary is conventionally drawn as bow-shaped rather than as a straight line. Can you interpret the meaning of a bow shape in terms of what happens to opportunity cost as production of a good is increased? Would it be plausible to draw the boundary as a straight line instead?

4 In December 1988 a highly publicized report linked the consumption of eggs with the incidence of food poisoning symptoms. Many people decided that breakfast cereals would be better for breakfast than eggs. Trace carefully what would happen in the markets for eggs and breakfast cereals (both immediately and subsequently) given such a change in demand conditions. (Assume that the government makes no attempt to influence the outcomes: the possibility of government intervention is taken up in later chapters.)

5 'Firms decide how much should be produced of each commodity. Only a minority of citizens own firms. Therefore, allocating resources by the market system is undemocratic.' Comment on the view expressed.

6 Under the pre-1989 system of rent controls in Britain, local committees were told by the relevant Act of Parliament to fix rents in their district at a level that would prevail in the absence of scarcity. Explain why economists found this provision puzzling and hard to apply in practice.

CHAPTER 2
Economics as a Social Science

POSITIVE AND NORMATIVE STATEMENTS

In this important section, Lipsey stresses the importance of distinguishing between different categories of statement – primarily the *positive* statement, the *normative* statement, and the *analytic* statement. Examples of these three types are:

(a) Tax cuts for businesses raise the employment level of people from poor families.
(b) Tax policy should have as its goal improving the wellbeing of the poor.
(c) Raising employment levels is one way of improving the wellbeing of the poor.

Some statements may contain elements of more than one of these categories. Consider:

(d) In the forthcoming budget, we recommend that the Chancellor cut taxes on businesses in order to improve the wellbeing of the poor.

Within this proposition, there is the positive (and testable) statement that cutting taxes for businesses helps the poor. The view that this is more effective than other policies could also be testable; but another proposition embedded in the sentence, that the wellbeing of the poor should be a consideration in government policy, is clearly a normative one.

Q1 Here are five statements. Which are *positive*, which are *normative*, which are *analytic*, and which contain elements both of the *positive* and the *normative*?

(1) In Britain, ethnic Asians have a higher mean I.Q. than whites but their mean examination grades are lower. P/N/A/P + N

(2) The method of allocating university places should be designed solely to ensure that they are filled by the most intelligent. P/N/A/P + N

(3) If the evidence on mean I.Q.s and examination performance is correct and if the government's goal is to ensure that university places go to the most intelligent, lower examination grades should be required of Asians. P/N/A/P + N

(4) Mean incomes in the Asian community would be higher if more Asians went to University. P/N/A/P + N

(5) Taking into account the relative I.Q. levels of Asians and whites, more university places than now should be allocated to Asians. P/N/A/P + N

Check your answers so far. Do not be discouraged if you need more practice because the differences between the statements are sometimes subtle. E.g., statement (3) is *analytic* because the policy recommended follows logically if the two conditions noted in fact hold true; (5) has both *positive* and *normative* elements because it not only relies on a testable hypothesis about I.Q. levels but also goes on to imply something about what education policy goals ought to be.

In case you need more practice, here are four more statements. You may care to imagine them being made in France in 1789.

 (6) Peasants have lower living standards than the rest of the population. P/N/A/P + N

 (7) Peasants deserve higher living standards. P/N/A/P + N

 (8) If peasants have high living standards, they don't join revolutions. P/N/A/P + N

 (9) Peasants should be allowed higher living standards to prevent revolution. P/N/A/P + N

STOCKS VERSUS FLOWS

Lipsey explains the distinction on pp. 22–23.

Q2 If you were measuring each of the following, indicate where you would be measuring a stock and where a flow.

 (1) The number of houses in Northampton   stock/flow

 (2) The number of houses sold in Northampton   stock/flow

 (3) The rent of a typical house in Northampton   stock/flow

 (4) Michael Jackson's royalties from record sales   stock/flow

 (5) The value of Michael Jackson's shares in companies   stock/flow

 (6) The dividend income Michael Jackson has from his shares in companies   stock/flow

EXOGENOUS VERSUS ENDOGENOUS VARIABLES

Lipsey explains the distinction on p. 22.

Q3 (1) An economist hypothesizes that the price of fish at Grimsby on any day depends partly on sea conditions in the North Sea on the previous seven days. Sea conditions in the North Sea are an exogenous/endogenous variable.

 (2) A meteorologist hypothesizes that wind speeds in the North Sea depend partly on how far away the centre of the nearest area of low pressure is. Wind speeds in the North Sea are an exogenous/endogenous variable.

 (3) A marine scientist proposes that the height of waves in the North Sea depends partly on wind speeds in the North Sea. Wind speeds in the North Sea are an exogenous/endogenous variable.

QUESTIONS FOR DISCUSSION

1 Previous to 1988, entitlement to housing benefit in Britain was based on how well-off a tenant was, as judged by a flow measure (weekly income). From 1988, entitlement was determined by a combination of the same flow measure but also a stock measure of wellbeing (accumulated savings). Pensioners' organizations described the change as 'unfair' because it appeared to penalize those who had been thrifty.

 Is 'fairness' a positive or normative concept?

2 In eighteenth-century England, some taxes had liability based on stock measures (e.g. the number of windows in a house) and some had liability based on flow measures (e.g. the quantity of brandy imported). List some examples of modern taxes classified according to this distinction.

3 Read the correspondence page of a popular daily newspaper. Is there a single letter which does not contain a normative element?

4 'If the scientist finds that the issue is framed in such terms that it is impossible to gather evidence for or against it, he will then try to reword it, so that it can be answered by an appeal to the evidence.' How might you begin to do this in the case of the following set of assertions?

'British justice is the best in the world.'
'More guilty people are given proper punishment and more innocent ones freed in Britain than anywhere else.'
'British justice doesn't provide enough deterrence.'

CHAPTER 3
The Tools of Economics

FUNCTIONAL RELATIONSHIPS

On p. 28, Lipsey makes the point that statements about functional relations can be in verbal, algebraic or graphical form. None of these is inherently superior, since they just employ different languages to describe the same thing. However, in economics, we often find it more straightforward to draw conclusions when a relationship is pictured in a graph or written in the form of an equation (this is illustrated by Lipsey's manipulation of the household consumption function on pp. 30–31). For this reason, the textbook asks you to become comfortable with the idea of expressing ideas using simple graphs or school-level algebra.

Q1 Suppose that British Rail has experimented with different fare levels for the route from Plymouth to London. On the basis of the experience, the B.R. statistician tells you that 'at £80 return, no one would travel at all; every £1 reduction from that level would raise sales by 20 extra return tickets per day'.

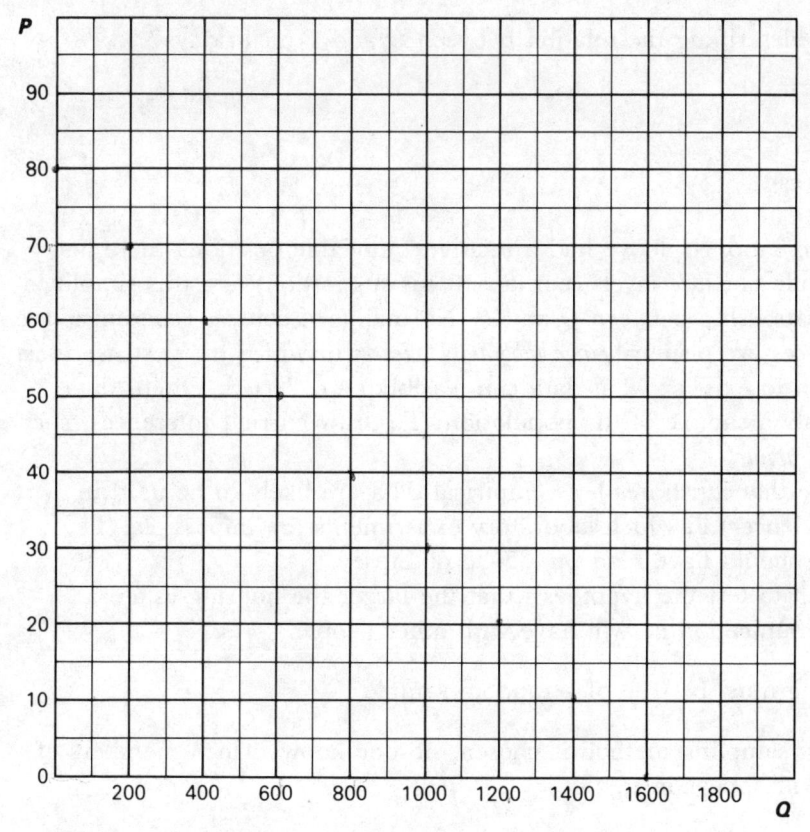

Fig. 1

The statistician makes a (verbal) hypothesis that there is a *negative* relation between the number (or quantity) of return tickets people choose to buy (Q) and the price in pounds at which the tickets are offered (P). He not only makes a general proposition that $Q = f(P)$; he also makes explicit the form of relationship he believes exists. Draw on to Fig. 1 a graph which expresses his estimate of the relation between Q and P (measure Q on the horizontal axis and P on the vertical).

Q2   Assuming that the relation specified is accepted without qualification, how many return journeys per day would be predicted if the fare was zero? _____

Q3   It is possible to find a precise algebraic equation that represents the relationship. It will be of the form $Q = a - bP$, where a and b are some numbers. Find what a and b are. Hint: if $P = 0$, $Q = a$. Your answer to Q2 therefore gives you a. It is not too difficult then to find b.

If you found Q3 too difficult, look up the answer from the back of the book. Then, trying different values for P, write down what is the corresponding predicted value for Q. Check the answer against what your graph on Fig. 1 tells you. Do this for as long as is necessary to convince yourself that the equation and the graph convey exactly the same set of information. Even if you did not find the correct answer to the question, it is important to understand that equations are nothing more than concise ways of conveying sets of information.

Q4   There is now new information given. The statistician reveals that ticket sales seem to depend not only on price (P) but also on time of week (T). He now believes that Q is some function of P and T. In particular, he says that if the time of week is Friday, 100 more people than predicted before are likely to travel at any given price. Draw a new line on Fig. 1 to represent the relation between Q and P on Fridays.

Q5   What is the equation describing the relation between Q and P on Fridays?
$Q =$ _____

STATISTICAL TESTING

The British Rail statistician mentioned above had a relatively enviable position: there had been experimentation with different fare levels (perhaps at his suggestion) and this simplified the task of estimating the relationship between Q and P. Normally, of course, economists are not so fortunate: social sciences are primarily *non-laboratory sciences* in which the best use must be made of what data happen to exist or what data can feasibly be collected. Often, data collected has to pertain to only a sample of the population. To draw current inferences, such a sample has to be a *random sample*.

We now follow an example that illustrates how empirical data are likely to be used in subjects (such as the social sciences) in which laboratory experiments are impossible. To appreciate this example, you should have read pp. 35–38 of Lipsey.

Let us assume that we wish to test the hypothesis that the larger the housing estate a person lives in, the less communication he will have with other people.

Q6   Which of the following must be true of a random sample?

   (a) Before the actual sampling method is chosen, no one knows which members of the population will appear in it.

(b) Every member of the population has an equal chance of being chosen.

☐

(c) A random sample is an accurate microcosm of the population.

☐

Q7   If you know the exact characteristics of the population, can you deduce the exact characteristics of a random sample of that population? Yes/No

Check your answer. If you were wrong, do Q8. If not, carry on with Q9.

Q8   Can we deduce whether the method by which a sample has been taken was random by inspecting the sample? Yes/No

The point of all this is that the randomness of a sample has to do with the method by which the sample is chosen. Just seeing what the sample looks like does not tell us about this. Of course, if we happen to know what the population is like, and we know that the sample is in fact very unrepresentative, then we may *suspect* that our selection procedure was not random, especially if, when the same procedure is used to select other samples, they are also similarly unrepresentative.

Q9   Why (in this study of size of housing estate and communication with others) would you reject the selection method of sticking pins in a telephone directory?

_____

_____

We decide on a suitable method, and pick out our sample. We are aware of the size of the housing estate the members of our sample live on, and the number of their acquaintances.

(For the purposes of this illustrative example we will take the unrealistically small sample size of 12: in a research project we would require a much larger sample before we would consider generalizing on the basis of the results.)

We then tabulate our information: for ease of reference, we arbitrarily label the persons sampled from A to L.

Individual	Size of estate (in no. of houses)	No. of acquaintances
A	30	50
B	100	32
C	100	28
D	72	32
E	65	34
F	90	17
G	60	42
H	82	35
I	38	44
J	50	43
K	137	17
L	65	55

We now express the information in a scatter diagram. Label the axes, and plot the points in Fig. 2.

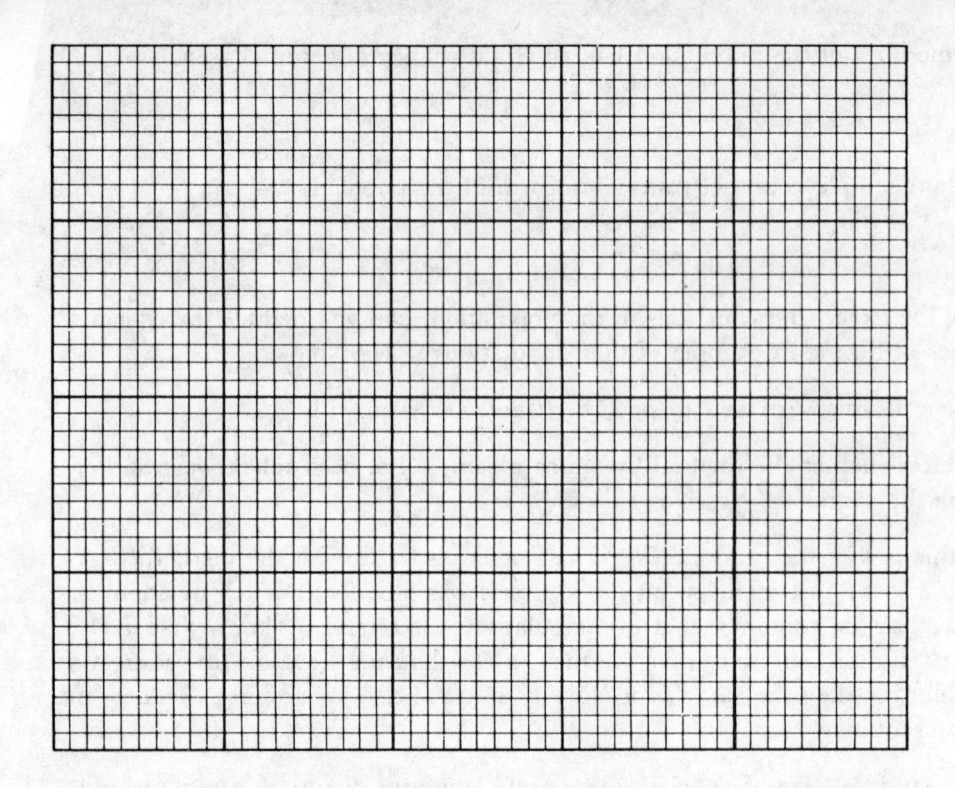

Fig. 2

Q 10 Why can you be sure that, assuming that your information is accurate, the number of one's acquaintances is not completely explained by the size of one's housing estate?

_____

_____

We formulate the second hypothesis, therefore, that the number of one's acquaintances also depends on the number of gardens which one's own back garden joins. We return to our sample, and find the following data.

Individual	No. of neighbouring gardens	Individual	No. of neighbouring gardens
A	3	G	3
B	3	H	3
C	2	I	3
D	3	J	2
E	2	K	3
F	1	L	4

As we had hoped, we see that the number of gardens backed on by individual C is less than those backed on by individual B; that the number is higher than average for L (who has the highest number of acquaintances) and lower than average for F (who has the lowest number of acquaintances). We can classify these data as in Table 3.2, p. 38 of Lipsey.

Q 11   Complete this table.
Average number of acquaintances known, classified by estate-size and number of neighbouring gardens

		No. of gardens			
		1	2	3	4
	0—40				
Estate Size	41—80				
	81—120				
	121—140				

Q 12   Read down column 3, and interpret the information verbally.

Q 13   Now do the same, reading across row 3.

   This is really as far as we can go without statistical techniques. If we used multiple regression analysis we could find out what would be the likely effect of a change in the number of back-gardens, keeping estate-size constant, or vice versa. (By the use of various results and assumptions we can also form a measure of the reliance which we can place upon the representativeness of our sample.)
   Statistical methods can be very useful indeed. But, like most techniques, they have limitations. For example, no matter how close the relationships found here seem to be, it can never conclusively *prove* a hypothesis. We can only establish with what probability the observations are consistent with given hypotheses (see Lipsey, pp. 38–40).

QUESTIONS FOR DISCUSSION

1   The chief officer of a major British police force has presented statistics which appear to show that the number of crimes committed per person by black youths is very much higher than the corresponding figure for white youths. Here are two (of many) possible interpretations.

   (a)   Black people are inherently less respectful of the law than white people.
   (b)   Black youths in Britain happen to come from mainly low-income backgrounds. Tendencies to crime depend heavily on family background in terms of income; race is not *of itself* relevant to explaining crime figures.

   Write down these two interpretations using the functional notation learned in this chapter (and indicating what your symbols mean). Is it possible to decide which of the interpretations is the more accurate? What information would you need to collect and what tools of analysis would be used?

2   'All this about smoking being bad for you is nonsense. All my aunts and uncles smoked but every one lived to a ripe old age.' Explain in the clearest language you can what is wrong with the speaker's reasoning.

3   You are asked to test the hypothesis that the first-term economics course grades of a polytechnic student depend on how many hours per week is spent reading the textbook. You are to use a sample interviewed during the second term. Why would it be wrong to gather your sample by knocking on every tenth door in your hall of residence? How should you choose your sample? What questions would you put to its members?

Appendix to Chapter 3

Q1 Take an equation, $Y = 10 + 2X$. Use the same steps as Lipsey uses in section (5), pp. 44–45, to demonstrate that when X changes by n units, Y will change by $2n$ units.

Q2 This question should only be attempted after close study of Lipsey, pp. 45–49. The total ticket revenue (in pounds per day) on a railway is given by the equation $TR = 80q - 1/20q^2$, where q is tickets sold per day. By how much does revenue per day change if the price is lowered so $q = 420$ instead of $q = 400$?
£ _____ .

Note: you could do this by first substituting into the TR equation for $q = 400$; then substituting for $q = 420$; and then performing the subtraction. However, if you know the calculus, it is a little easier to use the marginal revenue curve. Its equation is $MR = $ _____. This gives you a *general formula* for all such calculations. It tells you the change in TR when q changes by 1 unit. In *this* example, $\Delta q = 20$. Therefore, here you find MR for $q = 410$ (the midpoint between the two values of q); *then* you multiply by 20 to find ΔTR.

CHAPTER 4
Basic Economic Concepts

DECISION-TAKERS

We distinguish three main sets of actors on the economic stage: *households, firms* and the *central authorities*.

Q1   Wherever a person, group or institution is taking a decision on how much to consume of one or more commodities, it is acting as a household/firm.

Q2   What is the minimum number of persons in a household? _____

Q3   Wherever a person, group or institution is taking a decision about the production and sale of one or more commodities, it is acting as a household/firm.

Q4   Could Robinson Crusoe be a firm? Yes/No

Q5   We assume that households seek to maximize _____ and firms seek to maximize _____.

Q6   Households and firms are intimately linked in the economic system: households are the main owners of _____ of which _____ are the main purchasers.

Q7   Which of the following fall into the category of 'central authorities'?
(a) the authors of this Workbook, (b) the Bank of England, (c) the Midland Bank, (d) the Government of the United Kingdom, (e) Clwyd County Council.

MARKETS

Q8   Define a market.
_____
_____

Q9   What geographical area is likely to be covered by the market for Lancashire evening papers? _____

Q10   What geographical area is likely to be covered by the market for oil?
_____

Q11   What geographical area is likely to be covered by the market for French wine?
_____

Q12   What factors may separate the markets for French wine and Australian wine?
_____
_____

15

Q 13   In a goods market, _____ are usually the sellers, buyers can be _____. In a factor market, sellers are usually _____ and buyers are usually _____.

Q 14   What do we call a market where there is a large number of buyers and sellers such that no one buyer or seller has an appreciable influence on price? Free/controlled/competitive/open.

Q 15   An economy in which the decisions that determine the pattern of production and consumption are largely under the control of firms and households is called a _____ economy.

Q 16   British Gas is in the public/private sector.

Q 17   British Gas is in the market/non-market sector.

Q 18   The Victoria and Albert Museum is in the public/private sector. When it began to charge admission fees, it moved from being wholly in the public/private/market/non-market sector to being partly in the private/market sector.

MICROECONOMICS AND MACROECONOMICS

Q 19   'The UK price level rose by 7% last year.'
'Beer prices could fall by 7% as a result of more competition in brewing.'
   The first of these two news reports falls under the heading of microeconomics/macroeconomics; the second falls under the heading of microeconomics/macroeconomics.

Q 20   The main income flow from firms to households is payment for _____. The main income flow from households to firms is payment for _____.

Q 21   A business tax levied on firms is an addition to/leakage from the circular flow of income.

QUESTIONS FOR DISCUSSION

1   A declared policy goal of the European Community is that by 1992 there should be a 'single European market'. Is this likely to mean that the market for every individual commodity will cover the whole of the Community area? If not, why not?

2   In 1989, a British government which was associated with support for the idea of a free-market economy promised legislation to prohibit any individual from selling his or her kidney for transplant purposes. Can we conclude that the government did not really support the idea of free markets?

3   Why are households forced to send their children to school until age 16? What arguments would you mention for and against a new system in which all schools would become private but parents would receive a voucher to spend at the school of their choice?

4   Heathrow and Gatwick Airports changed in 1987 from being in the public sector to being owned by private-sector firms. Do you think that any differences result when such a change occurs?

CHAPTER 5

Demand, Supply and Price

DEMAND

Q1 The total *quantity demanded* in any market (i.e. the amount per period that all households together wish to buy) depends on these factors:

(1) the price of the commodity being sold

(2)

(3) total household income

(4) the distribution of income among households

(5) tastes

Fill in the blank.

Q2 The *demand curve* is drawn on the assumption that we hold constant all of the above factors except one. Which one? _____

Q3 The market demand curve is derived from the demand curves of individual households by vertical/horizontal summation.

Let us now consider the demand curve for peas. This shows what amount of peas all households together would wish to buy at each possible price, *ceteris paribus*.

Q4 What does *ceteris paribus* mean here? _____

Q5 To draw the graph, we would need to decide which *units to use*. We could not simply decide on, e.g., kilos and pence. We would have to add two words after both 'kilos' and 'pence'. Given an example of such words _____ and _____.

Now refer to Fig. 1. Like most such constructions, this demand curve (for peas) is drawn to be *continuous*. This is a convenient approximation: we know, in fact, that price is unlikely to be quoted to the nearest penny, but for the sake of a straightforward picture, we show a curve which gives a quantity for *every* price.

Q6 At what price per ton will quantity demanded be 10 tons per week? _____

Q7 What price per ton would be needed for purchases to be restricted to 14 tons per week? _____

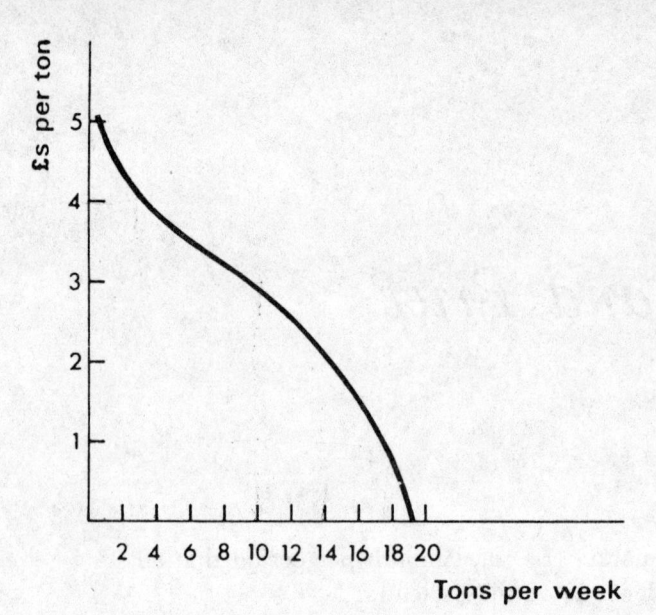

Fig. 1

Q8 If the price were £4 per ton, how much would households wish to buy (per week)? _____

Q9 How much (in tons per week) would households choose to buy at a price of £1 per ton? _____

Q10 Sketch on Fig. 1 the new demand curve if quantity demanded is reduced by 4 tons per week at each and every possible price.

Q11 If peas are a normal good, which (one or more) of the following could cause such a *leftward shift* in the demand curve?

(a) a rise in the price of peas
(b) a rise in the price of sprouts
(c) a fall in the price of peas
(d) a fall in the price of sprouts
(e) a rise in total incomes
(f) a fall in total incomes.

Q12 A normal good is defined as one where the slope of the demand curve is negative. True/False

Q13 Define an inferior good. _____

Q14 Complete this sentence.
It would be very implausible to suggest that all goods were inferior because it would imply that, as household incomes increased, _____

Q15 How will the market demand curve of a 'normal' good shift if

(1) The price of a substitute falls? right/*left*/not/indeterminate

(2) Population rises? *right*/left/not/indeterminate

(3) Tastes shift away from the commodity? right/*left*/not/indeterminate

(4) The prices of complements fall? right/left/not/indeterminate

(5) The distribution of income becomes more even? right/left/not/indeterminate

(6) National income rises? right/left/not/indeterminate

(7) Complements become more expensive? right/left/not/indeterminate

(8) Substitutes become more expensive? right/left/not/indeterminate

Q 16 Which one of these answers (to Q 15) would change if we talked about an 'inferior' good instead? _____

Q 17 Consider the market for jeans. Which of the following would result in a shift in the demand curve, and which in a movement along it?

(1) Foreign imports of jeans are banned. Shift/movement along

(2) The percentage of the population under age 30 falls. Shift/movement along

(3) Textile workers' wages fall after minimum wage regulations are abolished. Shift/movement along

(4) State schools are prohibited from enforcing dress codes on pupils. Shift/movement along

SUPPLY

Q 18 The total *quantity supplied* in any market (i.e. the amount per period that all firms together wish to sell) depends on these principal factors:

(1) the price of the commodity being sold

(2) P ops

(3) the goals of producing firms

(4) the state of technology

Fill in the blank.

The *supply curve* is drawn on the assumption that we hold constant all of the above factors except the price of the commodity itself. Fig. 2 depicts the supply curve of metal girders: for each possible price, it shows how many miles of metal girders all producing firms together would wish to sell per month. It so happens that the form of this particular supply curve is *linear* (i.e. it is a straight line).

Q 19 What quantity of metal girders (in miles per month) would firms wish to sell at a price of £375 per mile? _____

Q 20 What price (in pounds per mile) would have to be reached for 1,900 miles of girders to be offered for sale each month? _____

Q 21 Which way would this curve shift as a result of:

(1) a rise in the cost of iron ore? left/right/not at all

(2) a fall in the price of metal girders? left/right/not at all

(3) a house-building boom that causes builders to order more girders? left/right/not at all

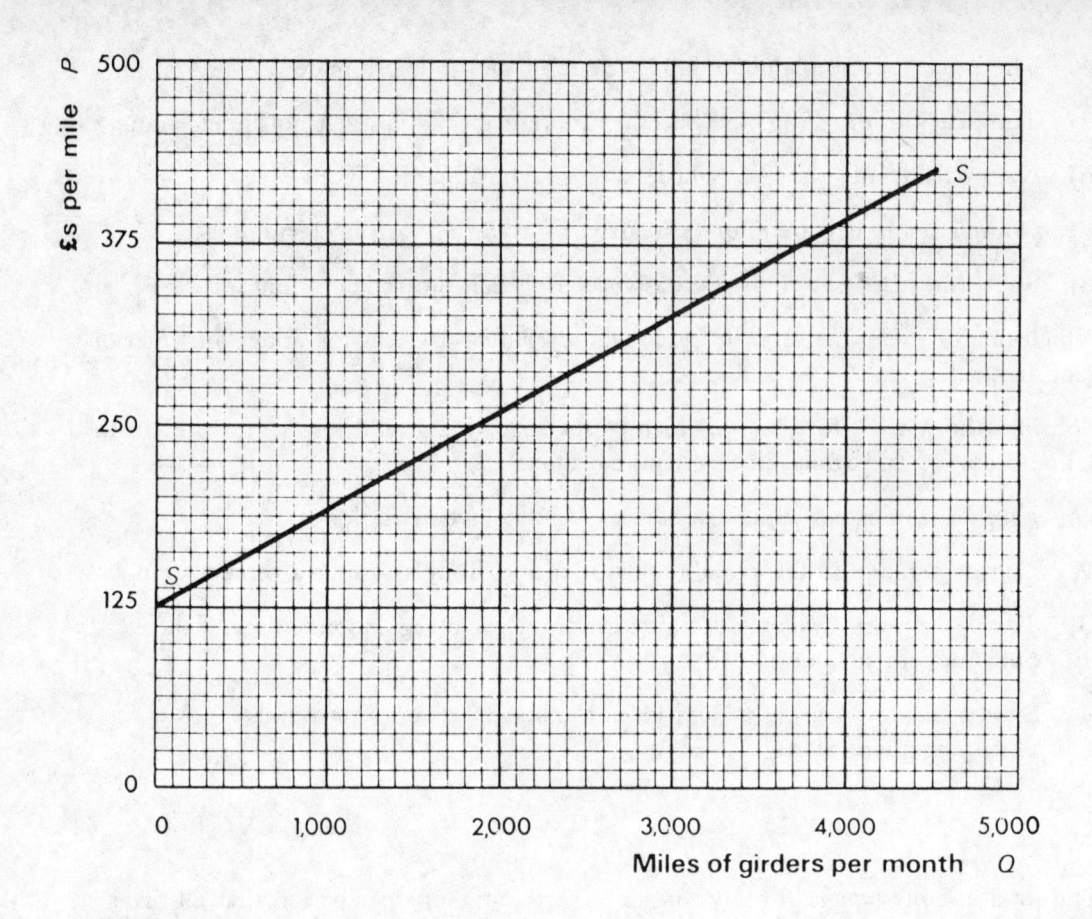

Fig. 2

If you got (2) wrong, you are still confused between *movements along* the curve and *shifts* of the whole curve. A fall in the price of metal girders could be *caused by* a shift of the supply curve but *does not bring about* such a shift. This distinction is vital to the analysis. So also is the conceptual distinction between demand and supply: (3) refers to something that would shift the demand curve, not the supply curve.

Q 22 A shift to the right in the supply curve would indicate that

(a) a higher price is necessary to call forth any given quantity supplied than before the shift.
(b) less will be supplied at each possible market price.
(c) the willingness of the producers to supply the commodity has diminished.
(d) more will be supplied at any given market price.
(e) none of the above answers is correct.

THE DETERMINATION OF PRICE

In the first part of this chapter we expressed demand as a function of price, holding constant all the other factors which influence demand, and supply also as a function of price, holding constant all the other factors which influence supply.

For any given value of all the other factors (variables) that influence demand and supply, therefore, we can show on one diagram the various amounts supplied and demanded at any price.

Table 1 shows the market demand and supply schedules for a commodity.

TABLE 1

Price (£s per ton)	Quantity demanded (tons per year)	Price (£ per ton)	Quantity supplied (tons per year)
5	0	1	0
4.50	2.25	1.50	0
4	3.35	2	0
3.50	4	2.50	1.6
3	4.75	3	3
2.50	5	3.50	4
2	5.5	4	4.75
1.50	5.75	4.50	5.5
1	6	5	6.25
0.50	6.25	5.50	6.9
0.00	6.5	6	7.7

Plot the schedules of Table 1 on to Fig. 3. Choose your own scales for the axes.

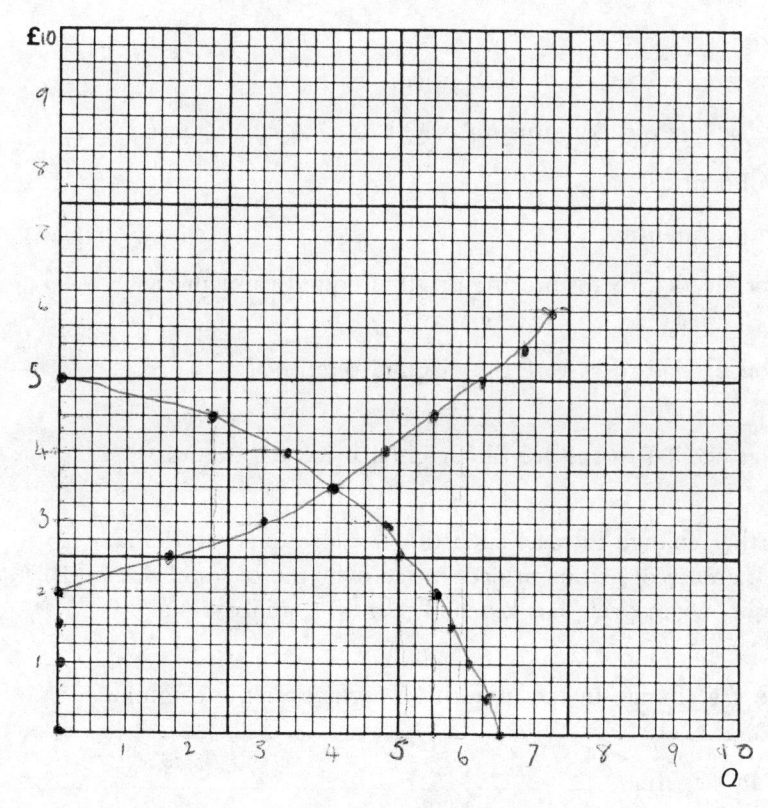

Fig. 3

Q23 Define equilibrium price. _____

Q24 What is the equilibrium price in our example? _____

Q25 What is the equilibrium quantity? _____

So far we have no theory to explain why the equilibrium price should prevail – why the market mechanism works, in fact. We will first introduce the concepts of *excess demand* and *excess supply*.

21

Excess demand is the difference between quantity demanded (q^d) and quantity supplied (q^s), i.e. excess demand = $q^d - q^s$.

Excess supply is merely $q^s - q^d$ and hence is just excess demand with the sign reversed.

Often people talk about excess demand when $q^d > q^s$ and excess supply when $q^s > q^d$. But it is also acceptable to speak only of excess demand, allowing it to be positive when $q^d > q^s$ and negative when $q^d < q^s$.

Q 26 To make a statement about the amount of excess demand, is it necessary to mention a price? Yes/No

Q 27 When there is negative excess supply, there is upward/downward pressure on price.

Q 28 When there is positive excess supply, there is upward/downward pressure on price.

Q 29 From Fig. 3, estimate the excess demand at:

  (1) £2 per ton _____

  (2) £3 per ton _____

  (3) £4 per ton _____

  (4) £5 per ton _____

Assume now that two extra tons are demanded at each price.

Q 30 What is the excess demand at the old equilibrium price? _____

Q 31 Estimate the new equilibrium price. _____

Q 32 Estimate the new equilibrium quantity. _____

Q 33 What supply shift would be needed to restore the original equilibrium price? right/left/impossible

Q 34 What supply shift would be needed to restore the original quantity? right/left/impossible

Q 35 What supply shift would be needed to restore the original price *and* quantity? right/left/impossible

Q 36 Assume that there is a further change in taste such that 2 more tons are demanded at each price (making an increase of 4 tons at each price over the original demand). What is the quantity bought, when price has reached its new equilibrium? _____

Q 37 What, therefore, would be the change in the quantity bought over the original equilibrium? _____

Q 38 Why is the change less than 4? _____

Q 39 Consider the market for fish, in particular the effects of each of the following changes.

  (1) To avoid depletion of fish populations, Britain signs an agreement under which no fishing will occur in certain sections of the North Sea for a year. The demand/supply curve will shift left/right, and there will be a movement along the demand/supply curve to a higher/lower price and a higher/lower quantity.

  (2) Foot and mouth disease in cattle pushes up the price of meat. The *fish* demand/supply curve will shift left/right, and there will be a movement along the demand/supply curve to a higher/lower price and a higher/lower quantity.

(3) Income-tax rates on households are substantially reduced. *If* fish were an inferior good, the demand/supply curve would shift to the left/right and there would be a movement along the demand/supply curve to a higher/lower price and a higher/lower quantity.

(4) *Simultaneously*, two things happen. A report on the health benefits of consumption shifts preferences in favour of fish; and there is a wage increase for trawlermen. There will be a rise/fall/indeterminate change in the price of fish and a rise/fall/indeterminate change in the quantity of fish sold.

Q 40   Between two years, the average of all prices in an economy rose by 20%: this was the *inflation rate*. Rail fares, however, rose by more than the rate of inflation: they increased by 50%. What was the percentage increase in the relative price of rail fares? _____

QUESTIONS FOR DISCUSSION

1 The bus industry in Britain has been subject to long-term decline: the number of passenger-miles per annum has decreased steadily since 1945. One view is that this is explained by bus travel being an inferior good. Another possibility is that rising prices have deterred potential passengers. Comment on whether these explanations contradict each other or whether each has a contribution to make to understanding the trend in the industry.

2 How do you reconcile the hypothesis that the quantity demanded varies inversely with the price, with the statement that a rise in demand will lead to a rise in price?

3 'Wine is a normal good.'
'Mean incomes in France are much lower than in the USA.'
'Americans must drink more wine per person per year than Frenchmen.'
Why does the third statement not follow from the first two?

4 For British and EC students, there is no tuition fee charged for economics degrees at UK universities. However, the total number of places has been (indirectly) fixed by central educational policies and these have had to be rationed by a 'price' set in terms of how many A-Level points (grade A = 5 points, grade B = 4, etc.) students require to secure admission to a typical course. Illustrate this situation using a supply-demand diagram. How would entry standards be affected by (i) a fall in the number of 18-year-olds, (ii) a rise in the wages of economics graduates relative to other graduates, and (iii) the replacement of a student grant by a student loan system? On the loans issue, given that the (A-Level grades) admission price will change as well as the financial arrangements, do you think there would be a rise or fall in the proportion of students from low-income backgrounds?

CHAPTER 6
Elasticity and Consumers' Surplus

ELASTICITY

Suppose an airline is thinking of buying a new plane which would double the number of seats available each day between two cities. In deciding whether to make the purchase, the company will wish to estimate the fare reduction that would be required to sell the extra seats. In other words, it will need to know how responsive quantity demanded will be to changes in price.

Take now the rental housing market. New legislation in 1989 allowed the typical price per week to rise above its previous (controlled) level. The government was hoping thereby to bring about a rise in the available number of rental houses. The success of the policy will depend on how responsive quantity supplied is to changes in price.

These are just two illustrations of circumstances in which economists would be interested in the responsiveness of quantities demanded or supplied to price changes. So often do we encounter these sorts of issues that we have a special terminology with which to describe such responsiveness: this terminology is that of *elasticities*.

We could measure responsiveness by the ratio of the actual change in quantity (e.g. an increase of 1,000 per week) to the actual change in price (e.g. a drop of 4p per unit). However, it is more useful to compare *proportional* changes.

'The percentage change in x brought about by a percentage change in y' defines the term 'y-elasticity of x'.

In the first paragraph we were referring to the 'price elasticity of demand'; in the second to the 'price elasticity of supply'. We could also have such measures as the 'income elasticity of demand', 'the population elasticity of demand', 'the factor-cost elasticity of supply', and so on.

Price elasticity of demand is defined as the percentage change in quantity demanded divided by the percentage change in price that brought it about. For a negatively sloped demand curve, this will always be a negative number. However, in this one particular (but most common) type of elasticity measure, we often just drop the minus sign and talk about absolute values only. In this section of the Workbook, we do just this and ignore the sign when referring to price elasticity of demand.

Q1   Define income elasticity of demand _____

_____

If you were wrong, read the explanation above and then do Q2.

Q2   Define price elasticity of supply _____

_____

Q3   From which of the following sets of information can you deduce the elasticity of either demand or supply for the given commodities over the relevant range? Where you can make the deduction, what value is the particular elasticity?

(1) At a total level of production of 100 gallons per day, a change in price of 5p per pint will produce a change in quantity demanded of 1 gallon per day.

(2) An increase in price from 9p to 11p will cause the amount offered by suppliers to double. _____

(3) An extra 4p per lb will be needed to reduce the demand for butter at 40p per lb by 30 cwt per day. _____

(4) At a price of £11 per book, the publisher needs to drop his price by £2 to sell one tenth as many again. _____

Adopt in Q3 and from now on, the convention that a percentage change in price is to be measured by dividing the change in price by the *average* of the old and new prices. A similar convention should be applied on the quantity side. The advantage of defining percentage changes in this particular way is discussed on p. 81 of Lipsey.

If you had difficulty with Q3, you are probably not adopting a sufficiently systematic approach. Although it may seem a bore, try drawing a rough Table like table 6.3 in Lipsey. When you can't fill in an element in this table, it is obviously a case where extra information is needed to calculate elasticity.

Since all the necessary information for the determination of demand elasticity is contained in the demand curve, we can deduce elasticity from it.

Q4 Fig. 1 shows us a demand curve for a commodity.

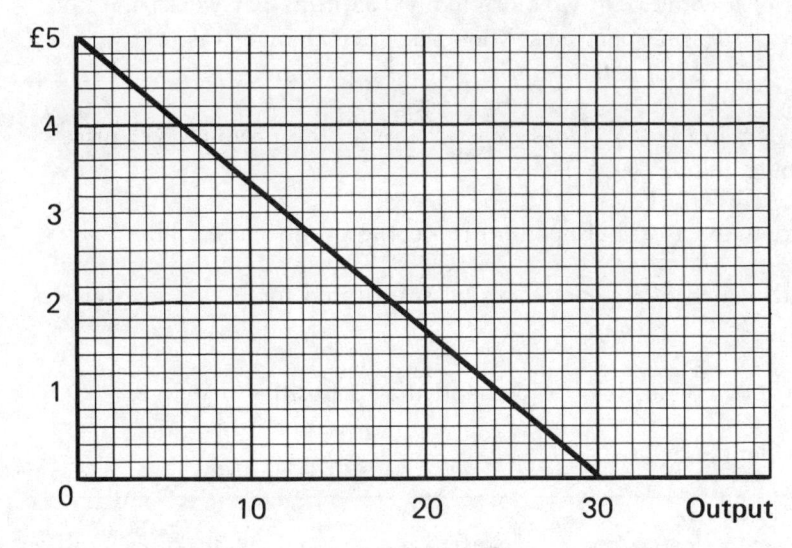

Fig. 1

(1) Can we assign a single elasticity to the whole curve? Yes/No

(2) Estimate the elasticity at a price of £3. _____

If you answered Q4(1) wrongly, convince yourself of the right answer by doing Q5.

Q5 (1) From Fig. 1, estimate the elasticity of demand at £2. _____

(2) and at £4. _____

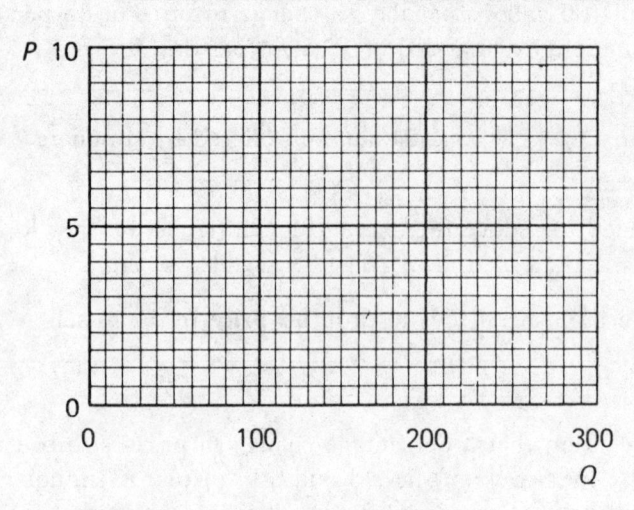

Q6 What does a perfectly elastic supply curve at price *x* mean? _____
_____

P 10 |
5 |
0 |_____
  0   100   200   300 *Q*

Fig. 2

Q7 Draw in Fig. 2 a supply curve of infinite elasticity at a price of £5. Then draw in a demand curve with elasticity of infinity at a price of £4. Will this commodity be traded? Yes/No
If yes, at what price and quantity? If no, why not?
_____
_____

Q8 The quantity demanded of a commodity was originally 105 units per week; the fall in quantity demanded was 10 units per week when the price change was +10 pence; elasticity of demand was 0.5. What was the price before the change? _____

Q9 Price rises; elasticity of demand is 0.8. Does expenditure on the product (i.e. price times quantity) rise or fall? Rise/Fall

Q10 Price falls; elasticity of demand is 2.3. Expenditure on the product rises/falls.

Q11 The greater the ease with which other goods can be substituted for it, the greater/less its elasticity of demand.

Q12 An inferior good has an income elasticity of demand that is positive/negative.

Q13 Define cross-elasticity of demand. _____
_____

Q14 Consider Pepsi-Cola and Coca-Cola. Their cross-elasticities will probably be positive/negative.

Q15 When two supply curves pass through the same point, the flatter is less elastic at that point. T/F

Q16 Suppose a demand curve is of such a shape that, as price changes through the whole of its range, quantity demanded changes in such a way that expenditure on the product (i.e. quantity × price) remains the same. We can assign to this curve the same elasticity at every point, and that elasticity is one. T/F

Q17 If the government raises the costs of egg farmers by forcing them to pay a tax for each egg sold, and if the aim of this policy is to reduce consumption for health reasons, then this policy will be more successful the less elastic is demand.   T/F

Q18 As you travel down a linear demand curve, demand becomes more elastic.   T/F

Q19 The less elastic the demand for cigarettes, the more successful an increase in the tobacco-tax will be if

(a) the aim is to increase government revenue.
(b) the aim is to reduce smoking-related diseases.

Q20 A rightward shift in the demand curve for a commodity is predicted to increase the equilibrium quantity to a greater degree

(a) the more inelastic is the supply curve.
(b) the more elastic is the supply curve.
(c) the closer the elasticity of supply is to unity.
(d) the more the elasticity of supply diverges from unity in either direction.

Q21 A demand curve which is a horizontal straight line has an elasticity that is

(a) zero.
(b) greater than zero but less than one.
(c) one.
(d) between one and infinity.
(e) infinite.

CONSUMER SURPLUS

Consumer surplus measures the net benefit consumers get from purchasing a commodity. Take the case of chocolate. If the price of chocolate is 40 pence per bar, I will increase my weekly purchases until the perceived value of the *last* bar bought in the week is just 40 pence. However, I would still have purchased *some* chocolate if the price had been more than 40 pence. The first bar of the week may, for instance, be 'worth' a lot to me if it is eaten on a weekly cinema trip. Consumers gain a net benefit from consumption to the extent that, for many of the bars of chocolate that they buy, the value placed on those particular bars (the maximum they would be willing to pay) exceeds the amount which they actually have to pay.

Q22 I decide to buy my daily newspaper for 40 pence but I would cancel the order if the charge were even a penny more. What can you say about my consumer surplus from this commodity?

Q23 (1) Refer back to Fig. 1. What is the value of consumer surplus per period if price is £3 per unit of output? _____ You could spend a lot of time on this question by considering each unit sold separately, but Lipsey's Fig. 6.8 indicates a rapid means of calculation: you shade in the appropriate area on the graph and then measure it.
(2) Using consumer surplus as your yardstick, what is the benefit per period to consumers if the price were reduced to £2 per unit of output?

Q24 If the demand curve is perfectly elastic at the current price, consumer surplus is

    (a) zero.
    (b) infinity.
    (c) indeterminate.

Q25 If a commodity is given away to customers at no charge, consumer surplus is

    (a) zero.
    (b) infinity.
    (c) the whole area under the demand curve to the point where it intersects the quantity axis.

QUESTIONS FOR DISCUSSION

1 A local newspaper writes: 'local farmers will be even more thankful than usual at Ambridge Parish Church Harvest Celebration next Sunday. Record sunshine in August has ensured a bumper harvest locally and throughout the country.' Under what demand conditions might this bumper harvest cause the farmers in fact to feel less than thankful?

2 When compact-disc technology was invented and put on to the market, what do you think happened to the values of (a) the elasticity of demand for record-players, and (b) the income elasticity of demand for records?

3 A study (by Joskow and Baughman) of the demand for gas in the USA estimated the following elasticities.

	short-run (one year)	long-run
price elasticity of demand	0.15	1.01
cross-price elasticity of demand (with respect to electricity)	+0.01	+0.17

Explain what these numbers mean and consider why the long-run measures are larger than those reported where one year is taken as the time-horizon.

4 What do you think the elasticity of supply of fresh fish would be on any one day (i.e. if we compared the price change to the consequent change in the amount offered for sale the same day)? How is this elasticity likely to be influenced by the available methods of refrigeration?

5 Suppose evidence has been building up that the drinking of spirits such as rum and gin is injurious to health. Most of the price of these goods is composed of tax. If demand is elastic, why might there be a conflict between the Minister of Health and the Chancellor of the Exchequer about future tax changes on spirits?

6 'If water metering is introduced, demand will prove to be inelastic because no one can do without water.' Comment.

Appendix to Chapter 6

Q1 We want to be able to award a unique elasticity to each point on a demand curve. The result which we get when we use the formula 'percentage change in Q divided by percentage change in P' will, however, depend upon how large a ΔP we choose.

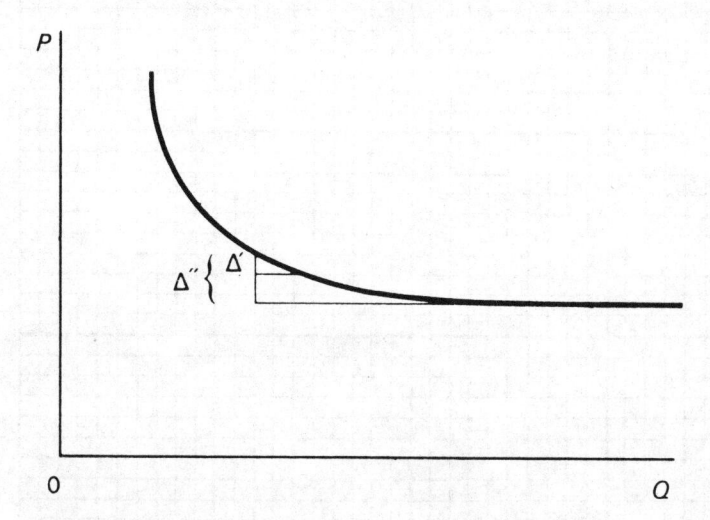

Fig. 1

For example in this diagram the choice of Δ' willl clearly give us a different result from Δ''. But how big a ΔP should be chosen? Let us take a curve where we know in advance what the elasticity is. We choose a curve where elasticity is always 1, i.e. where the percentage change in quantity demanded always equals the percentage change in price, and where revenue, therefore, remains constant (consider – if the price of Fords increases by 1%, and the number sold drops by 1% (strictly speaking 0.99%), Fords will receive the same revenue). Since revenue equals price × quantity, the formula for such a curve (do you remember what it is called? Read Lipsey, p. 82, if not) can be written $p \times q = k$, where k represents the constant revenue.

The formula for the demand curve in Fig. 2 is $pq = 1,440$.

TABLE 1

Initial price	Change in price	Initial quantity	Change in quantity	Elasticity
12	+5	120		
12	+2	120		
12	+1	120		
12	−1	120		
12	−2	120		
12	−5	120		

Now use the method to calculate the elasticity at $p = 12$, $q = 120$ (we know, of course, that it should be 1 – at that point, and at all others). Calculate the elasticity for the 6 price changes in Table 1, filling in all the blanks. Calculate the change in quantity to 1 decimal place.

Therefore, the smaller the ΔP, the better is the approximation to the value of the elasticity. The techniques of calculus enable us to assign a unique value to the elasticity. (See Appendix – Lipsey, pp. 99–100.)

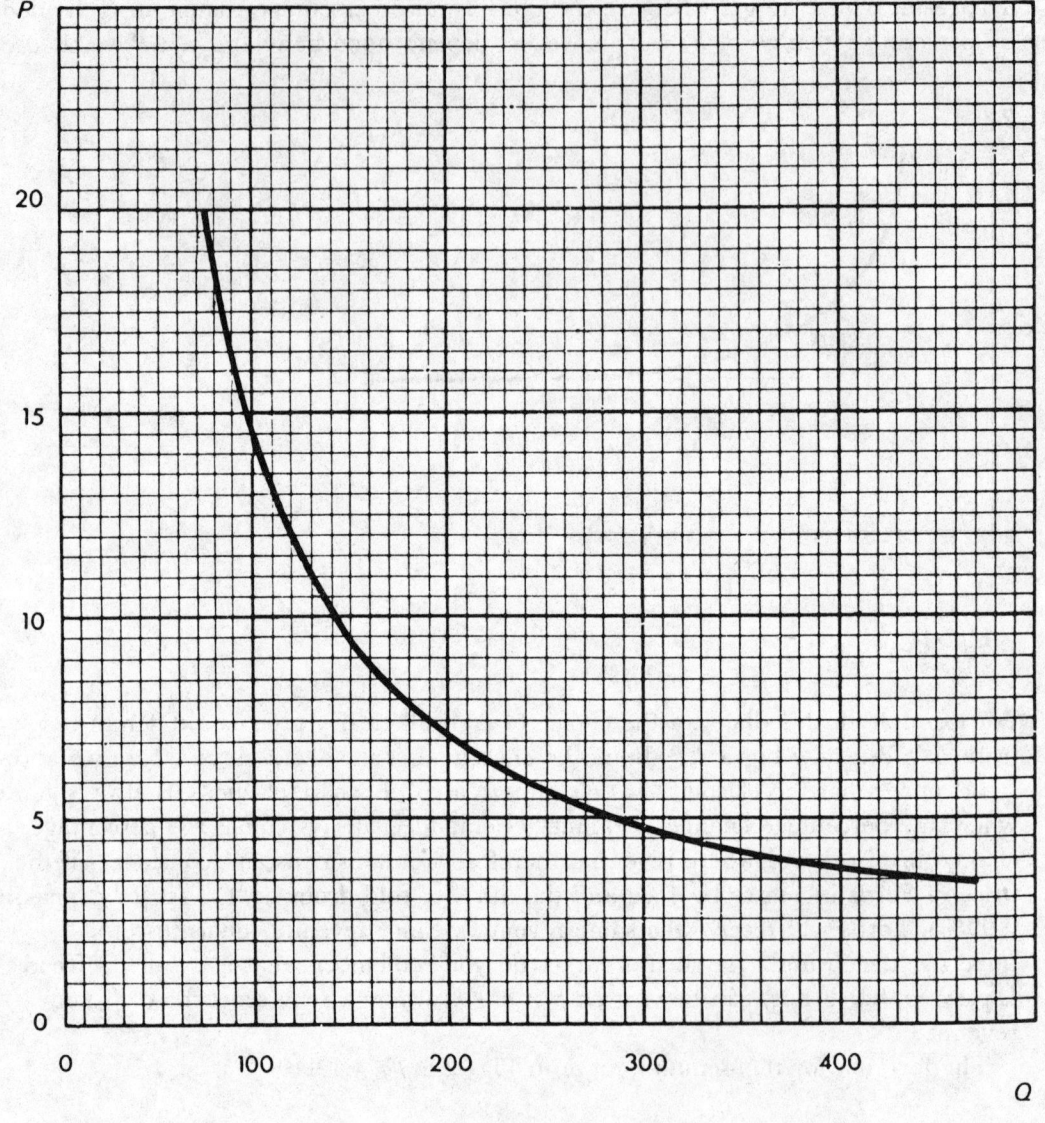

Fig. 2

Q2 Over what price range does the demand curve in Fig. 3 have less than unit elasticity? _____
(*Hint*: Calculate $\Delta Q/\Delta P$, which is a constant, and substitute into the elasticity formula to discover the price and quantity for which elasticity equals 1.)

Q3 Over what price range does the demand curve in Fig. 3 have more than unit elasticity? _____

Q4 In Fig. 3, how would elasticity at £7.50 be altered if the figures on the output axis were doubled? doubled/halved/not changed

Q5 If two linear supply curves pass through the origin, the steeper is the less elastic. T/F

Q6 A supply curve is linear and passes through both the origin and the point P = £4, Q = 2 units. Is the elasticity of supply the same at every point on the curve? Yes/No If yes, what is its value? _____

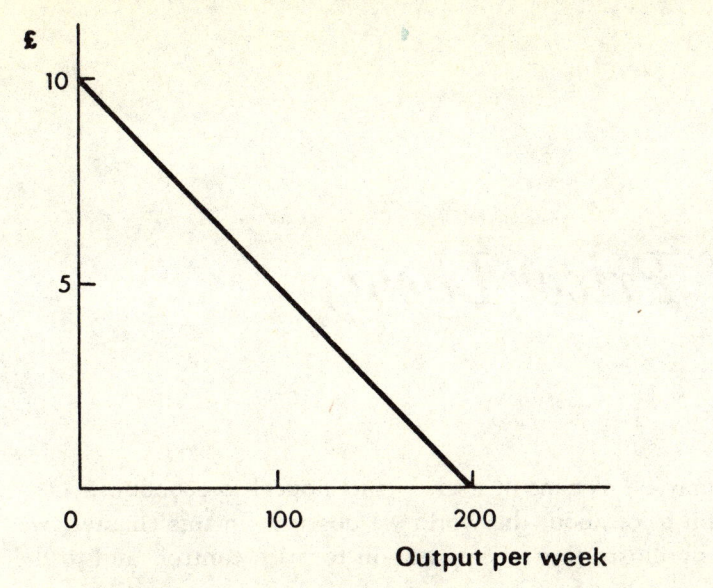

Fig. 3

CHAPTER 7
Applications of Price Theory

The theory of supply and demand may be elegant in itself but its appeal to economists can only be based on its ability to explain a lot about the world we observe. In this chapter, we see how powerful its use can prove by illustrating its application to price controls and to the problems of the agricultural sector.

Q1 Which of the following diagrams show in continuous lines the parts of the supply and demand diagram which determine quantity traded in disequilibrium?

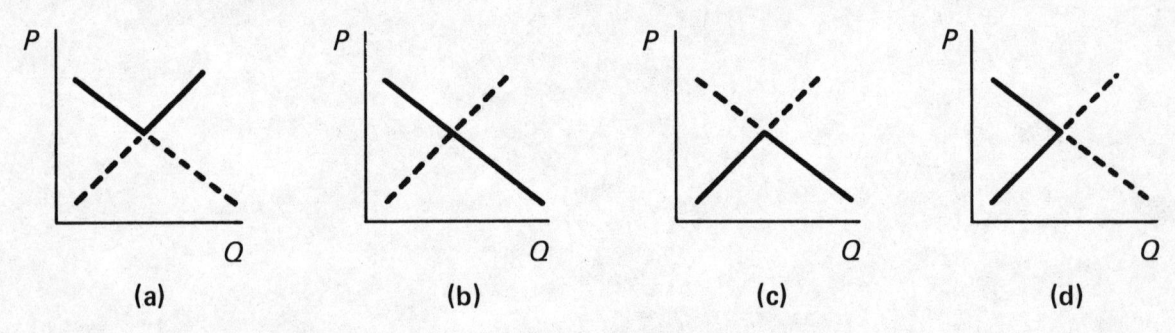

(a) (b) (c) (d)

Fig. 1

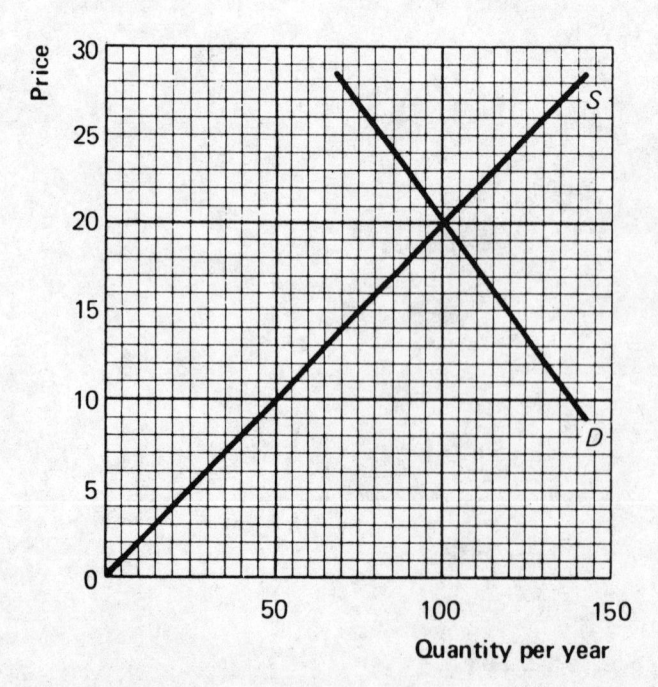

Fig. 2

Refer to Fig. 2.

Q 2   Over what range will a maximum price be ineffective? _____

Q 3   When the maximum price is set at £16, the excess demand will be
      _____ per year.

Q 4   What price would consumers be willing to pay for the amount actually supplied at
      the controlled price of £16? _____

Consider now the setting of a MINIMUM price, using the example of labour.

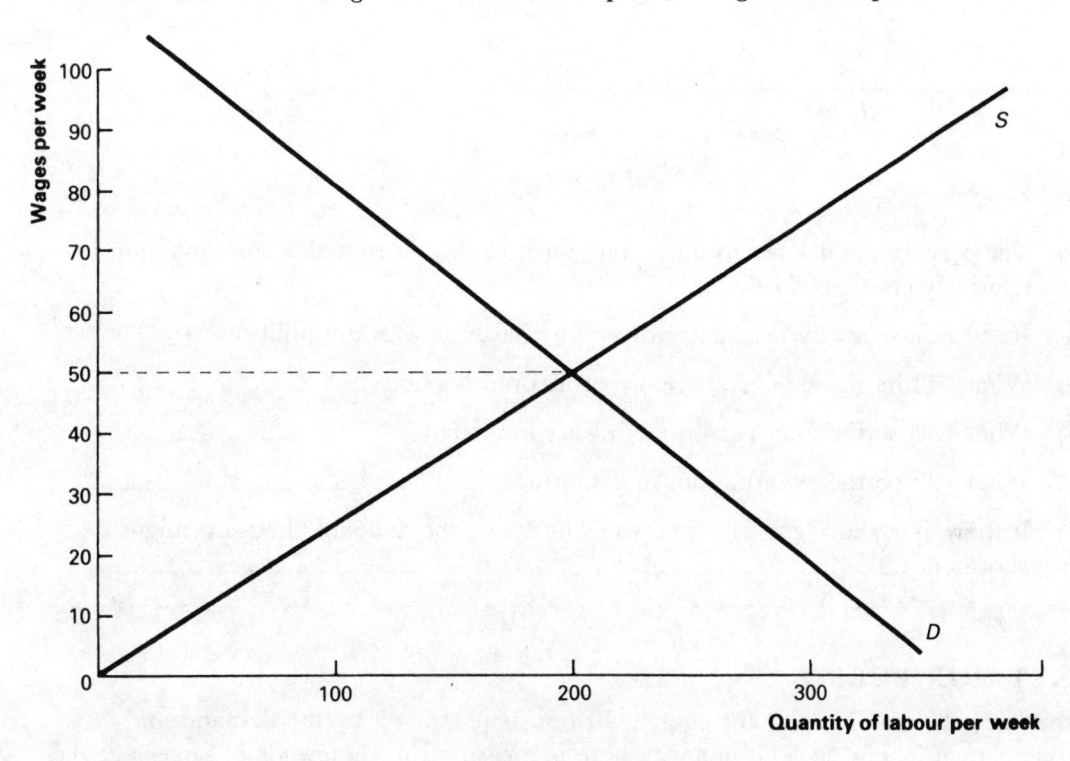

Fig. 3

Refer to Fig. 3.

Q 5   Over what range will the minimum price be ineffective? _____

Q 6   If the minimum wage is set at £75.00 per week, the wages of those employed will
      fall/rise.

Q 7   The employment level will rise/fall if the minimum wage is set at £75.

Q 8   What will be the *size* of this change in employment? _____

Q 9   Here, the total wage bill rises/falls. This is because the elasticity of demand is
      _____.

Q 10 Under what conditions would the total wage bill rise? _____

Q 11 Fig. 4 shows a market for private rented accommodation.

      (1) Label the curves. (Check in Lipsey p. 106 if necessary)

      (2) Illustrate what would be the effect of an increase in population.

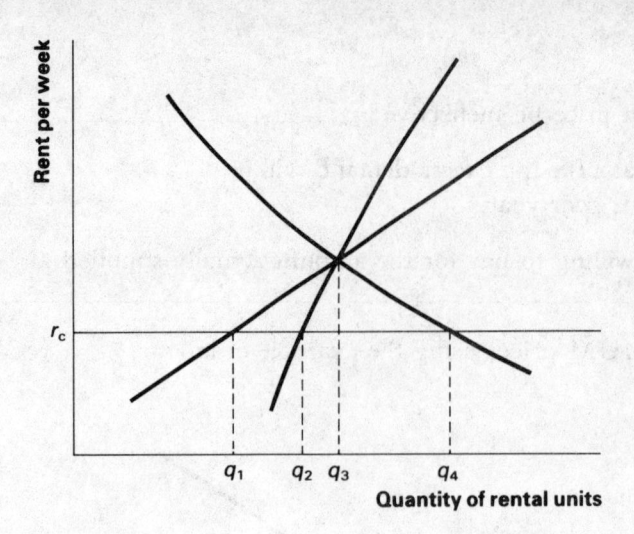

Fig. 4

(3) The S_L curve is flat because the long-term supply of rented accommodation is relatively elastic/inelastic.

If the rent is set by law at r_c (where previously it was at equilibrium):

(4) What will be the short-run supply of accommodation? _____

(5) What will be the long-run supply of accommodation? _____

(6) What will be the eventual housing shortage? _____

(7) If there is a shortage, list some ways in which the available housing might be allocated. _____

A MARKET FOR EGGS

Suppose that the wholesale market for eggs in Britain is portrayed by the demand and supply curves shown in Fig. 5. The quantity here is measured in thousands of boxes per day (a box is a 100-egg unit) and price is measured in £s per box.

Q 12 What is the equilibrium price (in £s per box) in this market? _____

Q 13 What is the equilibrium quantity (in boxes)? _____

Q 14 An Egg Control Authority is now established and is instructed to ensure that sellers receive at least £7 per box for eggs. It is to purchase and destroy whatever quantity of eggs is necessary to maintain a price of £7. With this policy introduced, by how many boxes per day will consumption of eggs fall? _____

Q 15 How many boxes per day would the Authority need to purchase from the market? _____

Q 16 What would be the expenditure per day on such purchases? £_____

Q 17 An alternative policy to the Egg Control Authority would be to set legally enforceable quotas on egg farmers, so that quantity supplied would equal quantity demanded at a price of £7 per box. What would be the total daily production (in boxes) that such a policy would require? _____

Q 18 Compared with the original situation, when price was £6, egg farmers in aggregate would earn greater/smaller revenue with quotas in force. This result arises because demand is elastic/inelastic.

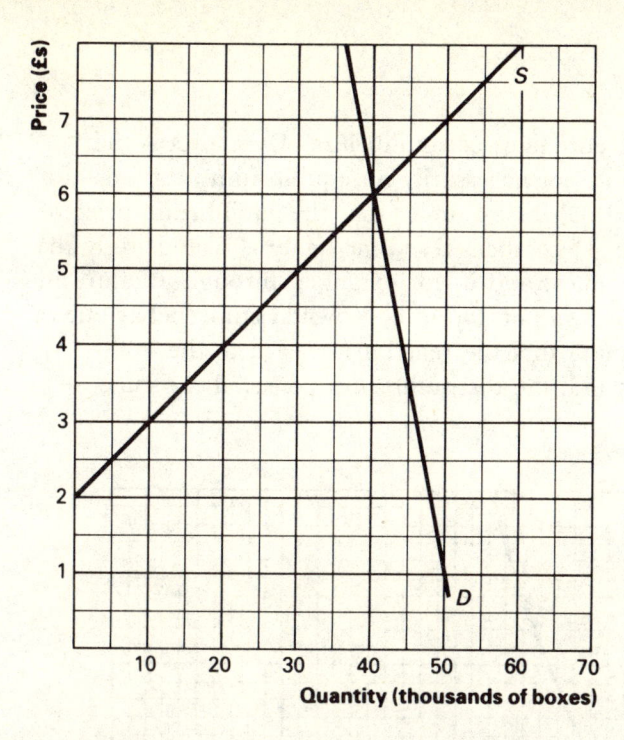

Fig. 5

QUESTIONS FOR DISCUSSION

1. Milton and Rose Friedman, in their book *Free to Choose*, write about the US minimum-wage law as 'one of the most, if not the most, antiblack laws on the statute book'. Why did they expect minimum-wage laws to result in unemployment, and why did they expect the unemployment to be concentrated amongst racial minorities?

2. It has been claimed that rent control has destroyed more housing than did Hitler's bombs. What is meant? If rent control is really so destructive, why did Britain have it in force for all but a few years of the 1914–1989 period?

3. Housing benefit in Britain is a contribution to weekly rent by government to eligible low-income households. If the level of benefits were increased, which group, landlords or tenants, would you expect to gain more as a result? (To answer this question, you need to take a view on relevant elasticities.)

4. Why has the working of the Common Agricultural Policy in the last decade required the sale of large amounts of butter to the Soviet Union at a price far below the cost of producing it?

5. Milk quotas have been enforced rigorously on British dairy farmers in recent years. Why are such quotas necessary? If a free market in quota entitlements were allowed, why would quotas command a high price?

6. Three airlines operate on a particular route. A Civil Aviation Board is established and succeeds in fixing the fare to be charged at a level well above the equilibrium. What would you predict would happen to the numbers of passengers choosing air, the frequency of flights and the standard of in-flight catering?

7. What (if anything) is wrong with Cup Final ticket touts?

Appendix to Chapter 7

Comparative statics is the comparison of different states of equilibrium. Dynamics is the study of the movement from one position – and not necessarily an equilibrium position – to another. Comparative-static analysis might tell us, for example, that the equilibrium price of strawberries is 25p per lb in June and 200p in December. Dynamic analysis would study the movement in the actual prices between those times, and if, for example, through a failure in the crop in June there was persistent excess demand at 25p a lb, it would study behaviour of producers, customers and market price, assuming that the reactions of each to the disequilibrium situation took time to occur so that the disequilibrium persisted for some period of time.

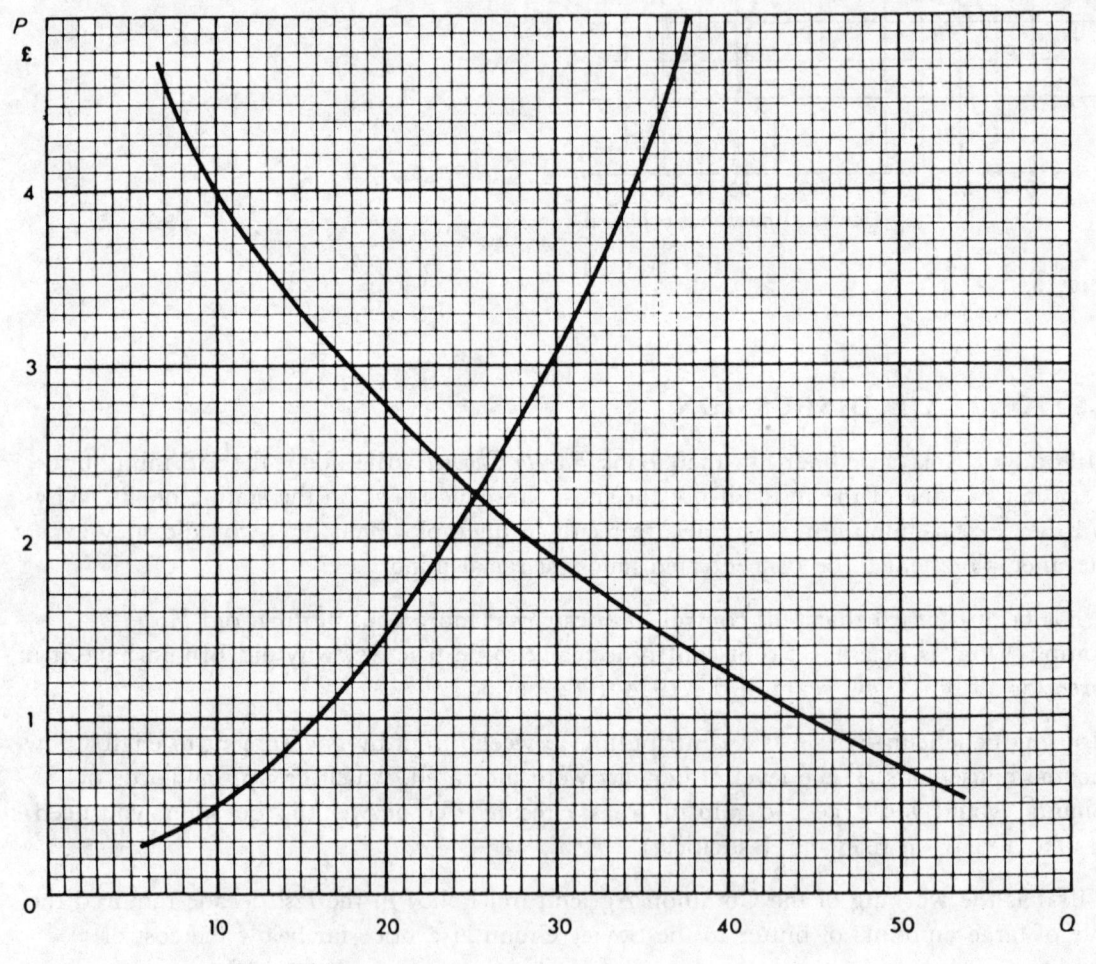

Fig. 1

THE COBWEB

Assume that Fig. 1 is a cobweb diagram of a market for strawberries. Assume also that suppliers expect that the present market price will prevail next year, and that the size of one year's crop must be planned a whole year in advance.

Q1   A drought in year t causes 10 tons to be supplied instead of 25.5.

    (1)   What is the price in year t? _____

(2) In what year will price be £2.65p? $t+$ _____

(3) In what year will quantity supplied be 24? $t+$ _____

Now go back to the static equilibrium, and assume that, instead of the drought, marvellous weather in year t causes 35 tons to be supplied.

(4) What price will clear the market? _____

(5) What quantity will be supplied in year $t+1$? _____

(6) What price will clear the market in year $t+1$? _____

(7) How much will be supplied in year $t+2$? _____

(8) What price will clear the market in year $t+2$? _____

(9) What quantity will be supplied in year $t+3$? _____

Q2 Is this a stable or unstable adjustment mechanism? _____

Q3 A demand curve which is flatter than the supply curve will yield a stable/unstable adjustment mechanism.

Q4 If the slope of the demand curve is equal to minus the slope of the supply curve, prices and quantities will alternate between 2/4/3 levels each, and will _____ reach equilibrium.

Q5 If the supply curve is, over the relevant range, less elastic than the demand curve, the process is stable/unstable.

Q6 The stability of the process depends on the relative slopes of the demand and supply curves, and on nothing else. T/F

QUESTION FOR DISCUSSION

1 What is the difference between static and dynamic analysis? What are some of the limitations of statics?

2 Draw a graph from the following equations:
$D_t = 100 - 6p_t$
$S_t = 4p_{t-1}$
where S and D are supply and demand and where the subscripts t refer to time-periods. Is the system stable or unstable? Formulate a different demand equation that would change your conclusion.

3 In the early 1980s, hotel space in Singapore was described as 'in very short supply'. In the late 1980s, it was known as one of the cheapest and easiest places to find a high-class hotel room. Formulate a simple explanation based on the analysis you have studied of why the situation changed so drastically.

4 The simple cobweb assumes that producers base their production plan for next year's output on this year's prices. They are not assumed to learn anything from previous price fluctuations. One way of changing this assumption to one perhaps more realistic is to introduce the idea of a normal price, and to assume that future production plans are based upon some average of actual market price and this 'normal' price.

Construct a supply-demand schedule on graph paper, and let the 'normal' price be the equilibrium price. Start off a cobweb with an unforeseen drop in supply, caused perhaps by unusually bad weather, but assume that the price which producers expect to receive in the next time-period equals actual price + normal price, all divided by two.

Trace out the cobweb process. Is it more or less stable than the simpler version? What are the stability/instability conditions now?

CHAPTER 8
Indifference–Preference Theory

Behind every market demand curve – and remember, all the demand curves in the Workbook so far have described the total, i.e. market, demand for a commodity – there are all the independent decisions made by all the people who form the market.

Q1   What do we take as the basic decision unit for the theory of demand?
_____

THE BUDGET LINE

The budget line represents the sets of purchases that the household *could* make given the constraints implied by its income and the prices of the goods available to it.

Q2   The price of x is £5 each, of y 50p each. These are the only goods that I consume, and I receive an income of £15 a week. I neither borrow nor save. Construct a budget-line diagram for one week's purchases on Fig. 1.

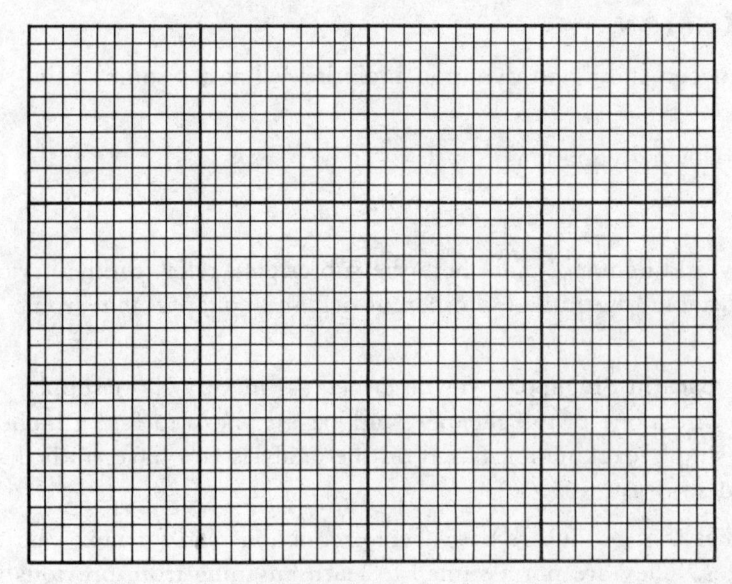

Fig. 1

(1) Which combinations of x and y can I buy that do not lie on the budget line? Those lying above the line/below the line/neither.

(2) My income rises to £20 a week. Which good, or goods, will have to change price in order to restore my original budget line? *x/y*/both.

(3) On the original budget line I decided to consume $10y$ (how much x did I consume? _____). My income then fell by £5. Draw in my new budget line. By how much will the price of x have to change (given that y remains

constant) in order to make it possible for me to consume the same amount of *x* and *y* as before? up/down by £_____

(4) The budget line shifts its intercepts to 5*x* and 20*y*. Could this be the consequence of one price change from the original data in (2) above? Yes/No.

(5) ... of an income change only? Yes/No

(6) ... of two price changes? Yes/No

(7) ... of one price change and an income change? Yes/No

Q3 If all money prices are multiplied by p, by what must income be multiplied in order to restore your original command over goods? _____

Q4 In the budget line of Q2(4), what is the opportunity cost (in terms of *x* forgone) of 10*y*? _____.

Check your answers, and if you got any wrong, re-read pp. 124–26 and 133–35 and do Q5.

Q5 Construct a budget line on Fig. 2.

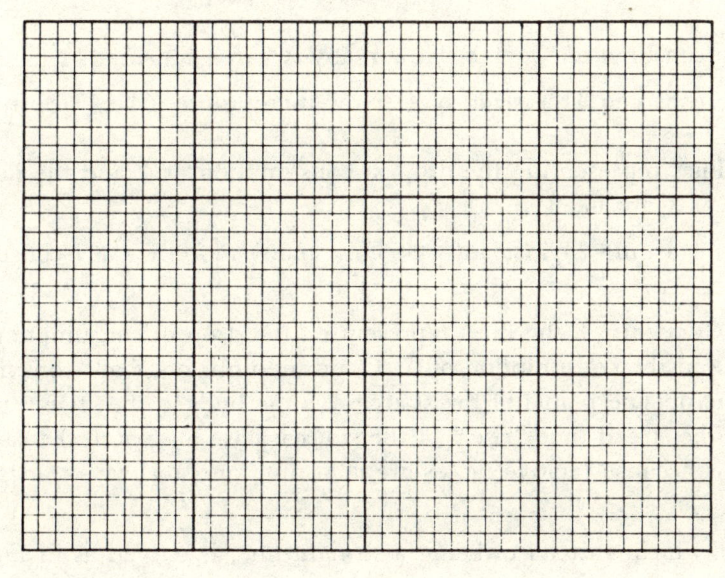

Fig. 2

(1) Assume that the price of the good measured along the horizontal axis doubles. The budget line will cut the horizontal axis

 (a) half the previous distance from the origin.
 (b) twice the previous distance from the origin.

(2) Assume that the change in Q5(1) takes place, but income doubles.

 (a) The original budget line will be restored.
 (b) The new budget line will cut the vertical axis half the original distance from the origin, and the horizontal axis at the original distance.
 (c) The new budget line will cut the vertical axis twice the original distance from the origin, and the horizontal axis at the original distance.

Consider for a moment why we normally draw budget lines straight. If you understand this, do question 7. If not, do question 6.

Q6 Look at Fig. 3.

The price of *Y* is £2, the price of *X* is £1. My income is £10 per consumption period. Assume I start by consuming 5*Y*.

(1) How many *X* do I consume? _____

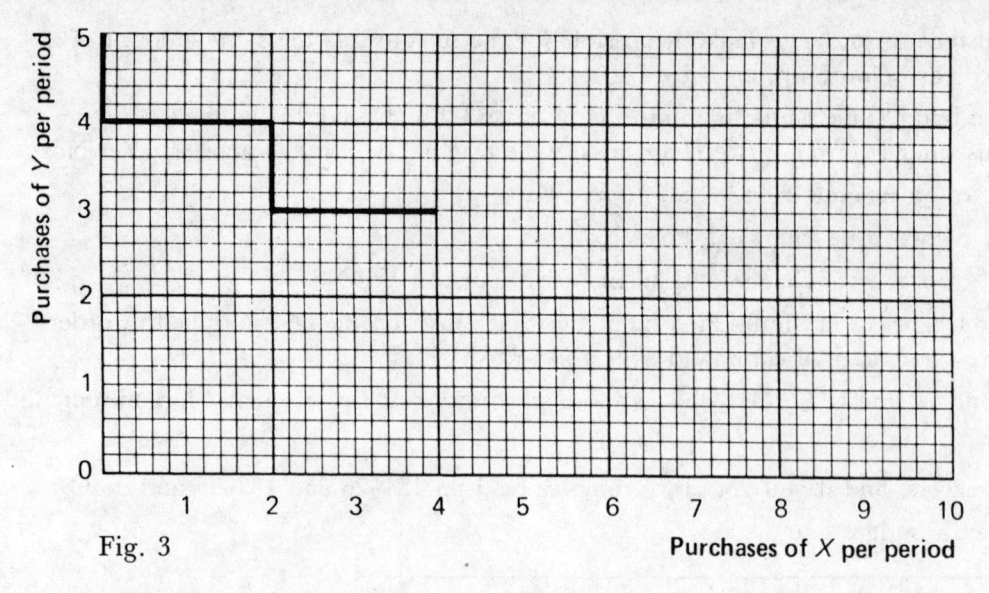

Fig. 3 — Purchases of Y per period vs Purchases of X per period

(2) Now I decide to consume one less Y. How many X can I consume? _____

(3) Now I decide to consume 3Y instead of 4. How many more X can I consume? _____

(On Fig. 3 the lines representing the drop in consumption of Y and the increase in consumption of X are filled in.)

(4) Now I decide to consume 2Y instead of 3. How many more X can I consume? _____

Check your answers. Sketch on Fig. 3 the lines representing the drop in consumption of Y from 3 to 2, and the increase in the consumption of X. Continue until no Y are consumed, and 10X. The line joining the outside points of the staircase is the budget line. It is straight, just like a staircase, because the 'tread' and 'riser' of the staircase are always in the same relation to each other. This is because relative prices are constant; one Y always trades for 2X. Now do Q7.

Q7 Assume a budget line which, instead of being a straight line, is curved as in Fig. 4. This would mean

    (a) the more of one good I consume, the cheaper it gets.
    (b) the more of one good I consume, the more expensive it gets.
    (c) the goods' relative prices are constant, but my income is changing.

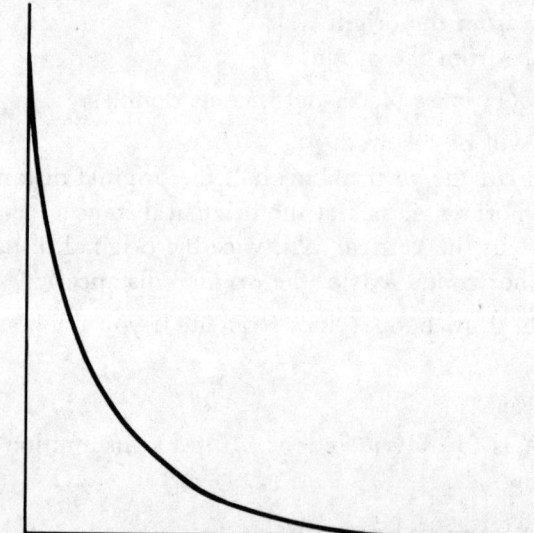

Fig. 4

Check your answers. If you were right, carry on. If not, go back to Q6.

So one individual's budget line is straight because prices are what he finds in the shops, and do not change according to the level or pattern of his purchases.

INDIFFERENCE MAPS

Indifference maps are a way of portraying the *preferences* of a household. A single *indifference curve* shows all the combinations of goods that will give the household a certain level of satisfaction. There are an infinite number of indifference curves, because each one would correspond to a *different* level of satisfaction. When we represent a selection of these curves on a diagram to show the household's tastes, we are presenting its *indifference map*.

Q8 Sketch on to each pair of axes in Fig. 5 a single indifference curve appropriate to the description of tastes given below.

(1) x is supposed to taste much better than y according to taste tests shown in TV commercials but I think it's all nonsense. I could never even tell which one I was drinking.

(2) I like x but I hate y and it's only because of my parents' nagging that I use it at all.

(3) I like x and y. As I have more of one of them, though, I get more and more bored with the extra – not that I'd never refuse some more if it were free!

(4) I would only ever use x and y in one particular recipe. It calls for 2 ounces of x for every 1 ounce of y you put in.

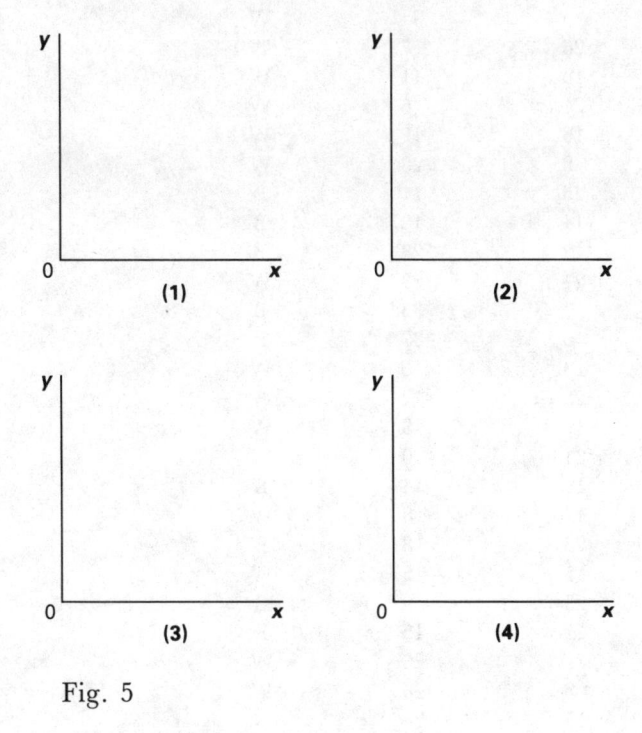

Fig. 5

HOUSEHOLD EQUILIBRIUM

The budget line (representing what choices of expenditure are *feasible* for the household) and the indifference curve (representing its *preferences* between different choices) are put together in one diagram to illustrate what influences the final consumption decision.

Q9 A utility-maximizing household may allocate its weekly income between the purchase of X and Y. It chooses to buy $22Y$ and $10X$.

(1) It is questioned about the bundles of X and Y which would leave it better off, or worse off, than its choice of $22Y$ and $10X$. The question, and its answers, are tabulated in Table 1. 'W' in the 'Evaluation' column means that the bundle would leave it worse off, 'B' means that the bundle would leave it better off, and 'I' means that it would be indifferent between that bundle and its original choice of $22Y$ and $10X$.

From the data in Table 1, construct its indifference curve on Fig. 6, plotting the bundles of X and Y which would give it equal utility to $22Y$ and $10X$.

(2) From the data given so far, can you infer the relative prices of X and Y? Yes/No. If yes, X cost about _____ as much as Y.

(3) The price of Y doubles and the price of X falls to one-third of its previous value; the household's money income remains the same. Can the household move to a higher indifference curve? Yes/No

Are you able to say that the household will definitely decrease its consumption of Y? Yes/No

If yes, can you say that it will fall below any particular level?

If yes, below (roughly) what level? _____

TABLE 1

Amount of Y	Amount of X	Evaluation
5	34	W
26	7	W
18	11	W
24	6	W
16	12	W
8	28	W
25	11	B
14	18	B
12	22	B
24	8	W
7	33	B
6	37	B
13	16	W
25	12	B
17	13	W
21	10	W
19	14	B
11	18	W
28	8	B
15	15	W
25	9	B
17	15	B
12	20	W
8	18	W
13	24	B
9	30	B
21	11	I
11	22	W
6	40	B
9	22	W
6	32	W

TABLE 1 (contd.)

Amount of Y	Amount of X	Evaluation
15	17	B
20	12	B
13	23	B
9	25	W
17	17	B
7	28	W
11	25	B
7	31	I
22	12	B
12	28	B
29	7	B
6	33	W
5	37	W
5	36	W
9	28	B

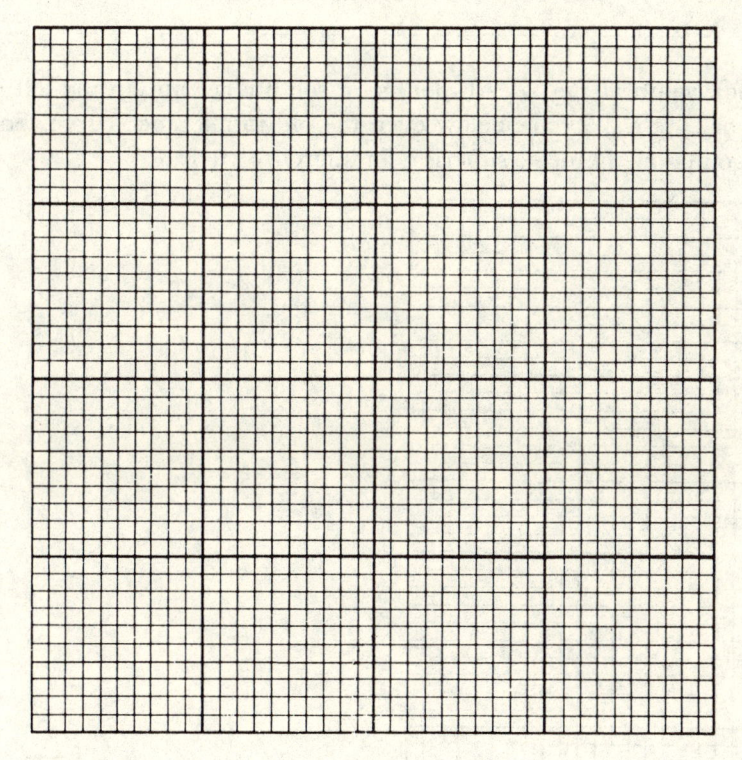

Fig. 6

Q10 The following bundles of clothes and food give a household the same level of satisfaction, when consumed during a given period of time.

Bundle no.	Quantity of food	Quantity of clothes
1	30	10
2	25	12
3	20	14
4	15	17
5	12	20
6	7	40

(1) Construct the appropriate indifference curve on Fig. 7.

(2) The household would prefer any point to the right/left of the curve.

(3) Assume that the household is a utility maximizer, and consumes 10 units of food and 23 units of clothes. What are the relative prices of clothes and good? Clothes are roughly _____ as cheap as food.

(4) Draw in a budget line which corresponds to 35 units of food if no clothes are consumed, given that food and clothes cost the same price per unit.

    (a) If the household is a utility maximizer, will it consume on the indifference curve which you have already drawn? Yes/No
    (b) Have you enough information to tell where the new point of utility-maximizing consumption will be? Yes/No
    (c) Can you at least say that there are any parts of the budget line which cannot contain the new point of consumption? Yes/No
    (d) If your answer to (c) was Yes, what parts are they?

If your answer was No, look again at Fig. 7. All points on the budget line to the left of Clothes, 13 and to the right of Clothes, 25 are below even the old indifference curve. So they must be inferior to all points on the new, superior, indifference curve.

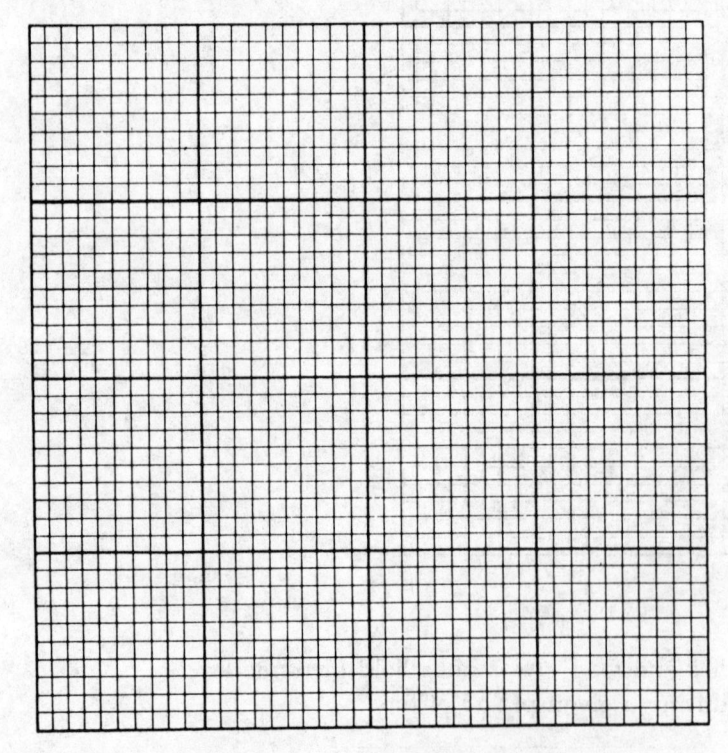

Fig. 7

Q11 If income and prices all increase by the same percentage, the equilibrium quantity of each commodity purchased will be unchanged. T/F

Q12 I spend 50% of my income on x and 50% on y. My income is about to increase by 10% but at the same time the price of x is increasing by 15% and of y by 5%. My purchasing decisions will, therefore, be unaltered. T/F

Q 13 Sketch onto Fig. 8., an *income-consumption line* for a world where y is a normal good throughout the income range but x becomes an inferior good beyond a certain income level.

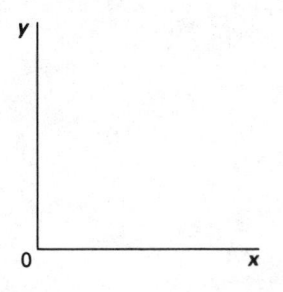

Fig. 8

You should now re-read the section on the derivation of demand curves from indifference maps.

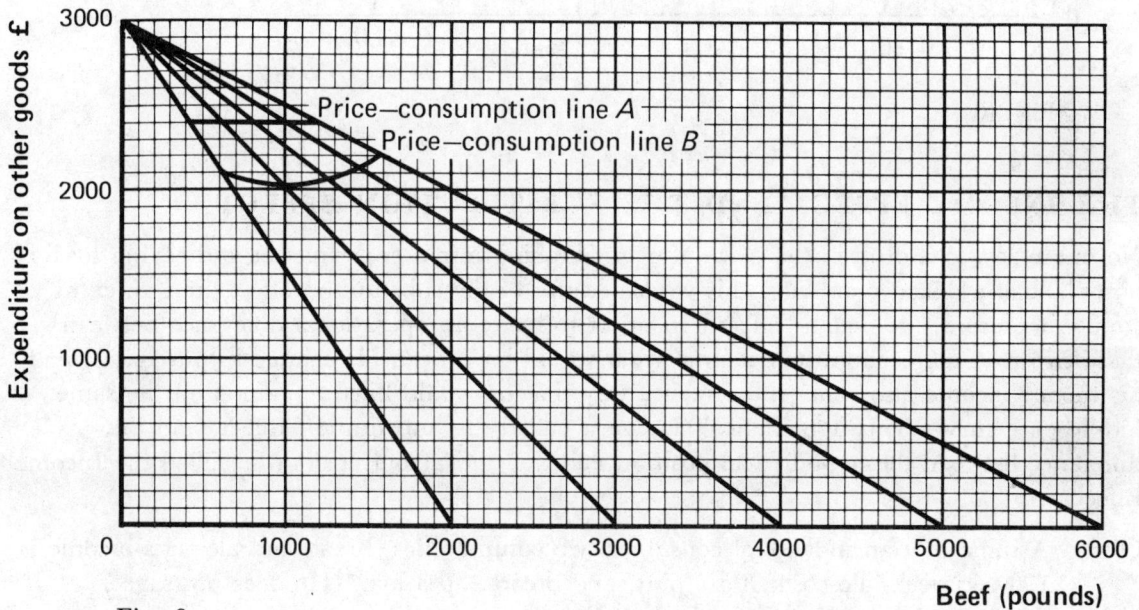

Fig. 9

Q 14 On Fig. 9 sketch in (using two different colours) indifference maps that could lead to price-consumption lines A and B.

From the price-consumption lines, derive demand curves A and B and enter on Fig. 10 below.

(1) For the demand curve derived from price-consumption line B, how much beef will be consumed if its price is £0.80? _____

(2) For the demand curve derived from price-consumption line B, how much beef will be consumed if its price is £1.25? _____

Q 15 Households could never attain a higher indifference curve in which of the following cases?

    (a) An increase in money income.
    (b) A reduction in absolute prices.
    (c) A proportionate increase in money income and in absolute prices.
    (d) A change in relative prices caused by a reduction in one price.

45

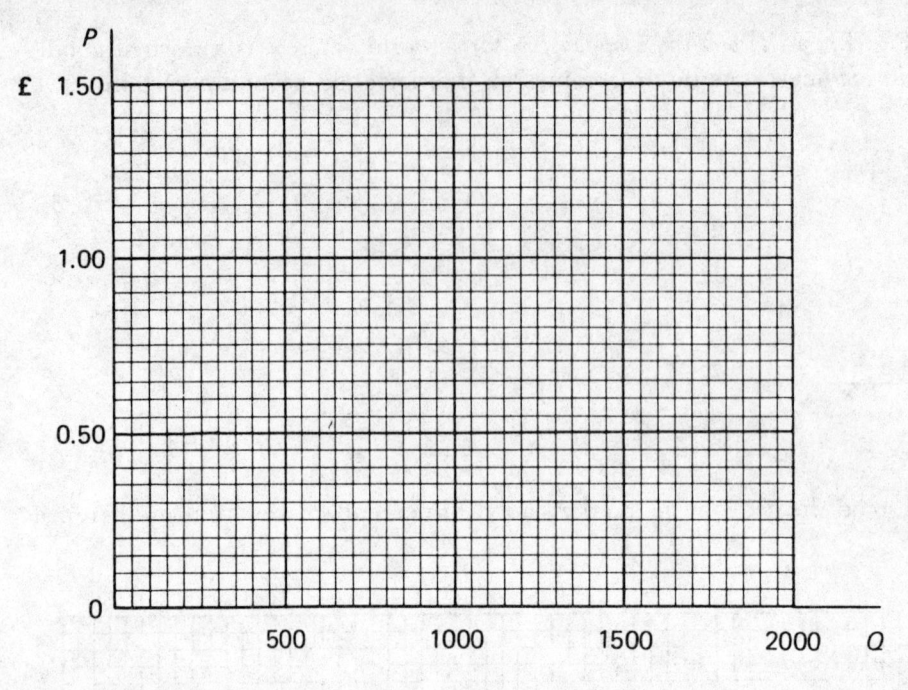

Fig. 10

THE INCOME EFFECT AND THE SUBSTITUTION EFFECT

No one reacts to a drop in the price of eggs by going into a supermarket and saying to himself 'half a dozen more eggs this week because of the substitution effect, and an extra couple because of the income effect'. In order to make an operational difference between these two reasons, economists examine what would have been his change in purchases, had his money income also changed in such a way that he would have remained on the same indifference curve. This hypothetical change is called the Substitution Effect, and the difference between the hypothetical position and the new actual position is called the Income Effect.

Q 16 Assume that an individual consumes two commodities, bread and ale. His income is £90 per week, ale costs 90p a pint, and bread 45p a loaf. (He does not save.) Construct his weekly budget line on Fig. 11, which is an indifference map.

(1) How much bread does he eat? _____

Now assume that a shortage of wheat causes the price of bread to double. Draw in his new budget line, and construct the notional budget line required to analyse his change in consumption into its two components.

(2) What is the substitution effect on his consumption of bread? _____

(3) What is the income effect on his consumption of bread? _____

(4) What is the substitution effect on his consumption of ale? _____

(5) What is the income effect on his consumption of ale? _____

Q 17 For a normal good, the substitution and income effects reinforce each other. T/F

Q 18 For an inferior good, the substitution and income effects reinforce each other. T/F

Q 19 A normal good could, on rare occasions, be a Giffen good. T/F

Q 20 All inferior goods have positively sloped demand curves. T/F

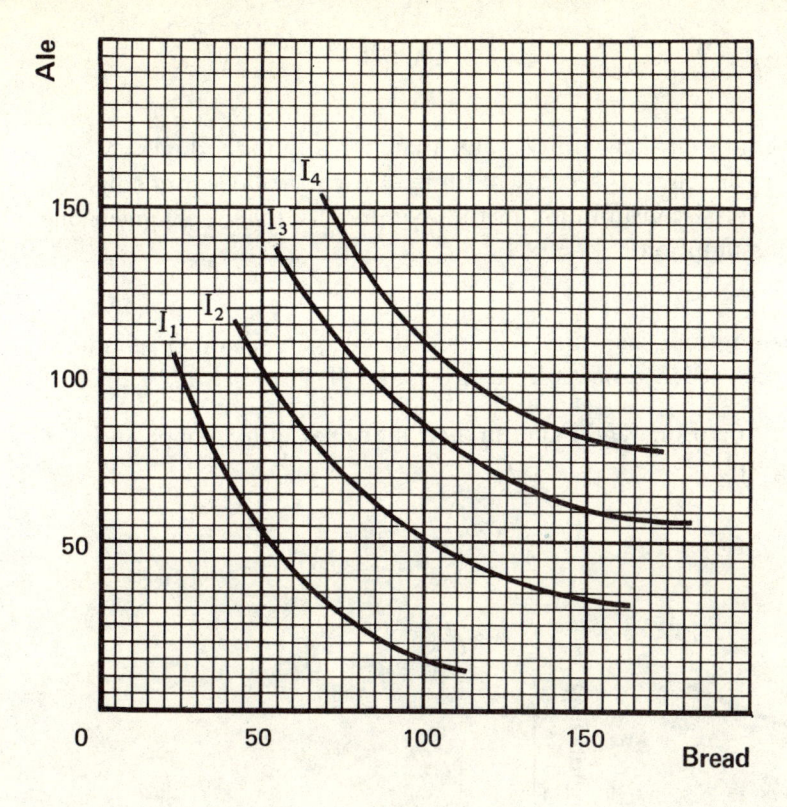

Fig. 11

QUESTIONS FOR DISCUSSION

1 'I like both x and y but I would always prefer a combination with more x in it no matter how much y there was.' Demonstrate why it is said that no indifference curves exist if preferences are of this category (known as *lexicographic*).

2 Draw a budget line assuming some given income and money prices of two goods, X and Y. Show a 10% rise in the money price of X. Show a 10% fall in the money price of Y. Compare these two cases with respect to the substitution effect, the income effect and the total effect of the change.

3 The original good for which it was claimed that the demand curve was positively sloped was that of wheat in the diet of farm labourers in England in the nineteenth century. Explain why more wheat might be consumed when its price rose and less when its price fell. What conditions are necessary for such 'Giffen goods' to exist?

4 A typical student has an income of £2,200 and pays £1,200 of it as his residence-hall rent. Residence includes vouchers for an evening meal on each of the 200 days of the academic session. The college authorities decide to make meals optional. Fees will be reduced to £600 and students can in future purchase a meal any evening for £3 cash. Show, using indifference analysis, why students are likely to favour this change. Could the college authorities retain student support if they proposed to charge more than £3 cash per meal?

Appendix to Chapter 8

Q1 The hypothesis of diminishing marginal utility states that, for any individual consumer, the value that he attaches to successive units of a particular commodity will diminish steadily as his total consumption of that commodity increases, given one assumption. What is that assumption? _____

Q2 'The hypothesis of diminishing marginal utility implies that I gain six times as much satisfaction from my first bun at tea time as from my sixth.' T/F

Q3 Derive from the total utility map on Fig. 1 the implied marginal utility map, and draw it in on the second graph.

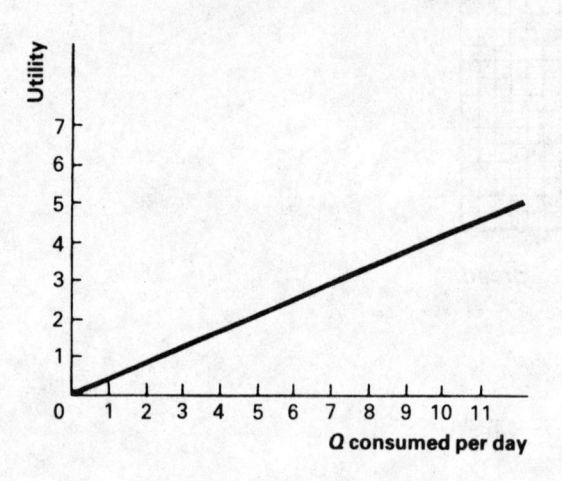

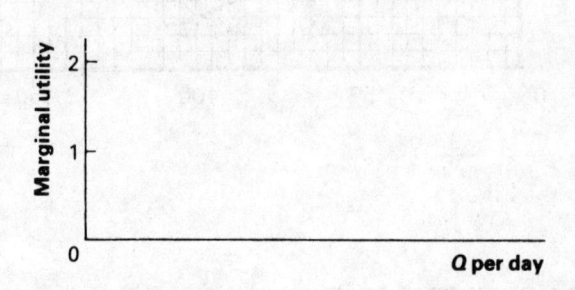

Fig. 1

(1) What is the marginal utility of the third unit? _____

(2) What is the marginal utility of the fifth unit? _____

(3) Does the behaviour of the individual support or oppose our hypothesis? _____

Check your answers. If you got Q3 wrong (or are not confident that you know why you got it right), do Q4. If not, go on to Q5.

Q4 (1) The hypothesis of diminishing marginal utility states that, as you add to your consumption of a particular good, the extra utility which you derive gets progressively larger/smaller.

(2) Which of the two diagrams in Fig. 2 represents diminishing marginal utility? (a)/(b).

(3) Diminishing marginal utility means that total utility

    (a) rises at a constant rate.
    (b) rises at first, then falls.
    (c) rises, but at a decreasing rate.

(4) Which of the two diagrams in Fig. 3 corresponds to diminishing marginal utility? _____

Fig. 2 (a) (b)

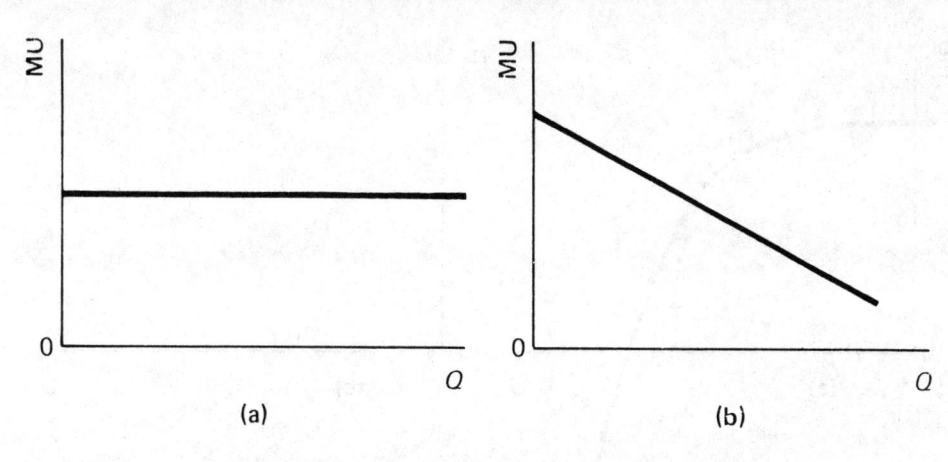

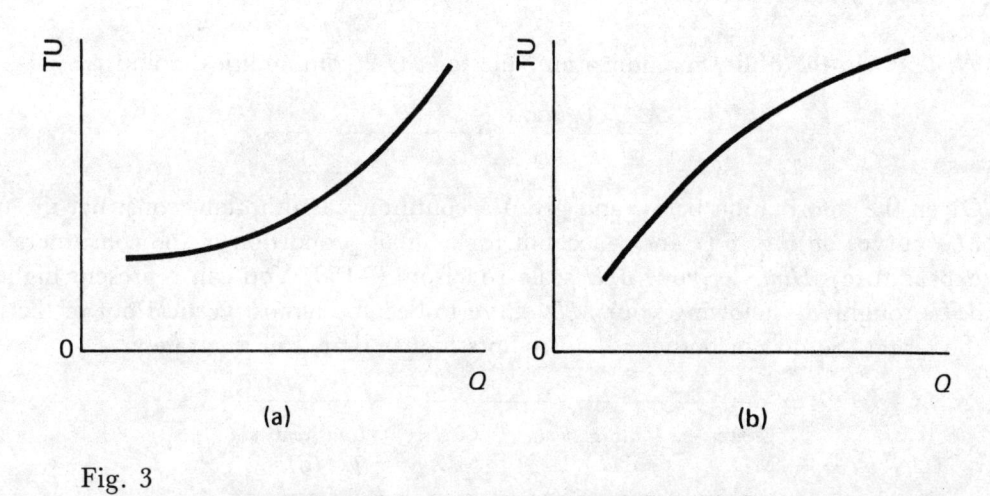

Fig. 3 (a) (b)

Q5 (1) Draw on Fig. 4(b) the approximate total utility curve derived from Fig. 4(a).

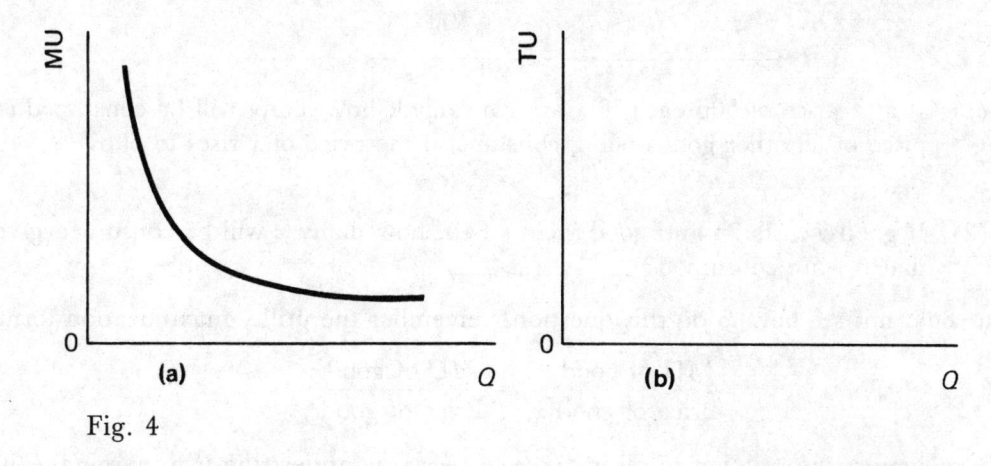

Fig. 4 (a) (b)

(2) Draw on Fig. 5(b) the approximate total utility curve derived from Fig. 5(a).

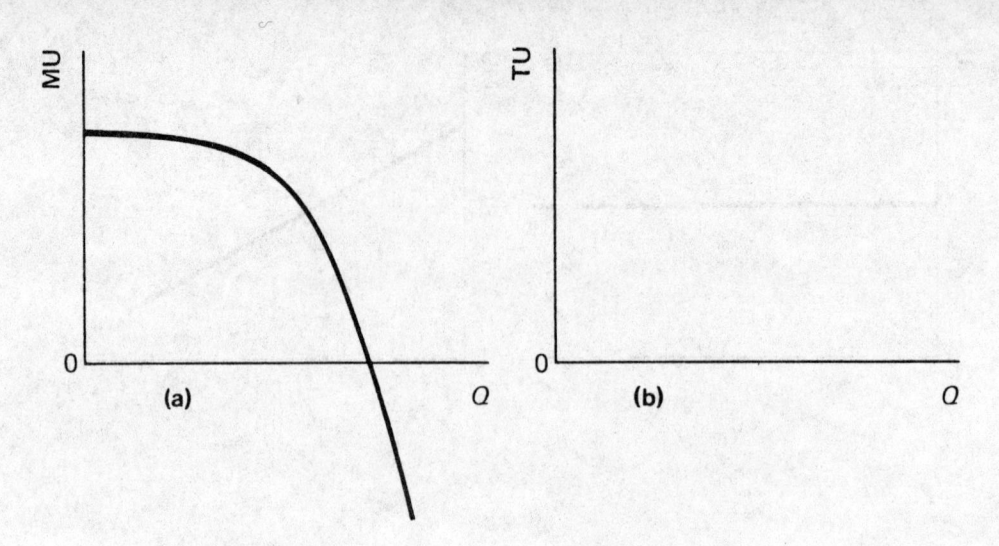

Fig. 5

Q 6 Write down the utility maximization rule for *any* 2 commodities, *x* and *y*.

$$\frac{MU \text{ of good } x}{\qquad} = \underline{\qquad\qquad}.$$

Q 7 Given the information below and given a continuity assumption, construct the two *MU* curves on Fig. 6 (*x* and *y* account for a small proportion of the consumers' total expenditure). *Hint:* let your *MU* scale run from 0–150. You can represent higher *MU*s roughly by allowing your *MU* curve to become almost vertical out of the top of the graph. So do not bother to plot points higher than 150 accurately.

Good x MU	Units consumed (per day)	Good y MU	Units consumed (per day)
∞	1	200	1
500	3	150	2
70	4	110	3
60	5	50	5
51	6	10	6
50	8	5	8
47	10	0	10

(1) If at a price of 50p each, 8 *x* are consumed, how many will be consumed (the price of all other goods being constant) if the price of *x* rises to 60p?

_____

(2) If good *y* costs 7p and good *x* costs 84p, how many *x* will be consumed given that 8 *y* are consumed? _____

If you could not see how to do this question, remember the utility-maximization formula

$$\frac{MU \text{ of good } x}{\text{Price of good } x} = \frac{MU \text{ of good } y}{\text{Price of good } y}$$

If you have enough information to fill in three of these quantities (the two marginal utilities and the two prices), then you can calculate the fourth. It merely means working out a simple equation like, for example, $6/4 = z/3$. The table in Q 7 gives this information. Look again at Q 7(2). Straightaway we can fill in the price of *y* and the price of *x*:

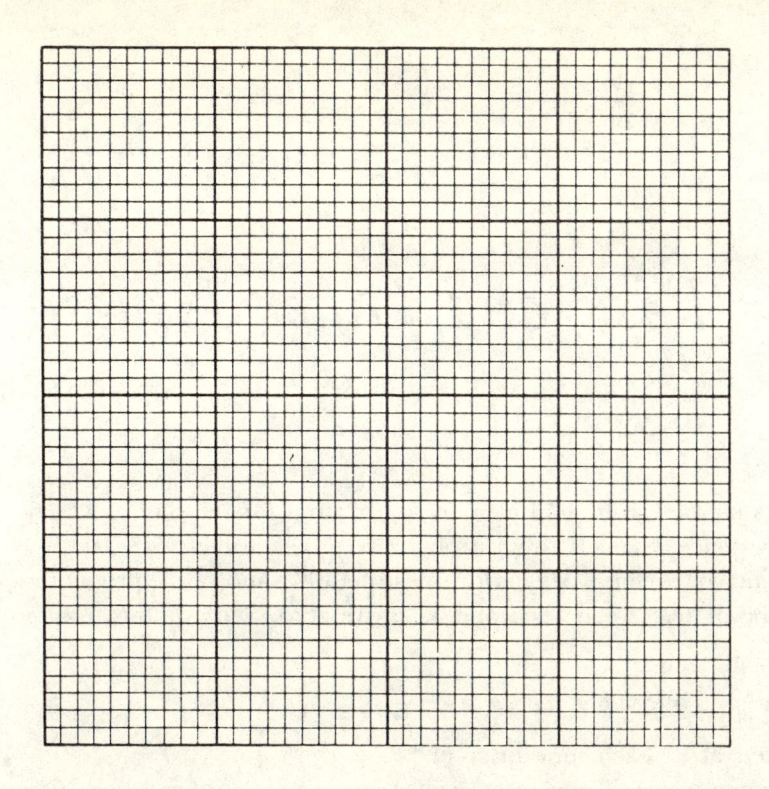

Fig. 6

$$\frac{\quad}{84} = \frac{\quad}{7}$$

The table for the *MU* of good *y* says that if 8 *y* are consumed daily, the *MU* of *y* will be 5. So we have now:

$$\frac{\quad}{84} = \frac{5}{7}$$

We can work out by algebra that the *MU* of good *x* must be 60.

Looking back at the *MU* table for good *x*, we see that if the *MU* is 60, then 5 units are consumed daily. And this is the answer. If you got it wrong, try Q 8.

Q 8   (1)   Using the data of Q 7, what is the *MU* of *x* if at a price of 11p three *y* are consumed per day, and *x* cost 5p each? _____

      (2)   What is the daily consumption of *x*? _____

As you can see, the part of the graph where the curves shoot up and away is irrelevant to these considerations. This illustrates one of the reasons why bread is cheaper than caviare.

CHAPTER 9
Uncertainty, Risk and Other Issues

Q1 A businessman rents an ice-cream stall at a cricket ground for the day of a major match. On past experience, there is a 0.5 probability of a fine day with sales of £800; a 0.4 probability of a cloudy day with sales of £400; and a 0.1 probability of so much rain that the match is cancelled and sales are zero. What is the *expected value* of sales? _____

Q2 Which of the following is offering a *fair game*?

  (a) ten lottery tickets at £1 each, one prize of £6.
  (b) £1 stake in a game where if you toss a coin twice and it's a head both times, you win £3 (plus your stake returned).
  (c) an insurance policy which costs £100 per year and pays you £30,000 if your home burns down (the probability of a house burning down here in a given year may be taken as 0.001).

Q3 The fact that people buy insurance suggests an increasing/constant/diminishing marginal utility of income.

Q4 Increasing marginal utility of income is inconsistent with purchasing tickets in a profit-making lottery. T/F

Q5 The demand for food as a whole has been found to be elastic/inelastic.

Q6 Demand tends to be more elastic the greater/the less the number of close substitutes.

Q7 If bus travel is an inferior good, its price elasticity of demand has to be close to zero. T/F

Q8 Figure 1 shows two observations (for successive years) of the price and quantity sold of a particular commodity. Which of the following could *not* be a possible explanation of the observations?

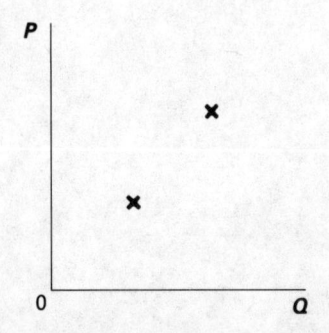

Fig. 1

(a) The supply and demand curves both shifted.
(b) The supply curve did not shift, but the demand curve shifted right.
(c) The supply curve is positively sloped but shifted right, the negatively sloped demand curve being unaltered.
(d) The commodity in question is a Giffen good.

QUESTIONS FOR DISCUSSION

1 Historically, the gambler who has staked a £1 bet on every ride by the jockey who had most winners in that particular season has not lost any less money per bet than the one who staked the same on the second (or tenth) most successful jockey. Why?

2 Is it inconsistent behaviour to insure your house *and* gamble on the football pools each week?

3 In any year, low-income households consume more cigarettes per week on average than high-income households. Does this imply the shrinking of the industry if the aggregate income of the country rises?

4 What do we mean when we say that there is a ready-made alibi to explain away any apparent refutation of some theory? Why do we say that tastes provide such an alibi in demand theory? What would we need to do to remove this particular alibi?

5 As measured in bed-nights, the British seaside hotel industry has declined substantially since 1960. Can we conclude that seaside holidays are an inferior good? If they are, are they likely to continue to be inferior as income growth continues over the next thirty years?

6 Both the price level and the total sales of fresh flowers reach a peak in the week before Mother's day. Can one conclude anything about the shapes of the demand and supply curves for fresh flowers?

CHAPTER 10
The Firm, Production and Cost

Q1 In the *market sector* of the economy, we distinguish four types of enterprise. For each of the definitions below, indicate the name normally used for that category of firm.

(a) One owner – legally responsible for everything the firm does.

(b) Two or more owners – each is legally responsible for *all* the firm's debts.

(c) The firm is a separate legal entity and the owners are not legally liable for any debts or actions of the firm (thus their maximum potential loss is their original investment in the firm).

(d) A state-owned firm with a separate legal entity.

Q2 In a joint-stock company, the *shareholders* own the firm. Firms raise funds initially by selling the shares (ownership certificates); but a further major source of funds in modern economies arises because much of the subsequent profit is not paid out in dividends but is used for further investment. This is known as distributed/undistributed profit.

Q3 Traditional economic theory predicts how firms behave by making a simplifying assumption about what motivates its decisions. What is this assumed goal of firms?

For this assumption to be appropriate, it is not necessary that all firms follow it all the time. An assumption is judged by its ability to generate empirically successful predictions.

A firm's *profit* in a period is defined as the difference between its total revenue and its total cost. However, costs are a particularly difficult concept, so that a firm's profits as defined by economists may be different from that recorded by accountants or tax authorities. An economist's assessment of profits will be based on defining costs in terms of *opportunity cost*.

Q4 If a firm can fund an investment from its own sources rather than having to borrow, the opportunity cost of its investment is zero. T/F. Explain.

Q5 If the rate of interest available to lenders were significantly less than that charged to borrowers, the opportunity cost of an investment is different according to whether the firm uses its own funds or whether it has to borrow. T/F. Explain.

Q6 A firm buys a machine for £5,000 which can produce at a constant rate of output for five years. Government safety regulations allow it to be *in use* for only five years and after that it has no value. The second-hand value of the machine depends solely on how much time remains when it can legally be used – i.e. the second-hand price is £1,000 times t, where t is the number of years of possible further use.

(1) What is the depreciation cost of the first six months' use of the machine? _____

(2) What is the depreciation cost of the last six months' use of the machine? _____

(3) What is the depreciation cost of the machine when the firm leaves it idle for six months? _____

Now assume that safety regulations enforce the scrapping of the machine after five years, regardless of whether it has actually been in use for the whole of the period.

(4) What is the depreciation cost of the first year's use of the machine?

(5) What is the depreciation cost of the machine when the firm leaves it idle for six months? _____

(6) If there is no second-hand market in these machines, what is the depreciation cost of the first six months' use? _____

Return now to just the original assumptions (i.e. ignore those for parts (4), (5) and (6)). After two years of continuous use, a technical innovation lowers the price of new machines to £2,500.

(7) What happens to the resale value of the existing machine? _____

(8) The firm suffers a once-and-for-all capital loss. T/F

(9) Will there be a change in the depreciation cost of using the machine for another six months from now? Yes/No. If yes, what is the new depreciation cost? If no, explain.
_____

If you got (9) wrong, you are forgetting that *bygones are bygones*. In planning actions for the next period, it is future costs that matter – past costs are irrelevant.

Q7 Explain why the cost to farmers of using manure as a fertiliser might be negative.
_____

Q8 Define *economic profit* (also known as *pure profit* or, in some basic texts, *supernormal profit*). _____

QUESTIONS FOR DISCUSSION

1 Why do single proprietorships dominate some industries (e.g., garages), whereas joint-stock companies are dominant elsewhere (e.g. in motor manufacturing)?

2 Most large retailing chains are joint-stock companies but began life as single proprietorships or partnerships. What circumstances would yield the switch and determine its timing?

3 Explain why a permanent rise in interest rates would raise the economic cost of production most severely for products like timber and whisky even if firms in these industries never borrow from a bank.

4 How do you think the managers of a large firm would decide on the speed with which they choose to pay the bills presented by their suppliers? Explain the role of the level of interest rates in the decision.

5 Your Uncle Joe wins £120,000 on the football pools. He considers using the money to buy a fast-food franchise in which he and his wife would work alongside some paid help. He tells you that after paying his staff, suppliers and tax he would make a 'clear profit' of £14,000 per year. Advise him on any appropriate modification to this figure that should be made before any final decision is taken.

CHAPTER 11
Cost and Output

THE PRODUCTION FUNCTION

Q1 Define the production function. _____

Q2 The production function will be affected by changes in the prices of inputs/outputs/neither.

Check your answer to Q2. We are at the moment only concerned with the physical relationship between, for example, tons of steel and motorcars, not the price of either.

Q3 Define the 'short run'. _____
_____

Q4 This question uses information shown in Table 1.

TABLE 1

(1) Quantity of labour per day	(2) Total product per day	(3) Average product (to nearest whole number)	(4) Marginal product
1	10		
2	27		
3	49		
4	73		
5	96		
6	112		
7	119		
8	121		
9	122		

Note. Variations of output per week with one fixed, one variable factor (land and labour). Land fixed at 1,000 acres.

(1) Does this Table show a short- or long-run production function? _____

(2) Fill in columns (3) and (4) of the Table.

(3) Plot the average and marginal product curves on Fig. 1 (label the vertical axis *Product*, the horizontal axis *No. of men*).

(4) Are the data in Table 1 consistent with the law of diminishing returns? Yes/No

(5) After what level of *total output* do diminishing marginal returns set in?
_____

(6) After what level of total output do diminishing *average* returns set in? _____
(For this answer, compare average products to one decimal place).

Check your answers. If you feel the need for more practice at this sort of curve-building, take the marginal product column given for Table 1 in the Answers section and derive the other two columns from it. Total product for any given quantity of labour input is just the sum of all the marginal products up to that point. For example, total product of the first 3 men is 10 + 17 + 22 = 49.

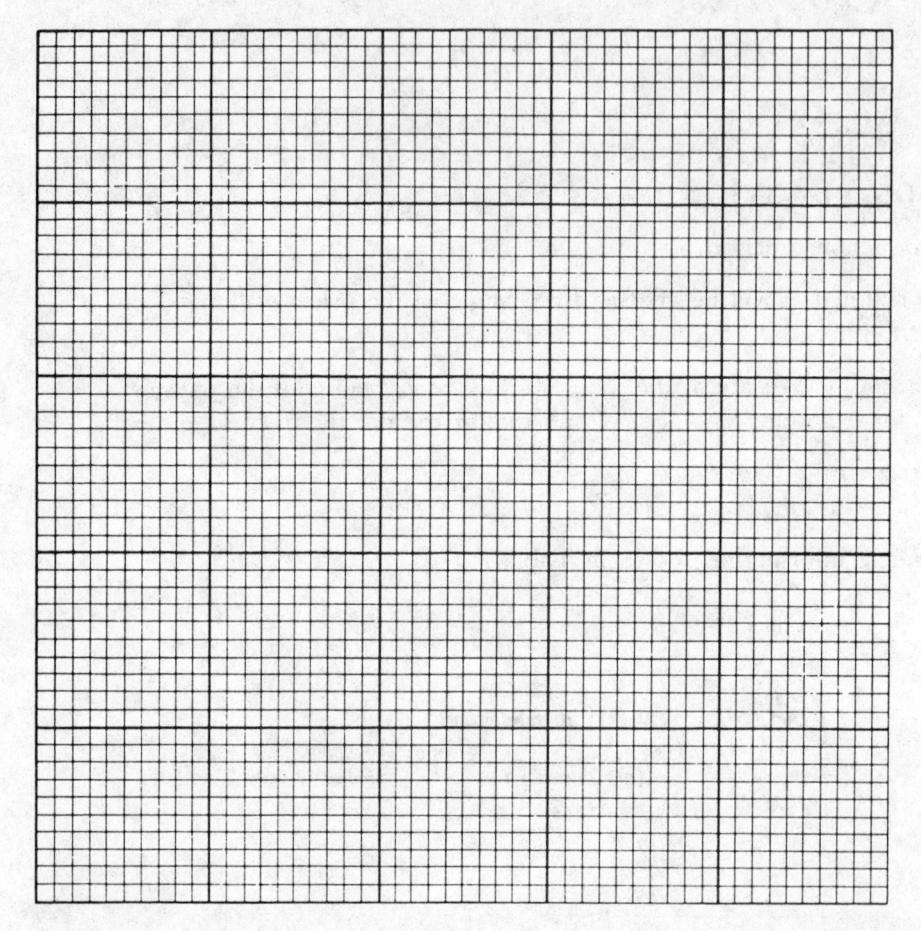

Fig. 1

SHORT-RUN VARIATIONS IN COSTS

Inputs have a cost; we assume that the unit cost is always the same to the firm. In terms of the example of Table 1, this means that if the wage rate for the first man is £18 per day, so is the wage rate for the tenth man.

You should now re-read Lipsey, pp. 182–85.

Q5 Average variable cost is always equal to or below average total cost. T/F

Q6 (1) Given that land costs £26 per acre per year rent, and that the weekly wage rate is £20, fill in the following weekly cost schedule on Table 2 using the data in Table 1.

TABLE 2

Quantity of labour	Total output	Total fixed cost	Total variable cost	Total cost	Average fixed cost	Average variable cost	Average total cost	Marginal* cost
1	10	500	20	520	50	2	52	2
2	27	500	40	540	18.5	1.5	20	1.18
3								
4								
5								
6								
7								
8								
9								

*For a working method of arriving at a figure of marginal cost, in this situation where inputs of the variable factor are not infinitely divisible (that is, they come in man-days only), divide the cost of each unit of labour by its marginal product. For graphical purposes, plot this at the level of output halfway between total output *including* the marginal unit, and *excluding* it. E.g. MC of 1.18 should be plotted against an output of 18.5.

(2) Plot the average and marginal cost curves on Fig. 2.

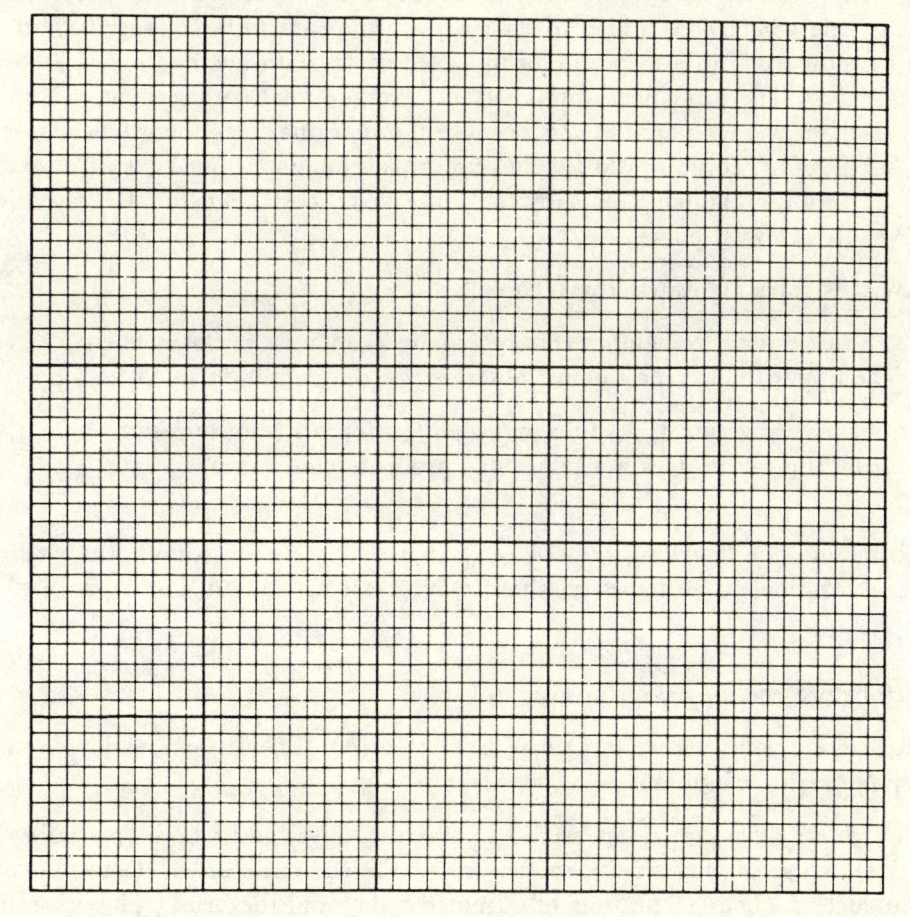

Fig. 2

(3) After what level of total output do increasing marginal costs set in?

(4) After what level of total output do increasing average total costs set in? _____

(5) After what level of total output do increasing average variable costs set in? _____

(6) After what level of total output do increasing average fixed costs set in? _____

Check your answers. The answers to Q6 parts (3) and (5) are the same as the answers to Q4(5) and (6). If you do not see why this should be, you should look again at Lipsey's Table 11.2.

(7) If you have plotted your graph correctly, the marginal cost curve should cut both AVC and ATC curves at their _____ point. If you find it difficult to see why this must always happen, and not be coincidence, you might think of cricket batting averages. So long as a batsman scores more runs than his previous average, his average rises. When he scores less, it falls. So if the average is falling, the marginal score must be below it, and if the average is rising, the marginal score must be above it. This means that when the average changes from falling to rising, the marginal score must change from below to above it – in other words it must cut it. And of course, the point where the average changes from falling to rising is the lowest point on the curve. This is true whatever is added to start with to the sum to be averaged. With average total costs, it is the value of the fixed costs; with average variable costs, it is zero. The principle is not affected. Average total cost will go on falling longer than average variable cost because the marginal increment which served to turn the AVC curve upward would not be so influential on the ATC curve, more heavily weighted as it is by the initial fixed costs. But the MC curve will cut it at its lowest point.

Q7 What is capacity output from Table 2? _____

If you got this wrong, remember that *capacity* in economics is not defined, as in ordinary usage, as the upper limit of productive ability – see the definition in Lipsey, pp. 184–85.

Q8 Profit maximization is a sufficient condition for cost minimization. T/F. Explain why cost minimization does not guarantee profit maximization.

_____

Q9 Rearrange the following symbols such that they state the condition for cost minimization (in an industry whose two factors are labour and capital).

$$P_L, = MP_K, MP_L, P$$

Do Q10 before checking your answer to Q9.

Q10 Rearrange your answer to Q9 in order to give a different expression to the cost-minimization conditions.

Q11 A firm employs capital (measured in machine-days) and labour (measured in man-days) as its only factors of production. At the current scale of operation, the marginal product of labour is 20 units of output per day and the price of labour is £10 per man-day. The marginal product of capital at the same output level is 200 units of output per day and its price is £50 per machine-day. *This firm is not cost-minimizing.* (Check for yourself.)

(1) At this output level, it should employ more/less labour and more/less capital.

(2) Suppose it employed five less labour units and used the saving to employ one more machine. Taking the marginal productivity figure as roughly constant over these ranges of employment, output per day would rise/fall by _____ units per day for the same total cost.

The significance of the assumption is that if the marginal productivity schedule is negatively sloped, each time one less man was employed, the impact on output would be greater than before. Indeed, this is what would eventually stop the process of switching expenditure from hiring one factor to hiring the other: once $MP_K/P_K = MP_L/P_L$, no further gains are to be made from substitution.

Q 12 Another firm employs capital (measured in machine-days) and labour (measured in man-days) as its only factors of production. At the current scale of operation, the marginal product of labour is 40 units of output per day and its price is £20 per man-day; the marginal product of capital is 80 units of output per day and its price is £40 per machine-day. Is the firm cost-minimizing? Yes/No. If the price of labour changed to £30 per man-day, then *for the same output level*, it would be appropriate to employ more/fewer machines.

Q 13 'A long-run average cost curve might be U-shaped because, as output is expanded,

(a) advantages of specialization are gained at first but managerial diseconomies set in later.
(b) the necessary machines get cheaper, then more expensive.
(c) spare floor space gets used up, thus spreading overheads better, but then runs out, and the consequent overcrowding produces inefficiency.'

One of these is wrong, which one? _____

If you made the wrong choice you must remember that since this is a long-run (minimum) cost curve, it is drawn to show costs when all factors are adjusted to be used in their cheapest combination for each rate of output.

So for points on the *LRAC* curve, there could never be any un-needed floor space. Could there be overcrowding? Yes, if we define overcrowding as a higher ratio of 'other factors' to floor space than for some lower level of output; no, if we define it as a situation in which the other factors are too close together to produce maximum efficiency for that level of output. The former possibility merely says that optimal factor proportions vary as output varies, which is quite possible; while the latter implies that the optimal proportions are not being employed. In this case we are not on the *LRAC* curve.

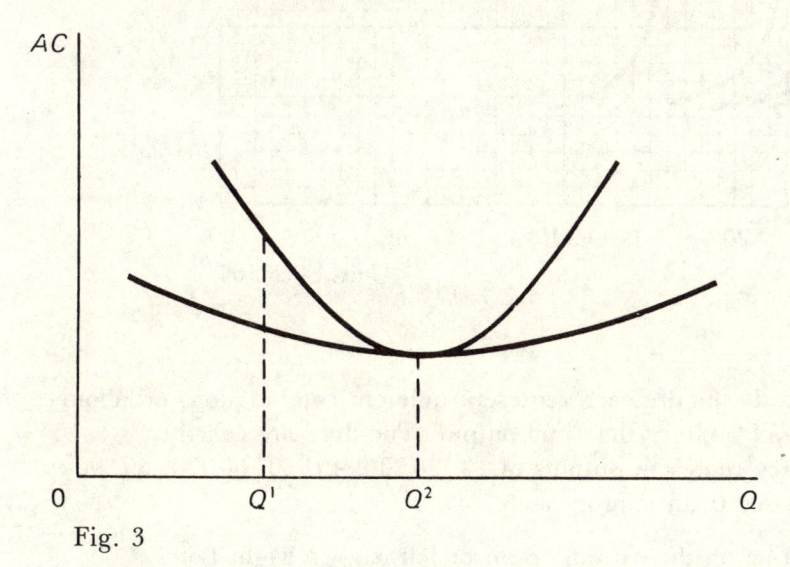

Fig. 3

Q14 (1) One of the curves in Fig. 3 is a *LRATC* curve, the other a *SRATC* curve. Which is the one underneath? _____

(2) How many levels of capital does the *SRATC* curve apply to? _____

(3) Why is it more expensive to produce Q^1 on the *SRATC* curve than on the *LRATC* curve?
_____
_____

Q15 Look at Fig. 4.

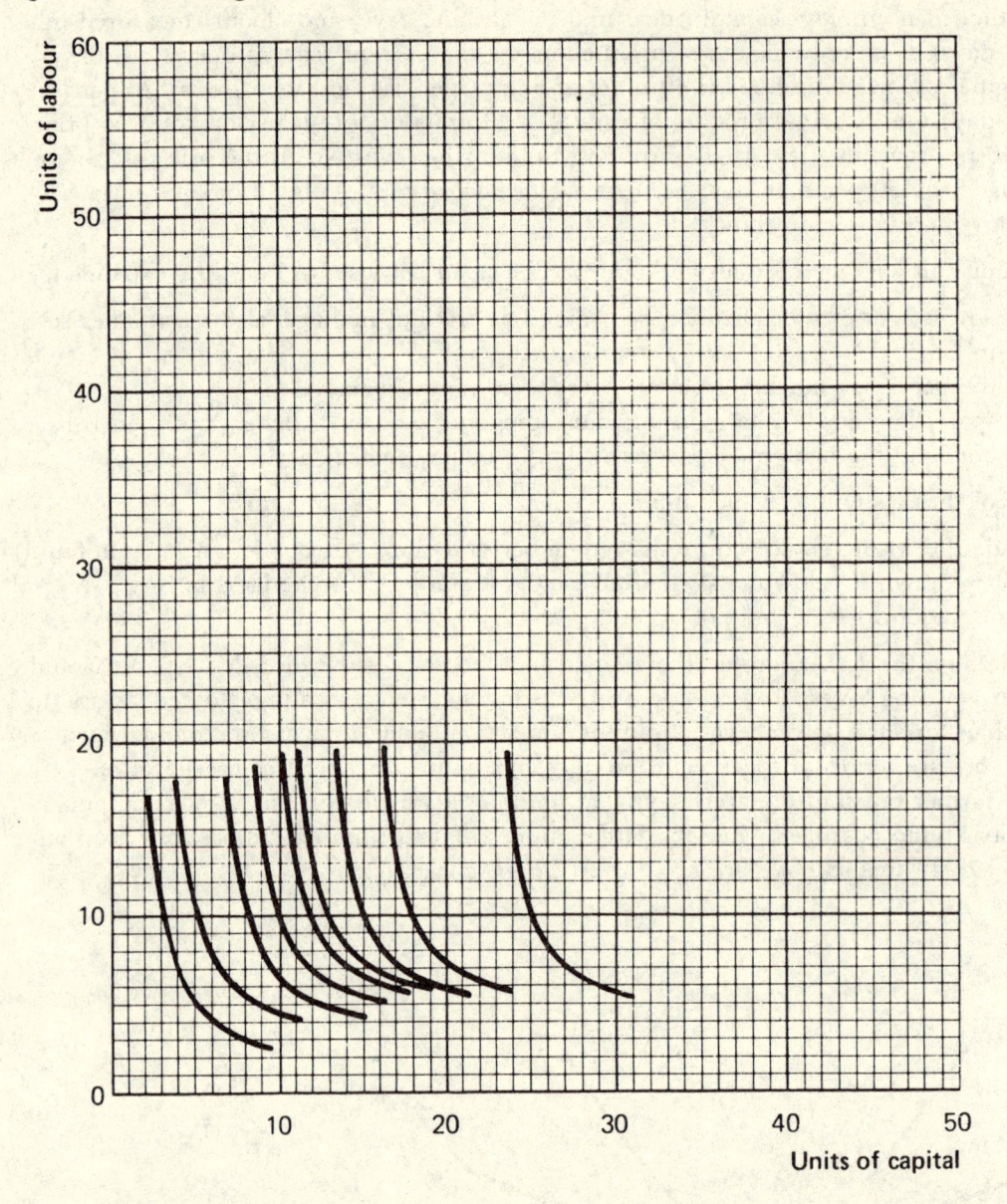

Fig. 4

(1) The lines drawn on the Figure each represent different combinations of labour and capital which will produce the same output. The lines are called _____. They represent outputs of 10, 20, 30, 40, 50, 60, 70, 80, 90 per unit of time. Label them appropriately.

(2) Should the 90 label be on the extreme right or left curve? Right/Left

Check your answer to 15(2) and, if you were wrong, think about it and correct your diagram.

(3) Labour costs £10 per unit, capital £20. Construct a set of isocost curves on Fig. 4 which will yield the cost-minimization points for the production levels of each isoquant. As output increases, relatively more capital/labour is used.

(4) What is the lowest cost at which an output of 30 per unit of time can be produced? _____

Check your answer to 15(4). If you were wrong, or could not do it, read on and do 15(5) and 15(6). If not, go on to 15(7).

All you have to do is to look at the point where the isocost curve, which you drew in order to answer 15(3), touches the 30 isoquant. You read off from this that 8½ units of labour are used and 9 units of capital. The cost is therefore 8½ × £10 + 9 × £20 = £265.

(5) What is the lowest cost at which an output of 50 per unit of time can be produced? _____

(6) What is the greatest output which can be produced for a total cost of £200? ____

(7) If the price of labour doubles – to £20 per unit – what will be the lowest cost at which 40 can be produced? _____

(8) What has been the change in the use of capital and labour in the production of 40 units, caused by this doubling of the price of labour?
capital up/down by _____ units
labour up/down by _____ units

(9) The effect shown in 15(8) exemplifies the principle of _____

Q 16 Plot a long-run average cost curve for the firm represented in Fig. 4 (with capital costing £20 and labour £10 regardless of how many units of each are employed) onto Fig. 5. Remember – it is an average cost curve, so you divide each total cost by the appropriate output.

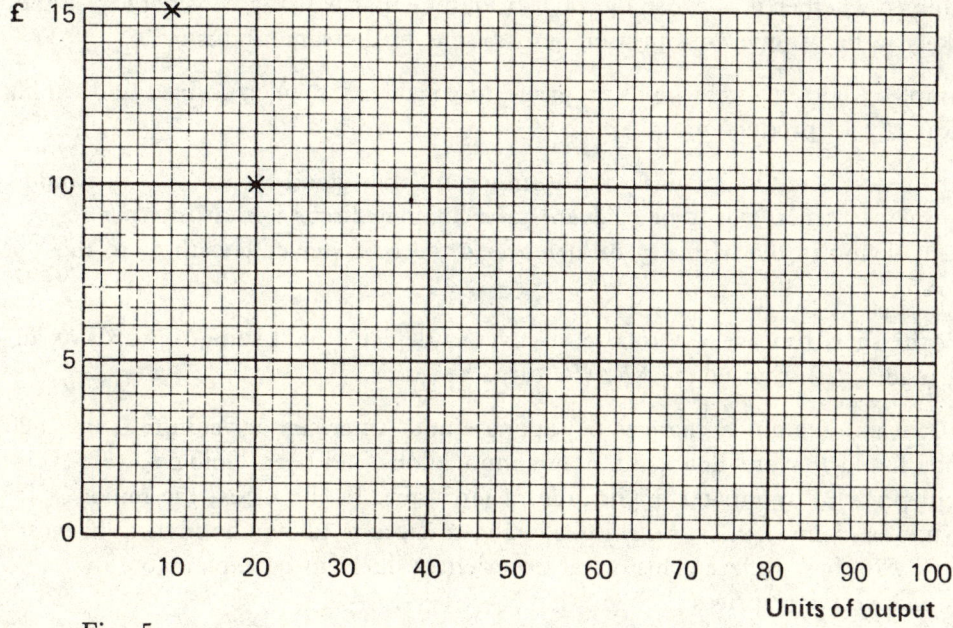

Fig. 5

(1) What is the minimum average cost of 60 units? _____

(2) Up to what output does this firm enjoy increasing returns? about _____

Q 17 The marginal cost curve cannot be deduced from the average cost curve, but can be deduced from the total cost curve. T/F

Q 18 If the *AC* curve is rising, the *MC* curve must be above it. T/F

Q 19 If the *AC* curve is above the *MC* curve, the latter might be either rising or falling. T/F

Q 20 The production function relates

(a) cost to input.
(b) cost to output.
(c) wages to profits.
(d) inputs to outputs.
(e) all of the above.

Q 21 Each short-run average cost curve

(a) never touches the long-run curve.
(b) always crosses the long-run curve.
(c) always lies above all points on the long-run curve.
(d) coincides with the long-run curve at one point.

Q 22 A change in factor prices

(a) changes long-run cost-curve positions.
(b) changes short-run cost-curve positions.
(c) alters the optimal factor proportions.
(d) is likely to do all of the above.

QUESTIONS FOR DISCUSSION

1 Is the 'short run' in a particular industry likely to correspond with a different length of time according to whether it is a rise or a fall in output that is being considered? Is the short run likely to be of different duration across firms in the same industry?

2 Suggest examples where it might be appropriate to consider labour as a fixed and capital as a variable factor of production.

3 'Good health in a country is obviously more important than good theatre'. Why would such an argument not necessarily be relevant to a Cabinet discussion on whether to allocate a £1m saving in the Ministry of Defence to the Minister of Health or to the Minister of Arts?

4 Explain why the short-run average total cost curve is depicted as turning upwards at an output level higher than that where *SRAVC* turns upwards.

5 Ruttan and Hayami examined changes in Japanese and American agriculture from 1880 to 1960. They found that in Japan, the major innovations had been biological (e.g. raising output per acre by greater application of fertiliser). In the USA, the major innovations had been mechanical (e.g. introducing tractors to allow one man to harvest vast acreages). Are these different historical experiences likely to be explainable by reference to relative factor prices?

CHAPTER 12

Perfect Competition

If we make two simplifying assumptions about the behaviour of firms, and the conditions under which they operate, we can use our previous supply and demand analysis together with the assumption of profit maximization to spell out in detail, but extremely succinctly, the logical implications of our theory. The use of the word 'perfect' to qualify the theory does not imply that a world in which the assumptions are true is a better world than one in which they are not true; it is merely meant to indicate a situation of 'extreme competition' or 'as much competition as is logically possible'.

Q1 The theory of perfect competition is based upon two assumptions, one about the firm, the other about the industry.
The firm is a _____
The industry has _____

TOTAL, AVERAGE AND MARGINAL REVENUE OF THE FIRM IN PERFECT COMPETITION

Q2 In perfect competition the average revenue curve and the firm's demand curve are all the _____

Q3 Given the information that a firm sells 200 units per period and has total revenue of £100 per period, draw on Fig. 1 the relevant firm demand curve.

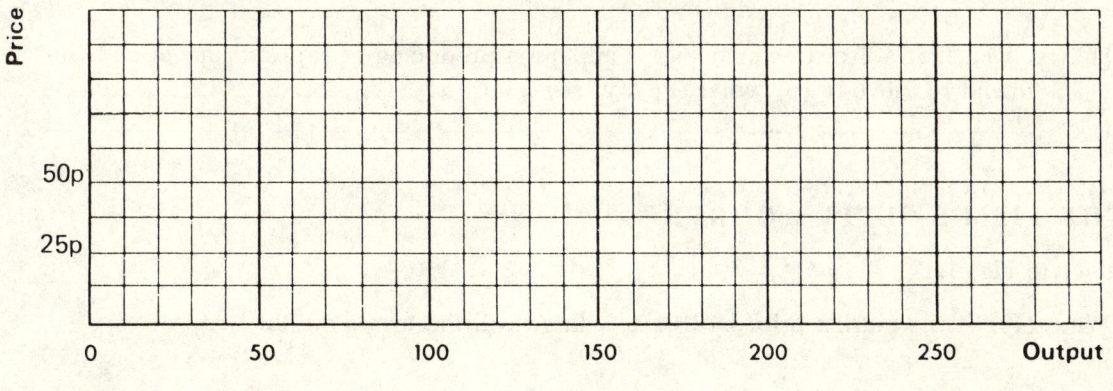

Fig. 1

Q4 Construct the total revenue curve, corresponding to the above diagram, on to Fig. 2.

(1) Can a *TR* curve in perfect competition be anything but a straight line? Yes/No

(2) What is *TR* at an output of 500? _____

Fig. 2

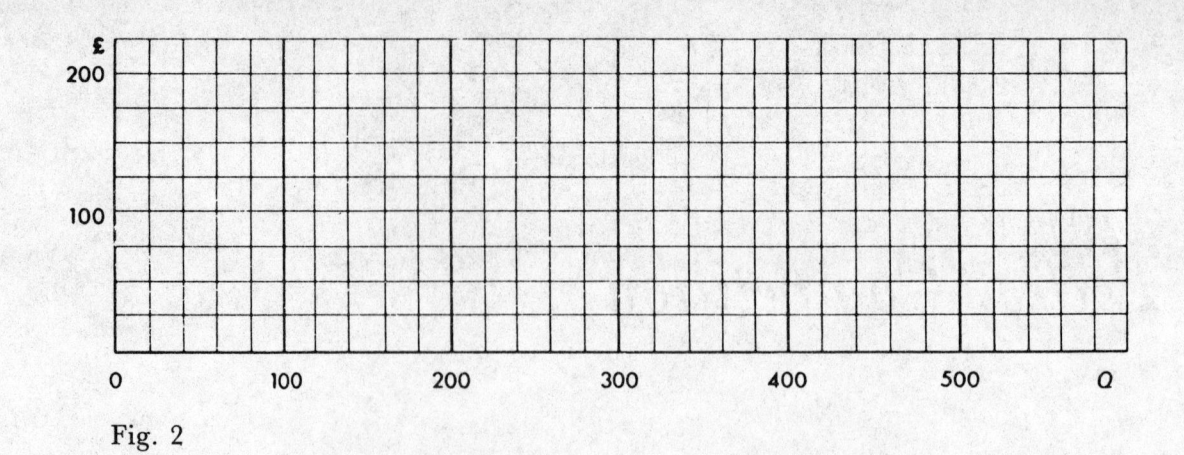

SHORT-RUN EQUILIBRIUM OF THE COMPETITIVE FIRM

Q5 If a firm maximizes profits, then in equilibrium marginal _____ is equal to marginal _____

If a firm is perfectly competitive, market price equals marginal revenue. Therefore, when a perfectly competitive, profit-maximizing firm is in equilibrium, price equals marginal/average/total cost.

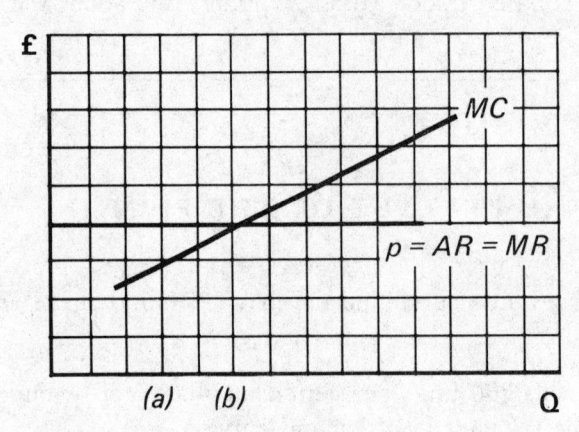

Fig. 3

Q6 Given that a firm to which Fig. 3 applies is producing at (a), and that it does not intend to move to (b), what can you say about it? _____

THE FIRM'S SUPPLY CURVE

Refer to Fig. 4.

Q7 (1) If the market price is £10, how large will the firm's output be? _____

(2) If the firm's output is 30, what is the market price? _____

(3) Below what price will the firm not produce? _____

(4) If the price is £8.25,
what is AVC? _____
what is output? _____

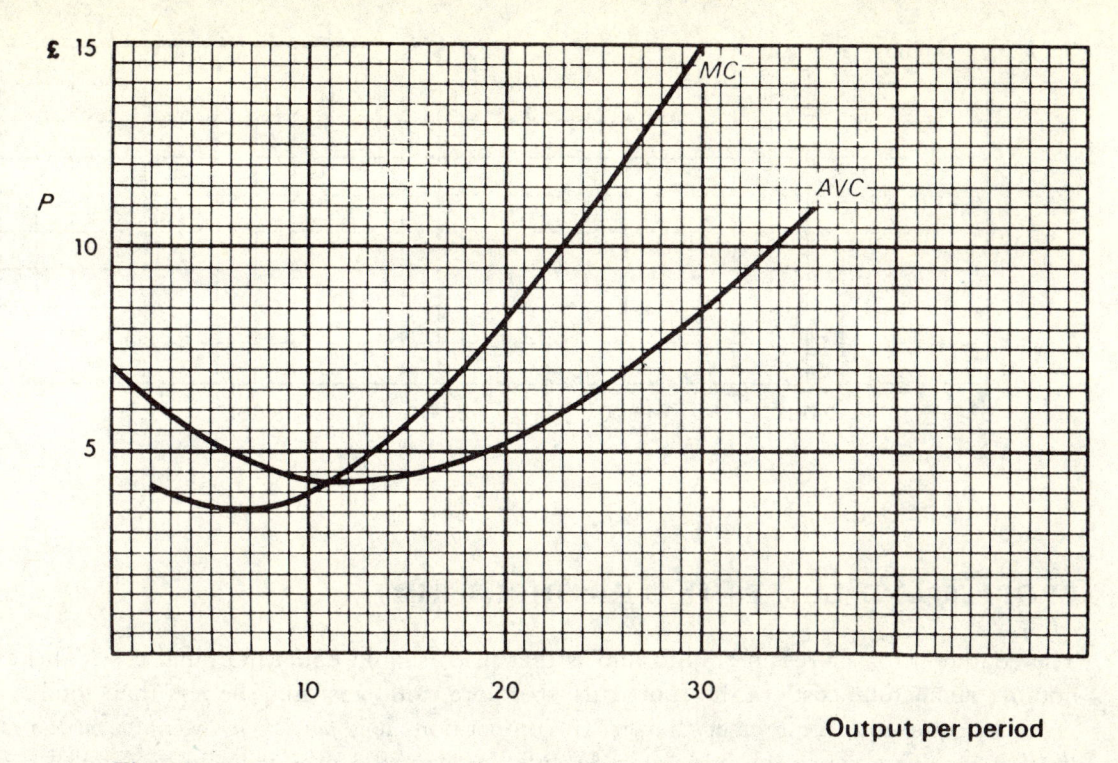

Fig. 4

what is, therefore, the total return on *fixed* costs (i.e. excess of revenue over *VC*)? _____

THE SHORT-RUN SUPPLY CURVE FOR A COMPETITIVE INDUSTRY

Q8 There are 520 firms in the schmoo industry. 200 have a supply curve as in Fig. 5, and 320 have a supply curve as in Fig. 6:

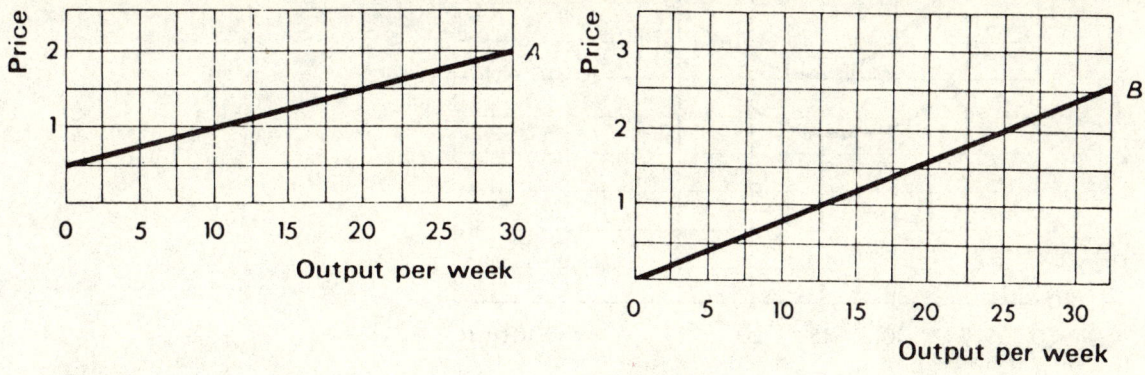

Fig. 5   Fig. 6

Construct the industry supply curve for schmoos on Fig. 7:

The industry is faced with a straight-line demand curve which is defined by the two points that at $p = 3$: 0 is demanded, and at $p = 2$: 3,000 are demanded.

(1) What is the equilibrium price and quantity? _____

(2) How much will each firm with supply curve A offer? _____

(3) How much will each firm with supply curve B offer? _____

67

Fig. 7

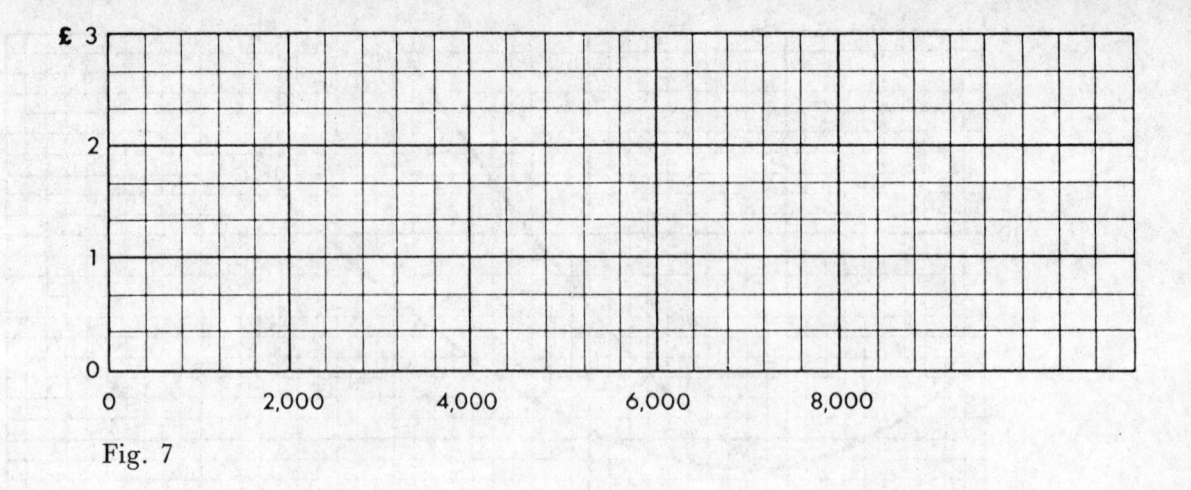

PROFITS AND LOSSES IN THE SHORT RUN

The condition for short-run equilibrium is that price should equal marginal cost. This says nothing about total cost. In the short run, therefore, total cost may be less than total revenue, equal to it, or greater than it. In competition, it is *possible for a firm to make a loss in the short run*. This may seem odd; why doesn't the firm stop producing immediately? Because, although it is making a loss, it is making the minimum possible loss. Were it to close down, it would still have to meet all its fixed contractual payments (unless, of course, it went bankrupt): these are *unavoidable* costs in the short run and, bygones being bygones, play no role in the short-run decision on whether to produce. So long as *variable* cost is less than revenue, it will pay the firm to remain in operation in order to offset some at least of its potential loss.

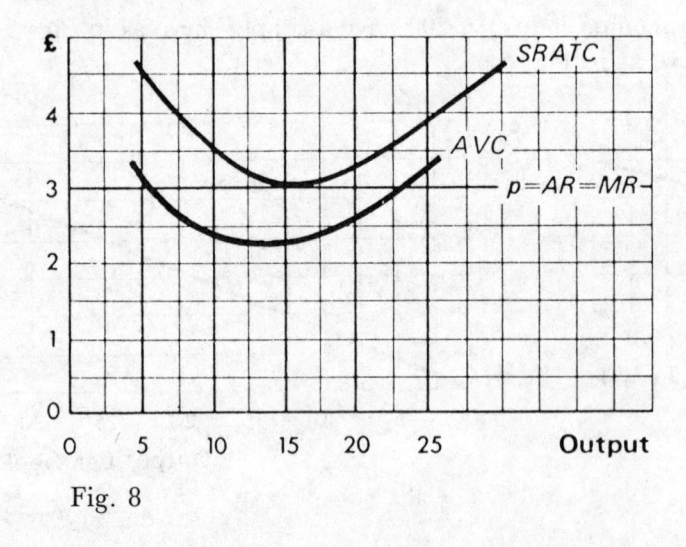

Fig. 8

Q9 Have you enough information in Fig. 8, which is the cost diagram for a profit-maximizing firm, to deduce immediately the output of the firm? Yes/No. If so, what is it? _____

The next question makes you think about a case in which the distinction between fixed and variable cost is less clear-cut; but the basic principles of considering what costs can be avoided in what circumstances are the same here as in the parable told by Lipsey in Box 12.2, p. 212.

Q10 A firm owns a factory (which it does not envisage selling). The firm bought the factory by borrowing funds and must pay a £1,000 mortgage payment on it each month. Furthermore, *if the factory is used for production*, it must pay a rates bill (a local business property tax) of £150 per month and heating costs of £200 per month. If the factory is not used, these bills are zero. Labour is the only variable input, and use of the factory involves no wear and tear on the equipment.

(1) If there is no possibility of leasing the factory to another firm, what is the minimum amount by which total revenue per month must exceed total labour costs per month before the firm will choose to engage in production? £____

(2) Suppose there is in fact no output level at which revenue would cover labour costs. However, leasing the plant to another firm is feasible. Under the lease, the factory owner would be responsible for the rates bill and the tenant firm for the heating bill. Above what level would the rent per month have to be, for the owner of the factory to agree to lease it out? £____

(3) Consider now the same type of leasing possibility but a situation in which the firm owning the factory could locate at its short-run profit-maximizing output and make a £500 per month return on fixed costs (i.e. excess of revenue over labour costs would be £500). In this situation, above what level would rent have to be, to lease the factory instead? £____

Q11 What is the second key assumption of perfect competition? _____
_____

Q12 Consider the position of the firm shown in Fig. 9.

(1) The firm is currently producing output Q. Is it in short-run equilibrium? Yes/No

(2) If all firms in the industry were in the same position, then in the long run capital will move into/out of the industry and the price of the product will fall/rise/stay the same.

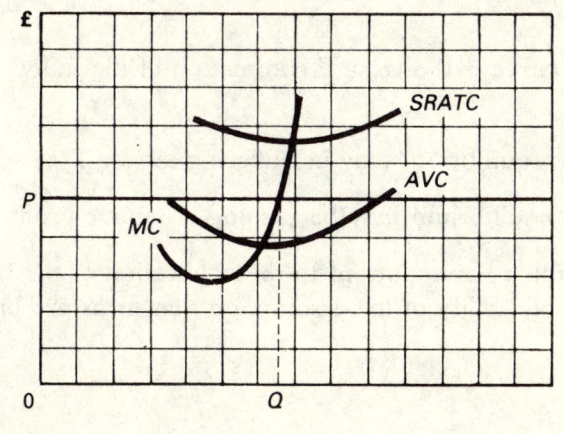

Fig. 9

REVISION

As this is another central chapter to the exposition of traditional microeconomic theory, we include again a selection of revision questions covering the whole range of material.

Q13 In short-run competitive equilibrium, we predict that:

    (a) marginal cost is rising.
    (b) $P = MC$.
    (c) there is no incentive for firms to enter the industry.
    (d) all of the above answers are satisfactory.
    (e) both (a) and (b) are satisfactory.
    (f) none of the above answers is satisfactory.

Q14 If more firms enter a competitive industry, our theory predicts that:

    (a) marginal cost curves rise.
    (b) the industry supply curve shifts to the right.
    (c) output of all existing firms increases.
    (d) product price falls.
    (e) all of the above answers are correct.
    (f) both (b) and (d) are satisfactory.
    (g) none of the above answers is satisfactory.

Q15 In long-run competitive equilibrium, the theory predicts that:

    (a) $TC = TR$.
    (b) firms operate at minimum average total cost.
    (c) $MC = MR$.
    (d) there is no incentive for entry or exit of firms.
    (e) all of the above answers are satisfactory.
    (f) none of the above answers is satisfactory.

Q16 If firms are suffering losses in a short-run competitive equilibrium, we predict that:

    (a) production will be stopped by the industry.
    (b) some firms will exit from the industry.
    (c) more efficient new firms will enter the industry.
    (d) both (b) and (c) are satisfactory.
    (e) none of the above answers is satisfactory.

Q17 For a price-taker, $P = MR$. T/F

Q18 The long-run industry supply curve is the vertical summation of the individual firms' supply curves. T/F

Q19 Firms in short-run competitive equilibrium may be suffering losses. T/F

Q20 Firms in long-run competitive equilibrium may be earning economic profits. T/F

Q21 The number of firms in an industry is important to the application of the competitive model because it affects the applicability of the assumption that firms are price-takers. T/F

QUESTIONS FOR DISCUSSION

1 The two assumptions of perfect competition are that each firm is a price-taker and that the industry has freedom of entry and exit. Some elementary texts have, however, published longer lists of assumptions including 'many firms', 'identical firms' and 'homogeneous product'. Explain why these can be interpreted as a set of sufficient conditions yielding a state of perfect competition as properly understood.

2 Why do we say that perfect competition and decreasing costs (over the entire relevant output) are incompatible in long-run equilibrium? If we observed an industry with many firms, each one of which had unexploited economies of scale, would you conclude that the industry was not perfectly competitive? Would your answer be affected by the added information that (a) the industry was not growing in size, or (b) the industry was growing in size?

3 The demand for a product shifts left, reflecting changed tastes in the community. Trace through the consequent short- and long-run changes in the industry and in the individual firms that comprise it. At each stage, pay special attention to price, quantity and the level of profit.

4 When changes in an industry's demand bring about an outflow of capital, what determines which firms exit?

5 In a long-run perfectly competitive equilibrium, is it possible for *some* firms to earn positive economic profits or must *all* firms earn zero economic profits?

CHAPTER 13
Monopoly

This chapter should seem simpler than the previous one. This is because by now you should be thoroughly familiar with all the important concepts used in our analysis.

Q1 In order to review your understanding of these, you should provide one-sentence definitions of each of the following:

(1) Demand _____

(2) Marginal revenue _____
_____

(3) Short-run average total cost _____
_____

(4) Long-run average total cost _____
_____

(5) Average variable cost _____
_____

(6) Marginal cost _____
_____

(7) Profits _____
_____

All the conclusions of the theory of monopoly that differ from the conclusions of the theory of perfect competition stem from the alteration of one assumption. *Whereas a competitive firm faces a flat demand curve, a monopolistic firm faces a downward-sloping demand curve.* In other words, the monopolist is *not* a price-taker. We see from the argument of this chapter in Lipsey that, given normal assumptions about the shape of the various cost curves, a monopolist can make a profit in the long run. Long-run profits can only exist if capital is prevented from being transferred into the industry where they are being made. *Barriers to entry* are therefore an implication of the assumption that the monopolist's demand curve does not shift in the long run.

Q2 In perfect competition, $AR = MR = P$. In monopoly, are these all the same?
_____

Q3 Look at Fig. 1.
We will now construct the marginal revenue curve. Let us look at the marginal revenue when output changes from 4 to 5 units. Total (weekly) revenue from the four units would have been $4 \times £24 = £96$. Total revenue from the five units, however, is $5 \times £22.50$, since in order to sell the extra unit price has had to drop

(by £1.50). Five times £22.50 is £112.50. The marginal revenue is, therefore, £112.50 – £96 = £16.50. This point is plotted on the graph at a point corresponding to 4.5 (i.e. midway between $Q = 4$ and $Q = 5$). Let us now look at the *MR* when output changes from 7 to 8 units.

(1) Total revenue from 7 units _____

(2) Total revenue from 8 units _____

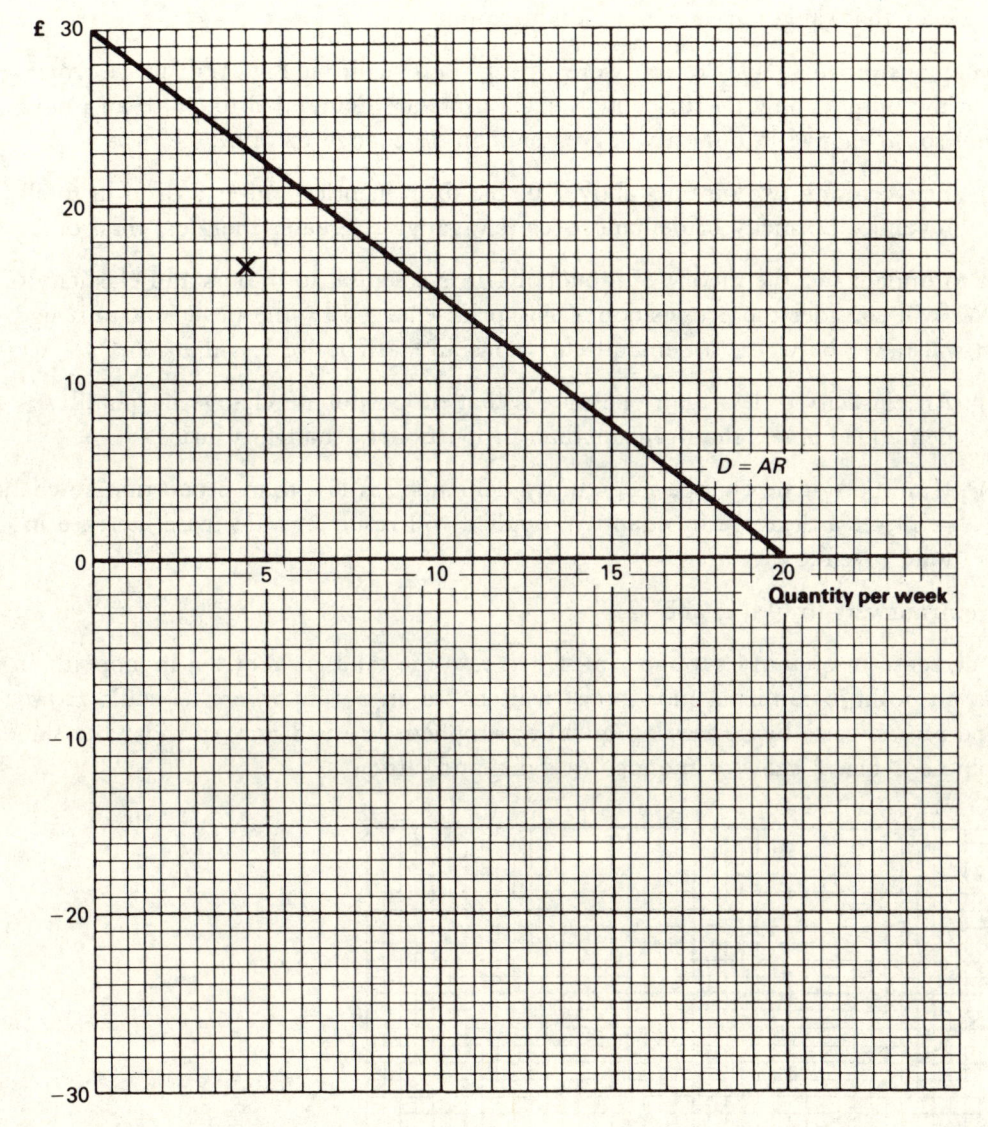

Fig. 1

(Check these answers – if you were wrong, work them out again.)

(3) Therefore, marginal revenue when output changes from 7 to 8 units is

_____

Plot this point on the graph.
Now, the *MR* of the 11th unit.

(4) *TR* from 10 units _____

(5) *TR* from 11 units _____

(Again, check these answers.)

(6) Therefore, *MR* when output changes from 10 to 11 units is _____
Now, draw a straight line through these points, and continue it below the horizontal axis. This is the *MR* curve. (N.B. Those well versed in mathematics could show that all the *MR* points lie on a straight line, which bisects exactly the distance from the origin to where the *AR* curve cuts the horizontal axis.)

(7) In our example, therefore, between any two outputs up to 10, the drop in price is actually associated with a rise in revenue. Elasticity of demand is therefore, over that range, greater than/less than one.

Check your answer to Q 3(7). If you were wrong, look again at Fig. 1. If price drops anywhere in the output range 1–10, enough extra units are demanded to cause an increase in revenue – so % change in quantity is greater than % change in price, i.e. $\eta > 1$.

(8) Between any two outputs above 10, the drop in price causes a drop in total revenue. Elasticity of demand over that range is greater than/less than one.

In order to understand the theory of monopoly, it is essential to understand elasticity of demand. We will consider the proposition: 'The price charged by the profit-maximizing monopolist will never be where a demand curve has an elasticity of less than one.'

Q4 (1) An elasticity of less than one means that proportionate change in quantity demanded is less than/greater than proportionate change in price.

(2) If proportionate change in quantity demanded is less than proportionate change in price, a decrease in quantity supplied will result in a decrease/increase in total revenue.

Check your answers to Q 4(1) and (2).

Since a decrease in quantity supplied must decrease the total costs of the monopolist in the short term, no profit-maximizing monopolist will choose an output where he could *increase* revenue and *decrease* costs by decreasing quantity supplied. We will now consider the same point graphically. Fig. 2 shows a monopolist's demand curve:

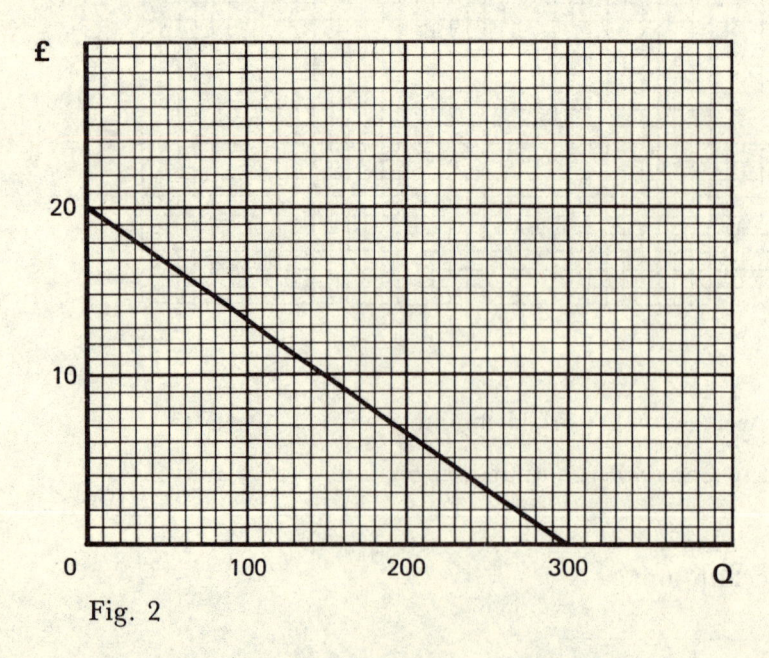

Fig. 2

(3) What is the level below which price will not be set? _____

Check your answer.

(4) On a straight-line demand curve, elasticity falls/rises as the curve falls.

(5) The point of unit elasticity is halfway down/a quarter from the top/a quarter from the bottom.

(6) Write down the formula for elasticity. _____

(7) What is elasticity at £8? _____

(8) What is elasticity at £12? _____

(9) What is the change in total revenue from a reduction in quantity supplied from 180 to 150? _____

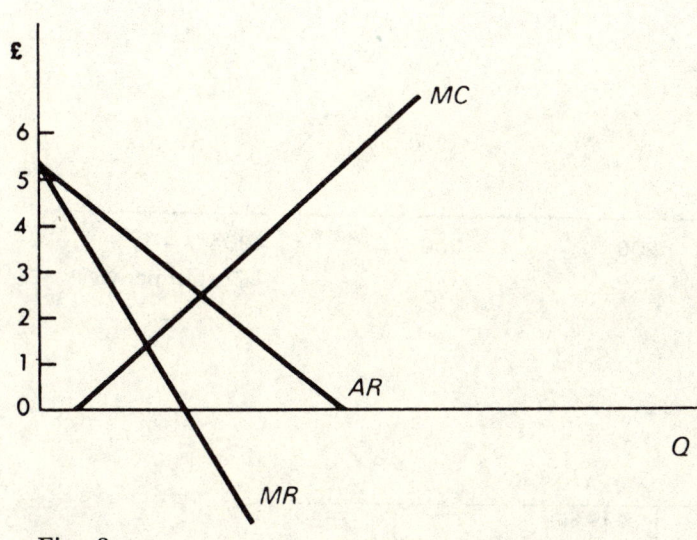

Fig. 3

Q5 Fig. 3 shows a monopolist's *MR*, *AR* and *MC* curves. What is the equilibrium price? _____

Q6 Does the marginal cost curve cut the *SRATC* curve, or the *AVC* curve, at its lowest point? _____

If you were wrong, re-read Lipsey, p. 184.

Q7 Superimpose on Fig. 4 the straight-line demand curve defined by the two points (0, £30) (300, £0). The marginal revenue curve corresponding to this is defined by the two points (0, £30), (150, £0). Draw this in also.

(1) What is the profit-maximizing quantity? _____

(2) What (approximately) is the total amount of profit? _____
Assume that the demand curve shifts until it is defined by (0, £20) (200, £0). Its *MR* curve is now defined by (0, £20) (100, £0).

(3) What will be the new price? _____

(4) For how long will it persist? _____

(5) Assume that the demand curve shifts until it is defined by (0, £21), (200, £0). What will be the new price? _____

(6) What will be the new level of profits? _____

(7) So a monopolist must/need not make profits.

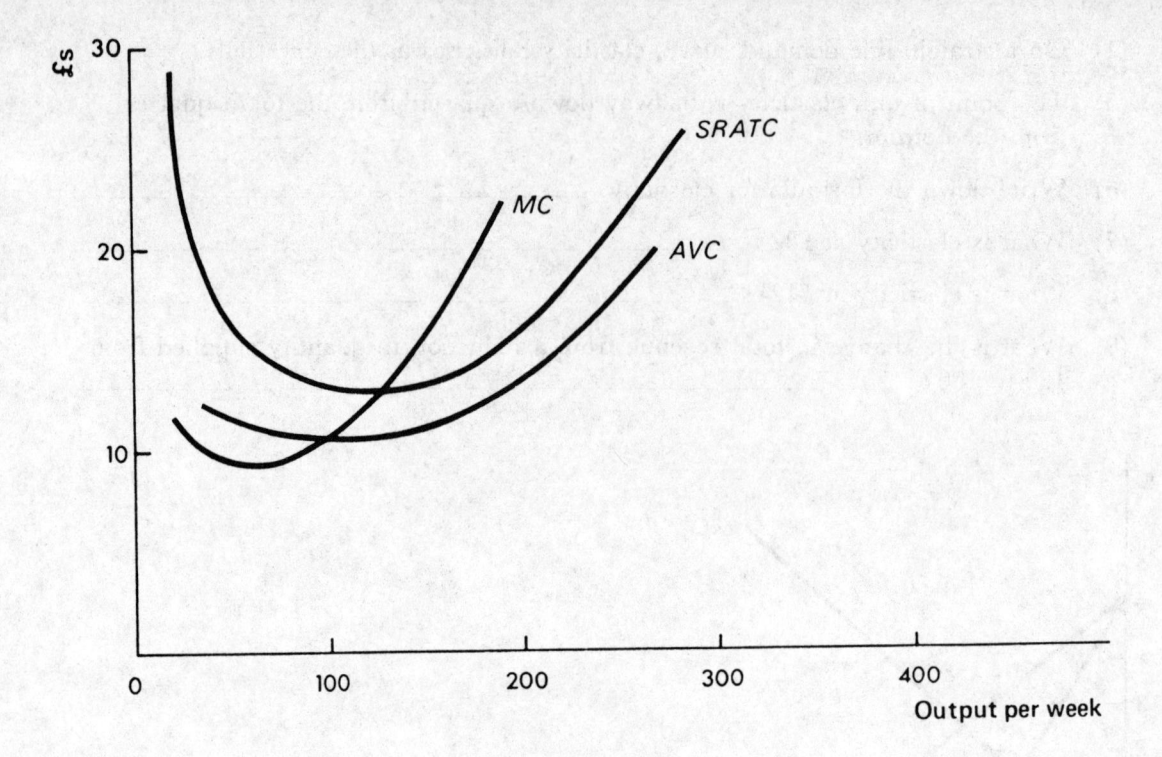

Fig. 4

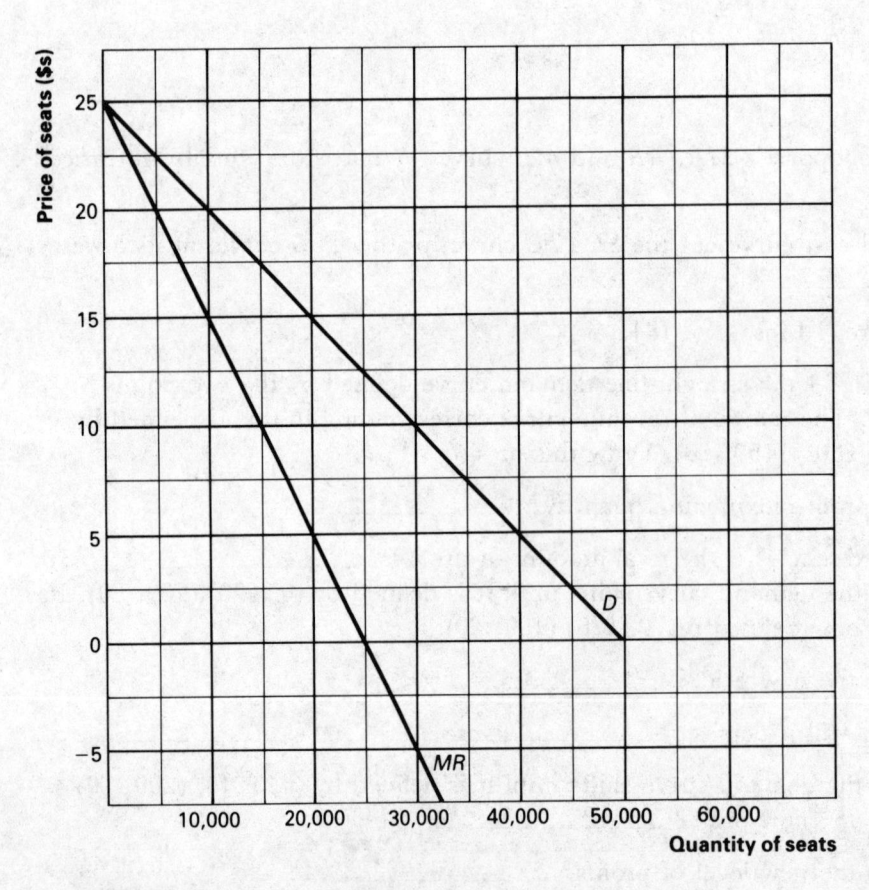

Fig. 5

Q 8 Suppose that the Manchester Morons play in a New England Football League in a 30,000 seat stadium (where all seats have an equally good view). For the weekly game, the demand and marginal revenue curves are as depicted in Fig. 5. The cost of putting on the game is the same no matter how many tickets are sold. The club owners are profit-maximizers.

  (1) The price charged for tickets will be $ _____

  (2) What will be the elasticity of demand at this price? _____

  (3) The League's central administration and school coaching programmes used to be funded by the sale of TV rights, but TV coverage is lost and it is decided to institute a levy of $1 per ticket sold on all clubs. After this change, the ticket price at the Morons' games will be $ _____ .

  (4) In this situation, demand will be elastic/inelastic.

THE ABSENCE OF A SUPPLY CURVE IN MONOPOLY (Read p. 223)

What is a supply curve? A supply curve joins all the points which show the quantity offered for sale by a supplier at a given price. One can therefore say, for a firm in competition, 'If the price is x, q will be offered for sale.' Why can this not be said for a monopolist? To start with, the monopolist is *not* faced with a market price to which he reacts. It is his behaviour which helps *make* the price. Secondly, different *shaped* demand curves (facing the monopolist with unchanged costs) might well result in different outputs but the *same* price. To summarize: in competition, only one output is associated with one price and vice versa. In monopoly, two or more prices may be associated with one output, or two or more outputs may be associated with one price.

Q 9 Patent laws, franchises, molotov cocktails and membership of the Royal Institute of British Architects have one thing in common. What is it? _____

Q 10 Overseas subscribers to a magazine are charged more than domestic subscribers, the excess reflecting higher mailing costs. Is this price discrimination? Yes/No. Explain.

Q 11 Student subscribers to a magazine are charged less than normal prices because they have low spending-power. Is this price discrimination? Yes/No. Explain.

Q 12 What must the seller be able to prevent in order to be able to practise price discrimination among buyers? _____

Q 13 Price discrimination among buyers is possible under perfect competition. T/F.

QUESTIONS FOR DISCUSSION

1 'Since the monopolist is the only firm in the industry, he can charge what he likes.' Comment.

2 In 1980, British legislation allowed bus companies to operate whatever pattern of inter-city coach services they liked. Previously a monopoly was enforced by licence on almost all routes; in most cases, it was granted to National Express. Ten years later, most routes are still served only by National Express. Does this imply the existence of barriers to entry? If so, what might they be?

3. In 1844, the French engineer, Dupuit, made a noted contribution to the economics of monopoly. His example was of a privately-owned bridge. Tolls could be levied on traffic but the structure was strong enough that no extra maintenance costs actually arose from allowing extra carts to pass. Sketch how the owner would decide on the level of toll. Would there be a gain from public ownership of the bridge with no toll charged?

4. A soccer club has a large enough stadium that it could not fill every seat even at zero price. All costs are fixed costs: no extra costs arise as the number of spectators increases. Under an agreement between the Football League and a television company, the TV company pays a levy to each club in the League based on a sum of 50 pence for every ticket sold by that club that week. To maximize profits, how should a club decide on the ticket price? What do you know about elasticity of demand at the profit-maximizing price?

5. Until 1989, British Gas negotiated individual tariffs with each of its industrial customers. This practice was then outlawed after a Monopolies and Mergers Commission Report. How do you think British Gas decided on the pattern of prices when it was able to discriminate? Who lost as a result of the Monopolies and Mergers Commission Report? Why did the Monopolies and Mergers Commission think that price discrimination was a barrier to entry by new gas suppliers?

Appendix to Chapter 13

Q1 Suppose that the London Louts football team play in a Canadian university city. The costs of putting on the weekly game are mainly fixed but there is a variable element of $5 per spectator associated with security, mailing of tickets, provision of programme, etc. The stadium capacity is 50,000. The townsfolk and students of London can be treated as separate markets since student tickets are clearly marked and must be supported by ID cards at the turnstile. Demand conditions are illustrated in Fig. 1(a) and (b). Owners are profit-maximizing. Use (c) to construct the combined *MR* curve and answer the following questions.

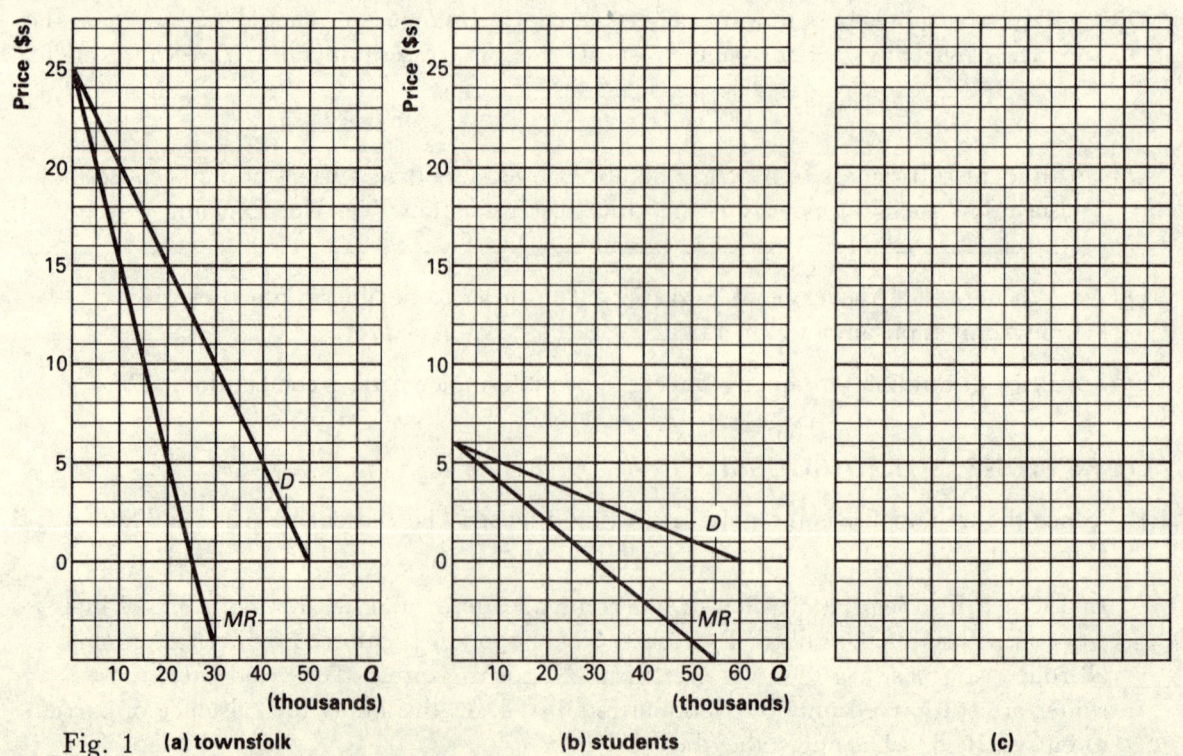

Fig. 1 (a) townsfolk   (b) students   (c)

(1) How many student tickets will be sold at each game? _____

(2) At what price? $_____

(3) How many non-student tickets will be sold at each game? _____

(4) At what price? $_____

(5) Why are ticket prices not lowered to fill the stadium? _____
_____

(a)

(b)

(c)

(d)

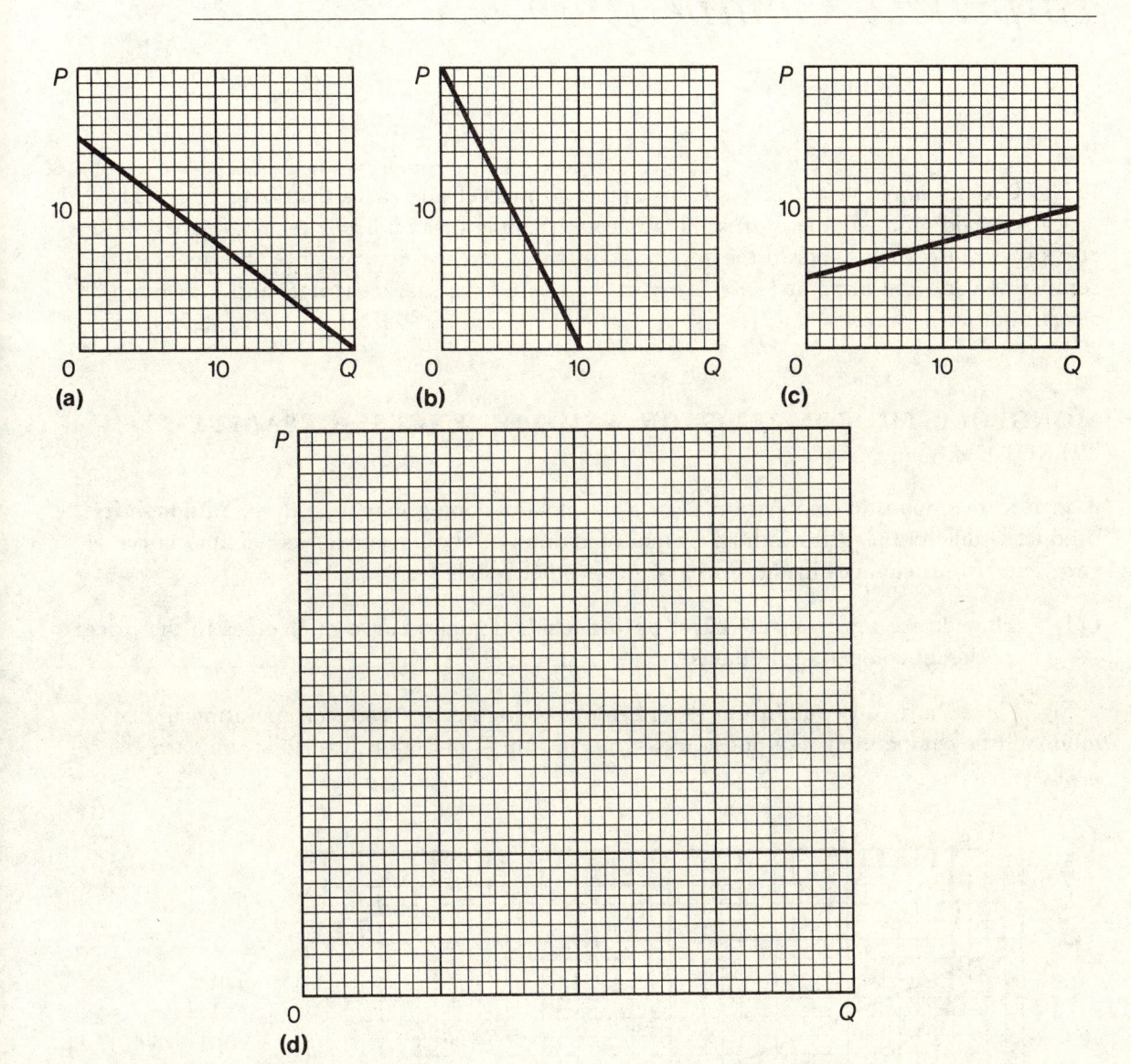

Fig. 2

Q2   The monopolist whose MC curve is given in Fig. 2(c) sells in the two separate markets, whose demand curves are given in Fig. 2(a) and (b). Construct on Fig. 2(d) the diagram which will show his equilibrium output.

     (1) What is the price in market (a)? _____

     (2) What is his price in market (b)? _____

     (3) What are his sales in market (a)? _____

     (4) What are his sales in market (b)? _____

CHAPTER 14
Imperfect Competition

In the UK, an apple producer sends his apples to market and takes the going price. The processed-food giant, Lyons, turns the apples into apple pies and sells them to supermarkets at a price which they quote to the supermarket chain. In the first instance, the market is competitive and the firms are *price-takers*, in the second the market is not, and a system of *administered prices* prevails.

MONOPOLISTIC COMPETITION AND THE EXCESS-CAPACITY THEOREM

A firm in monopolistic competition faces a downward-sloping demand curve. Although its product is differentiated from those of manufacturers of similar goods, its demand curve is very sensitive to changes in the prices of these other goods.

Q1   How do we represent the effect on the firm's demand curve of changes in the prices of closely competing products? _____

Fig. 1 is a short-run equilibrium diagram for a potato-crisp producer operating under monopolistic competition. Output is measured in 'units' of 100 grams (four standard packets).

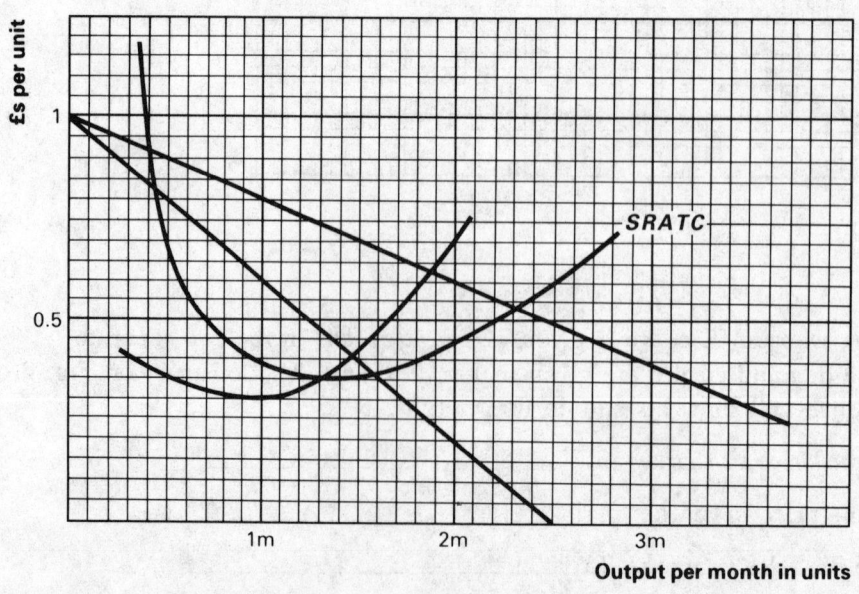

Fig. 1

Q2 (1) Label the curves.

(2) Estimate the SR equilibrium price. _____ pence per unit.

(3) Estimate the SR equilibrium quantity. _____ units per month.

(4) Estimate the SR equilibrium profit. £ _____ per month.

Q3 Because the company is now making profits, what will be the reaction of at least some other firms? _____

Q4 (1) The increase in the number of firms among whom total demand has to be shared will cause the company's demand curve to shift to the right/left.

(2) The immediate influx of new firms means that, to start with, the AR curve shifts 1m units to the left, parallel to its old position. Will there be an incentive for even more firms to enter the industry? Yes/No

(3) Assume that the next influx were to cause an *additional* shift to the left of 1.2m units. Now what will some firms do? _____

Q5 What will the price be when the firm is in equilibrium, assuming that the demand curve shifts parallel to its previous position?

Q6 Look at Fig. 2, which shows the short-run equilibrium of a firm in monopolistic competition. Its correct output is 12 units per period.

Draw in a possible marginal cost curve. It must pass through two points. These points are

(1) £ _____ Q _____

(2) £ _____ Q _____

(3) Equilibrium price is £ _____

Check your answers. If you were wrong on (1) and (2), then re-read Lipsey, pp. 182–84. You should know that MC curves always cut AC curves at their lowest point – look again at p. 60 of the Workbook. And in any position of equilibrium, MC = MR, otherwise the firm would make more profits by simply producing more, or less.

Q7 Is Fig. 2 consistent with the situation being one of long-run equilibrium? Yes/No. Explain _____

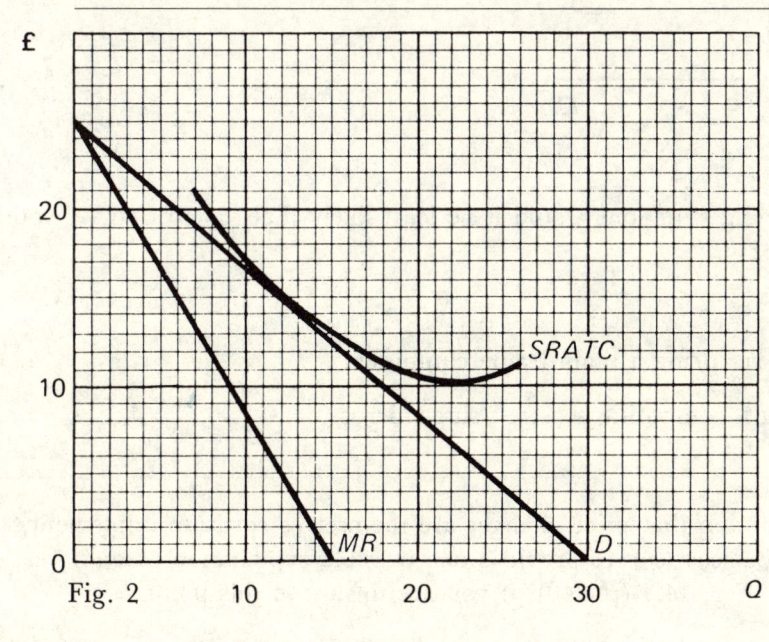

Fig. 2

Q8 The firm shown in Fig. 2 produces an output level lower than that which would minimize average total cost: this result is the _____ (1) theorem and holds in the short run and the long run. In the short run, it is easy to understand.

A profit-making firm, with the optimal capital equipment, finds that its profits _____ (2) other firms into the industry and this causes its sales to _____ (3) (its demand curve shifts to the right/left) (4). Its capital stock is therefore appropriate to a larger output than its equilibrium output. So it has excess capacity because it has *not* got the optimal capital stock.

But in the long run, as it seeks to reduce costs, it must move to its _____ (5) curve. And, as we have seen, it must move to that part of this curve where it is best to use a capital stock which could be operated even more cheaply at a higher level of output. (This is the point made on Lipsey, pp. 235–36, which you should re-read if necessary.) So in this case, although the firm has excess capacity, it is on its optimal *SRATC* curve.

(6) Why doesn't the firm use its equilibrium capital stock to produce a higher output, since we have deduced that the higher output will have a lower average cost? _____
_____

IMPERFECT COMPETITION AMONG THE FEW: OLIGOPOLY

Q9 Label the curves in Fig. 3. Point *b* is referred to as (1) _____, and point *c* as (2) _____

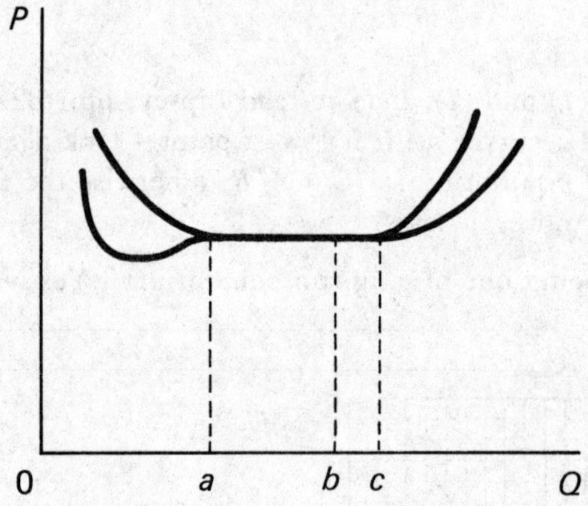

Fig. 3

Q10 In which of the following situations would it be least likely that the cost curve would be as shown in Fig. 3?

(1) A typing agency.

(2) A computer bureau using a main-frame computer.

(3) A firm providing a computing service using micros.

Why? _____

Once one makes the assumption that price changes are themselves costly to implement, the flatness of these *saucer-shaped* cost curves provides one possible explanation of *sticky oligopoly prices*: review Lipsey, Fig. 14.4 (p. 240), if you are unsure of this point.

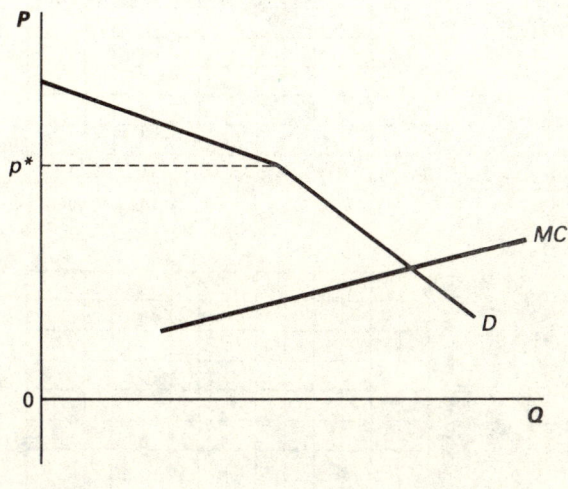

Q11 Another approach to understanding the alleged 'stickiness' of prices under oligopoly, this time in the context of cost changes, is illustrated by Fig. 4. This shows a _____ (1) demand curve. The current price is p^* and the construction assumes that the firm thinks its rivals would copy any reduction in price it might make but would not follow any price increase. (2) Sketch onto Fig. 4 the firm's marginal revenue curve. (3) If the MC curve shifted upwards in a parallel fashion, show on Fig. 4 how far it could move before the firm would decide to raise price.

Fig. 4

Firms under oligopoly are *inter-dependent*. The outcome in an industry will depend on whether they follow cooperative or non-cooperative behaviour. A well-known model of a non-cooperating oligopoly was provided by Cournot in 1838.

Q12 The *Cournot Model* is based on each firm choosing its profit-maximizing output on the assumption that the other firm _____

Q13 Two identical firms comprise a certain industry. The industry demand curve is drawn on Fig. 5(a). The marginal cost of production is £30 per unit, however many units are currently being produced.

   (1) Use Fig. 5(a) to predict what output Firm A will choose if Firm B currently produces no output at all. Q_A = _____ units per week. (Remember here that if the firm's demand curve is linear, the corresponding marginal revenue curve has the same intercept on the vertical axis but has twice the slope.)

   (2) Redraw the market demand curve on Fig. 5(b) and show how large the output of A will be if Q_B = 20 units per week. Q_A = _____ units per week.

   (3) On Fig. 5(c), repeat the exercise to show that if Q_B = 40, Q_A = _____

   (4) On Fig. 5(d), draw Firm A's *reaction curve*.

   (5) Now draw, on Fig. 5(d), Firm B's reaction curve.

   (6) In the Cournot equilibrium, Firm A will produce _____ units per week and Firm B will produce _____ units per week. Industry price will be £_____ per unit.

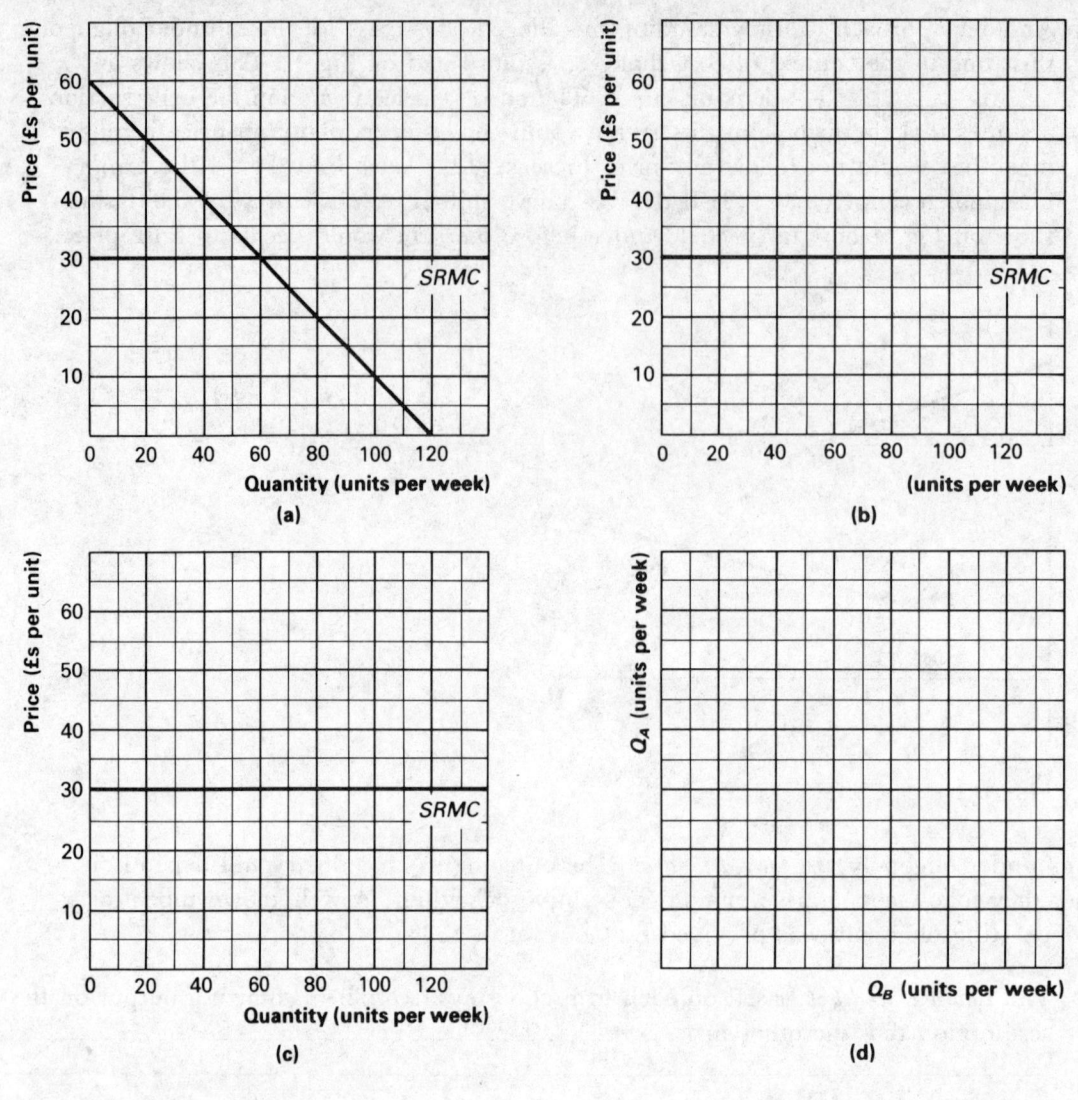

Fig. 5

(7) This compares with a price of £_____ if one firm were left as a monopoly.

(8) *Bertrand* made an alternative assumption to Cournot. He took it that each firm would choose its best *price* on the assumption that the other firm's *price* would be held constant. What would price be in equilibrium in this case if the industry behaved according to the *Bertrand* model? £_____

(9) Each firm would then be failing to cover its fixed costs and would exit from the industry in the long run. True/False?

The Cournot and Bertrand models provide results which suggest that all firms *could* gain by bringing about a cooperative solution. Should all firms make and keep to an agreement to act as a single monopolist, the total profit to the industry will be maximized. But it will still be in the interests of the *individual* firm to lower its price and increase its sales at the expense of the others, if it can get away with it.

But the recognition of the importance of its competitors' reactions differentiates this case from the case of the perfectly competitive producer. Unfortunately there is no simple theory that predicts precisely how close a group of oligopolistic competitors will come to the monopoly position of joint profit-maximization. What we do instead is to outline some of the conditions which, it is hypothesized, will permit the firms to move in the direction of joint profit-maximization. These conditions are outlined in Lipsey, p. 248.

LONG-RUN CONSIDERATIONS

Q15 Which of the average total cost curves of Fig. 6(a) and (b) will inhibit the entry of new firms more?

Q16 Firms in an oligopolistic industry have production costs per unit as in Fig. 6(c). They decide to embark on an advertising programme in order to raise the barriers to entry which

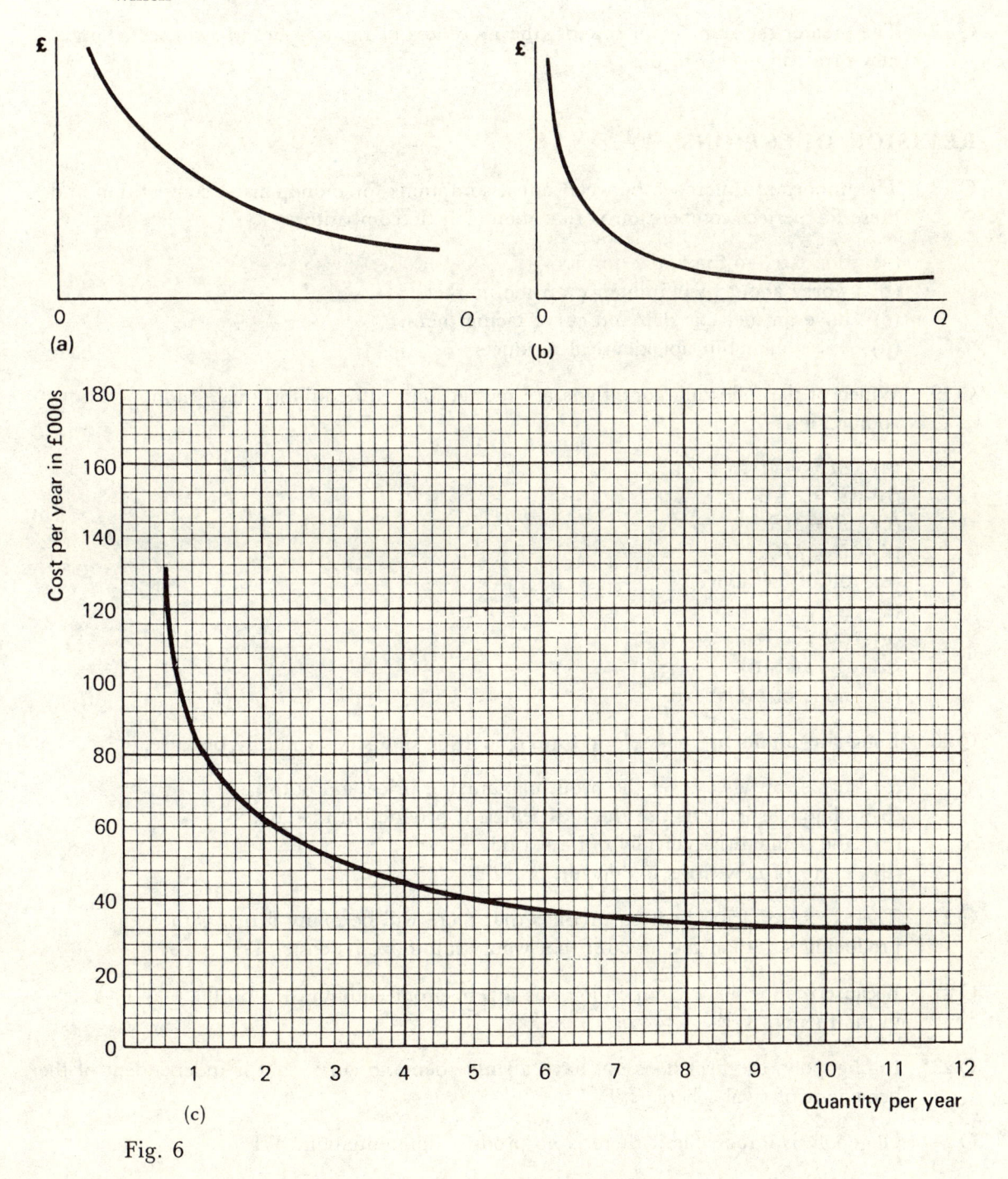

Fig. 6

new firms would face. Assume that they each undertake £200,000 worth of advertising per year. Sketch in their *new ATC* curve. (*Hint:* draw in the average advertising cost curve first, then add the two curves vertically.)

(1) What is the new *ATC* at an output of 2 per year? _____

(2) What is the new *ATC* at an output of 5 per year? _____

(3) What is the new *ATC* at an output of 10 per year? _____

Brand proliferation refers to the multitude of different brand-names for one firm's product. The explanation may have something to do with catering to individual tastes but, like advertising, it can also be used to create an effective barrier to entry.

Q17 The greater the number of brands, the more/less of random brand switches a single new firm can expect to pick up.

REVISION QUESTIONS

Q18 The important difference between our assumptions for monopolistic competition and those for perfect competition is that monopolistic competitors:

(a) don't try to maximize profits.
(b) worry about their influence on the market.
(c) have an inelastic demand curve facing them.
(d) sell similar but not identical products.

Q19 Which of the following conditions are met at long-run equilibrium in monopolistic competition?

(a) $MR = MC$.
(b) $P = ATC$.
(c) $P = MR$.
(d) $P = MC$.
(e) all of the above.
(f) (b) and (c).
(g) (a) and (b).
(h) (b) and (d).
(i) none of the above.

Q20 Long-run profits are possible in an oligopolistic industry primarily because:

(a) firms can always set the profit-maximizing price and output.
(b) oligopolistic firms use the most efficient production methods.
(c) the demand is typically quite elastic.
(d) entry of new firms is difficult.

Q21 The excess-capacity theorem predicts that there will be many firms, with each producing less than the amount that would minimize its costs. T/F

Q22 Because monopolistic competition has a zero-profit equilibrium, profits play no role in the theory. T/F

Q23 In oligopoly, the firm does not have a single demand curve that is independent of the behaviour of rival sellers. T/F

Q24 Oligopoly is impossible if there is no product differentiation. T/F

QUESTIONS FOR DISCUSSION

1. Many large cities have Chinatowns or 'Little Indias' where several streets are devoted almost entirely to restaurants of the particular ethnic type. Observed characteristics often include similarity in menus and prices, high turnover in ownership as a result of financial failures and low table-occupancy rates in particular restaurants. What model of market structure might be appropriate to analyse these situations?

2. Once product differentiation is introduced into our models, must we discard the concept of an industry and replace it with a view in which all firms compete with all other firms in the whole economy?

3. Look back to the information in discussion question 2 of this Workbook's Chapter 13. Despite National Express maintaining its dominance in the market, the price level (adjusted for inflation) on major inter-city bus routes was significantly lower at the end of the 1980s than at the beginning. Is this market 'contestable'? Does the theory of contestable markets enable us to understand what has happened in the industry?

4. In 1978, there was a substantial deregulation of North Atlantic air services. Fares fell and, with fuel cost rises occurring soon afterwards, most carriers showed large losses in 1979–81. Rigas Doganis in an article on the period wrote that the absence of controls 'makes it difficult for airlines to climb out of a crisis. With no multilateral agreement on tariffs, no single airline is prepared to increase its tariff unilaterally for fear of losing traffic. If one airline reduces its tariffs, the others feel they have to match them.' What model characterises such a situation? How do you think the situation would be resolved?

5. Advertising can be a weapon to deter entry into oligopolistic industries. The British cigarette and banking industries are both oligopolies, but the former devotes far more resources to advertising than the latter. Why?

CHAPTER 15
Applications

In this chapter the logical implications of the two sets of assumptions that constitute the basis of the theory of perfect competition and the theory of monopoly are examined.

THE DRIVE TO MONOPOLIZE PERFECTLY COMPETITIVE INDUSTRIES

An implication of the theory of perfect competition is that, at the equilibrium industrial output, price equals marginal cost. Fig. 1 shows such an equilibrium.

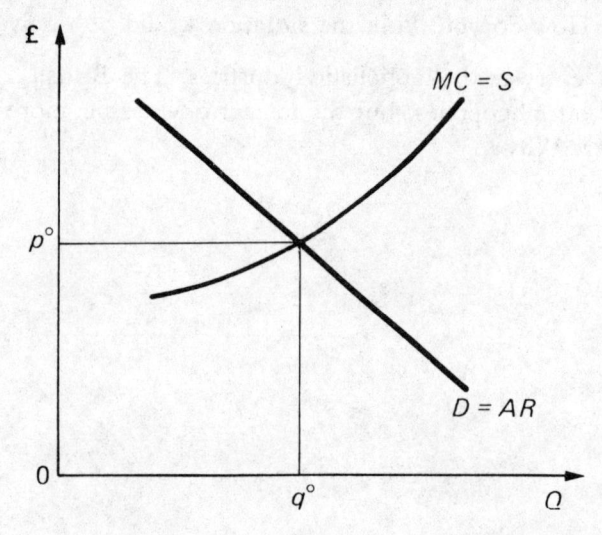

Fig. 1

Q1 Total Revenue to the industry equals _____

Q2 Must there *necessarily* be a different price, such that when it is multiplied by its corresponding quantity, total revenue is larger? Yes/No

Q3 Must there *necessarily* be a different price, such that with the corresponding sales, greater profits would accrue to the industry as a whole? Yes/No

Check your answers to Q2 and Q3. If you were wrong on Q2, remember that revenue might fall depending on the value of demand elasticity. Costs, of course, would fall *further*, and this is how the greater profit would be earned.

Q4 Assume that the members of the industry represented by Fig. 1 form a restrictive co-operative. Sketch in how the industry would make a profit.

(1) Under what conditions would total revenue fall? _____

Check your answer to Q4(1). If you were wrong, do parts (2) and (3). If not, go on to Q5.

(2) If two demand curves pass through the same point, which is the more elastic, the steeper or the shallower? Steeper/Shallower

(If you can't answer (2), you must re-read Lipsey, pp. 80–3, on elasticity. You cannot afford to be unsure about this.)

(3) Sketch in on Fig. 1 a shallower demand curve, passing through point p^0, q^0. You can see immediately that for a change from q^0 to any q less than q^0, total revenue from the shallower increases more/less than that from the steeper curve. And if the curve is so shallow as to have elasticity greater than one, total revenue actually decreases.

If you still find this confusing, try and think of it 'in reverse'. Elasticity greater than one means that if a producer *drops* his price he sells enough more to *increase* his revenue. It therefore also means that an *increase* in price is accompanied by a *decrease* in revenue. And now, to drive the point of this section home,

(4) If revenue decreases after monopolization, how can it be to the firm's advantage? _____

Q5 Under the Common Agricultural Policy, farmers have been prosecuted for producing too much milk. Why was it in their interest to risk fines? _____

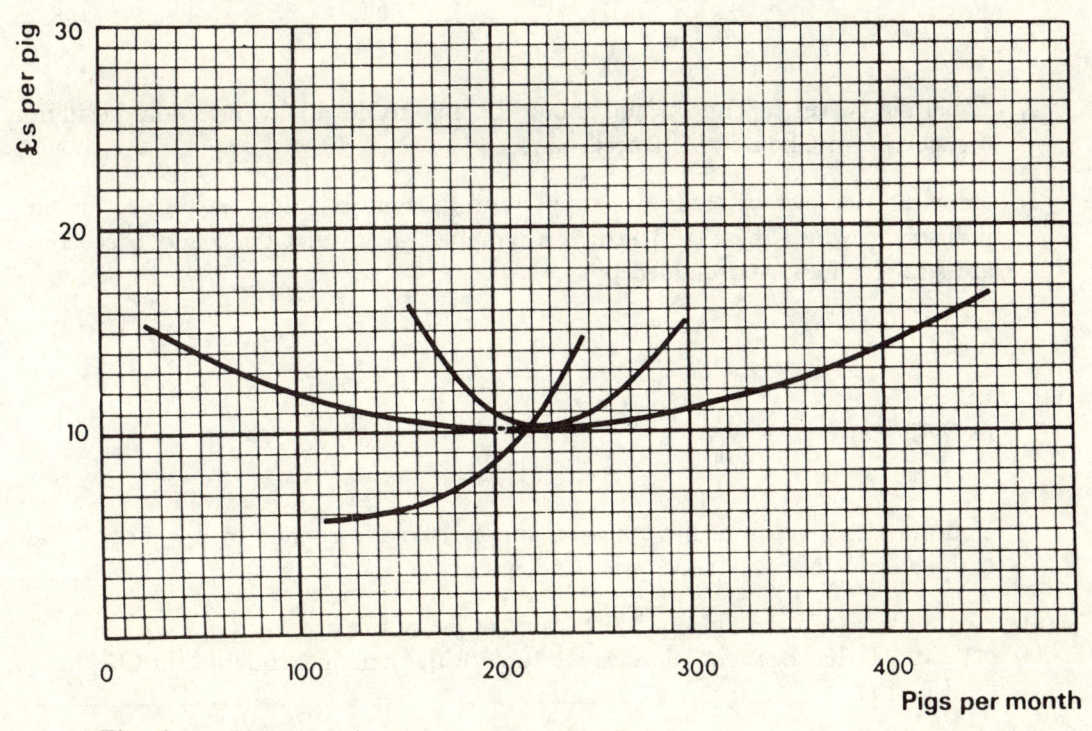

Fig. 2

Q6 Here is a pig farm in long-run competitive equilibrium (Fig. 2).

(1) Label the curves.

(2) Assume a quota of 140 pigs per month is imposed on this farm. By how much *must* price rise for the farm to stay in business in the long run?

(3) Assume price actually rises by £3 per pig. How much long-run profit will this farm now make given the price of 140 pigs per month? _____

(4) How much short-run profit *could* it make (on the original short-run curves), if it could successfully deceive the quota-imposing authority and *no one else did so*?

A CHANGE IN DEMAND: COMPETITION

Q7 Here is a firm in long-run competitive equilibrium.

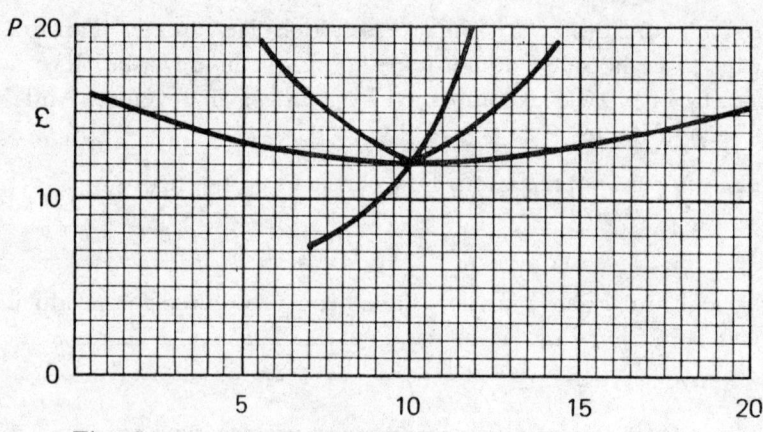

Fig. 3

(1) Label the curves in Fig. 3. You should be able to do this without any hesitation – check up in Chapter 11 if necessary.

(2) Construct the *industry* short-run supply and demand schedule on Fig. 4, for the industry of which the Fig. 3 firm is a member, given that the S and D schedules are straight lines, and defined by;

$S: p$ (in £s) $= \dfrac{Q}{250}$

$D: p$ (in £s) $= 27 - \dfrac{Q}{200}$

You are also given that the long-run supply curve is defined by $p = £12$. What is the short-run equilibrium price and quantity? _____

(3) Assume a rise in demand of 1,000 units at every price.
   (1) With what new equation do we replace the demand equation in Q7, part (2)? _____

   (2) Draw in the new demand curve on Fig. 4 (extend graph if necessary).

   (3) What is the immediate change in price? _____

   (4) Construct a new price line appropriate to this on Fig. 3.

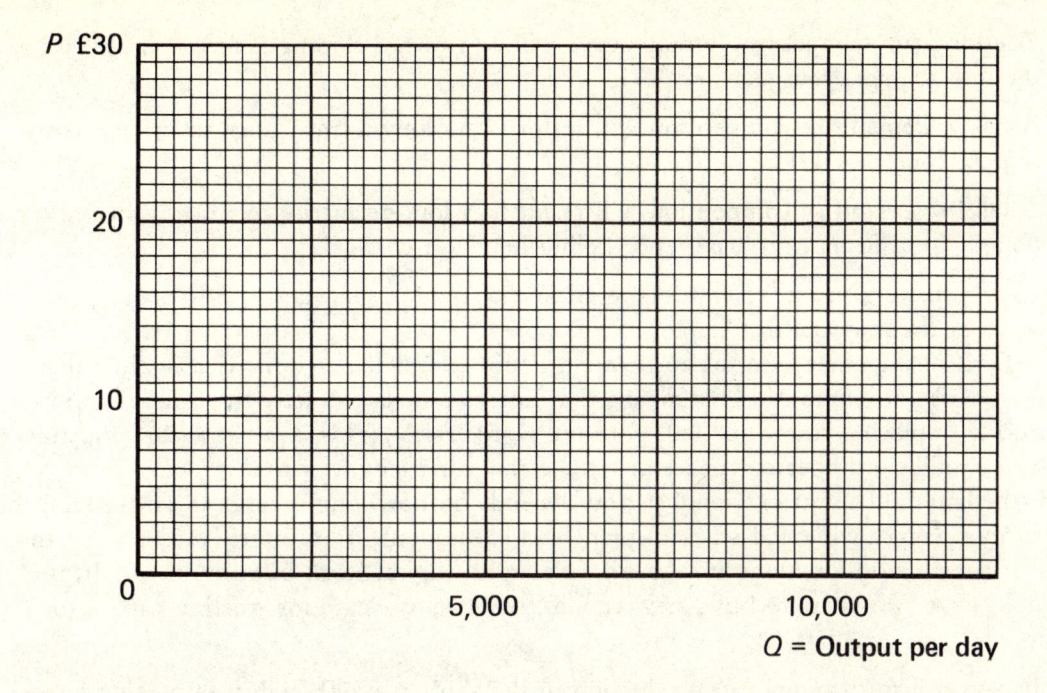

Fig. 4

The firm depicted on Fig. 3 is now making profits.

(5) Approximately what will be its total profits *in the short-run*? _____

The firm will now seek to maximize its profits, and it will do this in the long-run by moving to the right along the *LRAC* curve. Say this means that it produces at 15 units per day. Draw in an *AVC* and a *MC* curve for this output. There are, however, two reasons why this cannot be an equilibrium position. One is that this increase in production, and that of other firms in a similar position, must itself lower the price from the level to which it rose initially.

Q 8   What is the second reason? _____

The new price line therefore falls, and, as it falls, in order to continue making profits the firm will be moved along its *LRAC* curve until, when the price line eventually merges with the original one, it will have returned to its old position.

Recap: As long as the price line lies above the minimum point of the *LRAC* curve, profits can be made. As long as profits are made, firms will enter this industry and lower the price line.

Q 9   What assumption in Q 7 has excluded the possibility that the firm's *LRAC* curve might have *shifted* during this process? _____

Q 10   Since each firm is now producing at its old output, how is the increased output necessary to meet the increased demand attained? _____

Q 11   The theory of perfect competition implies, therefore, that in a constant-costs industry an increase in demand will in the long run result in a change/no change in price, and an increase in the size of the firm/the number of firms in the industry.

Q 12 The long-run competitive supply curve will be upward-sloping if factor prices rise as the industry total output rises. T/F

Q 13 A fall in demand in competition will result in no long-term change in price if costs remain constant. T/F

Q 14 A fall in demand in competition will result in a long-term rise in price if factors are bought from firms who experience falling long-run costs. T/F

Check your answers so far. If you answered any of the last six questions wrongly you should re-check the material in Chapter 12 of Lipsey.

The analysis of the effect of a fall in demand is not completely symmetrical with that of the effect of a rise in demand. (This means that one cannot use exactly the same description of the process, replacing the word 'fall' with the word 'rise'.) This is because the adjustment to long-run equilibrium does not necessarily take the same length of time. For a rise in demand, the length of the transitional period depends on how long it takes to go through the process of increasing the capital stock of plant and equipment in an industry. For a fall in demand, it depends on how long it takes to reduce the capital stock in an industry. It might, for example, take two years to build new capital, but twenty years for existing capital to wear out.

Q 15 It pays a firm to remain in production in the short run although it is making losses, as long as total revenue exceeds total fixed/variable cost.

Q 16 In a competitive industry which has a downward-sloping long-run supply curve, a decrease in demand will result in a rise/fall in price.

Q 17 In an industry with an upward-sloping long-run supply curve, a decrease in demand will result in a rise/fall in price.

A CHANGE IN DEMAND: MONOPOLY

Q 18 You might like to try constructing in the space below a diagram for a monopolist, showing an *increase* in demand, at all prices, but a *fall* in equilibrium price.

Hints: Make your *MC* curve shallow, your initial *AR* curve steep and your subsequent *AR* shallow. (Don't spend too long over this, and don't worry too much if you can't do it.)

CHANGES IN COSTS

Q 19 Fig. 5 shows the short-run industrial supply and demand diagram for a competitive industry (ignore the *MR* curve).

(1) Costs increase by £2 per unit. Draw in the new *MC* curve. What is the change in the short-run equilibrium price and quantity? _____

(2) Now assume instead that the diagram represents the demand and marginal cost curves of a monopolist. Again, costs increase by £2 per unit. What is the change in the equilibrium price and quantity? _____

(3) Conclusion – a cost change produces a greater effect on price and quantity in monopoly/competition.

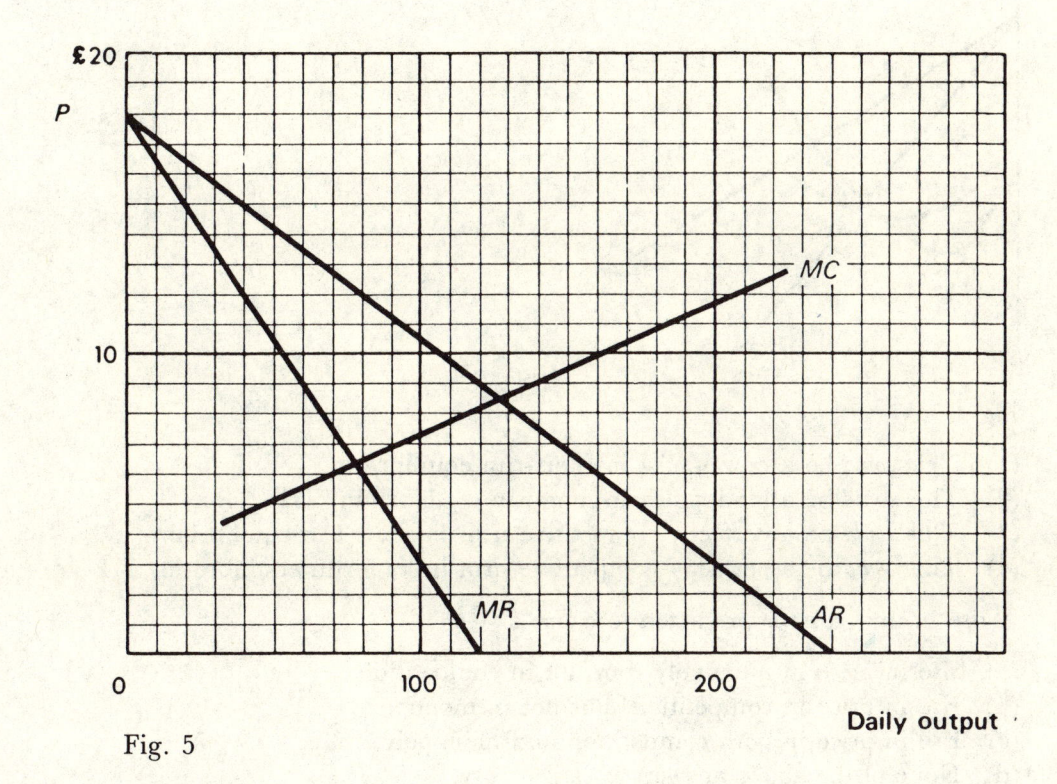

Fig. 5

TAXES

Q 20 In the long run, the whole burden of a per-unit tax must always fall on the producer. True/False

Q 21 What will be the short-run effect of a lump-sum tax levied on a competitive industry? Raise price/lower price/neither.

Q 22 What will be the total long-run effects of a lump-sum tax on a competitive industry? All passed on/none passed on/some passed on.

Q 23 Explain your answer to Q 22. _____

Q 24 Since a competitive industry does not make profits, what is the use of a profits tax on such an industry? _____

Q25 A monopolist has control of the price he charges for his product. He will thus be able to maximize his profits by:

(a) raising his price by the whole amount of a tax, thus passing it all on to his customers.
(b) absorbing the whole of any cost reductions into his profits, thus passing on to his customers none of the benefit.
(c) neither (a) nor (b).

REVISION QUESTIONS

Q26 Consider the firm represented by Fig. 6. Current output is Q^* and price P^*.

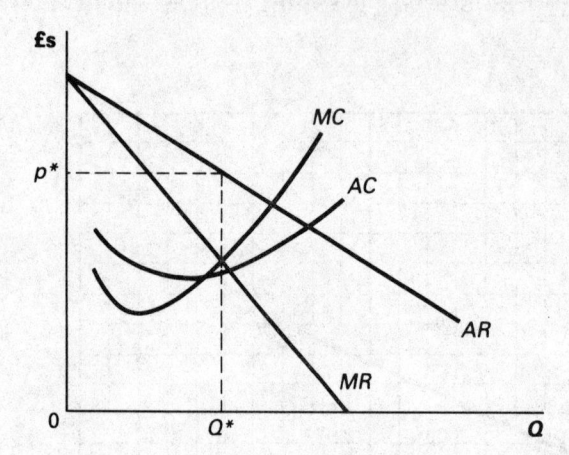

Fig. 6

(1) This *could* be a monopolist in short-run equilibrium. T/F
(2) This *could* be a monopolist in long-run equilibrium. T/F
(3) This *could* be a perfectly competitive firm in short-run equilibrium. T/F
(4) This *could* be a perfectly competitive firm in long-run equilibrium. T/F

Q27 A rise in unit costs is predicted to cause a

(a) rise in price in monopoly, but not in competition.
(b) rise in price in competition, but not in monopoly.
(c) rise in price in both competition and monopoly.
(d) None of the above answers is satisfactory.

Q28 In monopoly, a cost change is a necessary condition for a price change. T/F

Q29 In monopoly, a cost change is a sufficient condition for a price change. T/F

Q30 The market demand curve plays a role both in the theory of competition and in the theory of monopoly. T/F

Q31 The market supply curve plays a role both in the theory of competition and in the theory of monopoly. T/F

Q32 No industry in the economy will produce an output where its own elasticity of demand is less than 1. T/F

Q33 No profit-maximizing monopolist will produce where demand is inelastic. T/F

QUESTIONS FOR DISCUSSION

1. In the mid-1970s when OPEC forced oil prices to rise substantially, the Canadian and American governments sought to protect domestic consumers from the effects with price controls. Would this have helped the goals of the OPEC cartel?

2. In 1980, Milton and Rose Friedman wrote that it is close to impossible for international cartels to succeed; they break down under the pressure of international competition – 'a fate that we believe awaits OPEC as well'. In the light of the relatively low price of oil for much of the 1980s, were the Friedmans right? Was the failure of OPEC in the 1980s inevitable?

3. Why did European farmers need the Common Agricultural Policy to raise their incomes? Given inelasticity of demand for most agricultural products, could they not have achieved higher income via private arrangements rather than through the action of governments?

4. If several airlines operate on a route where prices are fixed by international agreement, what form would you expect competition between them to take? Would this non-price competition benefit consumers?

5. Suppose the Chancellor of the Exchequer raises the duty on cigarettes by twenty pence per packet. 'Cigarette prices to rise by twenty pence' is a newspaper headline next day. Comment on the headline.

6. 'The burden of a per-unit tax is shared between consumers and producers.' Is this true in the long run?

7. For a time in the 1980s, British students, almost all of whom qualified on income grounds, were allowed to claim housing benefit; they could reclaim from the government a percentage of the weekly rent paid to private landlords. A year after this scheme was introduced, a student newspaper commented that students were as poor as ever because rents in the market had risen sharply. Was the rent rise a coincidence? Who gained from the housing benefit scheme?

CHAPTER 16
Criticisms and Tests

Q1 (a) You go to a travel agent and ask to buy the cheapest ticket to New York. Because of lack of information, you take the ticket offered but it is not in fact the cheapest: the clerk sells you a more expensive type because his firm's commission is on a percentage basis.

(b) You go to a doctor during your visit to New York. He recommends an operation and pockets a high fee. Back home, the family doctor tells you that treatment with drugs would have been cheaper, less risky and just as effective. Both (a) and (b) are instances where the person acting on your instructions follows his own interests rather than yours. They are examples of which general class of problem? _____

Q2 In which of these two cases are the interests of the shareholders more likely to be different from the interests of the managers?

(a) Managers' salaries are a given fraction of profits.
(b) Managers' salaries are a given fraction of the firm's sales.

Q3 If managers seek to maximize sales revenue, output will be higher/lower than that which would maximize profit.

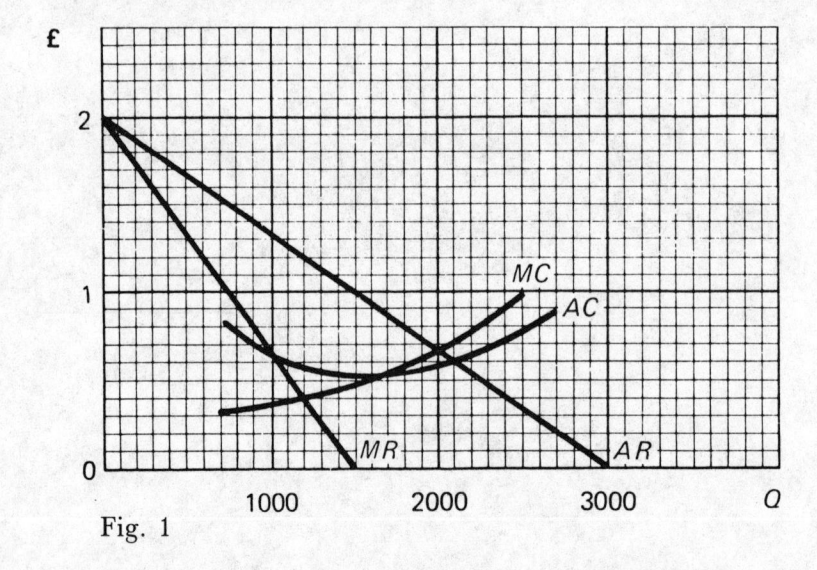

Fig. 1

Q4 (1) Fig. 1 shows the usual data for a monopolist. (*AC* now includes a return on capital.) Assume that the wages of management increase with the physical level of sales, and that the management's interest is to maximize its own wages. What would be the difference in the level of sales between the profit-maximizing output, and the management's wages-maximizing output? _____

(2) Why would it not be in the interests of management for sales to increase to a steady level greater than 2,100? _____

Q5 A profit-maximizing monopolist firm faces an increase in fixed costs. Output will rise/fall/stay the same. (Assume here and in Q6 that the rise in fixed cost is insufficient to cause exit from the industry.)

Q6 The managers of a firm choose to maximize the volume of sales subject to profit reaching a minimum level required by shareholders. If there is an increase in fixed costs, output will rise/fall/stay the same.

Q7 Is it possible for a businessman to maximize his profits without being aware that he is doing so? Yes/No

Q8 'If a firm does not seem to be maximizing its profits, then we can always say that it is nursing its market position, and is really seeking to maximize its *long-term* profits.' Is this a useful approach? Yes/No. Explain.
_____

Q9 Is full-cost pricing consistent with competitive behaviour? Yes/No

Q10 Assume that a full-cost pricer is a member of an industry whose equilibrium price is 50p per article. His conventional mark-up is 1/7 of his average costs, and his output is 500 articles a day. What are his total daily costs?

QUESTIONS FOR DISCUSSION

1 It is suggested that most managers, when asked directly, deny being profit maximizers because it would be a disreputable admission. But is the pursuit of maximum profits in fact likely to be against the public interest?

2 Many enterprises – housing associations, for example – are forbidden to make profits. What goals do you think managers would pursue in non-profit-making enterprises? How is the lack of a profit motive likely to affect efficiency?

3 How is the existence of the Stock Exchange argued to prevent managers sacrificing shareholders' interests for their own? Are the managers of a company like British Telecom likely to pursue cost-cutting more rigorously as a result of being made a private Stock Exchange-listed company?

4 Students asking their career advisers about a 'socially useful' career are unlikely to be directed to the advertising industry. Is the implied view of advertising justified?

CHAPTER 17
Factor Incomes in Competitive Markets

Q1 The *size distribution of income* refers to the relative incomes received by different individuals; the *functional distribution of income* refers to _____

Q2 The degree of inequality can be shown by a *Lorenz curve* (Lipsey, Fig. 17.1). What would you know about income distribution if the Lorenz curve for a particular society were exactly coincident with the diagonal line joining the top right and bottom left corners of the box?

Q3 Fig. 1 shows Lorenz curves for a particular country in 1979 and 1989. The earlier Lorenz curve is indicated by a solid line and the later one by a broken line. Between these years, the income distribution changed in the direction of greater/less inequality.

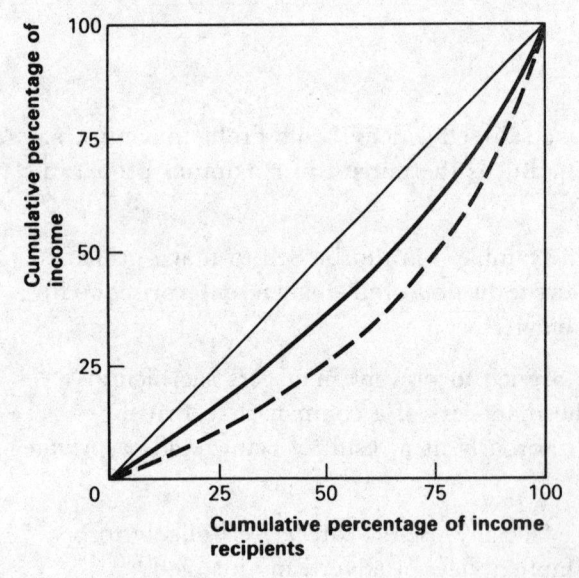

Fig. 1

Q4 The two Lorenz curves in Fig. 2 show the situation in another country in 1979 and 1989. This time the curves cross, so no unambiguous statement about greater or less inequality is possible. However, we can make certain statements about the relative positions of different income groups.

   (1) The income share of the bottom quarter of income recipients increased/decreased/stayed the same.

   (2) The income share of the middle fifty per cent of income recipients increased/decreased/stayed the same.

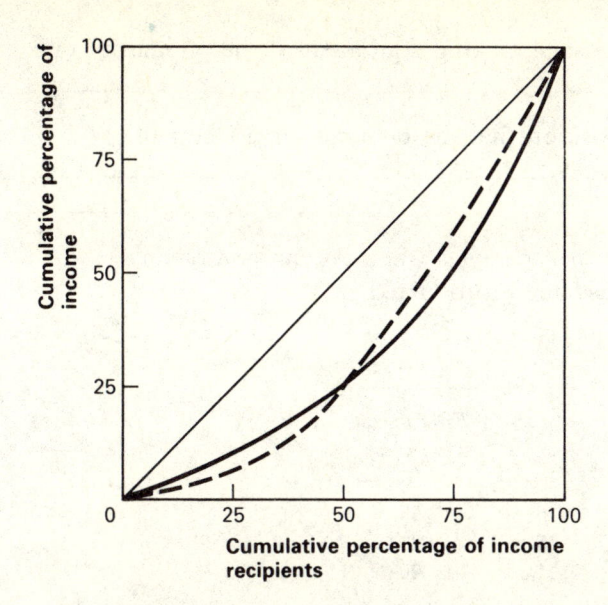

Fig. 2

(3) The income share of the top quarter of income recipients increased/decreased/ stayed the same.

Income distribution is explained in traditional models by ordinary theory applied to factor markets. The income of the owner of a factor of production depends on the price a factor commands in the market and on the quantity of the factor used. Prices and quantities of factors of production are analysed employing the same tools as in the study of commodity markets.

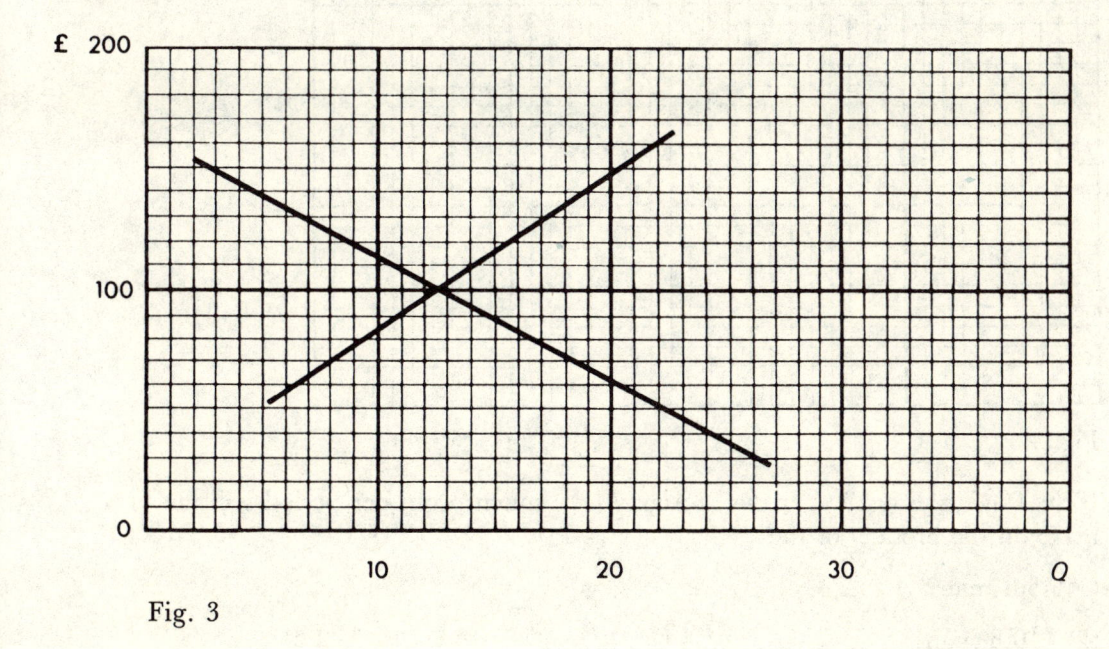

Fig. 3

Q5 Fig. 3 is a demand and supply diagram for a factor of production. What is the equilibrium total income per period of that factor? _____

Q6 Substitutes for the factor become much cheaper, with the result that the demand curve shifts right/left by 6 units. What is the new equilibrium income? _____

Q7 What will happen to the demand for sausage-making equipment if the popularity of the 'Great British Breakfast' declines? _____

Q8 This is an example of the general proposition that the demand for a factor of production is derived from _____

Table 1 shows how much the revenue of the firm changes when an extra worker is employed. All other factors of production are assumed to be fixed.

TABLE 1

Worker no.	Extra revenue (£s per day)	Worker no.	Extra revenue (£s per day)
7	60	16	38
24	30	35	23
12	44	41	20
28	26	50	19

Plot these points on Fig. 4 and construct by interpolation the curve fitting them. This curve is called the _____ (Q9) curve.

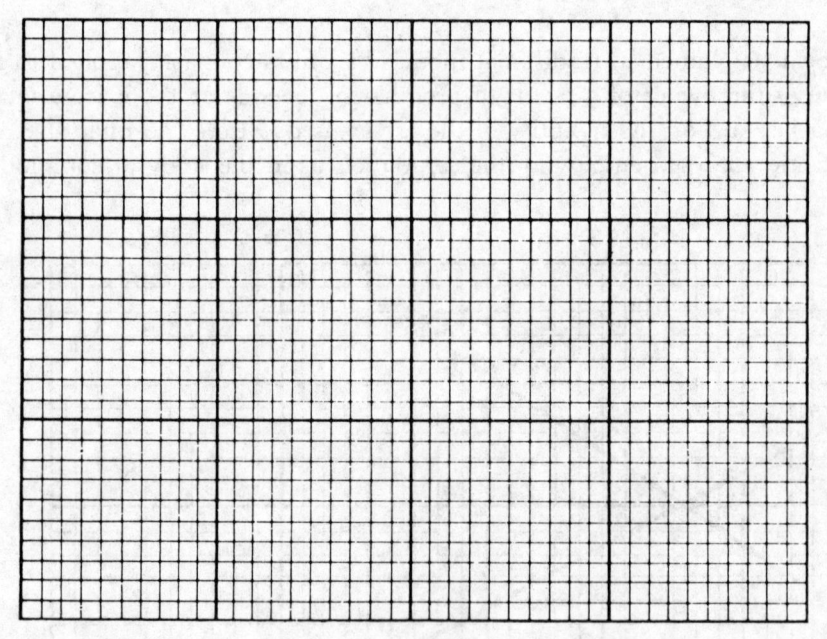

Fig. 4

Q10 If the wage rate is £30 per day, roughly how much profit per period will the firm make on the product of the

(1) 5th man? _____

(2) 10th man? _____

(3) 15th man? _____

(4) 20th man? _____

(5) 25th man? _____

(6) How many men will the firm employ in equilibrium? _____

Q 11 What will be the firm's excess demand for labour if it is employing 30 men, and the wage rate per day is:

(1) £36? _____

(2) £32? _____

(3) £20? _____

(4) £19? _____

Q 12 How many workers will be employed in equilibrium if the wage rate which the firm must pay is:

(1) £40? _____

(2) £32? _____

(3) £20? _____

(4) £60? _____

Q 13 In equilibrium, if a firm is maximizing its profit, the marginal revenue product of the variable factor is equal to the _____ of the variable factor. In competition this is merely the _____. In equilibrium this relationship must hold for all/at least one/only one factor(s).

We have illustrated the cardinal proposition that the marginal revenue product curve of a factor is the demand curve for that factor.

But we have not yet explained how we can determine what the shape of the *MRP* curve is. We have assumed, for the purpose of Questions 10–13, the data in Table 1, and we have seen that when this is translated into a graph, the *MRP* curve has a negative slope. But how are the data in Table 1 derived? This is what we shall now explain.

First of all, we will leave value aside, and look at the purely physical relationship between inputs and outputs. We already have a hypothesis which deals with this. Assume that the only variable factor is the factor whose *MRP* curve we wish to find, and the law of _____ (Q 14) predicts that the extra output produced by successive increments of the variable factor will decline. Examples jump to the mind – farm labourers and fields, detergent and washing machines, car workers and production lines.

So we have so far assumed and illustrated a declining marginal physical product curve. (Its actual shape, of course, depends upon the factual situation in the industry in question.)

The next step is to reintroduce value, and to derive the marginal revenue product curve from the marginal physical product curve.

We shall restrict our analysis to perfect competition, and our method shall be, first, to make a simplifying assumption in order to demonstrate the way in which the *MRP* is derived from the *MPP*, and then to relax this assumption and make the appropriate changes in our deduction.

The simplifying assumption: the output of all other firms is constant.

Q 15 Changes in one perfectly competitive firm's output, as it employs more factors, cause product price to change upwards/downwards/not at all.

Q 16 'Therefore the price of the firm's physical product will be the same at all points on the *MPP* curve, and the *MRP* curve is obtained by multiplying each *MPP* by the constant price'. Correct/Incorrect

So far, the analysis has not really been very difficult. Translating a relationship between inputs and outputs, where the outputs are measured in physical terms, into one where the outputs are measured in value terms, presents no problems if, at any level of input and output, the price of the output remains the same.

It gets tricky now, when we relax this simplifying assumption and take into account that a change in the price of the variable factor will result in a change in the equilibrium market price of the final product.

The rather complex analysis is covered in Lipsey's Box 17.1 (p. 290) and those who are happy to proceed without going through it should proceed to Q.33 below.

We will go through the process step by step.

Step 1 – Determine the market price of the commodity for some particular price of the variable factor. To determine the market price we need to know the industry supply curve, and the demand curve. Chapter 12 has taught us how to do this; what we have to do now is to show how the marginal cost curves which we need can be derived from the marginal physical product curves.

Fig. 5 is an *MPP* curve for a firm in a competitive industry. The only variable factor is labour. Fig. 6 is the graph on which we shall plot marginal cost. (We shall do it rather crudely, since the inputs of labour are not infinitely divisible, but come in chunks of one man-day.)

We will assume that the cost of labour is £10 per man-day.

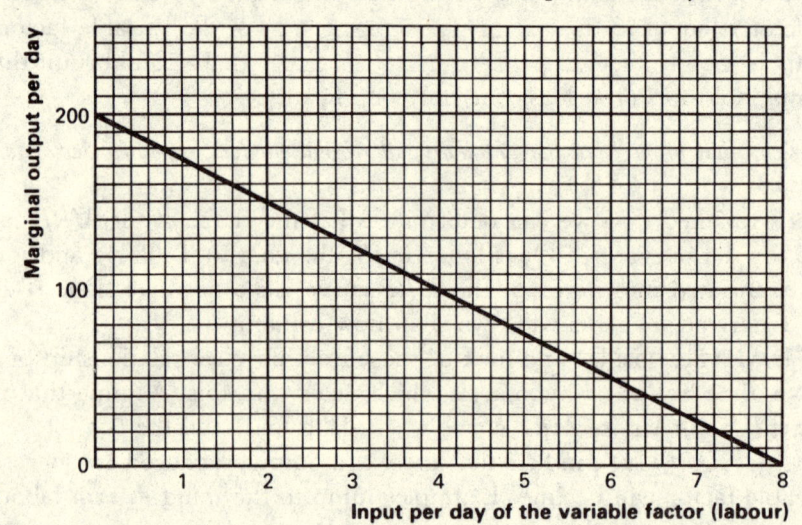

Fig. 5

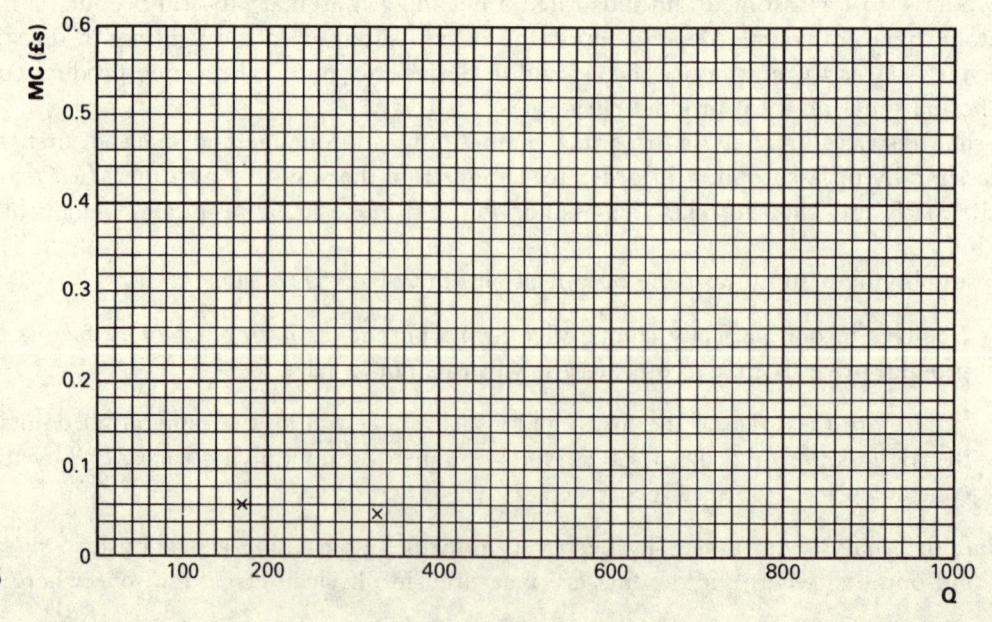

Fig. 6

The first man yields an output of 175 articles. He costs £10, so we can say that each article costs £10 ÷ 175 = £0.06 (roughly). On Fig. 6 the point 175, £0.06 is marked.

The second man yields an output of _____ (Q17). He costs £10 also, so each article costs £0.07. Total output is now 175 + 150 = 325, and between 175 and 325 the *MC* is £0.07. The point 325, £0.07 is marked.

The third man yields an output of _____ (Q18). He costs £10, so each article costs £0.08. Total output is now 325 + 125 = 450, and between 325 and 450 the *MC* is £0.08. Mark in the point 450, £0.08.

The fourth man yields an output of _____ (Q19). He costs £10, so each article costs _____ (Q20). Total output is now _____ (Q21), and between 450 and 550 the *MC* is _____ (Q22). Mark in the point _____ (Q23).

The fifth man yields an output of _____ (Q24). Each article costs _____ (Q25). Total output is now _____ (Q26). Mark in the point _____ (Q27).

For the sixth man, mark in the point _____ (Q28). For the seventh man, mark in the point _____ (Q29).

The eighth man produces nothing, in no circumstances would be employed, and so we'll forget about him.

Draw a continuous line through the points. You have drawn the firm's *MC* curve. Assume there are 100 firms in the industry, with identical *MC* curves. Re-label the horizontal axis of Fig. 6 to convert it to the industry short-run supply curve. (If you can't do this, look at the caption to Fig. 12.5 (Lipsey p. 208)).

The demand curve for this industry is a straight line, defined by the two points demand = zero when price = £0.28, and demand = 24,000 when price is £0.20.

Draw in this curve and label it. Now it can be seen that equilibrium price is _____ (Q30). (Check your answer and if you were wrong, find where your mistake was before going on.)

Step 1 is now complete.

Step 2 – Multiply every point on the marginal physical product curve by this price, £0.10. All this means is that the output figures on the vertical axis of Fig. 5 are replaced by their value equivalents. So 100 articles at £0.10 each are worth £10, and £200 articles are worth £20. Pencil in on to Fig. 7 the Marginal Revenue Product curve. (Q31) What is the *MRP* of the sixth man? _____ Do not continue until you are sure about the (very simple) relationship between Fig. 5 and Fig. 7.

This is the 'demand curve for labour' given that labour costs £10 per unit. A strange curve indeed! The only point on it which has any significance is the point (4, £10). All the others are pretty meaningless, at this level of analysis, since the only admissible point on the vertical axis is £10.

Nevertheless, we now have the information that *when labour costs £10, the firm will employ 4 units*. (If you're not sure why this is, then you haven't properly understood why an *MRP* curve is a demand curve, and you should look again at Q9–13.) So mark this point in. This is the end of Step 2.

Step 2½ – Go out and have a drink and return fortified for:

Step 3 – Go back to Step 1 and assume that the cost of labour is £20 per man-hour. Construct the appropriate *MC* curve on Fig. 6. (You don't have to go through the whole tedious procedure, if you notice that £20 = £10 × 2. Each point you mark on the graph will be twice the height of the point for a cost of £10.) Find out the equilibrium price. (Q32) What is the equilibrium price? _____ Check your answer (making allowances for difficulty in reading the graph).

Now go through Step 2 for a price of £0.15, and pencil in the appropriate curve on to

Fig. 7. This time, the only point in which we are interested is the point _____ (Q 33). Check your answer. If you were wrong and can't see why, then you should work through Step 2 again, making sure you've pencilled in the correct *MRP* line. In this case, of course, the only admissible point on the vertical axis is £20.

If you now go through Steps 1 and 2 again for a number of different labour costs and then join together the different 'admissible points', you will have built up the firm's demand curve for labour. The industry demand curve is obtained by aggregating across all 100 firms (i.e. the industry demand curve can be shown on Fig. 7 by multiplying the figures on the horizontal axis by 100).

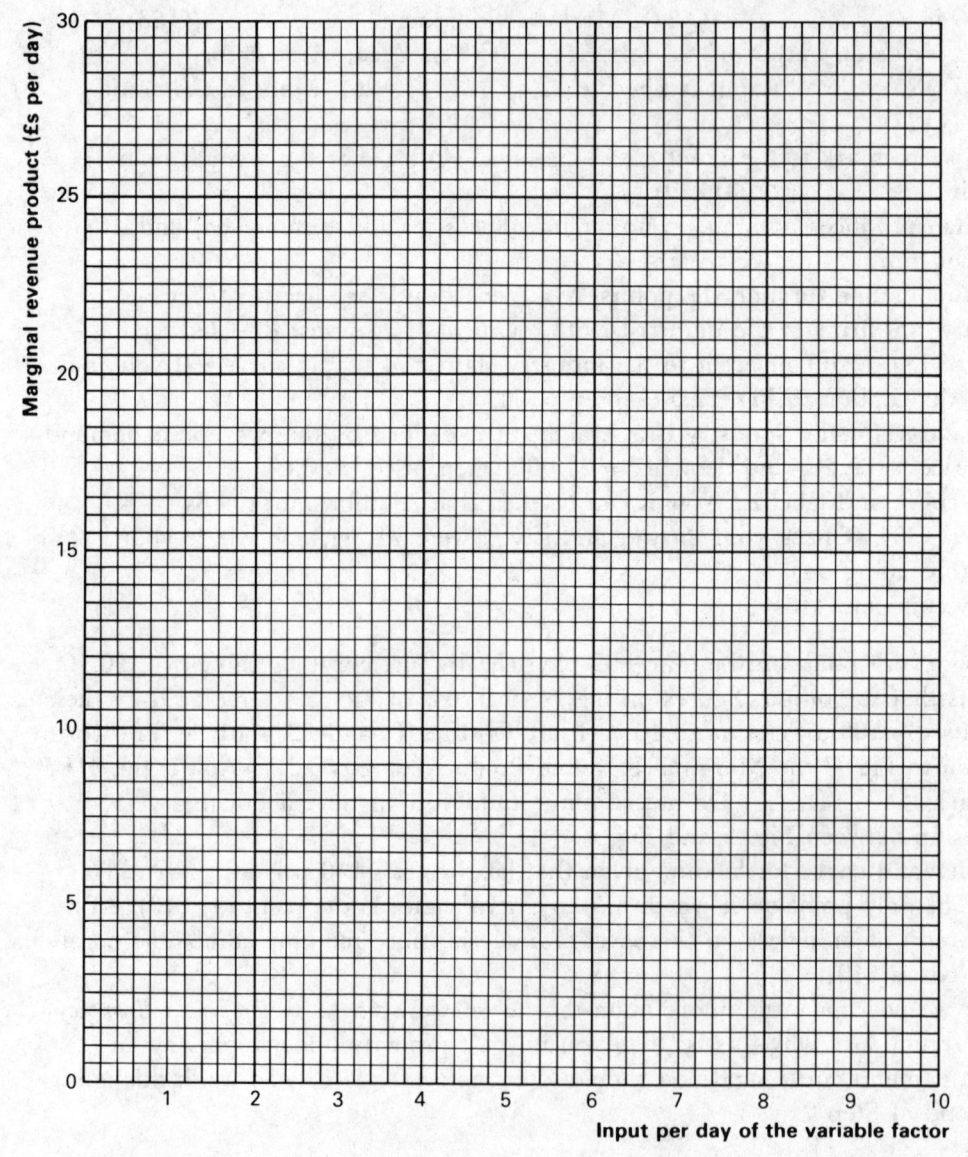

Fig. 7

Q 34 Because the change in the quantity of the factor demanded by a firm consequent upon a change in the factor's price is always reduced by the shifting of the *MRP* curve, the resulting demand curve must be flatter/steeper than any of the *MRP* curves.

Q 35 As factor price falls, the industry supply curve for the commodity will shift right/left. Price will therefore rise/fall, and the *MRP* curve will shift right/left.

Q36 Two neighbouring tenant farmers grow wheat for sale on the world market. The farms are *identical* and use only land and labour as factors of production. Farmer A rents his farm on a lease under which the rent is fixed in pounds per month. Farmer B is a share-tenant, i.e. his rent is a certain percentage of the value of the wheat output he sells.

  (1) Farmer A will employ more/less labour than Farmer B.

  (2) *Ceteris paribus*, a reduction in A's rent would raise his employment of labour. T/F

  (3) *Ceteris paribus*, a reduction in the rent share payable by B to his landlord would raise his employment of labour. T/F

Q37 If the price of a factor rises, its employment will fall by more/less the higher the elasticity of demand for its final product.

Q38 If the demand for the final product is perfectly inelastic, the employment of a factor that it uses must be unaffected by variations in that factor's price. T/F

Q39 You are told that, although a particular factor only accounts for 1% of the cost of production of a commodity, the factor's elasticity of demand is nevertheless very high. You conclude that other factors can be easily/only with difficulty substituted for it.

Q40 If factor proportions in an industry are fixed by the nature of the technology, the elasticity of the industry's demand for all factors must be zero. T/F

THE SUPPLY OF FACTORS OF PRODUCTION

Q41 We first consider the influence of wages on hours worked by labour. Assume that an individual can choose how many hours per day to work and has a fixed wage per hour available. Fig. 8 analyses the choice of a particular individual. Curves I and II are indifference curves. Initially the wage rate is £5 per hour but the worker then faces a reduction to £2.50 per hour.

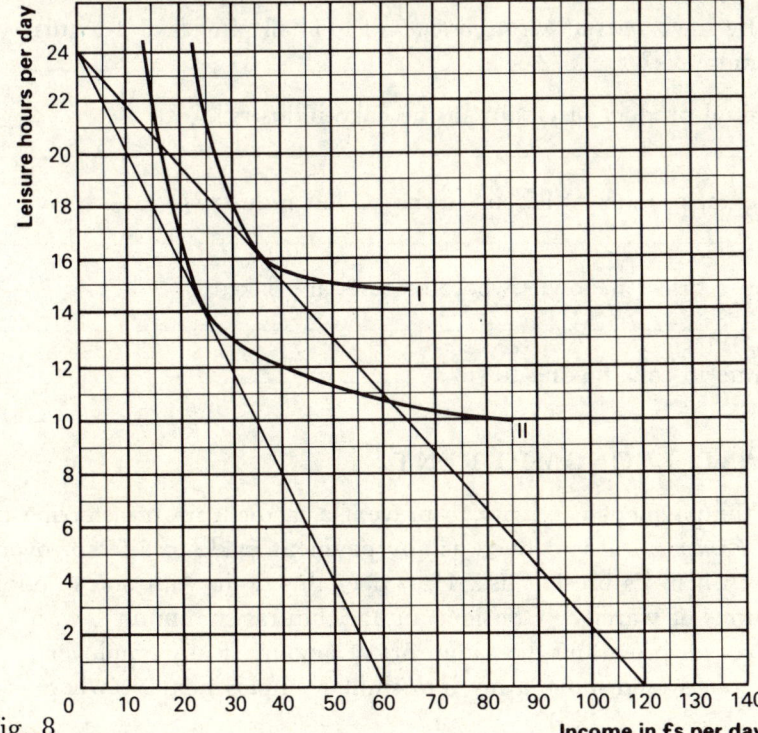

Fig. 8

(1) At the original wage rate, daily income is _____

(2) To earn this, _____ hours work is undertaken.

(3) Following the wage reductions, hours worked are changed to _____ per day and daily income is _____

(4) From the fact that hours worked have risen/fallen, we know that the substitution/income effect has been dominant.

Q 42 The hypothesis of equal net advantage (p. 297) would become testable as it stands if we could _____ non-monetary advantages. We cannot at the moment do this, so we make a particular assumption about monetary and non-monetary advantages.

Q 43 What is this assumption? _____

Q 44 Fig. 9 shows a hypothetical supply curve of labour to the biscuit industry. How would you represent on this diagram the effects of:

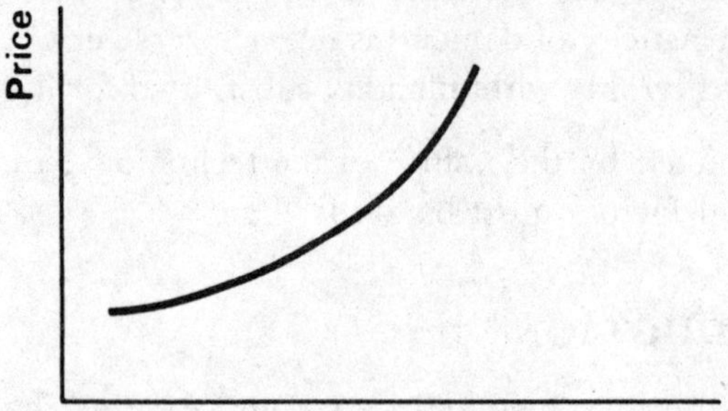

Fig. 9

(1) A rise in the marginal product of labour in the cake-baking industry?

(2) The construction by the *owners of biscuit factories* of football pitches and tennis courts for their employees?

(3) A fall in the marginal product of labour in the cake industry?

(4) A rise in the marginal product of labour in the biscuit industry?

(5) An increase in house prices in towns where biscuits are baked?

(6) An increase in crime in cake-baking towns?

TRANSFER EARNINGS AND ECONOMIC RENT

Transfer earnings are defined as the payment necessary to prevent a factor from transferring to some alternative employment. *Economic rent* is defined as any payment made to a factor over and above that necessary to keep it in its present use. How does this tie in with one's notion that rents are earned in conditions of scarcity? Consider an agricultural community, with everyone earning the same wage, all providing the same sort of labour. If any employer were to offer less wages, his labour would move away into similar employment elsewhere. So all earnings are _____ (Q 45).

Then an agricultural college is set up, and a small number of the most able farm workers are trained in more efficient agricultural techniques. All the farm owners compete for the services of the few graduates of this college, and bid up their wages. The other farm workers would have an incentive to acquire the training, but they are unable to do so. The graduates' *transfer earnings* are therefore the standard wage, and all their additional income is *rent*.

Q 46 Assume the rate of interest on safe securities is 5%, that repairs to my £40,000 house, plus insurance to cover the difference in risk between securities and the house, cost my landlord £2,000 per year, and that my rent is £4,000 per year. How much economic rent does he receive? _____

Q 47 Substitute repair and insurance costs of £1,000 a year in the above question. Now how much economic rent? _____

Q 48 Is it possible for an economic rent to be negative? Yes/No

Q 49 A pop singer is offered two contracts by agents, one at £100,000 a year and one at £200,000. He accepts the larger. His alternative employment would be as a bus driver at £120 per week. How much rent, and how much transfer earnings does he receive (both inter and intra industry)? _____

Q 50 Fig. 10 is the supply curve of a factor. What is the rent of the unit of the factor which would accept work at (1) £150 per week, when 200 are employed in equilibrium; (2) £200 per week when 300 are employed?

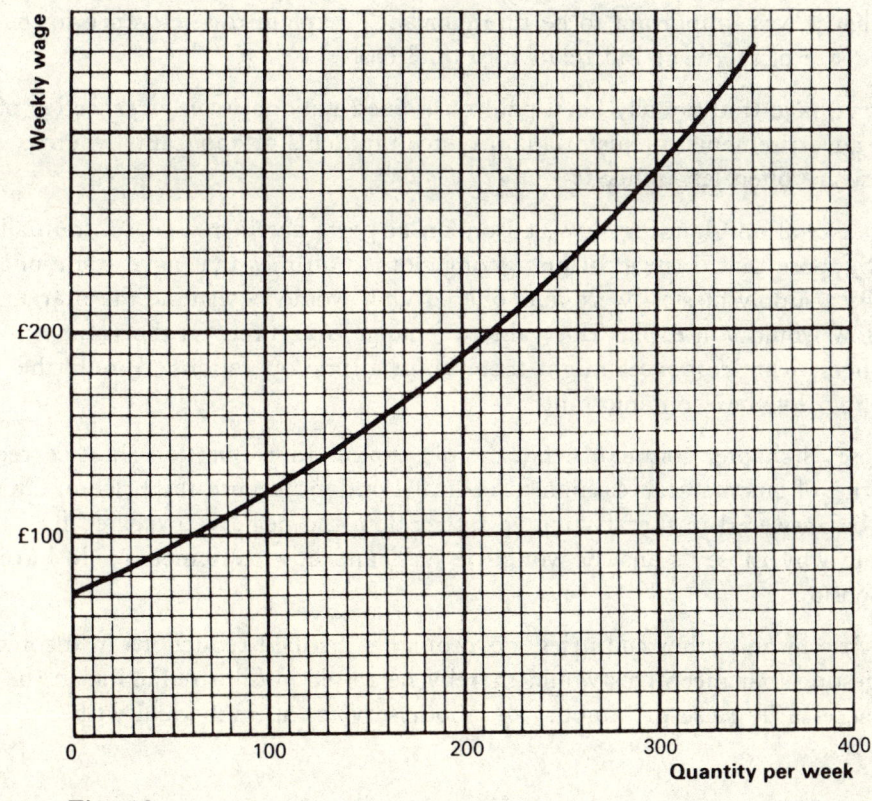

Fig. 10

Once an oil well has been sunk, the machinery on the rig has no alternative use – all the income from it is rent. But, when the decision comes whether to replace the machinery and to continue pumping, the amount of income earned – which has been rent – is a major factor in the decision whether or not to use the new machinery elsewhere. If, during its life, it had yielded less than the current marginal return to capital, it will not be replaced. If it yielded more, then it was earning a _____ (Q 51) equivalent to the marginal return to capital, plus a pure rent equivalent to the excess, and it will be replaced.

Q 52 Define quasi rent. _____

ECONOMIC RENT AND LAND RENT

It is important not to confuse these two concepts. The reason for the similarity in name is explained in Box 17.3 in Lipsey, p. 300.

Q 53 In 1971, the UK government was considering giving tenants of furnished rooms – perhaps in the landlord's own house – security of tenure at a 'fixed rent', perhaps lower than the rent already being paid. They decided against it, because they believed that the result would be fewer rooms offered to let. All such 'rents' are subject to UK taxation. Would all such 'rents' be rents in the economic sense? Yes/No. Explain. _____

QUESTIONS FOR DISCUSSION

1 The power of trade unions to raise wages without generating substantial job losses depends on the elasticity of demand for the relevant labour group. For power to be great, Marshall wrote that it was 'important to be unimportant'. Explain this reference to the significance of the size of the wage bill relative to total costs.

2 University lecturers have traditionally been paid on a fixed national scale irrespective of subject. Why do advertisements for historians produce big fields of applicants whereas lectureships in law are often left unfilled?

3 The demand for take-off and landing slots at London airports has increased substantially in recent years. Suppose that, instead of just giving slots to airlines that have traditionally used them, the fixed supply of slots were auctioned. What would determine the market value of slots? How would you expect this value to change over time? If the value of landing slots changes, what responses might there be in airline operations? Would the revenue from selling slots be economic rent?

4 A footnote in Lipsey's chapter comments that the old examination question (Is it correct to say that the price of cinema seats is high in central London because the price of land is high?) should be answered in the affirmative rather than the negative expected by examiners. Explain why Lipsey's answer would be 'yes' and how examiners could have conceived the opposite.

5 In the 1980s, in Britain and other countries, governments justified reductions in income-tax rates by suggesting that incentives would thereby be raised. Will a reduction in the income-tax rate necessarily raise the amount of labour services an individual wishes to sell?

CHAPTER 18

The Income of Labour

Lipsey lists various reasons why wage differentials exist as an equilibrium (and not only as a disequilibrium) phenomenon. One of them is that different workers possess different amounts of *human capital*. Two principal ways in which human capital is acquired are through formal education and on-the-job training.

Q1 Staying on at school to study for A-levels is an investment decision. Ignoring the consumption benefits (or disbenefits) of study, the principal cost of the decision is _____ and the principal benefit is _____.

Q2 On-the-job training may be *specific* or *general*. Define 'general' training.
_____
_____

Q3 Workers undergoing general training must be paid the same wage rate as would be paid to them in alternative occupations. T/F. Explain.
_____
_____

WAGE DETERMINATION WITH AND WITHOUT UNIONS

Q4 Fig. 1 represents conditions in a certain labour market.

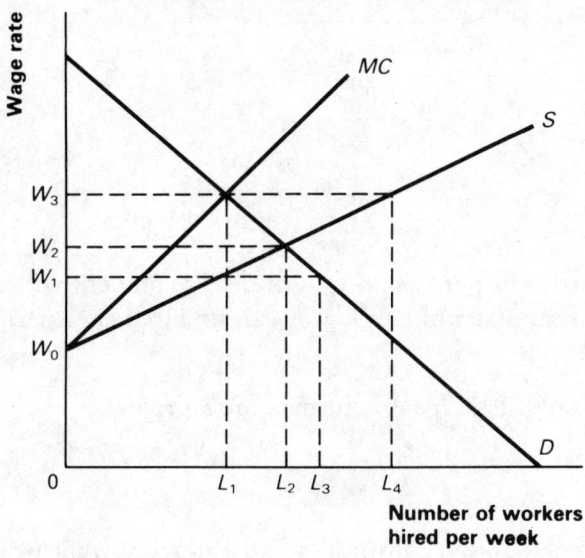

Fig. 1

(1) Under perfectly competitive conditions, the number of workers hired will be L_2 and the wage rate will be _____.

(2) A union could force the wage rate to W_3 if it could use entry restrictions so that only _____ workers were able to be hired each week.

(3) Suppose that, instead of a competitive, this were a *monopsonistic* labour market. The equilibrium wage would be _____ and the equilibrium employment level would be _____.

(4) A trade union is formed in this monopsonistic labour market. It can enforce whatever wage rate it chooses but cannot control how many jobs are offered. Any wage increase from the original monopsonistic equilibrium level would reduce employment. T/F. Explain. _____
_____
_____

(5) What level of wage rate in this situation would maximize employment?
_____

(6) What is the maximum wage rate consistent with maintaining employment at its original monopsonistic equilibrium level? _____

(7) What would be the excess supply of labour at this wage rate? _____

Q5 In a perfectly competitive labour market, the setting of a minimum wage above the equilibrium wage will reduce employment. T/F

Q6 In a monopsonistic labour market, the setting of a minimum wage above the equilibrium wage may increase employment. T/F

Q7 A firm operates in a local labour market where it knows that each increase in its labout force could require it to offer a more attractive wage rate. The relevant labour supply schedule and the total output figures for each size of work force are given below.

Wage rate per day (£s)	Number of employees	Total number of units of output produced per day
15.00	1	55
17.50	2	100
20.00	3	135
22.50	4	160
25.00	5	175
27.50	6	180

No other variable factor of production is used. Output is sold in a perfectly competitive national market for £1 per unit. Only whole numbers of employees can be hired (i.e. part-timers are not available).

(1) How many employees will be hired if the goal is to maximize profits?
_____

(2) What will be the wage rate per day? _____

(3) If a minimum wage of £22.50 per day were instituted and enforced, what would then be the number of employees hired? _____

(4) If a minimum wage of £40 per day were instituted, what would be the number of employees hired? _____

(5) If there were no minimum wage but the product price increased to £2, the employment level would be _____ and the wage rate would be _____.

Q8 *Ceteris paribus*, monopsonistic conditions will yield a lower employment level than competitive conditions. T/F

Q9 The answer to Q8 would change if a monopsonist could avoid a common wage rate and instead pay each worker just the amount sufficient to attract him to work for that particular firm. T/F

Check your answer to Q9. It was intended to underline that a monopsonist restricts employment because, if he increases the wage he offers in order to attract more labour, he has to pay that increased wage to all his existing workers as well. There is an analogy in product markets: if a *monopolist* could be a perfect price discriminator, his output would be less than/equal to/greater than the competitive level (Q10).

QUESTIONS FOR DISCUSSION

1 In the depression of the early- and mid-1980s, there was a substantial increase in the proportion of 18-year-olds applying for places in higher education. Formulate possible explanations within the framework of viewing education as an investment for which a relevant rate of return may be calculated.

2 Government-sponsored training schemes have replaced formal apprenticeships as the typical medium through which young British workers learn craft skills. Was this an inevitable result of trade unions forcing up youth wage rates relative to the adult wage?

3 School teachers' organizations have succeeded in making it mandatory for a teacher in a British state school to possess a teaching qualification. Does this rule serve a public interest, a private interest or both?

4 At one British university hall of residence, a student may not change the lightbulb in his room. He must send for a university electrician because electricians insist that electrical jobs need safety-conscious experts. Are the electricians being childish?

5 Discuss the effect on the amount of gas used in Britain if oil companies operating in the UK sector of the North Sea were compelled by law to sell their gas to British Gas and to no other company whatsoever. Note that this restriction to *only one buyer* actually had legal force until the late 1980s and there is still only one significant buyer because of a prohibition on pipelines to neighbouring European countries.

CHAPTER 19
The Income of Capital

Capitalists are heroes or villains according to different schools of political and social thought. But whether the society is capitalist or socialist, it is undeniable that capital goods play an important role in enhancing the flow of consumption goods and services that can be produced. The acquisition of capital goods, however, usually requires some sacrifice of present consumption in order to secure this future gain. In Chapter 19, Lipsey explores methods available for comparing present cost with future benefits.

THE RATE OF RETURN ON CAPITAL

The annual gross return on capital is the revenue generated by the output produced less the payments that have to be made to other factors of production. To obtain the net return we subtract _____ (Q1) from this figure.

The net return can notionally be divided into the pure return on capital, the risk premium and economic profit. Where an industry is in long-run equilibrium, economic profit will be _____ (Q2). If economic profits were negative, those who supplied the capital will be earning less reward than is available from alternative uses of capital with a similar degree of risk and the industry will _____ (Q3). We say then that the role of economic profit is to _____ (Q4).

In long-run equilibrium, in a world of certainty, the net return to capital would comprise only the pure return on capital. How the pure return is determined is considered in this Chapter.

PRESENT VALUES

Discussing the returns on capital investment is complicated by the fact that on many projects the benefits occur as an uneven flow over a long period of time. This matters because people perceive the value of a given sum of money differently according to when it is due to be received. If the annual rate of interest were 5%, and you were offered by a fairy godmother the choice of £100 now, or £103 in a year's time, you would choose £100 now, because even if you didn't want to spend it, it would accumulate to £105 in a year, and you'd be better off by £2 than if you accepted the £103. Conversely, if you were offered £100 now or £107 in a year's time you'd accept the latter; if you wanted to spend £100 now you could borrow £100 for a year, pay back the £105 which you would owe your creditor in a year's time, and have £2 over.

You would be indifferent between £100 now, and £105 in a year's time. Both would give you exactly the same command over possible purchases, either now, or in a year. This reasoning yields the present value technique, which allows us to cope with costs and benefits occurring at different points in time.

So if the rate of interest is 5%, £100 is worth £105 in a year's time.

Q5 Write this in equation form, putting X equal to what £100 is worth in a year's time.
X = £100 × _____ (Equation A)

Check your answer.

Q6 You leave this X invested for another year. Put Y equal to what X will be worth after this year has elapsed. $Y = X \times$ _____ (Equation B)

Check your answer.

Q7 You leave this Y invested for another year. Put Z equal to what Y will be worth after this year has elapsed. $Z =$ _____ (Equation C)

Check your answer.

Now, Equation A tells you that Y = £100 × 1.05. Substitute this expression into Equation B, and you get:

$$Y = (100 \times 1.05) \times 1.05 = £100 \times 1.05^2$$

Q8 Substitute this expression for Y in Equation C. $Z =$ _____

This states that, if the rate of interest is 5%, £Z in three years' time has the same value as £100 now. That is, the present value of Z is £100. We can state it more generally, putting i for the rate of interest, and K for the sum invested:

Q9 $Z =$ _____

Check your answer.

Often, we want to answer the question, 'What is the value of £X in Y years' time?' In this case we know the values of Z, i and t, and have to solve the equation for K.

Q10 $K =$ _____

Check your answer.

Sometimes we know the values of K, Z and t, and we want to find what interest rate makes K and Z have the same value. We can do this, solving the equation for i.

Q11 The rate of interest is 10%.

(1) What is the PV of £100 received in 1 years' time? _____

(2) What is the PV of £130 received in 3 years' time? _____

(3) What is the PV of £90 received in 5 years' time? _____

Check your answer.

(4) What is the PV, when i = 10%, of the following income stream? Received at end of:

Year	1	2	3	4	5	6	7...∞
	100	0	130	0	90	0	0 0 _____

Q12 Look at the irregular income flow of Q8. What regular yearly flow, received every year from year 1 onwards, has the same PV? _____

Check your answer. It is just the yearly income you would get if you invested £244.42 at 10%. Present Value calculations are usually made with the help of a table, part of which is reproduced in Table 1.

TABLE 1

Years hence (t)	1%	2%	4%	6%	8%	10%
1	0.990	0.980	0.962	0.943	0.926	0.909
2	0.980	0.961	0.925	0.890	0.857	0.826
3	0.971	0.942	0.889	0.840	0.794	0.751
4	0.961	0.924	0.855	0.792	0.735	0.683
5	0.951	0.906	0.822	0.747	0.681	0.621
6	0.942	0.888	0.790	0.705	0.630	0.564
7	0.933	0.871	0.760	0.665	0.583	0.513
8	0.923	0.853	0.731	0.627	0.540	0.467
9	0.914	0.837	0.703	0.592	0.500	0.424
10	0.905	0.820	0.676	0.558	0.463	0.386
11	0.896	0.804	0.650	0.527	0.429	0.350
12	0.887	0.788	0.625	0.497	0.397	0.319
13	0.879	0.773	0.601	0.469	0.368	0.290
14	0.870	0.758	0.577	0.442	0.340	0.263
15	0.861	0.743	0.555	0.417	0.315	0.239

Present value of £1.0

$$PV = \left(\frac{1}{1+i}\right)^t$$

Q 13 To calculate, for example, the PV, at 6%, of £4,326 in 13 years' time, you look for the entry common to the 6% column, and the 13-year row. It is _____.
This is the PV of £1, so to get the PV of £4,328 you multiply 0.469 by £4,328, which is £2,030.

Q 14 You are given two income streams:

(a) £50 per year for ever

(b) £120 after 1 year
£140 after 2 years
£620 after 4 years

The rate of interest is 8%. Which is more valuable, (a) or (b)?

THE DEMAND FOR CAPITAL BY A FIRM

Q 15 Construct a firm's marginal efficiency schedule for capital on Fig. 1, given

(a) on its 1,500th pound invested it will earn 20%.
(b) on its 3,500th pound invested it will earn 15%.
(c) it is a straight line (the relation between quantity of capital and productivity is linear).

(1) What is the marginal efficiency of the 5,000th pound? _____

(2) At what point does marginal efficiency become zero? _____

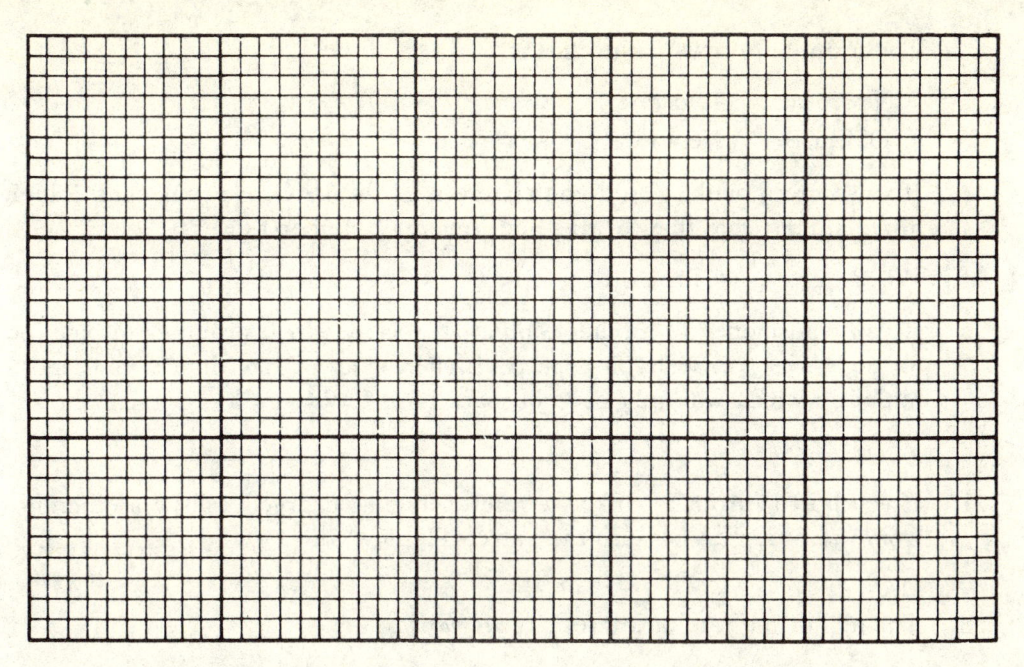

Fig. 1

(3) How much will the firm wish to borrow at a rate of interest of 10%?
_____

(4) If the firm is rationed by its bank (the only source of its funds) to £7,000 credit, will this limit have any effect with the interest rate at 9%? Yes/No
Will it have any effect if the interest rate is 5%? Yes/No

Q16 When comparing *capital cost* with *income stream* you should, in addition, deduct *depreciation* from the latter. T/F

THE AGGREGATE DEMAND FOR THE CAPITAL STOCK

Q17 If the economy is at the equilibrium point $i = MEC$, and i falls and remains at a lower level, equilibrium can only be restored by a fall/rise in the capital stock.

Q18 If technological innovation has shifted the *MEC* schedule to the right, this will have had a raising/lowering effect on equilibrium interest rates.

Q19 With inflation at 15% per year, what is the real rate of interest on a mortgage at a nominal 12%? _____

Q20 Governments in many countries have debts much larger than those of the whole private sector. In these countries, governments gain from an unexpected rise in inflation if their debt is in the form of long-term bonds with fixed interest rates. T/F

Q21 When the rate of interest was 5% I bought a perpetual bond for £2,000, giving me an income stream of £100 a year. The rate of interest now rises to 7½%. What has been my capital gain or loss? _____

Q22 I have bought a bond for £1,000 which yields 2½% for ever – i.e. £25 per year. The government makes an issue of bonds at 5%. How much could I sell mine for now? _____

The formula for calculating this is

$$\frac{\text{New price}}{\text{Old price}} = \frac{\text{Old rate}}{\text{New rate}}$$

Q 23 If you were a bank, would you charge a Ladbroke Grove junk shop a higher or lower interest rate than Marks and Spencer? Higher/Lower

Q 24 Why? _____

Q 25 If you lend money to a reliable building society which promises to pay you back at a fortnight's notice, will you expect a higher or lower rate than if you lend to a local authority which will only pay you back after two years? _____

Q 26 Why? _____

Q 27 If you borrow from a bank, the rate of interest charged will be a different number from the pure rate because the bank will allow for (1) _____ and (2) _____.

Q 28 The higher the rate of interest, *ceteris paribus*,

(a) the more investment opportunities will be profitable.
(b) the higher the necessary rate of return on any investment.
(c) the lower the amount of borrowing by the national government.
(d) the greater the demand for investment funds.

Q 29 The *MEC* schedule has a negative slope because

(a) the additional labour needed to work with the additional machines is of progressively lower quality.
(b) capital is subject to diminishing returns.
(c) with fully employed resources, the opportunity cost of increments of capital rises.

Q 30 Explain why the price of a British government bond, redeemable for £1,000 in 1998, was £1,325 in May 1989. 'Because the (1) _____ had (2) risen/fallen since the bond was issued.'

QUESTIONS FOR DISCUSSION

1 Suppose you were considering purchasing capital equipment for a company. How would you decide on the appropriate rate of discount for use in calculating present value? Would the rate differ if you had access to your own accumulated funds rather than having to borrow from a bank?

2 Some firms rank the priority of investment projects according to their payback periods. The payback period is the number of years before the unweighted sum of expected future profits from an investment reaches the cost of the original project. E.g., if double-glazing a property costs £2,000 and saves £400 per annum heating bills, the payback period is 5 years. Explain the weaknesses of evaluating investments by this technique.

3 In the 1970s, the nominal rate of interest offered by UK building societies was consistently lower than the inflation rate and at times the gap was larger than ten percentage points. Was it surprising that depositers were still found at these heavily negative real interest rates?

CHAPTER 20
Criticisms and Tests

The theory of distribution maintains that factor prices can be explained by the same supply-demand analysis as was used in analysing goods markets. Its particular predictions arise from assumptions about supply and about demand. On the supply side, factors are assumed to move among uses in pursuit of the highest net advantage for their owners. On the demand side, firms are assumed to be willing to employ factors in whatever quantities are consistent with profit maximization. These two assumptions generate the prediction that *in equilibrium*, in factor markets where firms are price-takers, the price of the factor equals its marginal revenue product.

Q1   If a firm has monopoly power in the market for its output, this invalidates a prediction that the price it pays to a factor will be equal to the factor's marginal revenue product. T/F

Q2   If a firm has monopsony power in a factor market, this invalidates a prediction that the price it pays to a factor will be equal to the factor's marginal revenue product. T/F

Q3   A firm is a price-taker in factor markets and a monopolist in the output market. If it chooses to maximize sales revenue rather than profits, the equilibrium wage-rate of its labour will be greater than/equal to/less than the marginal revenue product.

Q4   New legislation makes it easier to prove negligence by doctors when operations go wrong. In the short run, this will raise/lower the fees of lawyers specializing in medical law. In the long run, the number of such specialists will rise/fall. Assuming all specialisms are equally attractive in themselves and with no entry barriers by specialism, fees will/will not become the same as the average level in the legal profession. Medical specialists now win larger amounts in damages: is the long-run behaviour of fees consistent with marginal productivity theory? Yes/No

THE MACRO DISTRIBUTION OF INCOME

Q5   If technology and the amount of capital and land in an economy were fixed, whereas the labour force was growing, would you regard marginal productivity theory as refuted if the percentage of national income going to labour were to rise? Yes/No. Explain. _____

_____

Q6   You are told that, in our example of Q5, the percentage of national income going to land, which is in constant supply, is falling. Does this refute marginal productivity theory. Yes/No. Explain. _____

Q7   Again in the example of Q5, you have the information that the total income of capital has fallen. Does this refute marginal productivity theory? Yes/No. Explain.

QUESTIONS FOR DISCUSSION

1   'Given competitive markets, the equilibrium price of a factor equals its marginal revenue product.' 'Marginal productivity theory predicts that people are paid what they deserve.' Does the first statement justify the second?

2   Wage rates are different across UK regions. Would you expect these differentials to disappear in the long run?

3   In some jurisdictions, taxi licences are fixed in number but are transferable and sell openly for large sums. What will determine the precise price of a licence on the open market? What might cause fluctuations in the price of a licence over time?

4   In Britain and most other countries, local authorities use planning legislation to zone different areas to different uses (e.g. residential, agricultural, industrial). What effect do you think such regulations have on the spatial pattern of land prices?

5   Environmental scientists predict that permanent climatic changes may occur in the next century as a result of worldwide industrialization. What implications might there be for the world pattern of land prices?

CHAPTER 21
The Gains from Trade

Some countries are better at producing certain commodities than other countries; Britain can produce Land-Rovers more cheaply than Kenya, and Kenya can produce coffee beans more cheaply than Britain. In this case, it is obvious that trade in coffee beans and Land-Rovers could benefit both countries.

Q1 Look at Table 1. This shows the possible production of Land-Rovers and coffee beans in Britain and Kenya.

TABLE 1

	One unit of resources (e.g. 5 man-years) can produce:	
	Land-Rovers	Coffee beans (bushels)
Britain	10	50
Kenya	1	1,000

(1) In order to increase *total* production of both Land-Rovers and coffee beans, Britain must transfer resources from _____ into _____, and Kenya must transfer resources from _____ into _____.

(2) A transfer of *five* units by each country in the above directions will result in Britain producing _____ more _____, and _____ less _____, and in Kenya producing _____ more _____, and _____ less _____.

(3) After the transfer of 5 units in each country, total (Kenyan and British) production of coffee beans rises by _____, and of Land-Rovers by _____.

Q2 In the above example, the gains from specialization are clear – each country has an absolute/relative/proportionate advantage in the production of one commodity.

Q3 These are called conditions of _____.

In fact, the gains from trade do not depend upon reciprocal absolute advantage. Otherwise, there would be much less trade between East and West Europe, for example.

Look at Table 2, which shows the resources required to produce hi-fi loud-speakers and amplifiers in Britain and Japan.

TABLE 2

	One unit of resources (e.g. 5 man-years) can produce:	
	Speakers	Amplifiers
Britain	800	600
Japan	1,000	2,000

Q4 Does Table 2 represent a situation of reciprocal absolute advantage? Yes/No

Q5 Since Japan is more efficient in the production of both speakers and amplifiers, specialization by each country cannot increase total production of *both*. T/F

Check your answer so far. It is explained on Lipsey pp. 348–49 that gains from trade depend, not upon absolute advantage, but upon _____ (Q6) advantage.

Q7 In the example of Table 2, Japan has comparative advantage in _____, Britain in _____.

Q8 By moving five units of resources in each country, Japan will produce _____ more _____, and _____ less _____, and Britain will produce _____ more _____, and _____ less _____.

Q9 The net change in total production, after the transfer of Q8, is _____ more/fewer speakers, and _____ more/fewer amplifiers.

In these circumstances a simple shift of the same number of resources in each country will not result in an increase in the production of *both* commodities. The less efficient country must shift more resources.

Q10 In addition to the changes in Q8, assume that Britain shifts another five units of resources from amplifiers to speakers. British production of speakers increases, again, by _____ and that of amplifiers falls by _____.

Q11 The net change in total production, after the shifts of Q8 and Q10, is _____ more/fewer speakers, and _____ more/fewer amplifiers.

Q12 Look at Table 3.

TABLE 3

	One unit of resources (e.g. 5 man-years) can produce:	
	Wine (litres)	Olive oil (litres)
Greece	20,000	8,000
Spain	50,000	10,000

By shifting 15 units in Greece, and 10 in Spain, total production of wine increases by _____ and total production of olive oil increases by _____.

On pp. 350–51 of Lipsey it is explained that the theory of comparative advantage can be formulated in opportunity-cost terms – this formulation avoids the irrelevance (at this level) of the *absolute* efficiency of the countries concerned. It also avoids the difficulties of defining 'units of resources' when the countries may use different combinations.

Q 13 Fill in the following opportunity-cost tables, which you should derive from Tables 1, 2 and 3. Part of the first two tables have been filled in for you.

    (1) Opportunity cost of *one Land-Rover* and *one bushel of coffee beans*:

        Britain   5   bushels of coffee beans   _____   Land-Rovers
        Kenya   _____ bushels of coffee beans   0.001 Land-Rover

    (2) Opportunity cost of one speaker and one amplifier:
        Britain
        Japan   0.5 speakers

    (3) Opportunity cost of one litre of wine and one litre of olive oil:
        Greece
        Spain

Q 14 In order to increase total production, countries should specialize in those commodities for which the opportunity cost is higher/lower.

In order to utilize this extra production possibility to the advantage of each country, trade must, of course, actually take place – otherwise there would be no point in specialization.

Q 15 What name is given to the amount of home-produced goods which must be given up in order to acquire one unit of foreign goods? _____

Q 16 In the example of Table 2, what terms of trade will make it worthwhile for Britain to sell speakers to Japan?
Below/above _____ speakers.

Q 17 In the same example, will trade benefit *both Britain and Japan* if international prices are such that:

    (1) One speaker has the same value as 2 amplifiers? Yes/No

    (2) One speaker has the same value as 3 amplifiers? Yes/No

    (3) One speaker has the same value as 1 amplifier? Yes/No

Q 18 In this example, both countries gain from trade only if the world price of one amplifier is between _____ and _____ times the world price of one speaker.

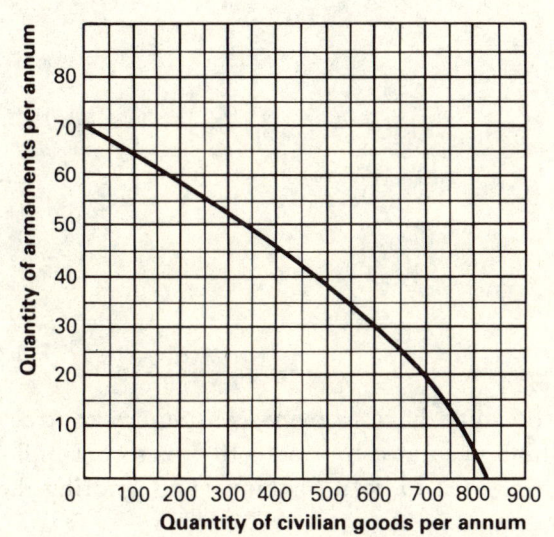

Fig. 1

Q19 Fig. 1 shows a production possibility boundary for a country which can produce armaments and civilian goods. The government has resolved that national security requires 50 units of armaments to be supplied to its forces each year. On world markets, one unit of armaments has a price 10 times as great as one unit of civilian goods.

(1) With no trade, how many units of civilian goods can be consumed each year given the requirement for 50 units of armaments? _____

(2) If the country is willing to purchase armaments from abroad, it could increase consumption of civilian goods to _____ units per annum and still have its target supply of armaments.

(3) In this situation, it would export _____ units of civilian goods and import _____ units of armaments.

(4) If self-sufficiency in armaments is judged to give greater security of supply, the opportunity cost of that benefit is _____ units of civilian goods per annum.

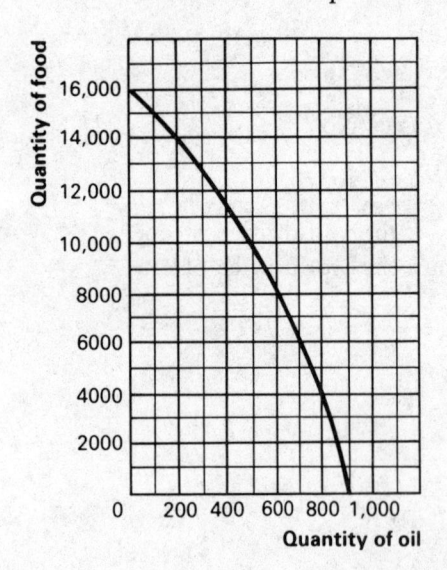

Q20 Fig. 2 shows a production possibility boundary for an economy which can produce oil and food. If the price of one unit of oil is (say) five times as great as a unit of food, it will not be appropriate for it to have an oil industry: it will produce (1) _____ units of food per annum and export some food to obtain oil. But if the price of oil becomes thirty times as great as the price of food (because of, e.g., the behaviour of OPEC), it will choose to produce (2) _____ units of oil per annum if it decides to take full advantage of trade opportunities. It will then have reduced its food production to (3) _____ units per annum.

Fig. 2

QUESTIONS FOR DISCUSSION

1 Professor Topping is a top economist who could have as many consultancy contracts as he cares to take. Mr Artist is a painter and decorator by trade. If Professor Topping paints his own house instead of hiring Mr Artist to do it for him, is he ignoring the fundamental theory of comparative advantage?

2   Through the 1970s and 1980s, Albania has followed policies designed almost to eliminate its participation in foreign trade. What form would the costs of this policy take? Could there be any benefits?

3   A government-owned liquor monopoly in Canada banned South African wine from its premises to show its distaste for apartheid policies. Discuss the proposition that this is likely to hurt both Canadian consumers and South African workers.

4   We normally represent a production possibility boundary with a curved rather than linear shape. If it were linear, would a country necessarily choose to produce only one of the two goods?

CHAPTER 22
Barriers to Trade

Despite the potential of free trade to raise consumption levels in all countries, the world nevertheless has countless instances where governments impose tariffs or quotas, or use other types of regulation, specifically to prevent trade taking place.

THE EFFECTS OF A TARIFF

Q1 Fig. 1 represents the (competitive) market for jeans in Britain. D_o and S_o are domestic demand and supply curves. Jeans are available on world markets at £15 per pair and this will be the price in Britain with free trade.

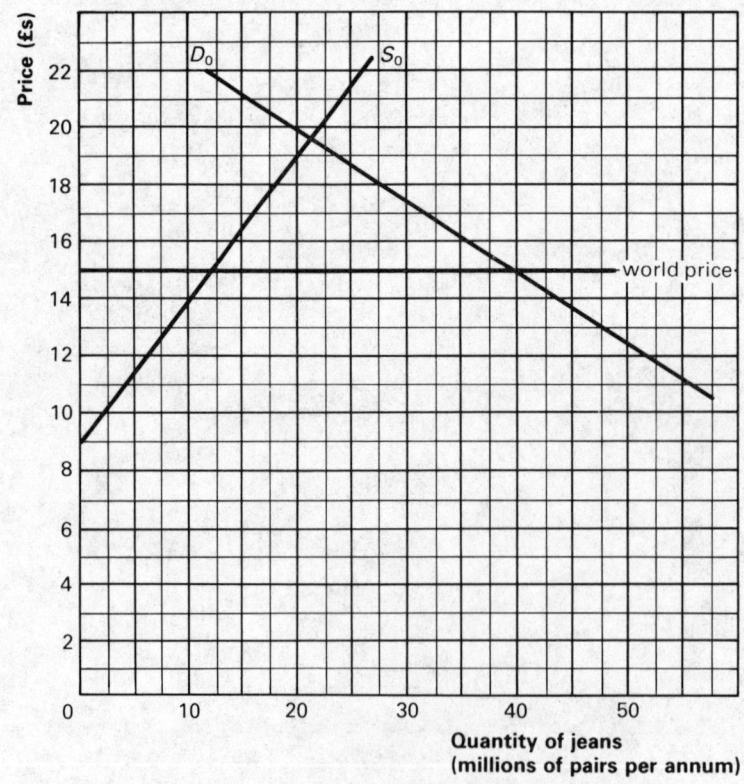

Fig. 1

(1) If imports were prohibited, estimate the equilibrium price of jeans in Britain.
_____

(2) With free trade, what is the equilibrium quantity sold in Britain?
_____ million pairs per annum.

(3) How many of these pairs will be British-produced? _____

(4) and how many imported? _____

(5) If Britain protects the domestic textiles industry by imposing a 20% tariff on jeans, what will be the new price in Britain? _____

(6) With this tariff, the equilibrium quantity purchased by British consumers will be _____ per annum.

(7) Domestic production will be _____ per annum.

(8) Leaving _____ to be supplied by foreign producers.

(9) The consumer surplus lost by British consumers will be _____ per annum.

(10) Tariff revenue for the British government will be _____ per annum.

The gain to British producers may notionally be divided into two parts. First, on jeans which they would have sold anyway, there is a revenue gain because the price is higher. Second, on jeans newly supplied, there is a gain equal to the difference between the revenue on those new sales and the extra production costs. If you recall that the competitive supply curve itself shows marginal costs, you will recognize that the area under curve S_o between the old and new production levels will measure the extra production cost. The reasoning will allow you to grasp why area (3) in Lipsey's Fig. 22.1 (p. 362) shows the gain to domestic firms from a tariff.

(11) What is the annual gain to the domestic producers in the example in this question? _____

(12) There is then a loss of consumer surplus of _____ per annum which is partly offset by a revenue gain of _____ to the government and a gain of _____ to domestic producers. This leaves a *deadweight* loss of _____ per annum. This figure measures the efficiency loss of the 20% tariff on jeans.

Q2 If tariffs were replaced by a voluntary agreement under which foreign firms agreed to restrict their sales in Britain, to what level would imports have to be held to have the same effect on domestic firms as the 20% tariff? _____ jeans per annum.

Q3 In the case of this voluntary restriction, the deadweight loss *in Britain* would be _____ per annum. Explain why the efficiency loss is greater than in the tariff case. _____

Q4 Consider the provision of canned peaches to Northland consumers. Possible suppliers include canning firms in Southland. They charge £1 per can, of which £0.80 is the payment to Southland farmers for the peaches themselves. Another source of supply is the Northland canning industry. It also relies on Southland farmers for the fresh peaches and also pays £0.80 per can for them. Northland has no tariff on imported fresh fruit but a 10% tariff on imported canned fruit. What is the *effective rate of tariff* protecting the Northland canning industry? _____ %

Q5 Explain in a sentence the economic meaning of this percentage.

Q6 Tariffs imposed by a country with a sufficient market share to affect the terms of trade can be beneficial for that country but will lower world consumption levels. T/F

Q7 A country operating on its production possibility boundary must gain if it increases the volume of exports while holding imports constant. T/F

QUESTIONS FOR DISCUSSION

1 Economists have called attention to the damaging effects of trade restrictions since at least the eighteenth century. Why are they still so pervasive?

2 '"Protection" really means exploiting the consumer' (Milton and Rose Friedman). Discuss.

3 Adam Smith wrote in *The Wealth of Nations* (1776) as follows: 'The case in which it may sometimes be a matter of deliberation how far it is proper to continue the free importation of certain foreign goods is when some foreign nation restrains by high duties the importation of some of our manufactures into their country.' In deliberating today on whether your government should retaliate in kind against foreign tariffs, what considerations would you have in mind?

4 'If an infant industry had good prospects, private firms would be willing to finance a period of losses in the expectation of long-run rewards. A tariff is then not needed. If private firms are not so confident, a tariff is not justified.' Discuss.

5 The Canadian general election of 1988 was bitterly fought on the issue of a free trade agreement with the USA. Opposition parties claimed such an agreement would threaten Canada's cultural and political identity. Are similar fears appropriate in Britain in respect of the EC goal of a 'Single European Market' in 1992?

6 EC regulators have tried amongst other things to force the sale of British beer in litres and the renaming of most British ice-cream on account of its low dairy content. Do such interventions reflect a bureaucratic love of meddling or are they necessary steps in pursuit of genuinely free trade?

7 In whose interests are voluntary export restrictions entered into by Japanese producers of electrical goods?

8 Nigeria invested heavily in steel plant that produced steel at $500 per ton when the world price was $250 per ton. Can one conceive of such an investment being justified?

CHAPTER 23

The Case for the Free Market

In the first part of the chapter, Lipsey presents the traditional case for the market system. The virtue emphasized is essentially that markets provide an effective mechanism by which patterns of production and consumption are modified in response to exogenous events. If rising incomes cause people in Britain to want to buy more holidays in Florida and fewer in Spain, no bureaucrat in a Ministry of Leisure has to recognize the new trends: price signals will induce holiday companies to change their offerings in pursuit of higher profits for themselves. *No great volume of national resources needs to be devoted to acquiring information on preferences* for use by central planners: production (in the case of the holiday) shifts in the direction of new preferences without any one individual needing to be aware of overall trends in the leisure market. There will of course be casualties – as profits in Spain contract, those who had trained as Spanish-speaking couriers will lose their jobs – but, overall, advocates of the market think that it has no rival as a coordinating mechanism in the economy.

ECONOMIC EFFICIENCY

The more formal case for the free market rests on a demonstration that (at least under universal perfect competition) efficiency is guaranteed once markets reach their equilibria. A conventional definition of efficiency (*Pareto efficiency*) is that it describes a situation where

_____
_____ (Q1).
Efficiency has two sides to it. We have achieved _____ (Q2) efficiency if whatever bundle of goods is produced is at the lowest possible resource cost; _____ (Q3) efficiency is achieved when the bundle being produced is an appropriate one.

Q4   Productive efficiency requires amongst other things that the marginal cost of product X should be the same in every firm involved in X production. That requirement is necessarily fulfilled under perfect competition. Why? _____
_____

Q5   If price is below marginal cost, efficiency criteria indicate that the relevant industry output is too large. T/F

The feature of perfect competition that yields allocative efficiency is that price is equal to marginal cost in equilibrium. This is *not* a feature of monopoly. Monopolistic output is below the allocatively efficient level and leads to a *deadweight loss*.

Q6   Fig. 1 shows the demand and marginal revenue curves facing a monopolist. Marginal cost is constant at £40 per unit whatever output per period is produced. There are no fixed costs.

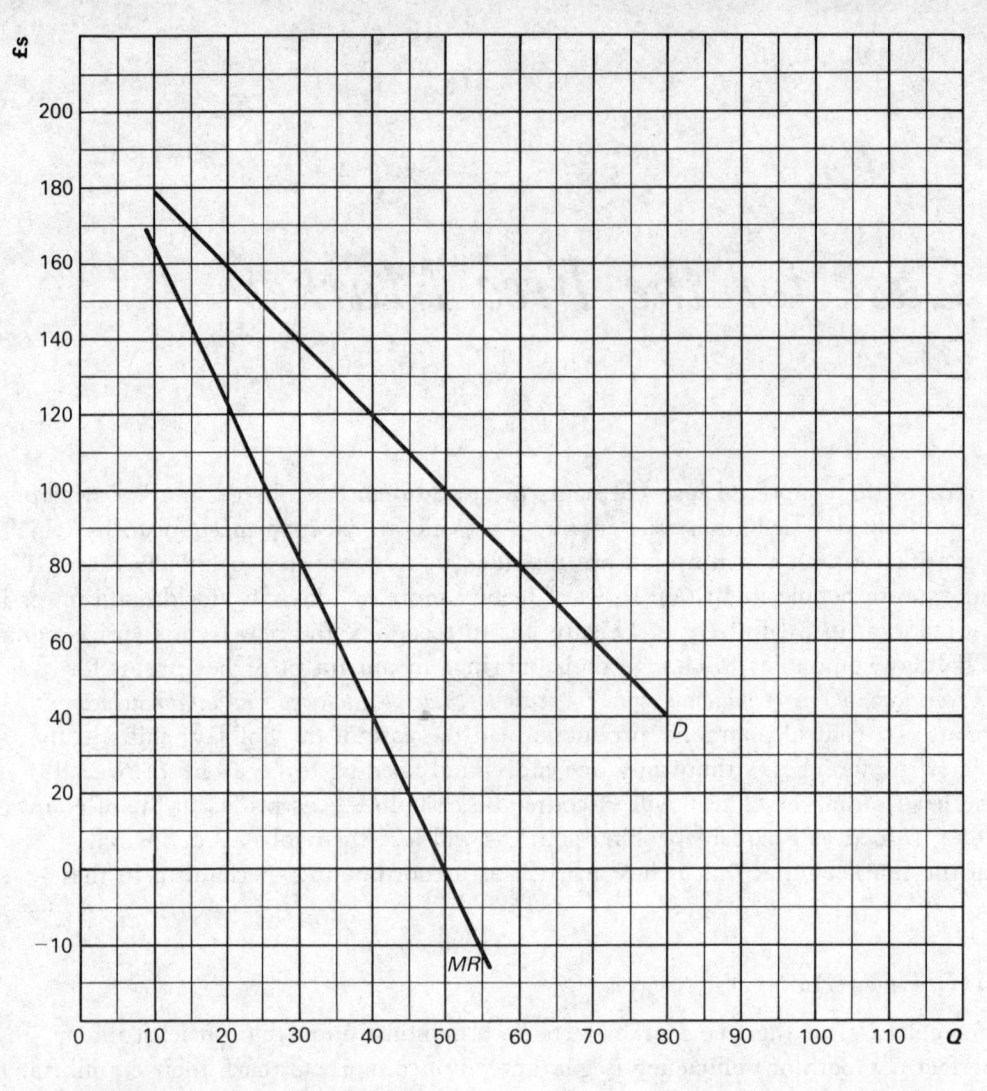

Fig. 1

(1) Draw in the marginal cost curve. What output per period will maximize profits? _____

(2) What price will be charged? _____

(3) If price were set equal to marginal cost instead, what would be the output per period? _____

(4) What would be the gain in consumer surplus per period as a result? _____

(5) What would be the loss of monopoly profit per period? _____

(6) Combining the effect on consumers and producers, what is the overall per period gain to society from marginal cost pricing? _____

This is a measure of the deadweight loss caused by monopolists maximizing profits and holding price above marginal cost.

Q7   Fig. 2 represents a monopoly which this time faces a rising marginal cost curve.

128

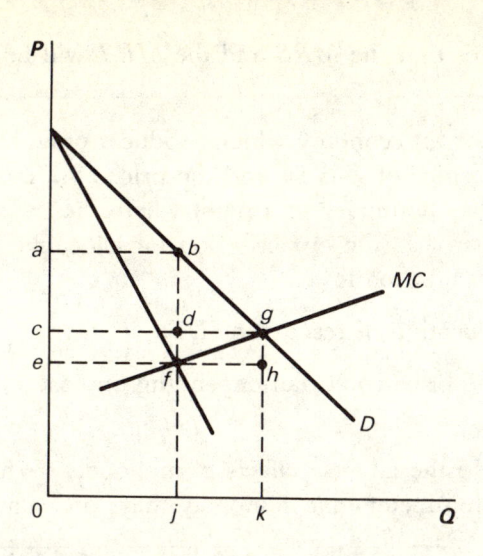

Fig. 2

(1) Using the letters indicated, monopoly output is at *j* and price is at _____

(2) If the cost of a given output were the same whether it was produced by one monopolist or by a collection of competitive firms, the *MC* curve would represent what the supply curve would be under perfect competition. In this case, price would fall to _____ and output rise to _____

(3) Indicate the consequent gain in consumer surplus per period by shading in the relevant area. This is bounded by the letters _____

(4) Part of the gain in consumer surplus consists of an amount indicated by area _____ which is transferred to them from producers.

(5) The loss of producer surplus is *partly* offset by a gain consisting of the difference between the sales value of the extra output and the extra cost of producing it: area _____

(6) Combining all the effects on consumer and producer surplus, there is a net gain of area _____ per period. This potential gain is forgone if monopoly prevails instead of competition. It is therefore the deadweight loss of monopoly.

If you got parts of this question wrong, study carefully Lipsey's Fig. 23.3 (p. 385). The caption that accompanies it has the same analysis as here except that it is explained in the context of a change from competition to monopoly rather than vice-versa.

THE GENERAL EQUILIBRIUM APPROACH

Q8 Define the marginal rate of transformation between goods *X* and *Y*.

_____

_____

Q9 Define the marginal rate of substitution between goods *X* and *Y*.

_____

_____

Q10 What condition is necessary to ensure that all consumers have the same *MRS* between *X* and *Y*?

_____

Q11 What feature of perfect competition ensures that the *MRS* and the *MRT* will be the same? _____

Q12 You are given the following information for an economy which produces only *X* and *Y*. All consumers are in equilibrium. The price of *X* is £4 and the price of *Y* is £2. The economy is on its production possibility boundary at a point where the opportunity cost of one unit of *X* is 3 units of *Y*. On our criterion for allocative efficiency, the output of *X* is too high/just right/too low.

Q13 Free markets always yield an optimum allocation of resources. T/F

Q14 If competitive industry is monopolized, the price could fall depending on cost conditions. T/F

Q15 Economists have usually drawn attention to the adverse effects of monopoly. What alleged feature of monopoly persuaded Schumpeter that monopoly may, on balance, have beneficial effects on living standards? _____

QUESTIONS FOR DISCUSSION

1 Newspapers hostile to Eastern Europe make frequent reference to long queues outside shops in the Soviet Union and other Communist bloc countries. Why are queues a relatively rare phenomenon in Western Europe?

2 Two new products of the early 1980s were the home video recorder and the small three-wheeled electric car known as the C5. The one product is now found in a majority of British households; the other has disappeared without trace. How have 'market forces' brought about these outcomes? Would there have been a different sequence of events in a command economy?

3 A patent confers a temporary monopoly on a firm registering a newly invented product with the relevant government agency. Explain why patents are said to raise the rate of innovation but ensure that any innovations are under-exploited from an efficiency perspective.

4 If BBC Radio were disbanded, do you think all stations would then be pop music orientated?

5 Look back to Chapter 13 of this Workbook. Discussion Question 3 on p. 78 asked about the effects of abolishing tolls on a bridge. Use the formal analysis of this chapter to show how the deadweight loss from charging tolls could be measured.

CHAPTER 24
The Case for Government Intervention

Market failure refers to situations where the market system fails to yield an optimal outcome. E.g., *public goods* (such as flood defences) are not produced at all by market systems because private firms cannot charge beneficiaries and, given this, are unable to recover costs. Where *externalities* exist, the amount of a commodity produced will be different from that required for allocative efficiency. In these cases, as in situations where equity issues are involved or where people are judged to need protecting from their own decisions, government intervention may be considered appropriate. Of course, the involvement of government does not guarantee an efficient outcome. *Government failure* can be as serious a problem as market failure.

EXTERNALITIES

Q1   Why would the number of people taking up innoculations against an infectious disease be lower than optimal if innoculations were sold only by profit-maximizing firms? _____
_____
_____

   Tools to correct this market failure would include rules (e.g. children must be innoculated), subsidies to private firms to bring down price, or provision of a cheap or zero-price programme as part of the National Health Service.
   Questions in Chapters 13 and 23 of this Workbook asked about the effects of bridge tolls. We expected students to respond that charging led to allocative inefficiency in that 'too little' traffic would use the facility with a toll in force. However, many parts of the road system, especially in urban areas, are subject to *congestion* (each extra car slows down other road users). In these cases, it can be argued that a toll would be socially beneficial.

Q2   Fig. 1 portrays the situation on a stretch of city centre road between 8 and 9 am. If up to 1,000 cars use the road in this period, traffic flows freely and it costs each road user £0.20 for his journey (this is made up of petrol costs and the value of the time spent on the journey). Beyond 1,000 cars, road space is under pressure and every extra car raises the journey cost of existing users by slowing them down, adding to their petrol and time costs. *AC* shows how cost per journey varies with the level of traffic flow. Marginal social cost shows the extra cost to society of one more journey being made. This consists of both the cost to the new driver (*AC*) *and* the extra cost borne by existing users as a result of the newcomer joining the queues. So, e.g., at a flow of 1,500 cars, the cost per journey is £0.24 but the 1,500th driver also adds a total of £0.10 extra costs to the existing users, making an *MSC* of £0.40.

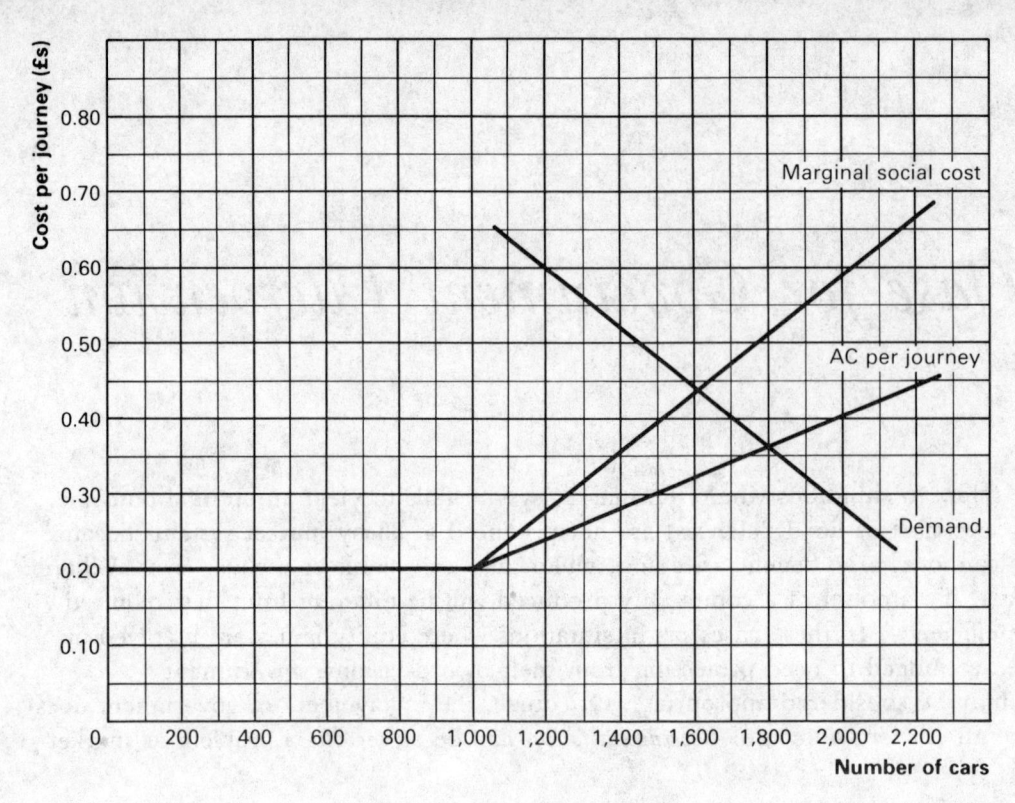

Fig. 1

(1) How many cars will use the road between 8 and 9 am if there is no toll system in force? _____

(2) What is the socially optimal number of cars in this hour? _____

(3) Explain in words why the actual number will exceed the social optimum.
_____
_____

(4) The Transport and Road Research Laboratory has devised relatively cheap systems for imposing tolls in such situations, using roadside electronic devices and in-car meters. What level of toll here would ensure that only the socially optimal numbers of journeys were undertaken? _____

(5) What deadweight loss is implied by a refusal to levy such a toll? _____ per hour.

Although the answer to (5) may appear small, in fact, across an entire urban road system like London's, the deadweight loss would amount to a very considerable sum. Such a sum represents the daily loss to society if there is no correction for the presence of the externality.

TAXES

Q3 Fig. 2 shows the demand and supply curves of whisky. Quantity is measured in barrels and price is measured in £s per barrel.

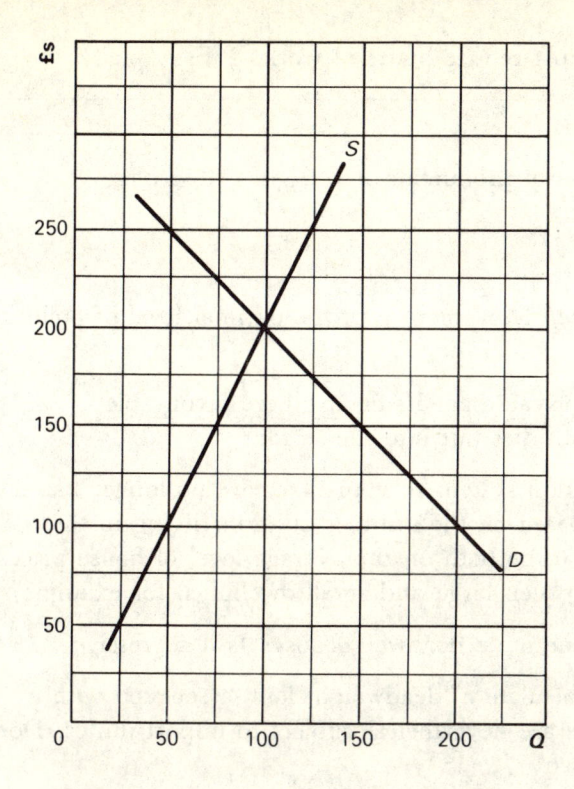

Fig. 2

(1) What is the equilibrium price and quantity? P = _____ Q = _____

(2) To what level would price rise if the government imposed an excise duty of £30 per barrel? _____

(3) How much is the fall in the price received by producers net of duty? _____

(4) What is the per-period loss of consumer surplus? _____

(5) What is the per-period loss of producer surplus? _____

(6) What is the per-period government revenue from the excise duty? _____

(7) What is the deadweight loss from this tax? _____

If you had wrong answers to this question, try again using Lipsey's Fig. 24.2 (p. 411) as a guideline.

Q4 *Ceteris paribus*, the deadweight loss from a tax is greater the lower the elasticity of demand. T/F

Q5 The average consumption of tobacco products falls as one considers higher and higher income groups. So the tax on cigarettes is progressive/regressive.

Q6 An unemployed unskilled labourer has a job offer for next week at £100 per week. Income tax at the rate of 25% is levied on all income over £60 per week. Benefit payable to the unemployed currently gives him £40 per week. What is the opportunity cost of spending next week at leisure? _____

Q7 If the labourer in Q6 were 18 years old and single, and if this made him ineligible for benefit, what would be the opportunity cost of leisure? _____

133

Q 8   An increase in the income tax rate must reduce hours of work. T/F. Explain.

Review Chapter 17 on the supply of factors of production if you got Q 8 wrong.

QUESTIONS FOR DISCUSSION

1 Explain to a friend who supports the Green Movement why the optimal level of pollution is not zero.

2 Does a university education confer only private benefits or are there favourable externalities to justify the high level of subsidies put into the sector?

3 Suppose a country changes the local taxation system so your taxes are no longer based on the value of your house but are instead based on the number of adults living in the house. What would you expect the effect to be both on the average level of house prices and on the pattern of house prices (as between large and small dwellings, for example).

4 Is the television licence a tax? Does it generate a deadweight loss? Is it regressive?

5 In Chapter 22 (Q 1) you were asked to calculate a 'deadweight loss' associated with a tariff on jeans. Despite such results, jeans are nevertheless subject to import duties. Does public-choice theory help us understand why?

CHAPTER 25

Aims and Objectives of Government Policy

In this chapter, Lipsey discusses a diverse set of issues on why and how governments may intervene in the economy.

Q1 The demand curve for a *private good* is the horizontal summation of the demand curves of individual consumers. T/F

Q2 The demand curve for a *public good* is the horizontal summation of the demand curves of individual consumers. T/F

Q3 A fishery downstream from a chemical plant suffers a fall in production as the chemical plant increases its effluent discharges into the river. This is an example of an _____ .

Q4 Suppose the fishery in fact owned the river. In this case, there would be more/less than the optimal amount of pollution of the river but this could be alleviated if there were a mechanism for selling pollution rights. T/F

Q5 A merger between the fishery and chemical companies would offer a means of securing the optimal level of pollution so long as the new firm was profit-maximizing. T/F. This would be an example of _____ .

Q6 If a nationalized industry follows marginal cost pricing and makes a profit, it must be on a rising part of its marginal cost curve. T/F

Q7 In the early 1980s, British Gas charged domestic consumers a price equivalent to short-run average cost. The average and marginal cost curves in the industry are upward-sloping because increasingly high-cost gas fields have to be tapped as more gas is required. Moreover, short-run average cost was artificially low because long-term contracts had been signed with North Sea oil companies which gave British Gas supplies at a cost which would not be maintained once the contracts came up for renewal. This situation gave rise to a deadweight loss because gas consumption was higher/lower than that indicated on allocative efficiency grounds. Consumers making long-term decisions on, e.g., central heating systems over-/under-invested in gas appliances.

Q8 If demand is perfectly inelastic, the *incidence* of an indirect tax is wholly on the producer. T/F

Q9 Define the *Laffer curve*. _____
_____
_____

QUESTIONS FOR DISCUSSION

1. A municipal swimming pool costs the same to run however many swimmers use it in any given session. Should it abolish charges for admission? Would your answer be different for summer Sunday mornings and winter Friday mornings if you knew that the former session already attracted large crowds? If there were no admission charges, why would it be difficult to assess proposals for new pools to be built in the future?

2. A dozen university lecturers go out for dinner to celebrate the end of marking examinations. If they split the bill equally rather than asking for each person to be billed separately, why would the bill be likely to be larger? Is the equal-split arrangement inefficient from the viewpoint of the whole group?

3. 'Legislation to outlaw smoking in the workplace is unnecessary. If non-smokers in an office felt enough discomfort, they would be willing to bribe their smoking colleagues to accept a local ban.' Comment.

4. If water were charged by meter at 10 pence per gallon, in what ways (if at all) would you expect your household to economize on its use? Note that average daily consumption in Britain is about 25 gallons.

5. Why does the Monopolies and Mergers Commission disapprove some mergers but not others?

6. Who would lose if mortgage tax relief were withdrawn?

7. Bus services in London are provided by a publicly owned organization but elsewhere in England privately owned companies are allowed to supply large numbers of services. Is there any argument for government provision of bus services? Is the case stronger in London?

8. Do you think your telephone service would be better if British Telecom were taken into public ownership?

CHAPTER 26
Macroeconomic Concepts and Variables

FROM MICRO TO MACRO ECONOMICS

One important lesson of this chapter is that the distinction between macro- and microeconomics is nothing like as clear-cut as it is sometimes represented. It is a platitude that a distinction within a science is a distinction of convenience, but it is worth explaining that although microeconomics and macroeconomics deal with some things that exhibit clear differences of type (the distinction, for example, between the effect of a rise in income tax on the income of the government and the effect on the price of peanuts of an improvement in the cashew nut crop), much of their subject matter is drawn from the same category of economic events, the difference being the level of aggregation at which they are treated. For example, the national level of expenditure on consumer goods is treated as a macro variable, whereas the expenditure of a family on a particular range of consumer goods is a micro variable. But what of the expenditure of a village on consumer goods? It doesn't really matter; we make a distinction between macro and micro variables because we have a hypothesis that variations in economic relations on the micro level are often cancelled out by other opposite variations on the micro level, such that at a certain level of aggregation the relation will be fairly stable. If this hypothesis is true for some level of aggregation, it will enable us to do economics without having to find out every detail of individuals' economic behaviour.

SOME KEY MACRO VARIABLES

Unemployment

Look at Fig. 26.1 on p. 447, which shows UK unemployment rates since 1930. As you can see, the unemployment rate has never been zero. Does this mean that we have never had full employment? It is difficult to conceive of an economy in which everyone who wants to work is in employment throughout the year. At any time there will be some people who are temporarily between jobs – perhaps because they have given notice and are waiting to take up their new job or are currently searching for a job that suits them. Other people may be unemployed because they have been laid off but are expecting to be recalled. When people are unemployed for relatively short periods between jobs, we call this frictional unemployment. When the unemployment rate is high, only a small proportion of unemployment will be due to people being out of work for fairly short periods between jobs, and when we talk of an economy being at the full-employment level, we mean that any unemployment is frictional unemployment.

Q1 When we talk of the unemployed we mean all people who are not working. T/F

Actual and Potential Output

Q2 The gap between actual and potential gross national product measures the difference between:

(a) what the economy is producing and what it could produce if the unemployment rate were zero.
(b) what the economy is producing and what it could produce if workers took shorter teabreaks, were more punctual and generally worked harder.
(c) what the economy is producing and what it could produce if the economy were kept at full employment.
(d) what the economy is currently producing and what it will produce in a year's time after investment plans have been completed.

Q3 Potential national product is what could be produced if the economy were on its production-possibility frontier. T/F

Price Indices

We often use GDP figures to compare total real output in different years. However, if a country is experiencing inflation over these years, part – or possibly all – of any increase in GDP measured in current prices may be due to the rising prices. We must therefore measure GDP in constant prices in order to separate out the change due to inflation from the change due to increase (or decrease) in real output. Real GDP is a measure of output obtained by evaluating the current year's output in terms of the prices of some base year.

Q4 Nominal GDP measures output in terms of current/constant prices.

On p. 451 several forms of price index are mentioned. The implied GDP deflator is calculated as

$$\frac{\text{GDP at current prices}}{\text{GDP at constant prices}} \times 100\%$$

Q5 Work out the implied GDP deflator for each year in the following table where the GDP figures are taken from CSO, *National Income and Expenditure*, HMSO 1988 (the 'Blue Book').

	Current prices (£ billion)	Constant prices (£ billion)	GDP Deflator
1978	149	275	_____
1979	172	283	_____
1980	200	276	_____
1981	218	273	_____
1982	237	278	_____
1983	260	289	_____
1984	279	294	_____
1985	305	305	_____
1986	322	314	_____
1987	352	327	_____

Q6   What is the base year? _____

Q7   By what percentage has real output risen between

  (a) 1978 and 1982? _____
  (b) 1978 and 1985? _____
  (c) 1985 and 1987? _____

Q8   If total UK population was 56 million in 1983 and 56¼ million in 1987, find whether real output *per capita* has risen. _____

Q9   GDP at current prices was £112 billion in 1976 and the index was 43. Find 1976 GDP at constant (1985) prices. _____

THE NATIONAL ACCOUNTS

National income is the total market value of all goods and services produced in an economy during some specific period of time. National income is also the total of all incomes earned over the same period of time, so

$$\text{gross national product} \equiv \text{national income}$$

Gross national product is the sum of the value-added of all firms over this same period; that is, the total value of *final* goods and sales. There is only one value of gross national product in any period but we can calculate it in different ways. We can measure GNP by taking the value of expenditure on goods and services produced (*the expenditure approach*). Alternatively, we can value output in terms of factor incomes (*the factor-income approach*), and yet another way is to measure GNP by summing value-added. These methods give us three different ways of looking at the value of the nation's output. The important point to grasp is that, whatever approach we use, the value of GNP will be the same because of the circular flow of income.

The *income approach* to national accounting adds together all the kinds of income earned by all households. The various categories of income are listed in column one of Table 26.2.

Q10 Gross company trading profits (Item 4) are equal to dividends paid by companies to shareholders. T/F

Q11 'Stock appreciation' in the GDP figures (Table 26.2) refers to the stock market/inventories.

In the *output approach* to measuring GNP, care must be taken to avoid double-counting of products. Most commodities go through several stages of production which may be undertaken by different firms. A commodity may be a finished product for one firm and raw material to another. Some commodities can be both intermediate and final products. In macroeconomics a firm's output is defined as its value-added.

Q12 Value-added = total value of sales less _____

Q13 From the following information, calculate:

  (a) value-added by each 'firm';
  (b) total value-added;
  (c) profits earned by each 'firm'.

Last year,

  (1) A group of fishermen sold their catch for £12,000. Materials purchased (nets,

etc.) cost £900, wages paid totalled £8,000, interest on a loan (for their boat) was £500 and harbour dues came to £100.

(2) A nearby food-processing factory had a total sales revenue of £60,000. Costs of raw materials were: fish £10,000, packaging materials £1,000. Rent came to £7,000, interest payments £6,000 and wages £15,000.

(3) A fishmonger sold £7,000 of frozen fishfingers and £3,000 of fresh fish. The frozen fish cost £5,000, while he paid £2,000 for the fresh fish. He ran his shop single-handed, paid a rent of £1,000 and valued his labour at £2,000. Interest payment on a bank loan came to £100.

The third way to measure GNP is based on categories of *expenditure*.

Q14 List the categories of expenditure which must be included when calculating GDP by the expenditure approach. _____

Q15 If you put some of your savings into an account with a building society, is this investment? Explain. _____

Q16 What are the three major components of investment? _____

Q17 Inventories are stocks of _____ goods held by the producer. If production exceeds sales, inventories are _____. If sales exceed production and such sales have been accurately forecast, inventory disinvestment is intentional/unintentional.

Q18 As inventories are stocks of goods that have not been sold by the producers, their value must be deducted from GDP. T/F

We distinguish between the total value of all goods produced, whether consumed or not, and the same value minus the value of all capital goods which have worn out during this period. This latter concept is called *net national product*.

Q19 NNP = GNP minus depreciation. T/F

When there are taxes on expenditure, VAT for example, the value of *national product at market prices* (i.e. sale price + tax) is not equal to national product valued in terms of income payments to factors of production. To find the value of *national product at factor cost*, expenditure taxes must be subtracted from national product at market prices.

Q20 National income is equal to national expenditure at factor cost. T/F

Q21 If instead of taxing goods, the government subsidizes them, national product valued at market prices will be greater/less than national product valued at factor cost.

At times we have referred to gross *domestic* product, and at other times to gross *national* product. Here are a couple of questions to check whether you understand the difference.

Q22 GNP = GDP + exports. T/F

Q23 Net property income = receipts by UK residents of overseas income *less* income from UK assets paid to UK citizens who live outside the UK. T/F

We need one further concept of income: *disposable income*. Disposable income is GDP *minus* any part of GDP not paid over to individuals, *minus* income tax, *plus* transfers.

Q24 Disposable income is the sum of all value-added in the economy. T/F

Q25 The following items appear in the 1987 national income accounts for an economy. Classify them into separate accounts of National Product, Expenditure and Income. (*Note*: as there is no net property income from abroad, national product = domestic product.)

	£ million
Wages and salaries	430
Imports of goods and services	220
Rent	50
Value-added in agriculture	100
Government current expenditure on goods and services	130
Capital consumption	70
Value-added in construction	120
Consumers' expenditure	450
Dividends	500
Income from self-employment*	60
Exports of goods and services	210
Undistributed profits*	110
Gross domestic fixed investment	150
Value-added in distributive trades	180
Value-added in manufacturing	700
Value-added in sectors not separately listed	290
Value of physical increase in stocks	10
Trading surplus of public corporations*	20

*Gross of depreciation

Q26 Unfortunately, due to recent disturbances in the country, much information on Ruritania's national income and expenditure is missing. All the available information is given below. You are able to reassure the Chancellor of the Exchequer that this information is sufficient for you to compute the national product in one of the conventional ways.

Find: (a) gross national product and net national product at factor cost;
(b) gross national product at market prices;
(c) disposable income.

	£ million
Dividends	40
Incomes of self-employed	780
Government expenditure on goods and services	300
Indirect taxes on expenditure	120
Value-added in manufacturing	1,000
Gross fixed capital formation	190
Wages and salaries	1,850
Gross trading profits of companies	170
Net fixed investment	150
Gross trading surplus of public corporations	40
Interest on the national debt	30
Rent	60
Retained profits of companies	130
Income tax	600

QUESTIONS FOR DISCUSSION

1 How do we distinguish between micro- and macroeconomics? Where do we draw the boundary?

2 What does microeconomics take as 'given' that macroeconomics considers? What would you say about the reverse question?

3 The retail price index (RPI) in Britain jumped unexpectedly from an annual rate of inflation of 3.3% to 7.7% during 1988. The increase in inflation was partly due to a rise in mortgage interest rates, which were included in the UK RPI. Keeping this in mind, list the likely effects of such inflation on the distribution of income.

4 We noted that only final goods and services are included in GDP. Does this mean that earnings of people producing intermediate goods and services are not part of GDP?

5 Are education and medical care intermediate or final goods? When education and medical care are not sold in the market, are they excluded from GDP?

6 Can one compare the standard of living in nineteenth-century Britain with the standard of living today, using national-income data? What adjustments would need to be made?

7 Why should subsidy payments be added to expenditure to get GDP at factor cost?

CHAPTER 27

National Income in a Two-sector Model

In this chapter we begin our analysis of the determinants of output and employment. In order not to have to think about many variables at once, we start by making some simplifying assumptions so that we can begin our study of the theory of national-income determination in a very simple economy; in later chapters we shall relax these assumptions.

Q1   Which of the following propositions are incompatible with the basic assumptions discussed on p. 468?
   (a) Increased demand for a commodity will not result in a price rise because new techniques will enable it to be produced more cheaply.
   (b) Even if the proportion of the population which constitutes the labour force increases, thereby increasing potential production, the price level will not fall.
   (c) If employment increases, production *must* only increase in the same proportion.

Q2   An increase in gross national expenditure always means an increase in both money and real gross national product. T/F

If you answered this question wrongly, consider the following case:

Q3   Total expenditure and money GNP increase by 6% in one year. Suppose that prices rose by 15% in the same period. Real GNP will have increased/remained constant/decreased.

If we want to find out about the behaviour of national income, we must start by separating out the change due to *price* changes so that we can concentrate on *output* changes – hence the important assumption on p. 468.

Q4   With a Keynesian aggregate supply schedule,
   (a) a rise in aggregate demand will raise price and income levels. T/F
   (b) a rise in aggregate demand will cause output to rise and unemployment to fall. T/F

Q5   When we say that income is demand-determined, we mean that the level of national income is determined by aggregate demand, firms producing whatever they can sell. T/F

THE BASIC MODEL

In the very simple model we study in this chapter, consumption and savings decisions are made by households; there is no business saving, no government expenditure and no government revenue from taxation. All consumption and investment goods are produced and sold within the country, so that there are no exports and imports.

Q6 In this basic model, disposable income = national income = net national product = net domestic product. T/F

Q7 What are the categories of expenditure which make up gross domestic expenditure? (List them in symbols) _____

Q8 There are two ways of expressing the equilibrium conditions. Can you remember what they are? (Write them as symbols.)

   (a) _____
   (b) _____

In the last chapter we learned that expenditure is equal to income. This is an identity: *actual* expenditure is equal to *actual* income through the circular flow of income. It is important to understand that this identity holds whether or not an economy is in equilibrium. For an economy to be in equilibrium, *desired* expenditure must be equal to income. To make quite sure you understand this point, we will look at the circular flow of income in a very simple economy where only one investment good is produced (canoes), all other goods being consumption goods.

Q9 Fill in the blanks in the following table:

(a)

OUTPUT (£000s)		EXPENDITURE (£000s)	
1. Breadfruit	100	*Consumption*	
2. Yams	80	1. Breadfruit	100
3. Pineapples	50	2. Yams	60
4. Fish	60	3. Pineapples	40
5. Canoes	120	4. Fish	60
		Investment	
		5. Planned fixed investment: Canoes	80
		6. Planned inventory investment: Pineapples	10
		7. Unplanned fixed investment: Canoes	—
		8. Unplanned inventory investment: Yams	—

   (b) What is the value of GDP and desired expenditure E? _____
   (c) What is the value of planned expenditure? _____
   (d) What is the value of planned investment? _____
   (e) What is the value of unplanned investment? _____
   (f) Aggregate demand is less than/equal to/greater than aggregate supply.

The important point is that goods which have been produced, but not yet sold, still exist. They don't vanish if nobody buys them; they pile up in firms' stockrooms and must be counted as part of total expenditure. Through the circular flow of income, expenditure is thus equal to national income.

Q10 When aggregate demand exceeds aggregate supply, inventory investment is rising/constant/falling.

Q11 GDP = Planned expenditure plus unplanned inventory investment. T/F

On p. 470 it was stressed that savings and investment decisions are made by different groups of people and that if, for example, firms wish to increase their investment, there is no automatic guarantee that households will be accommodating enough to increase their savings by a corresponding amount.

Q 12 Return to the table in Q 9. What is national income in this simple economy? _____

Q 13 How much did consumers save? _____

Q 14 Saving is less than/equal to/greater than planned investment and saving is less than/equal to/greater than actual investment.

In this example, actual expenditure is equal to national income (the identity of national-income accounts) but planned expenditure is not equal to income. For an equilibrium we require that planned expenditure equal actual output.

Q 15 In equilibrium, unplanned inventory investment will be positive/zero/negative and planned inventory investment may be positive/zero/negative.

This seems a good point at which to make sure you have grasped the difference between saving and investment. It is very important not to mix them up, so check your understanding by doing the following exercise.

Q 16 Group the following data as appropriate and check whether saving equals investment for the period concerned.

	£ million	Saving	Investment
Changes in business inventories	−10		
Expenditure on plant and equipment (net)	100		
Personal saving	90		
Total volume of transactions on the Stock Exchange	280		
Expenditure on residential construction (net)	50		
Undistributed business profits	60		
Value of individuals' building society deposits	120		

Q 17 Net investment in an economy can never be negative. T/F

EQUILIBRIUM IN THE BASIC MODEL

In equilibrium, desired expenditure is equal to national income. We will start by examining the two elements of aggregate expenditure: consumption and investment. You remember that every household will either spend its income on consumption or will save it.

Q 18 Fill in the gaps in the following table. (Figure are in £millions.)

National Income (Y)	Consumption (C)	Saving (S)
0	0	
20	12	
40	24	16
60		24
	42	28
100		40
120	72	
	75	50

145

Q 19 Using the data in the table, plot on Fig. 1 the amount spent on *consumption* and the amount *saved*. Join up the points and label the consumption function C and the saving function S.

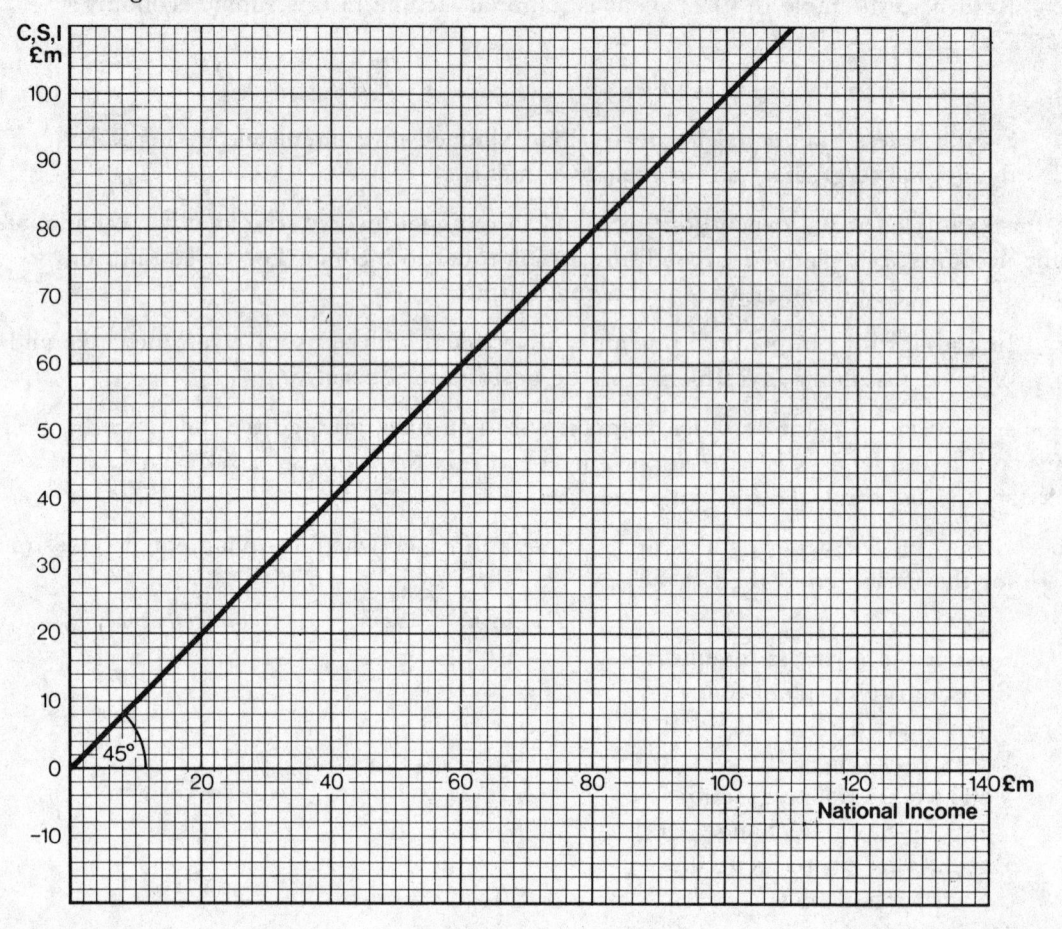

Fig. 1

Q 20 Investment is assumed to be fixed at a level of £18 million. Plot and label the investment function I on Fig. 1.

One way to find the equilibrium level of income is to find where aggregate expenditure is equal to income.

Q 21 How do we find aggregate expenditure? _____
Plot the aggregate expenditure function on Fig. 1 and label it E.

A 45° line has already been drawn on Fig. 1. This line shows all points at which annual expenditure is equal to annual income.

Q 22 The equilibrium level of national income can be found where intended consumption plus _____ equals national income; in other words, where _____ cuts the 45° line.

Another approach to finding the equilibrium level of income is to find the income at which intended saving equals intended investment. Find this point on Fig. 1 and check that both methods of establishing equilibrium income give the same result.

The consumption and savings functions which you have plotted on Fig. 1 are both straight lines. The equation for the consumption function is

$$C = \frac{3}{5} Y.$$

Q 23 Can you work out the equation for the savings function? _____

Q 24 Now that we have a specific consumption function, we could work out what consumption would be for any level of income. Find consumption when income is £80 million. _____ (Check this on Fig. 1.)

Q 25 What is saving when income is £50 million? _____

Q 26 Write out the equation for aggregate expenditure. _____

Q 27 Now find the equilibrium level of income, using this equation for aggregate expenditure. _____

Q 28 Remember that there is another way of finding equilibrium income and work out the answer using this other method. _____

Check that your answers to Questions 26 and 27 are the same as you found in Fig. 1.

In order to make quite sure you understand how to find equilibrium income without having to resort to plotting graphs, here is another example for you to work out:

$$C = 0.75\ Y$$
$$I = 100$$

Q 29 Find the equilibrium level of income using (a) the aggregate-expenditure-equals-income approach, and (b) the savings-equals-investment approach.
(a) _____
(b) _____

We shall return to our analysis of equilibrium income in a little while, but now we must examine more carefully the nature of the relationship between consumption and income.

THE CONSUMPTION FUNCTION

Q 30 Have another look at the consumption and savings functions which you drew in Fig. 1 and say which of the following statements are correct for these functions:

(a) As income falls, dissaving decreases.
(b) As income rises, the proportion of income spent on consumption increases.
(c) At no income level is consumption equal to income.
(d) As income rises from £60 million to £100 million, the amount saved increases.

Q 31 From Fig. 1, you can see that as income increases, consumption also increases by more than/the same amount as/less than income.

The propensity to consume (save) is the relationship between income and consumption (saving) levels.

Q 32 The average propensity to consume, *APC*, is defined as:
(a) (in words) _____
(b) (in symbols) _____

Q33 The marginal propensity to consume, *MPC*, is defined as:

(a) (in words) _____

(b) (in symbols) _____

CHANGES IN INCOME IN THE TWO-SECTOR MODEL

We now return to our simple model of the economy where there are only households and firms, and examine the causes of changes in the equilibrium level of income.

Q34 When the consumption function is given by $C = 0.8Y$ and investment is determined exogenously so that $I = £20$ million, find the equilibrium level of income.
_____

Q35 Suppose that producers are optimistic so that instead of producing at the equilibrium rate, they produce at a rate of £120 million. With national income at £120 million, aggregate expenditure would be £_____ million. Firms would find they had sold less than they had produced by an amount equal to £_____ million; this amount would be unintended investment in inventories. Saving would amount to £_____ million and *ex post* investment (i.e. including the unintended investment) would be £_____ million. In this situation firms would find it desirable to expand output/contract output/leave output unchanged.

Q36 Suppose instead that producers are pessimistic and decide to produce at a rate of £90 million. Intended consumption would be £_____ million; intended saving would be £_____ million; intended investment would be £_____ million; and aggregate demand would be £_____ million. Now if the firms are to meet all orders they would have to run down inventories by £_____ million. If they were to do this, realized saving would amount to £_____ million and realized investment would be £_____ million. However, let us suppose that firms are unable to run down inventories (or are unwilling to do so). This means they will only meet orders amounting to £90 million, of which £20 million are orders for investment goods. In this event, realized consumption would be £70 million, so unintended saving would amount to £_____ million. Total realized saving would be £_____ million, and realized investment would be £_____ million. Whether firms run down inventories or not, firms will find it desirable to expand output/contract output/leave output unchanged.

Q37 The only level of income at which desired saving is equal to desired investment and at which desired expenditure is equal to output is £_____ million.

We are now ready to consider what happens to the equilibrium level of income if there is a change in either or both of the two components of aggregate demand.

A shift in investment

Q38 Suppose that investment increases from £20 million to £22 million. What happens to the equilibrium level of income? _____

Q39 As a result of the rise in investment, the equilibrium level of income has risen. Suppose that producers continued to produce at a rate of £100 million. As a result of the shift in the investment schedule, aggregate demand is now £_____ million, of which intended consumption would be £_____ million. Firms will find it desirable to expand output/contract output/leave output unchanged. As income rises, savings fall/rise/remain constant until in equilibrium saving is £_____ million.

Q 40   Suppose that investment were to fall to £15 million. What would be the new equilibrium level of income? _____ At this new level, consumption is £_____ million and saving is £_____ million. The fall in investment of £5 million has resulted in the equilibrium level of income falling by £_____ million.

A change in the consumption function

Q 41   Suppose that the marginal propensity to consume falls from 0.8 to 0.75. If investment is £20 million, the new equilibrium level of income will be £_____ million and consumption has fallen from £80 million to £_____ million.

Q 42   The fall in the *MPC* shifts down/changes the slope of the consumption function and shifts down/changes the slope of the aggregate expenditure function.

Q 43   When we examine a fall in investment, this shifts down/changes the slope of the investment function and shifts down/changes the slope of the aggregate expenditure function.

Q 44   A rise in the *MPC* from 0.8 to 0.9 will result in an aggregate expenditure function with a slope of _____ and an intercept of £_____ million.

THE MULTIPLIER

So far we have discussed the *direction* of any change in equilibrium income. Can we say anything about the *magnitude* of such changes? Consider a change in investment: in Question 38, when $C = 0.8Y$ and $I = £20$ million, we found that a rise in investment (ΔI) of £2 million resulted in a rise in income (ΔY) of £10 million.

$$\frac{\Delta Y}{\Delta I} = \frac{£10 \text{ million}}{£2 \text{ million}} = 5$$

Thus a change in expenditure has led to a change in income five times the amount of the initial change in investment.

Q 45   The multiplier is defined as the ratio of _____ _____ to the _____ that brought it about.

Q 46   If the consumption function remains as $C = 0.8Y$ but investment falls from £20 million to £15 million, equilibrium income will fall by _____ million.

Remember, the multiplier describes the change in the *equilibrium* levels of national income between two different levels of expenditure. As it is a comparative-static theory, it does not say whether or not the new equilibrium level will actually be reached, or how long it will take to reach it.

Q 47   So far we have only defined the multiplier, but in the example above we found the value of the multiplier to be 5 when $C = 0.8Y$. The value of the multiplier is the reciprocal of the slope of the savings function.

   (a)   What is the savings function when $C = 0.8Y$? _____
   (b)   What determines the slope of the savings function? _____

Check that the multiplier in this case is equal to 5.

In this simple basic model, the multiplier is easily derived. In more complicated models, it is not quite so easy to work out the value at a quick glance and it is important, therefore, that you should be sure you can also work out the multiplier's value by using a little algebra.

Q 48   As the multiplier describes the change in equilibrium levels of income, start by writing out the equilibrium condition when $C = cY$: _____

If investment changes, we know that the equilibrium level of income changes, so we can write

$$\Delta Y = c\Delta Y + \Delta I^*$$

Re-arranging this we get $(1 - c) \Delta Y = \Delta I^*$

$$\text{and} \quad \frac{\Delta Y}{\Delta I^*} = \frac{1}{(1 - c)} = \frac{1}{s}$$

What do c and s represent? _____

Q 49   The slope of the savings function, s, is $\frac{\Delta Y}{\Delta I}$.   T/F

Q 50   If $C = 0.75 Y$ and investment is £5 million, find:
(a)   the value of the multiplier. _____
(b)   the effect of increasing investment by £1 million. _____
(c)   the new level of equilibrium income. _____

QUESTIONS FOR DISCUSSION

1   What assumptions underlie our theory?

2   Which variables are assumed to be endogenous and which exogenous?

3   Explain the process by which an economy will move towards the equilibrium level of income when
(a)   aggregate expenditure exceeds GDP.
(b)   withdrawals exceed injections.

4   What would be the value of the multiplier if the propensity to withdraw were
(a)   zero,
(b)   unity?

5   How can a household's annual consumption spending exceed its annual income?

6   Why may a firm experience *unplanned* inventory investment? Why may a firm *plan* an increase or a decrease in its inventory investment?

7   The following is an extract from a letter to *The Times* (13.10.78) from Sir John Partridge:

'Since the end of 1973 industrial earnings have risen by 106 per cent; prices by 101 per cent; Gross Domestic Product by 4 per cent. Within GDP, industrial production (including North Sea oil activities) has risen by 1½ per cent, and manufacturing production has fallen by 4 per cent. There are three elements in the equation: pay, prices, and output. It is the last of these which points most directly to the magnitude of our problems in the productivity field ... a nation or a business which pays itself vastly more for a relatively static volume of production is playing ducks and drakes with its future.'

How can a nation pay itself more than the value of its production? Is not GDP ≡ national income?

CHAPTER 28

The Consumption Function

We are now ready to make the consumption function more realistic by adding autonomous consumption to the Keynesian relation cY. The new, positive intercept allows for other determinants of consumption besides national income.

Q1 In the model on p. 491, what is the difference between A and a?

(a) (in words) _____

(b) (in symbols) _____

Q2 As A increases, the average propensity to consume must/may/cannot increase.

AVERAGE AND MARGINAL PROPENSITIES WITH AUTONOMOUS CONSUMPTION

When there is autonomous consumption, the marginal propensity to consume will be a different number from the average propensity to consume. Practise calculating these in the following questions.

Q3 Fill in the columns headed APC and MPC in the following table:

(a)

Y	C	APC	MPC	APS	MPS
0	50	___	___	___	___
100	130	___	___	___	___
200	210	___	___	___	___
300	290	___	___	___	___
400	370	___	___	___	___
500	450	___	___	___	___

(b) As income rises, the APC rises/remains constant/falls and the MPC rises/remains constant/falls.

(c) If income rises by £10, consumption spending will increase by £_____

(d) If income falls by £30, consumption spending will fall by £_____

Q4 The average propensity to save, APS, is defined as:

(a) (in words) _____
(b) (in symbols) _____

Q5 The marginal propensity to save, MPS, is defined as:

(a) (in words) _____
(b) (in symbols) _____

Q6   Fill in the columns headed *APS* and *MPS* for the table in Q3(a).

As $Y = C + S$, once we know what households decide to spend on consumption, we also know what they save. Any change in income (ΔY) must be allocated either to consumption, resulting in a change in consumption (ΔC), or to savings, resulting in a change in saving (ΔS). This means that

$$\Delta Y = \Delta C + \Delta S$$

Dividing this equation by ΔY, we get $\quad 1 = \dfrac{\Delta C}{\Delta Y} + \dfrac{\Delta S}{\Delta Y}$

$$\text{or} \quad 1 = MPC + MPS$$

Q7   Find the corresponding *MPS* or *MPC* for the following:

(a)   *MPC* = 0.75   *MPS* = _____
(b)   *MPC* = ⅔   *MPS* = _____
(c)   *MPS* = 0.28   *MPC* = _____

Q8   In Fig. 1, line *AC* is a community's consumption function.

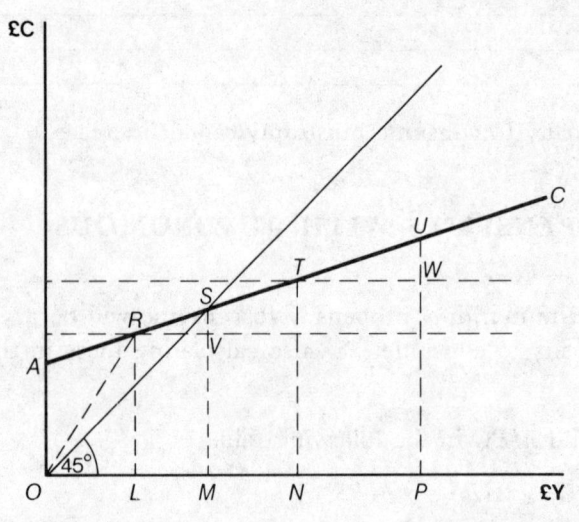

Fig. 1

Using letters, find:

(a)   The break-even level of income _____. At this income, the *APC* = _____ which is equal to the slope of line _____.
(b)   At income *OL*, the *APC* = _____ which is equal to the slope of line _____. At income *OL*, the *APC* is greater/less than 1.
(c)   At income *OP*, the *APC* = _____ which is equal to the slope of a line _____ and is greater/less than 1.
(d)   When income rises from *ON* to *OP*, the *MPC* = _____ which is equal to the slope of line _____.
(e)   When income falls from *OM* to *OL*, the *MPC* = _____ which is equal to the slope of line _____.
(f)   For the consumption function *AC*, the proportion of an increase in income spent on consumption is increasing/constant/decreasing and is greater than/equal to/less than 1, while the *APC* is falling/constant/rising.
(g)   At the break-even level of income, the *APC* is greater than/equal to/less than 1. At income levels below the break-even level of income, the *APC* is greater

than/equal to/less than 1; while at incomes above the break-even level, the *APC* is greater than/equal to/less than 1.

The consumption function in Fig. 1 and the functions you plotted in Fig. 1 are linear functions. The equation for a linear consumption function is $C = a + cY$ where

C is consumption

Y is income

a is autonomous consumption (i.e. that portion of consumption which is not determined by income. In other words, even if income is zero, consumption will occur and *a* is thus the *intercept* of the *C* line with the axis along which consumption spending is measured).

c is the *MPC* and is thus equal to the *slope* of the *C* line on the graph.

Q9 In Fig. 1,

(a) Autonomous consumption = _____
(b) When income is zero, dissaving is _____
(c) The *MPC* is equal to the slope of line _____

Q10 The consumption function you plotted in Fig. 1 on p. 152 was $C = \tfrac{3}{5} Y$.

(a) What is autonomous consumption? _____
(b) What is the *MPC*? _____

Q11 When the consumption function is given by $C = 0.75 Y$,

(a) What is autonomous consumption? _____
(b) What is the *APC*? _____
(c) What is the *MPC*? _____
(d) What is the *MPS*? _____
(e) What is the *APS*? _____

Q12 So far we have considered only linear consumption functions, which has meant that the *MPC* rises/remains constant/falls as income increases.

Q13 Consumption functions, however, are not necessarily linear and in Fig. 2 two consumption functions of different shapes have been drawn. Which curve is consistent with the following statements?

(a) *APC* and *MPC* fall as income rises;
(b) *APC* falls and *MPC* rises as income rises;
(c) *MPS* falls as income rises;
(d) *MPC* rises at low incomes and falls at high incomes.

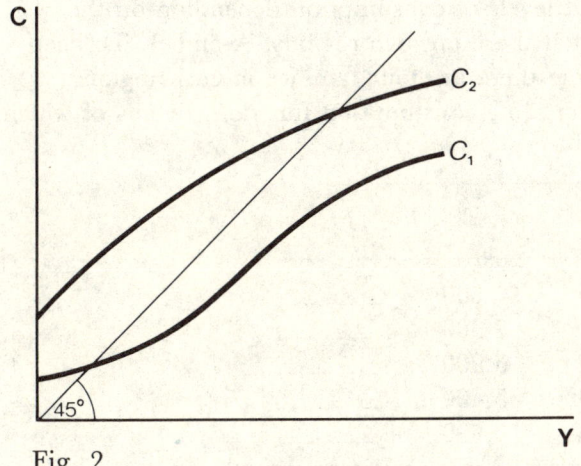

Fig. 2

Q14 To sum up, we hypothesize that all/part of an increase in income is always spent and that the *MPC* exceeds 0/1 but is less than _____.

THE MULTIPLIER WITH AUTONOMOUS CONSUMPTION

A change in the marginal propensity to consume affects the multiplier, but a change in autonomous consumption does not. The formula for the multiplier is therefore still $\frac{1}{1-c}$ in our two-sector model.

Q15 Consider now a consumption function where $C = 10 + 0.8Y$. If investment is equal to £20 million, equilibrium income will be £_____ million. The slope of the aggregate expenditure function will be _____ and the intercept will be at £_____ million. If autonomous consumption fell from £10 million to £5 million, this shifts down/changes the slope of the consumption function and the aggregate expenditure function.

Q16 What is the multiplier in the example above?

Q17 If the *MPS* rises, this changes the slope of the savings function in a clockwise/anti-clockwise direction and increases/decreases equilibrium income.

Q18 If the *MPS* falls, this changes the slope of the savings function in a clockwise/anti-clockwise direction and increases/decreases equilibrium income.

Q19 If autonomous consumption rises but the *MPC* is unchanged, this shifts the consumption function up/down and the savings function up/down and equilibrium income increases/decreases.

Q20 Aggregate demand rises as income rises at a rate equal to/greater than/less than the rise in income. This is because _____
_____.

Q21 If $C = 5 + 0.75Y$ and investment is £6 million, find:
   (a) the value of the multiplier. _____
   (b) the equilibrium level of income. _____
   (c) what would happen to equilibrium income if autonomous consumption fell by £1 million. _____

AGGREGATION PROBLEMS

Q22 On p. 491 it was pointed out that if households have different *MPC*s, then the same total income will result in different levels of consumption depending on the distribution of income. Suppose that there are two regions, A and B. To keep numbers manageable, let us assume there are four families in each region.

All families in region A have the same consumption function, details of which are as follows:

Y_d	C	*MPC*
£ 0	£ 600	_____
2,000	2,300	_____
4,000	3,900	_____
6,000	5,400	_____
8,000	6,800	_____

All families in region B have the following consumption function:

Y_d	C	MPC
£ 0	£ 500	_____
2,000	2,100	_____
4,000	3,700	_____
6,000	5,300	_____
8,000	6,900	_____

Fill in the gaps to show the marginal propensity to consume for each region.

Aggregate disposable income is £16,000 in each region. Consider three alternative ways in which this income might be distributed:

distribution I: each family has an income of £4,000,

distribution II: two families have £2,000 each and two have £6,000 each,

distribution III: two families have zero income and two have £8,000 each.

(a) In region A, aggregate consumption would be:

   (1) £_____ with distribution I

   (2) £_____ with distribution II

   (3) £_____ with distribution III.

(b) In region B, aggregate consumption would be:

   (1) £_____ with distribution I

   (2) £_____ with distribution II

   (3) £_____ with distribution III.

THE PERMANENT-INCOME AND LIFE-CYCLE HYPOTHESIS

Q23 (a) Suppose a man decides to become an accountant and calculates his life-time earnings as follows:

Age	Earnings per annum
19–23	£5,000
24–28	£8,000
29–34	£12,000
35–44	£15,000
45–64	£17,000
65–79	£8,000

Assuming that the interest rate is zero, calculate his annual permanent income.

(b) Now suppose that at the age of twenty-nine he wins £25,000 on the football pools. What effect will this have on his annual permanent income?

(c) Out of his winnings he buys a colour television for £500. Assuming the expected life of the set is ten years,

   (i) in the first year, actual consumption of this set was £_____ and saving £_____

   (ii) in the second year, actual consumption was £_____ and saving £_____

(d) As his career progresses, our man finds that he was over-cautious in his estimate of future earnings. He is so successful that he is able to set up his own firm when he is thirty-five. His income from then until he retires, at the end of his sixty-fourth year, is £25,000 p.a. On retirement his earnings are zero. What will be his new annual permanent income when he sets up in business on his own? £_____

Q 24 A construction worker expects to be unemployed for periods of six months to two years during recessions, until at the age of 40 he hopes to take a permanent job with a local firm. He also expects his wage to rise over time as he gains new skills. Draw, on Fig. 3, a diagram similar to Lipsey's Fig. 28.2, to show his actual and permanent income streams. Include unemployment benefit of one-third of his working wage during the unemployed periods.

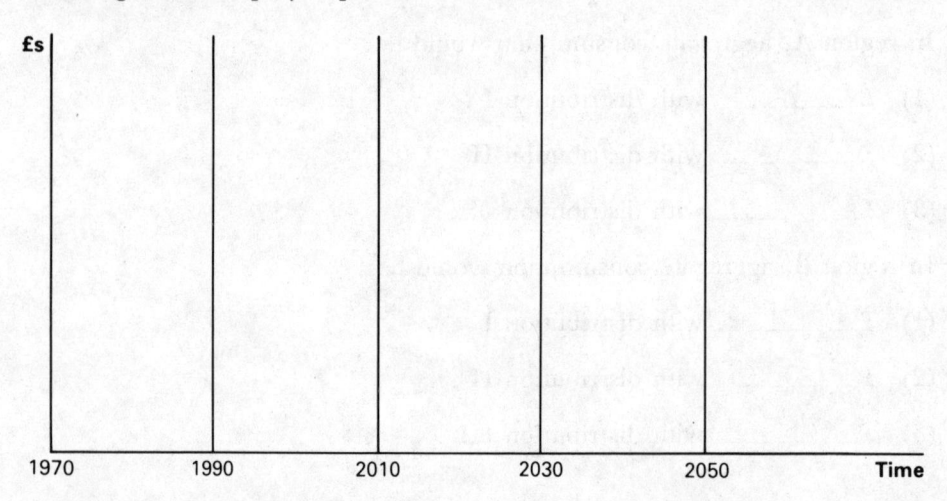

Fig. 3

QUESTIONS FOR DISCUSSION

1 Discuss the main factors, other than income, that might determine a household's consumption expenditure.

2 Suppose the government were to:

   (a) stipulate a higher minimum hire purchase deposit;
   or (b) shorten the maximum repayment period,

   what effect would this have on consumption and on the level of national income?

3 Many people today use credit cards, such as Access or Barclay cards. If the interest rate charged were to fall, how would this affect consumption?

4 Do you think the marginal propensity to consume of rich households is the same as that of poor households? What would be the probable effects on the equilibrium level of income of government policies redistributing income from the rich to the poor?

5   In permanent-income theories, you might expect to find a household's expenditure exceeding actual income when the household is first set up and also towards the end of its life. How does the household manage this?

6   Professor Duesenbery has suggested that consumption depends not upon absolute real income, but upon the *position* of the individual in the society's income scale – that is, upon relative income. This means, for example, that a person in the fifth income decile, i.e. in the 10% of the population compared with whom 40% are richer and 50% are poorer, consumes $1/x$th of his income, at one time. At another (perhaps later when everyone in the country is much richer) *as long as he is in the same 10%* he will still consume $1/x$th of his income. This position is often tacitly endorsed in the newspapers – cf. a letter to *The Times* (16.3.65): '... The emigrant (to the US) will almost certainly have greater purchasing power, but will he feel any richer? Eventually, his economic well-being depends distressingly on the level of other incomes in the community. What income do the Jones's have? What would they consider a good salary?'

How might you go about testing this?

7   In 1987–88 the British government advertised the sale of shares in British Petroleum, British Steel, and other large industries that were being transferred from public (national) to private ownership. Discuss how such advertising would affect autonomous investment, I^*, autonomous consumption, a, and total autonomous expenditure, A. Consider two cases: (i) where the advertising attracts new savings and reduces the marginal propensity to consume; and (ii) where the advertising simply shifts spending from autonomous consumption to investment. What would the C, I and E curves look like in each case?

CHAPTER 29
National Income in More Elaborate Models

When introducing microeconomics in Chapter 4, we saw two ways of breaking the economy into sectors. The market sector and the non-market sector together account for total national production; looking at it differently, the economy is made up of the public and private sectors. Sectoral breakdowns like these are useful in macroeconomics too, and they serve a similar purpose: to separate parts of the economy that behave differently so that we can examine that behaviour in detail without getting lost in complications. Hence the two-sector model of Chapter 27 separated consumers from investors and ignored all else. We now extend this approach by adding the government sector (in its taxing and spending capacity) and the foreign-trade sector.

The sectors in the two-, three-, and four-sector models do not correspond to the divisions used earlier in the text.

GOVERNMENT TAXING AND SPENDING

If a government builds roads, hospitals, etc. it must raise money to do these things – either by borrowing, or by increasing the money supply or by levying taxes. To keep matters simple at this stage, let us assume that all saving is done by households and that all government expenditure is financed by an income tax. The amount paid in taxes will depend on the tax rate (t), and tax revenue (T) will be equal to the tax rate × national income, i.e. $T = tY$.

Q1 If a person earns £5,000 and the tax rate is 30p in every £ earned, tax paid will be _____

The government also levies taxes in order to redistribute income from the rich to the poor, the healthy to the sick, the employed to the unemployed.

Q2 The government's budget is in deficit when tax revenue is less than/greater than the sum of _____

Q3 Disposable income (Y_d) is equal to _____

Q4 When Q stands for transfer payments, write (in symbols) disposable income as a function of national income. _____

We can now write consumption and saving functions as functions of either disposable or national income.

Q5 If c is the *MPC* out of disposable income, and Q stands for transfers:
  (a) write consumption as a function of national income. _____
  (b) write saving as a function of national income. _____

Q6 If the *MPC* out of disposable income is 0.8, the tax rate is 30% and transfers are £10 million, write

   (a) consumption as a function of national income. _____

   (b) If national income is £50 million, find consumption. _____
   (c) Is tax revenue sufficient to cover transfers? _____

   (d) What are savings? _____
   (e) What is disposable income? _____

National income in the three-sector model

Q7 For equilibrium we require that aggregate desired expenditure equals national income. What are the components of aggregate expenditure in the three-sector model (in symbols)? _____

Q8 Another way to find equilibrium is to see at what income level withdrawals equal injections. Write this condition (in symbols) listing each component. _____

Q9 From the information below, answer questions (a) to (i). You will find it helpful to complete the table as you work.

   (1) $C = 0.8Y_d$ C is consumption
   (2) $I = £78$ million Y_d is disposable income
   (3) $G = £70$ million I is investment
   (4) $Q = £40$ million G is government expenditure
   (5) $T = 0.25Y$ Q is transfer payments
                             T is tax revenue
                             Y is national income

   (a) Write out the equation for aggregate expenditure. _____
   (b) Its slope is _____ and its intercept is _____
   (c) What is the equilibrium level of income? _____

Level of national income (£m)	Disposable income (£m)	Consumption (£m)	Investment (£m)	Government expenditure (£m)	Tax revenue (£m)	Aggregate expenditure (£m)
0	___	___	___	___	___	___
150	___	___	___	___	___	___
250	___	___	___	___	___	___
350	___	___	___	___	___	___
450	___	___	___	___	___	___
550	___	___	___	___	___	___
650	___	___	___	___	___	___

   (d) At equilibrium, consumption is _____ and saving is _____ while disposable income is _____ .
   (e) At equilibrium is the government balancing its budget? _____
   (f) Graph the consumption, investment, government spending, and aggregate expenditure functions on Fig. 1.

The other way of finding the equilibrium level of income is to find the income level at which withdrawals equal injections. Here $W = s(1 - t)Y + sQ + tY$, while $J = I + G + Q$.

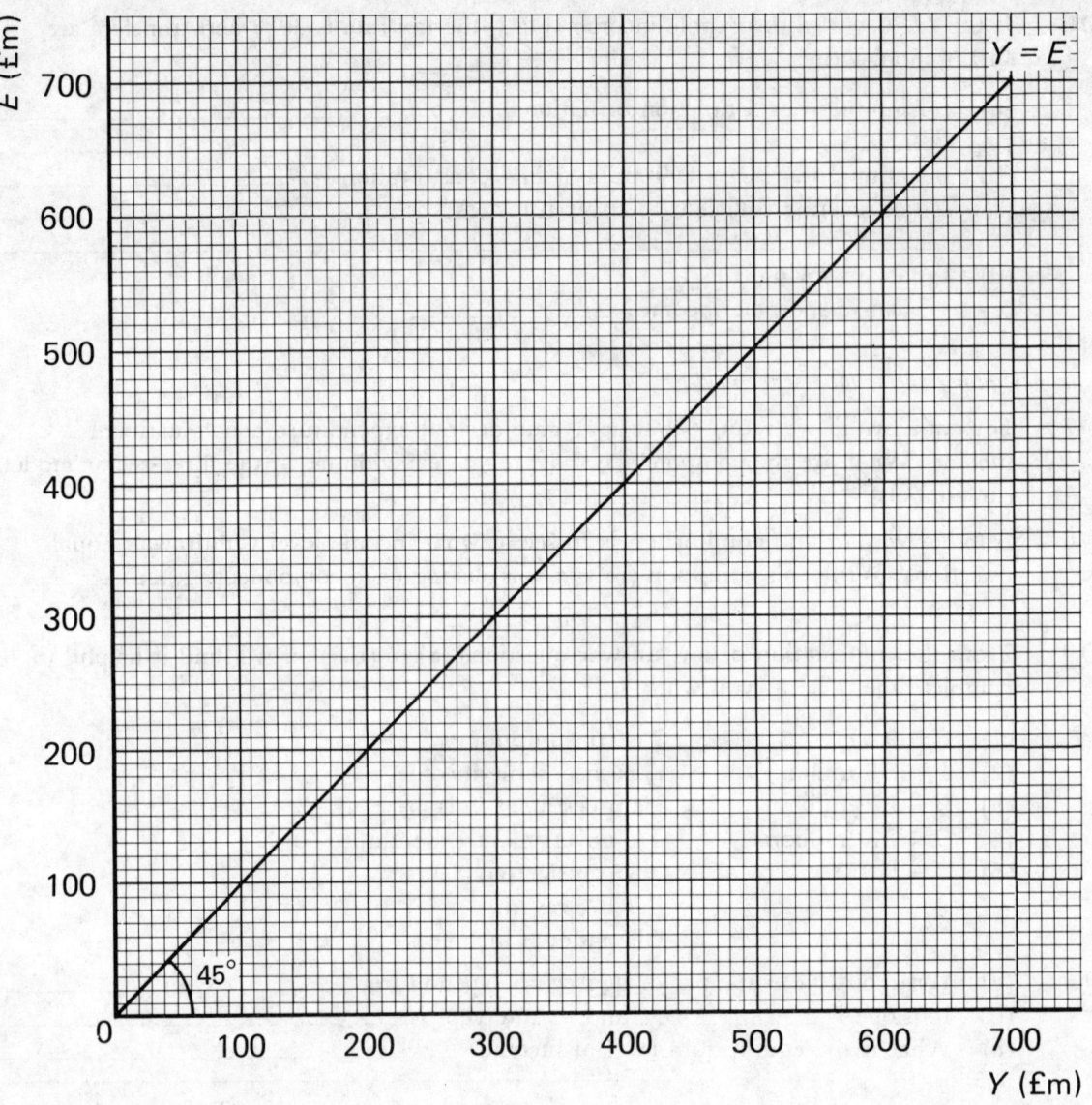

Fig. 1

Note that Q (transfers) appears both as a withdrawal (sQ) and injection (Q). When solving for equilibrium income, we include the *net* effect as an injection of cQ in the injections equation and delete sQ from withdrawals.

(g) Write the withdrawals and injections equations and plot the functions on Fig. 1. _____

Check that, at equilibrium, withdrawals equal injections.

(h) When national income is £250m, by how much do injections exceed withdrawals? _____

(i) When national income is £600m, by how much do withdrawals exceed injections? _____

By this time, you will have worked out the answers by both the graphical and algebraic methods. If you find algebra a bit difficult, it is worth persevering as not only will it help you to answer questions more quickly but it will also help you to understand and remember the theory.

Changes in Equilibrium Income in a Three-sector Model

Q10 Suppose now that the government were to raise the tax rate.

(a) What will happen to the consumption function? _____

(b) What will happen to the slope and the intercept of the aggregate expenditure function? _____

(c) What will happen to equilibrium income? _____

Q11 If the government raises the tax rate to 30% but all other equations set out in Question 9 are unchanged:

(a) what will be the slope of the consumption function? _____
(b) what will be the slope and the intercept of the aggregate expenditure function? _____

(c) what will happen to the level of equilibrium income? _____

(d) At the original level of equilibrium income (£450m), withdrawals are less than/greater than injections.
(e) At the new equilibrium what is tax revenue? _____

Q12 Suppose that instead of increasing taxes the government decreases its expenditure.

(a) What will be the slope and the intercept of the new aggregate expenditure function? _____

(b) What will happen to equilibrium income? _____

Q13 Assume that the government keeps the tax rate at 30% as in Question 11, but it also increases its expenditure by £12m.

(a) What will be the new equilibrium level of income? _____
(b) What will happen to the government's budget? _____

(c) Has the additional government expenditure offset the effects of the higher tax rate on the level of income? _____

Q14 Still keeping the tax rate at 30%, suppose that instead of increasing government expenditure by £12m, the government increases transfer payments by this amount.

(a) What will be the new equilibrium level of income? _____
(b) What will happen to the government's budget? _____

(c) Compare your findings with your answers to the previous question. Why has income increased by a smaller amount when the injection took the form of an increase in transfer payments rather than expenditure by the government on goods and services? _____

Q15 What would have happened to the level of income if investment had increased by £12m instead of government expenditure? _____

Q 16   A fall in the tax rate will mean that the *MPC* out of disposable income will rise/fall/remain unchanged, while the amount of disposable income will rise/fall/remain unchanged, consumption will rise/fall/remain unchanged and national income will rise/fall/remain unchanged.

Q 17   A fall in transfer payments will mean that the *MPC* out of income will rise/fall/remain unchanged, disposable income will rise/fall/remain unchanged, consumption will rise/fall/remain unchanged and national income will rise/fall/remain unchanged.

Multipliers in a Three-sector Model

We will start by reminding ourselves of the multiplier in the basic two-sector model we studied in Chapter 27 (remember: there was no government sector).

Q 18   If $C = cY$ and $I = I^*$, what is the marginal propensity to withdraw _____

Q 19   In this simple economy, what is the value of the expenditure multiplier? _____

In the three-sector model where $C = cY_d$, $Y_d = Y - T + Q$, $T = tY$, $I = I^*$, $G = G^*$ and $Q = Q^*$, finding the multiplier is just a bit more complicated.

Q 20   Start by assuming there are no transfer payments, i.e. $Q = 0$.

    (a) Withdrawals are equal to _____
    (b) Injections are equal to _____
    (c) Write savings as a function of national income. _____
    (d) Write the equation for withdrawals (W). _____
    (e) Write the equation for injections (J). _____
    (f) When $W = J$, then Y equals _____
    (g) The investment expenditure multiplier is $\dfrac{\Delta Y}{\Delta I}$ = _____
    (h) The government expenditure multiplier is $\dfrac{\Delta Y}{\Delta G}$ = _____

Q 21   We will now do the same exercise for the case when there are transfer payments, i.e. $Q = Q^*$.

    (a) Write down the savings function. _____
    (b) Write down the withdrawals function. _____
    (c) Write the injections function. _____
    (d) Set withdrawals equal to injections and solve for Y.

        _____

    (e) The transfer payments multiplier is $\dfrac{\Delta Y}{\Delta Q}$ = _____

Q 22   When $c = 0.8$ and $t = 0.25$, find the value of

    (a) the expenditure multiplier. _____
    (b) the transfer payments multiplier. _____

Q 23   When $c = 0.8$ but $t = 0$ (as in the two-sector model), what is the value of the multiplier? _____

Q 24   When $c = 0.8$ and $t = 0.25$,

    (a)   increasing government expenditure by £4m will result in income rising by _____
    (b)   increasing transfer payments by a similar amount will raise income by _____
    (c)   a fall in investment of £10m will change income by ____

Q 25   If the tax rate is cut, the value of the multiplier will rise/fall/remain unchanged.

Q 26   If people decide to save more of their income, the value of the expenditure multiplier will rise/fall/remain unchanged and the value of the transfer payments multiplier will rise/fall/remain unchanged.

Q 27   If we know that in a new equilibrium situation, brought about by a change in the rate of taxation, tax revenue has increased, then assuming no change in the propensity to save, we know that

    (a)   the level of income has risen/fallen.
    (b)   the level of saving has risen/fallen.

WITHDRAWALS AND INJECTIONS

You must develop an intuitive understanding of withdrawals and injections as well as a technical understanding of the model. A *withdrawal* is any income that is not passed on in the circular flow, e.g. savings.

Q 28   Define an injection, and state who controls the different types of injections. _____
_____
_____

Q 29   Which of the following are withdrawals, which injections, which are neither and which both?

    (a)   Payment to New Zealand for lamb imports? _____
    (b)   Firms increase the proportion of profits retained? _____
    (c)   Purchases of theatre tickets by foreign visitors? _____
    (d)   Payments into a private pension scheme? _____
    (e)   The construction of a sugar beet refinery, financed by a bank loan? _____
    (f)   My decision to remove my savings from a building society, and to put them in the National Savings Bank. _____
    (g)   A decision by the banks to loan more to exporters, and less to producers for the domestic market. _____
    (h)   The payment by the government of a motorway-construction gang. _____

Q 30   In the previous chapter, the only withdrawal in the basic model was _____ and the only injection was _____

Q 31   Withdrawals exert an expansionary/contractionary force on national income, while injections exert an expansionary/contractionary force.

Q 32   When withdrawals are greater than injections, the level of national income will rise/fall.

Q 33   Use algebra to show that the two multiplier formulae below are equal:

$$K = \frac{1}{1 - c(1 - t)} \quad \text{and} \quad K = \frac{1}{s(1 - t) + t}$$

(*Hint:* Substitute $(1 - s)$ for c, since they are equal.)

EQUILIBRIUM IN THE OPEN ECONOMY

Q 34 What are the four sectors that make up the open economy? _____

Q 35 In this economy, what are the main components which act as withdrawals from the system? Is any of them a declining function of income? _____

Q 36 What constitute injections? Are these variables exogenous or endogenous to our theory? _____

Q 37 In this more complex model, what are the conditions for equilibrium? _____

Q 38 Express these symbolically. _____

Q 39 In this chapter we assume that injections are unaffected by a change in income but withdrawals are affected by such a change. T/F

Q 40 Identify the following according to whether they are components of aggregate expenditure (C, I, G, X, M), factor payments (F), withdrawals (W), injections (J) or none of these (N):

	Expenditure/Factor payment	W or J
e.g. Construction of new motorway	G	J
(a) Car hire by foreign visitors	___	___
(b) Undistributed profits	___	___
(c) Residential construction	___	___
(d) Advice from a lawyer	___	___
(e) Change in inventories	___	___
(f) VAT	___	___
(g) Your holiday abroad	___	___
(h) Purchase of primary school computers	___	___

We now expand the model we used in Question 9 to include the foreign sector.

Q 41 The behavioural equations were:

(1) $C = 0.8Y_d$

(2) $I = £78$ million

(3) $G = £70$ million

(4) $Q = £40$ million

(5) $T = 0.25Y$

We now add:

(6) $X = £50$ million   where X is exports

(7) $M = mY = 0.1Y$ M is imports

(a) What is m? _____
(b) What is the equation for aggregate expenditure? _____
(c) The equilibrium level of income is _____

(d) What are net exports? _____
(e) What is the expenditure multiplier? _____

(f) If exports were to increase by £10m, by how much would income rise? _____

(g) Assuming exports remained at £50m but the marginal propensity to import were 0.2, what difference would this make to
 (i) income? _____
 (ii) net exports? _____

Q42 The introduction into the model of the foreign-trade sector increases/reduces the value of the multiplier as imports are an injection into/leakage from the domestic circular flow of income.

Q43 An increase in investment will cause national income to rise/fall. In an open economy the consequent change in national income will be greater than/the same as/less than a change in national income in a closed economy following an increase in investment of the same magnitude.

Q44 Who are the main exporters of goods? consumers/firms/government/all three.

Q45 Who are the main importers of goods? consumers/firms/government/all three.

Your answers to the above two questions should help you to see why exports can be taken as exogenous (outside the model) but imports cannot. Imports depend directly on national income in a way that exports do not.

Q46 Net exports are positively/not/negatively associated with real national income.

Q47 What does *ceteris paribus* mean?

QUESTIONS FOR DISCUSSION

1 What would be the effect on national income of each of the following:

(a) households save a greater proportion of their income;
(b) a rise in exports;
(c) a rise in imports.

Depict each graphically. Can you suggest any measures the government might adopt to offset any adverse effects on national income and employment of these changes?

2 What would be the effect on the value of the multiplier of:

(a) a rise in the income-tax rate;
(b) a fall in exports;
(c) a rise in the marginal propensity to import.

3 'Increases in national income will increase revenue from taxes, both income and sales taxes, and decrease that part of public spending which is not cash limited, principally social security and other transfer payments.'
Are tax revenue and government expenditure endogenous or exogenous?

4 On 11.3.83 the *Guardian* reported Mr Peter Shore, the Shadow Chancellor, as advocating an increase in public expenditure of not less than £10,000 million.
'Mr Shore's proposals rest upon four main planks. The two most important are an increase in public spending of £5,000 million on goods and services ... and an extra £4,000 million on measures to contain costs – such as action to tackle the National Insurance surcharge, or to cut VAT or to freeze rents.

'He also proposed a further £1,000 million spending in the coming financial year – £2,000 million in a full year – in increases on benefits and pensions. The fourth point in his programme is a self-financing tax package which includes a number of redistributive measures ...'

Analyse carefully the effect of these proposals on the level of income and on employment. Would the multiplier effect be the same for each of the proposals? Which of the proposals would have the most immediate effect?

5 'If the consumer spending spree is sustained ... then destocking will have to yield to an increase in actual output. This is bound to give some sort of boost to industrial production in the UK even if ... a lot of the stocks will be replaced by imports. What matters with stocks is not so much the absolute level as the pace of change. Even if destocking merely slows down in the first half of this year it will have beneficial effects on output.' (Victor Keegan, the *Guardian*, 7.3.83.)

What is 'destocking'? Why might stocks be replaced by imports? Do you agree with Keegan that it is not the level of stocks that is important but the rate at which they are rising or falling?

6 In the *Sunday Times* (6.2.83) Graham Searjeant wrote:

'... Britain is suffering from a chronic shortage of production ... we have three million producing nothing at all and extra income going into imports.

'Crude reflation, for instance by cutting VAT or raising benefits, would probably make matters worse, if only because we have lost many factories and product lines. We have plenty of spare capacity but it probably does not match what people want to buy with extra income.'

What must be the value of the marginal propensity to import if extra income from reflation is spent on imports? Is this realistic?

7 Mr John Major, Chief Secretary to the British Treasury, said in a parliamentary committee that 'the ratio of government spending to gross domestic product might rise in the event of a substantial slowdown in the economy' (*Financial Times*, 24.11.88). He emphasized that the Conservative government's policy was to continue reducing public spending as a proportion of GDP. Can you re-interpret his statements in terms of autonomous versus income-determined categories of expenditure?

8 Under the Conservative government of the 1980s, British government spending was reported as falling to below 40% of GDP for the first time in 20 years. Mr D. Soskin wrote to the *Financial Times* to complain about this report:

'This figure is highly misleading, understating the true level of public spending.

'Gross domestic product (GDP) is not a correct measure of national income. Net national product is the correct measure of national income.

'Measuring state expenditure against this measure shows that the state spends about 60% of the nation's income. The real issue is whether or not it is justifiable for the state to take and spend £6 of every £10 of a citizen's income.' (*Financial Times*, 8.11.88.)

Explain how GDP and NNP differ, and discuss Mr Soskin's point.

CHAPTER 30

Money and the Price Level

THE FUNCTIONS AND CHARACTERISTICS OF MONEY

Q1 List the three primary functions of money.

Q2 When Latin American debt is denominated in US dollars instead of in Pesos, etc., what functions are the US dollars serving?

Q3 What is the difference between paper money and fiat money?

Q4 When cigarettes are exchanged for other goods in jails, are cigarettes money? If so, which functions do they serve?

THE NATURE AND HISTORY OF MONEY

Q5 'A licence to print money.' We have seen that this was possessed by the old goldsmiths. Why was it, then, necessary for goldsmiths to keep any stock of gold at all?

Q6 Given that the public's desired ratio of gold to paper money remained constant at 1:3, what was there to prevent goldsmiths, in whom confidence reposed, from paying all their bills with paper claims on themselves which then merely added to the circulating money supply, and therefore living free?

Q7 'The natives of these parts use but the Cowrie shell for money, deluded into believing it valuable' (a missionary). Does the missionary understand the nature of money? Yes/No. Explain.

Q8 'The greater the propensity to pay bills by cash instead of cheque, the lower the level of cash reserves which a bank need keep.' T/F

Q9 The government creates as much money as it wants. What is this sort of currency called? _____

THE MODERN BANKING SYSTEM IN THE UK

Q10 What are the three *main* elements of the present-day banking system in the UK?
_____
_____

Q11 What are the main functions of the central bank? _____
_____
_____
_____

Q12 If a commercial bank (or discount house) was faced with a run on its cash reserves, and it could not call in enough loans quickly, what would it do? _____
_____
_____

THE CREATION OF DEPOSIT MONEY

Bank balance sheets play a role in the explanation of how banks 'create' money. The assets of a bank are its holdings of cash and other valuables as well as its claims on other banks and people, such as loans. The liabilities of a bank are the claims other banks and people have on the bank – mainly deposits for now, since money deposited with a bank can be claimed back at any time by its owner. The assets and liabilities of each bank will normally be equal.

It is very easy even for experienced economists to make mistakes about the creation of money, so read and work through this section carefully.

(a) A system containing a single bank

Q13 Assume a legal reserve ratio (which is above the 'prudent' ratio) of 10%. If a cash deposit of £50 is made, how much extra can the bank lend? _____

Q14 Express the final result in balance sheet form.

(1)   Assets   Liabilities
Initially _____
Subsequently _____

We have the assumption that there is

(a) no drain to any other bank, since there isn't any, and
(b) no drain of cash to the public.

If we add the assumptions that

(c) the bank is a profit-maximizer, and
(d) the marginal revenue from lending (taking into account risk of default) is always above the marginal cost (i.e. the rate of interest charged to borrowers is higher than the rate paid to depositors),

then it follows that a single bank will always adopt what policy in regard to its loans?

(2) _____
_____

(b) Many banks, a single new deposit

Assumption (a) above is now removed. It is a very common mistake to assume that all deposit creation takes place instantaneously, any bank receiving an extra deposit immediately expanding by the reciprocal of the reserve ratio. But think what would happen; assume that individual k deposits £100 in bank A, which lends £900 to individual 1. He pays his creditors m and n, by cheques drawn on bank A; but they bank with B and C; so £900 in cash has to be paid by bank A to banks B and C. Bank A now has to contract its loans by an extra £7,200. Meanwhile, B and C then lend an extra £8,100 to individual o, but his creditors bank with D ... and so on. The correct aggregate expansion is made, but goodness knows how many banks go into liquidation in the process!

Q 15 Assume that individual a places a deposit of £100 into bank A. Assume also that A lends what extra it can to individual b, who banks with B, which lends to individual c, and so on. (The reserve ratio is again 10%.) Fill in the changes in the banks' balance sheets above the line before they have expanded their loans, after, below it.

A		B		C		D		E	
A	L	A	L	A	L	A	L	A	L
100									

cash:
loans: _____   _____   _____   _____   _____

The series 100 + 90 + 81 + 72.9 ... sums to £1,000, as the series 10 + 9 + 8.1 ... sums to £100. This is, of course, no piece of mathematical luck – it is a straightforward implication of every bank's strict adherence to the 10% cash ratio.

If you got the answer wrong, try again, working it through on your own.

(c) Many banks, many deposits

This is easy, once you have mastered (b) above.

Q 16 (a) Assume a system with 10 banks in which a deposit of £300 cash accrues to bank I. There is a 10% cash ratio.

  (1) Show the initial changes in the balance sheet of this bank.

      L | A

  (2) Assume that bank I expands deposits up to the maximum possible; that 90% of all new deposits to any bank find their way into other banks (as cheques are passed between individuals for various transactions) and that other banks do *not* expand deposits when they obtain extra cash. Show the final changes in the balance sheet of bank I.

      Bank I
      L | A

  (3) *Conclusion:* One bank in a multi-bank system cannot engage in a large deposit expansion even when it gets new cash if the other banks do not do the same. T/F

(b) Assume that all banks expand deposits as soon as they obtain new cash.

(1) Show the final changes in the balance sheets of the system.

Bank I		Banks II to X	
L	A	L	A

(2) *Conclusion*: If all banks expand deposits together, the final result is the same as the monopoly-bank case. T/F

Q17 Suppose that the required reserve ratio is 15% and that a bank has cash reserves of £15m, loans and bonds of £85m, and demand deposits of £100m:

(a) By what additional amount can this bank expand its loans? _____

(b) If the reserve ratio is changed to 10%, the bank must reduce its lending by/can make additional loans up to _____

Q18 Suppose that you cash £300 from your grant cheque at your bank and keep all the money under your mattress (this is *not* a good idea!). If the required reserve ratio is 15%, what will be the effect on deposit money? _____

Q19 What have we assumed so far about the public's desired cash to deposit ratio?
_____
_____

Q20 If the public's desired cash ratio is zero, and the banks' reserve ratio is 15%:

(a) A new deposit of £300 would increase deposit money by _____

(b) If the public's desired cash ratio is 10% instead of zero, the increase in deposit money would be _____

(c) If the public's desired cash ratio is 15%, the increase would be _____

Q21 The higher the proportion of its money holdings the public wishes to take in cash, the larger/smaller the expansion of deposit money supported by new deposits.

DEFINITIONS OF MONEY

Q22 What are Post Office savings accounts, building society deposits, and gold wedding rings examples of? _____

Q23 What is the difference between *near money* and *money substitutes*?
_____
_____
_____
_____

Q24 In the table overleaf are listed various items which may or may not be classified as money, according to which money function they fulfil. Put a tick (or a cross) in the appropriate column if you think that the item listed does (or does not) fulfil that function.

Q25 Using the information in the previous question, what is the total value of the money supply under:

(a) the sterling M1 definition? _____

(b) the sterling M3 definition? _____

	Store of value	Medium of exchange	Value in £ million
Building society deposits	_____	_____	1,500
Company securities:			
– ordinary shares	_____	_____	867
– debenture and preference shares	_____	_____	105
Local authority bonds held by the private sector	_____	_____	340
Notes and coins	_____	_____	4,661
New domestic share issues	_____	_____	35
Deposits in current accounts at commercial banks	_____	_____	8,779
UK government bonds	_____	_____	477
Money held in deposit accounts at commercial banks	_____	_____	18,879

MONEY VALUES AND REAL VALUES

In Chapter 26, we saw that real GDP is nominal GDP adjusted for inflation. Real values are usually calculated by dividing the nominal (actual, current) value by a price index – i.e. by a weighted average of many prices. Going back to the base year when that price index was at 100, the real and nominal values are necessarily equal in the base year.

Q26   Suppose the nominal value of manufacturing output and the wholesale price index are as shown in the table below. From the data given, calculate the real value of manufacturing output, and state whether it is rising in real terms.

	Nominal value of output (£m)	Wholesale price index (1985 = 100)	Real value of output (£m in 1985 prices)
1985	4,000	100	_____
1986	4,410	105	_____
1987	4,620	110	_____
1988	5,040	120	_____
1989	5,460	130	_____
1990	5,670	135	_____

THE QUANTITY THEORY OF MONEY

Q27   'Whatever my expenditure, I only keep the same amount of cash, and the same level of my current account. I never like to "feel short of money".' This statement is/is not consistent with the transactions-demand assumption used by the quantity theory.

Q28   If the individual speaking in the previous question were given £100, might he spend it all on goods? Yes/No. Would the relationship between this individual's expenditure and his level of cash and current account be the same in the two time-periods both when he was spending his £100 and when he had spent it, and was back to his old level of expenditure? Yes/No

Q 29 In the quantity theory of money, $M_d = $ _____

Q 30 Is the money supply endogenous or exogenous in the quantity theory? _____

Q 31 What is meant by the velocity of circulation (V)? _____
_____

Q 32 What relation does V bear to k? _____

How do we explain this relationship? Well, consider what would happen if k were half its present level. This would mean, for example, that the amount of money in your wallet would be half what it actually is at the moment. But you are still going to make the same purchases, so the average length of stay in your wallet of the pounds in it would halve. Each pound note (on average) would 'move on' twice as quickly, which means that velocity would be double.

Q 33 Suppose that $V = 4$, $Y_F = $ £100m and $P = 1$.

  (a) Find the equilibrium money supply. _____
  (b) If the government buys bonds from the public to the value of £1m and if the banks expand to the limit (assume the cash ratio is 10%), what happens to P? _____
  (c) What is the value of GDP in current prices? _____
  (d) What is the value of GDP in real terms? _____

Q 34 The quantity theory predicts that increasing the money supply when there is an inflationary gap raises the real/money value of GDP through changes in _____ _____, and that increasing the money supply when there is an output gap raises the real/money value of GDP through changes in _____

QUESTIONS FOR DISCUSSION

1 During the Second World War, cigarettes were used as currency in prisoner-of-war camps. How well do you think cigarettes fulfilled the functions of money, and how easy would it be to debase the currency?

2 Mr Kovari, in a letter to *The Times* (20.7.78) wrote: 'Mr William Rees-Mogg advocates a return to the gold standard. What conceivable objection is there to a realistic monetary standard based upon useful commodities?'

   What do you think about Mr Kovari's idea? What useful commodities do you think he had in mind?

3 What do we mean when we say that banks can create money? Some people advocate that banks should be required to keep 100% cash reserves behind all their deposits. What would be the effects of such a policy?

4 Banking can be treated as business; shareholders in banks expect to receive dividends. A prominent British banker was quoted in the *Sunday Times* (28.2.71) as saying, 'There are times when we could pay more and charge more; the supply of advances would be rationed by price and those who can pay more are alleged to be the most efficient ... much bank money is still lent at rates of interest below those generally attainable in the markets, since we have been reluctant to exploit usuriously a scarcity of essential money.'

What might you, as a shareholder in the bank of this particular banker, say at a shareholders' meeting? What sort of reply might you expect? The *Sunday Times* financial journalist, Nicholas Firth, commented (the article concerned the relationship between the Conservative Government of Mr Heath, and industry in general):

'Faced with an attitude like this, in which money-lending to maximize profit is equated with usury and the doubting word "allegedly" is put ahead of the key notion that those able to pay the highest price for their capital are the most efficient, the Government should pause and wonder whether the country is worthy of it. We just cannot live up to the rarified notions of capitalism prevalent in the inner circles of government; and it is useless trying to make us revert to our nineteenth-century archetypes. We're too decadent – or should one say civilized – for such barbarities.'

5   What is the difference between the real and the nominal money supply?

CHAPTER 31
Monetary Equilibrium

Q1 Throughout this chapter we shall assume the money supply to be exogenously determined. What does this assumption mean? _____
_____
_____

MONEY DEMAND AND SUPPLY

Q2 Why do we say that keeping money under the mattress – or in a current account at the bank – has a cost? _____
_____
_____

Q3 What are the three main reasons for holding money? _____
_____

Q4 What determines the transactions demand for money? _____

Q5 As income rises, the demand for _____ balances will rise/fall and, as the interest rate falls, the demand for _____ _____ balances will rise/fall.

Q6 Define speculative balances. _____
_____

In Chapter 19, you can review the reasons why bond prices and interest rates are inversely related. You may find this helpful as you study the reasoning behind the *LM* curve.

Q7 When the price of interest-earning assets rises, the interest rate will rise/fall.

Q8 If people consider current bond prices are low and they expect them to rise, then they will tend to buy/sell bonds. Explain why. _____
_____
_____

Q9 The demand for money will vary directly/inversely with the level of income, directly/inversely with the level of wealth, and directly/inversely with the rate of interest.

Q10 Into which of the three categories of demand for money do the following fall (if any)?

(a) Money I keep in my current account to pay my rent. _____

174

(b) Money to pay a bill for a new car engine in case my claim on the guarantee does not come through quickly enough. _____
(c) The money which is deducted from wages in PAYE. _____
(d) The large cash balance held by a bookmaker. _____

The level of cash balances depends on income. The rich speculate more, spend more on their weekly grocery bill and have a larger number of uncertainly timed payments than do the poor.

Q11 What effect, on which of the categories, would the following have?

(a) Belief that the rate of inflation will increase. Raise/lower _____ balances.
(b) All unemployment and social security payments to be paid on a monthly, instead of a weekly, basis. Raise/lower _____ balances.
(c) Expectations that interest rates are about to rise. Raise/lower _____ balances.
(d) A salary rise. Raise/lower _____
(e) Go-slow by civil servants in settling firms' tax returns. Raise/lower _____
(f) Credit cards which grant you up to two months' credit. Raise/lower _____
(g) Authors' pessimism about the punctuality of royalty receipts. Raise/lower _____

Q12 When we talk about the liquidity-preference function of a firm we refer to the amount of cash held by the firm on its business premises instead of in the bank. T/F

Q13 What determines the real demand for money? (Write in symbols) _____

Q14 What is the difference between the real demand for money and the nominal demand for money? _____

Q15 If the price level rises by 10%, the nominal demand for money rises by ____%/is unchanged/falls by ____%, while real demand rises by ____%/is unchanged/falls by ____%.

Q16 In the short term, wealth is considered to be constant and the demand for money, therefore, depends on the level of income and the rate of interest.

(a) When income is rising, but the rate of interest is unchanged, the demand for money is rising/unchanged/falling.
(b) When income is rising and the rate of interest is falling, the demand for money is rising/unchanged/falling.

Q17 If the demand for money function is $M_d = 0.3Y - 20r$ (r expressed as %), find the amount of money demanded when:

(a) Income = £500m, r = 5% _____
(b) Income = £500m, r = 4% _____
(c) Income = £600m, r = 5% _____
(d) Income = £600m, r = 6% _____

Q18 Suppose that all workers are paid on a monthly, rather than weekly, basis. Income and the interest rate are unchanged.

(a) The demand for money rises/is unchanged/falls because the transactions/precautionary/speculative demand for money balances has risen/remained unchanged/fallen.

(b) If the demand-for-money function when workers were paid on a weekly basis was $M_d = 0.3Y - 20r$, which of the following functions is consistent with workers being paid on a monthly basis:

(i) $M_d = 0.3Y - 15r$;
(ii) $M_d = 0.4Y - 22r$;
(iii) $M_d = 0.4Y - 20r$;
(iv) $M_d = 0.2Y - 20r$.

Q 19 Fig. 1 shows the effects of the rate of interest on money balances. This refers to the marginal decision: 'is the extra liquidity gained from the addition of £x to my money balances worth the sacrifice of £rx per year?' It is assumed that the value to the individual of extra liquidity decreases with the amount held. This implies that the higher the rate of interest, the less cash will be held – *ceteris paribus*. (Note that the average level of money balances is a stock, not a flow – so we do not have to label the axis '... per period of time'.)

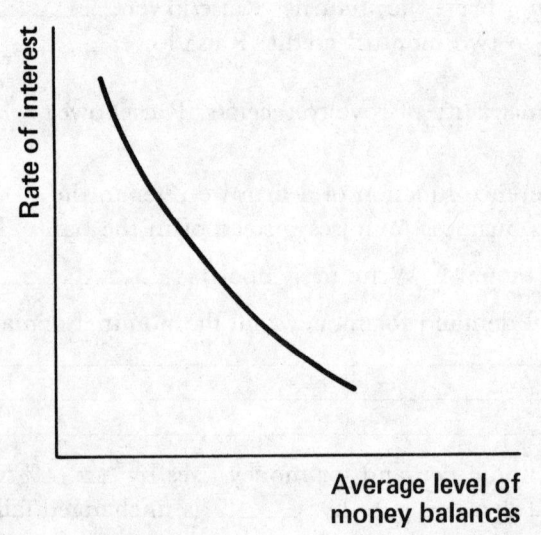

Fig. 1

(a) How would you represent on Fig. 1 an increase in the speculative demand for money?

(b) How would you represent a shortening of the payments period?

(c) How would you represent the immediate effect of a rise in interest rates?

Q 20 Equilibrium in the money market requires that the demand for money equal the supply of money. In our two-asset model, when this condition holds, it follows that

Q 21 If the demand-for-money function is $M_d = 0.4Y - 20r$, and the money supply is £80m, find whether $M_d = \dfrac{M^*}{P}$

(a) when Y = £600m and r = 10%.
(b) when Y = £600m and r = 8%.
(c) when Y = £600m and r = 5%.

PORTFOLIO BALANCE

Q 22 If the demand for money exceeds the supply of money, firms and households will seek to buy/sell bonds. As a result, bond prices will rise/fall and the interest rates will rise/fall until _____

Q 23 Following an increase in the money supply,

(a) the demand for transaction balances rises/falls/remains the same,
(b) which means there is more/less/the same money available for speculative purposes.
(c) the price of bonds will rise/fall as people attempt to sell/buy bonds and this causes a rise/fall in the interest rate.

Q 24 When the level of income rises but the interest rate and the money supply are unchanged,

(a) the demand for money will rise/fall.
(b) this means that the demand for money is now greater than/less than the supply of money (assuming that previously they were equal).
(c) for a return to equilibrium, the interest rate must rise/fall.
(d) alternatively, if the interest rate is to be maintained at its original level, equilibrium could be achieved by raising/lowering the money supply.

Q 25 Let $M_d = 0.4Y - 20r$ and $\dfrac{M^*}{P} = £80m$. With current $Y = £600m$ and $r = 8\%$, $M_d = \dfrac{M^*}{P}$.

(a) The level of income now rises to £625m, while r and $\dfrac{M^*}{P}$ are unchanged. Find M_d. _____
(b) If the money supply is unchanged and $Y = £625m$, what is the interest rate at which $M_d = \dfrac{M^*}{P}$? _____
(c) In order to maintain an interest rate of 8%, by how much would the supply of money have had to be increased? _____

THE *LM* CURVE

We have seen that different levels of income require different rates of interest in order to equate the demand for money with a constant money supply. More generally, we can now see that the rate of interest at which the demand for and supply of money are equal will depend on the level of income, the money supply and the size of the behavioural parameters of the demand-for-money function.

Q 26 The *LM* curve is the locus of all _____ combinations that yield equilibrium between the demand for and the supply of money.

Q 27 If the demand for money is $M_d = dY + er$, and the money supply is $M_s = M^*/P$, how is the *LM* curve derived? _____

Q 28 Suppose that the demand for money is given as $M_d = 0.4Y - 20r$ and $M_s = £80m$. Derive the equation for the *LM* curve. _____

Q 29   What is the slope of this curve? _____ And the intercept? _____

Q 30   What would be the effect on the *LM* curve of the following?

(a) A fall in the money supply. _____

(b) A rise in the level of income. _____

(c) The demand-for-money function changes as a result of an increase in the speculative demand for money balances (e.g. $M_d = 0.4Y - 10r$ instead of $M_d = 0.4Y - 20r$). _____

(d) A fall in the demand for transaction balances (e.g. $M_d = 0.35Y - 20r$). _____

When the position of the *LM* curve changes, monetary equilibrium can only be restored if the level of income and/or the rate of interest change. If the interest rate is held constant, the level of income must change. If the level of income is held constant, the rate of interest must change.

Q 31   When $M_d = 0.4Y - 20r$, $\dfrac{M^*}{P} = £80m$ and $Y = £700m$, what is the rate of interest at which there is monetary equilibrium? _____

Q 32   Now let the money supply fall to £79m. Keeping $Y = £700m$, the interest rate must rise/fall to _____. (Before you work out the answer, see if you can predict the direction of change correctly.) Holding the interest rate at its previous level, income must rise/fall to £_____ for equilibrium. Draw a diagram to illustrate your answer.

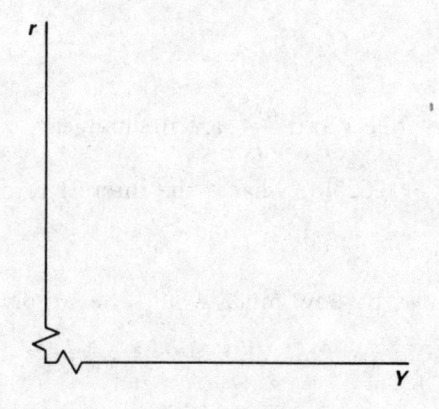

Q 33   Keeping $\dfrac{M^*}{P} = £80m$, let $M_d = 0.4Y - 10r$. Holding $Y = £700m$, the rate of interest must rise/fall to _____. Holding *r* at its original level, income must rise/fall to _____ for equilibrium. Draw a diagram to illustrate your answer.

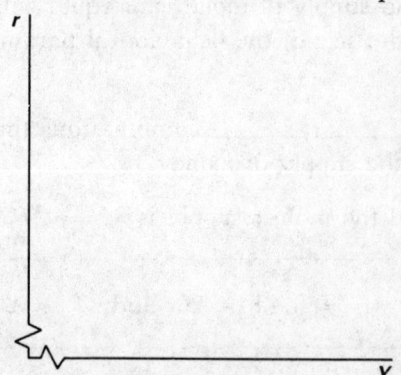

Q 34 With $\frac{M^*}{P}$ = £80m, let M_d = 0.35Y − 20r. Holding Y = £700m, the interest rate must rise/fall to _____ ; holding r at its original level, income must rise/fall to _____ for equilibrium. Draw a diagram to illustrate your answer.

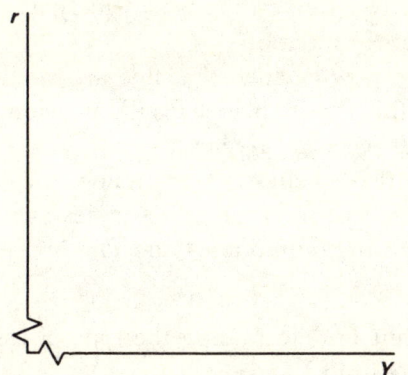

Q 35 If M_d = 0.4Y − 20r and $\frac{M^*}{P}$ = £100m.

(a) When Y = £700m and r = 8%, the demand for money is greater than/less than the supply of money and, therefore, the rate of interest will rise/fall when income is held constant.

(b) When Y = £500m and r = 6%, the demand for money is greater than/less than the supply of money, and the rate of interest will rise/fall when income is held constant.

QUESTIONS FOR DISCUSSION

1 If you keep all your money in your current account at your bank you do not earn any interest on it. What could you do with your money in order to earn interest? What transactions costs are involved?

2 'A rise in bank base rates is always welcome news for investors. Seven-day deposit accounts are now offering 8 per cent compared with under 7 per cent a week ago.

   'But this is still small beer compared with the more generous terms offered by the money funds ... Save & Prosper is offering a high-interest deposit account (currently paying 11.25 per cent) with the flexibility of a cheque book facility for withdrawals of £250 or more. Customers earn money market rates on relatively small sums with no penalties on withdrawal and no requirement to give notice.' (Report in *The Times*, 15.1.83.)

   (a) Are the 'investors' referred to in this report investors in the sense discussed by Lipsey?
   (b) In what ways does the Save & Prosper high-interest deposit account discussed here differ from other savings and deposit accounts?

   Do you think many people will transfer funds from existing accounts to this new account?

3 Outline the main forms wealth can take, and discuss the pros and cons of holding wealth in more than one type of asset.

4 On 19.3.79 Christine Moir reported in the *Financial Times* that British Rail's pension funds were to stop buying works of art:

'The Funds' purchases to date amount to £28m and include 12th-century candlesticks, Picasso's *Young Man in Blue* and Chinese and Egyptian antiquities.

'Since 1974 British Rail has been spending in the fine art auction rooms around 4 per cent of the new money flowing into its pension funds each year ... BR defended (these purchases) on the grounds that it needed to diversify its investments as widely as possible and to seek the maximum shelter from future inflation.

'(The general manager) said: "the trustees have now decided that fine art should not represent a major diversification in a portfolio of this size". British Rail's pension funds already total £750m and are growing at around 10 per cent a year.

'At present the funds' budget is to keep about 10 per cent of their money in cash and fixed securities, 40 per cent in UK equities, 10 per cent in overseas securities and 25 per cent in property. A further 8 per cent has been in commodities and fine art, leaving 7 per cent flexible.'

(a) What factors do you think will be important in determining the type of asset the fund acquires? (Remember this is a *pension* fund.)
(b) What are the advantages and disadvantages of works of art when compared with other types of asset held by the fund?
(c) What factors might determine the proportion of the fund's budget allocated to different types of asset?

5 This is an extract from a letter to the *Financial Times* (30.11.74):

'Now that the government is actually minting gold sovereigns, would it not be possible for these to be designated as alternative legal tender to the pound sterling, albeit at their free exchange rate?

'Investment should quickly be revitalized by such a measure, because a would-be house purchaser, who today pays £105 per month for a £10,000 mortgage at 11%, could probably borrow at 4% from a holder of gold sovereigns who now receives no interest at all. The repayments on a £10,000 mortgage at 4% would be less than £50 per month (in sovereigns) which example illustrates the beneficial effect of honest money, with its endemic low interest rates, on the vital process of investment for the future.'

What do you think of this suggestion?

6 'The demand for money is positively related to national income valued in current prices.' How is the demand for money related to national income when there is inflation?

7 What do we mean by money market equilibrium? Which markets are in equilibrium along the LM curve?

8 What would happen to the LM curve if:

(a) the money supply increases?
(b) the price level rises?
(c) the demand for transaction balances increases?

9 What would the LM curve look like if:

(a) money and bonds were perfect substitutes?
(b) money and bonds were non-substitutes?

10 Hamish McRae wrote an article for the *Guardian* (8.3.79) entitled 'Why some money is more "moneyish"'. Here are some extracts:

Money, money, money. One of the most puzzling aspects of the present debate on the money supply, with all its references to M1, M3 and M5, is to try and see in what way the various definitions of money supply differ from each other and why the definitions should matter anyway.

'The key to understanding about money, in its various guises, is to grasp the fact that some money is more "moneyish" than others. To explain: money in our pockets, the notes and coins, is clearly money. It can be spent straight away without the bother of having to go round to the Post Office or bank to draw it out. Money in current account at the bank is also money, but you could argue that it is not quite as "moneyish" as notes and coin. Try and give a taxi-driver a cheque and you will see what I mean.'

What McRae is talking about is the ease and cheapness with which one asset can be exchanged for another. The usual term for this is 'liquidity'. Obviously money in the form of notes and coins is the most liquid of all assets. McRae goes on to list other assets with varying degrees of liquidity.

(a) Here is a list for you to put in order of *decreasing* liquidity: shares in ICI; deposits with building societies; short-term government securities; time deposits with commercial banks; national savings certificates; long-term government securities; sight deposits with commercial banks; Picasso paintings; local authority bonds.

(b) What are the costs of exchanging the following for pound coins: ICI shares; building society deposits, time deposits with commercial banks and Picasso paintings?

(c) Which of the assets listed in (a) are included in the M1 and M3 definitions of money supply?

(d) Some people argue for a broader definition of money supply to include deposits with building societies. What do you think are the arguments for and against a broader definition?

CHAPTER 32

The IS–LM Model

INVESTMENT IN NATIONAL-INCOME THEORY

Up until now we have not considered what determines investment but have treated investment as an exogenous variable. We now have to examine the effect of the rate of interest on desired investment.

Any businessman making an investment decision has to weigh up many different factors. Clearly no one will undertake an investment unless the returns cover the cost. If these returns are yielded over a period of time, it is necessary to discount them to find the Present Value. The Net Present Value of any project is the difference between the capital cost of a project and the present value of the future cash flows to which the project will give rise. (If you cannot remember how to calculate the Present Value, you should have another look at Chapter 19 in the Workbook.)

Suppose that an investment project has a Net Present Value of zero when discounted at 13%. This means that 13% is the rate of discount which makes the expected stream of future net income equal to the cost of the investment. We say that the *rate of return* on this investment is 13% and this rate of yield is what Keynes called the *marginal efficiency of capital*. No project will be undertaken unless the rate of return is positive, but a positive rate of return is only a necessary, and not a sufficient, condition for investment. The firm must be sure that this rate is at least as high as the rate it could earn on any other asset. For example, a firm considering financing investment out of its business savings could use these savings to purchase government bonds, which yield a return, or it could deposit these savings in a bank account. Any investment project it undertakes must yield at least as much as these alternatives.

Q1 If the rate of interest falls, the value of an asset producing a given stream of income will also fall. T/F

Q2 The higher the rate of interest, the greater/smaller will be the amount of investment worth undertaking, other things being equal.

Q3 When interest rates rise, the amount firms could earn on money not invested falls. T/F

It is not possible to forecast precisely the expected income streams of an investment project: there are many unknown factors such as the state of the economy, technological developments, etc. The longer the time horizon, the less accurate forecasts are likely to be.

Q4 Suppose you are a producer of hosiery and are considering whether to introduce a new line of patterned tights. To do this you would need to purchase new and specialized machines. Would the following events be likely to *increase* or *decrease* the probability of your making this investment? When answering, make clear whether it is revenue or costs that are likely to be affected.

(a) Fashion magazines forecast a return of the mini-skirt.
(b) The Union of European Hosiery Workers has put in a claim for a 30% wage increase and threatens to strike if this is not granted.
(c) The Government announces that one of its major objectives will be to avoid any increase in the unemployment rate.
(d) There is a large explosion at the biggest nylon yarn producing plant in the UK.
(e) VAT on all clothing is cut by 2%.
(f) The rate of interest rises by 1%.
(g) You hear rumours that your main competitor has discovered a new technique which enables him to produce more hardwearing hosiery for the same price as his current products.

Q5 The marginal efficiency of capital schedule falls as the stock of capital rises because the rate of interest falls. T/F

Q6 The equilibrium amount of capital stock increases as the interest rate falls. T/F

Q7 Referring to Fig. 1 below, complete the following:

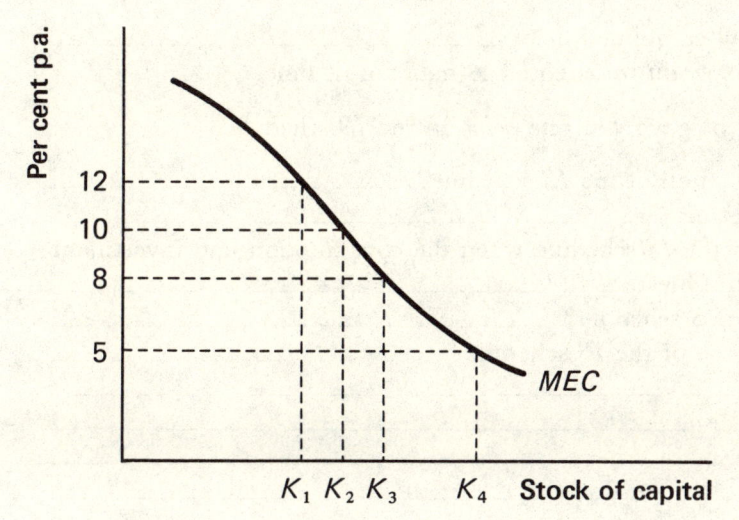

Fig. 1

(a) When capital stock equals K_1, the yield is _____
(b) If the rate of interest is 10%, the equilibrium amount of capital is _____
(c) A 2% fall in the rate of interest would require _____ of new investment to restore equilibrium.
(d) If the stock of capital is K_4, the yield is greater than/less than the new rate of interest (i.e. the rate in part (c)).
(e) If the rate of interest were to rise again to 12%, how can the equilibrium stock of capital be achieved? _____

Q8 Why may a fall in the rate of interest result in a *temporary*, and not permanent, increase in investment in plant and machinery? _____

Q9 List the main sources of funds for investment. _____

Q 10 What transactions take place when companies borrow directly from the public? _____

Q 11 What two transactions take place when companies borrow *indirectly* from the public? _____
_____

THE *IS* CURVE

Q 12 If aggregate expenditure is determined by consumption and investment, where

$$C = 4 + 0.8Y$$
$$I = 180 - 10r$$

(r is rate of interest expressed as a percentage, i.e. 6% interest rate implies $r = 6$; C and I are in £million.)

(a) What is the equation of the aggregate expenditure function? _____
(b) What is the equilibrium level of income when the rate of interest is 10%? _____

Q 13 The *IS* schedule represents all combinations of _____ at which desired aggregate expenditure is equal to national income.

Q 14 Your answer to Question 12(b) gave you one *point* on the *IS* schedule.

(a) How do we find the equation of the *IS* schedule? _____
(b) What is the equation of the *IS* schedule when the consumption and investment functions are as given in Question 12? _____
(c) What is the slope of the *IS* schedule? _____
(d) What determines the slope of the *IS* schedule? _____
_____
_____
_____

Q 15 In Question 12 you found that when the rate of interest was 10%, the equilibrium level of income was £420m.

(a) Now suppose that national income rises to £445m. What will consumption, investment and aggregate expenditure be, if the interest rate remains at 10%?
_____
(b) Thus, with the rate of interest constant, the rise in aggregate expenditure is greater than/equal to/less than the rise in income.
(c) For equilibrium at the higher level of income, the rate of interest must rise/fall, bringing about an increase/decrease in investment.
(d) Find the rate of interest required to equate desired aggregate expenditure with national income at £445m. _____
(e) What is investment now? _____

Q 16 Why is the slope of the *IS* schedule negative? _____
_____
_____
_____

Q17 Suppose that the level of income is £430m, and the rate of interest is 9%.

(a) Aggregate expenditure is greater/less than national income by an amount of _____

(b) For equilibrium at this level of income, the rate of interest must rise/fall to _____

(c) If the rate of interest were to remain at 9%, find the equilibrium level of income. _____

(d) Draw a diagram to illustrate your answer.

Q18 Given the following consumption and investment functions:

$$C = a_0 + cY$$
$$I = a_1 + br$$

(a) What restrictions do you have to put on the behavioural parameters and the autonomous elements of expenditure to ensure a positive value of equilibrium income? _____

(b) Derive the equation for the *IS* schedule. _____

What happens to the aggregate expenditure function and the *IS* schedule if:

(c) exogenous expenditure, A^*, falls? _____

(d) the marginal propensity to save falls? _____

(e) the value of b increases? _____

THE *IS-LM* MODEL

Q19 The *IS* curve shows all combinations of interest rates and income levels resulting in equilibrium in the _____ market, while the *LM* curve shows similar combinations satisfying the equilibrium condition for the _____ market.

Q20 For equilibrium in:

(a) the goods market we require: _____

(b) the asset market we require: _____

(c) both markets we require: _____

Q21 If $C = a_0 + cY$ $0 < c < 1, 0 < a_0$
        $I = a_1 + br$ $b < 0 < a_1$
        $M_d = dY + er$ $0 < d < 1, e < 0$
        $\dfrac{M^*}{P}$ is money supply.

(a) What is the equation of the *IS* curve? _____
(b) What is the equation of the *LM* curve? _____
(c) Now set the *IS* equation equal to the *LM* equation and solve for *Y*.
_____
(d) What is the *interest-constant* multiplier? _____
(e) What is the *interest-variable* multiplier? _____

Q22 Suppose there is an increase in autonomous investment, i.e. a_1 increases.

(a) At the original equilibrium values of income and rate of interest, desired aggregate expenditure is greater than/less than income.
(b) The injection raises/lowers income through the multiplier, shifting the *IS* schedule outwards/inwards.
(c) As income changes, the demand for transactions balances rises/falls.
(d) With the money supply unchanged, the demand for money will exceed/be less than the supply.
(e) As a consequence, the price of bonds will rise/fall and the interest rate will rise/fall.
(f) The change in the interest rate will curb/encourage investment spending.
(g) A new equilibrium level of income will be established that is higher than/lower than before but less high/low than the income level that would have occurred if expenditure had been insensitive to the interest rate.

Q23 Here is another sequence for you to work through:

(a) A fall in the money supply will shift the *LM* schedule upwards/downwards.
(b) This will leave the asset market in disequilibrium at the initial levels of *Y* and *r* as, with these unchanged, the demand for money will be greater than/less than the new supply.
(c) The public will seek to buy/sell bonds, thus raising/lowering the interest rate.
(d) The change in the interest rate will result in higher/lower investment and the *IS* curve will shift out/remain the same/shift in, while income will rise/fall.
(e) The rise/fall in the interest rate will not be as great as it would be if income were unchanged, as the rise/fall in income increases/decreases demand for transaction/speculative balances.
(f) The new equilibrium will be at a higher/lower rate of interest and a higher/lower level of income than existed before the change in the money supply.

Q24 Suppose the economy is in disequilibrium and at a point such as *A* in Fig. 2.

(a) At point *A*, the demand for money is greater than/less than the supply, and aggregate desired expenditure is greater/less than income.
(b) If income is unchanged, what will happen to *r*? _____
(c) Why is it unlikely that income will not change? _____
_____
_____

(d) For a new equilibrium to be established, income must rise/fall and the rate of interest must rise/fall.

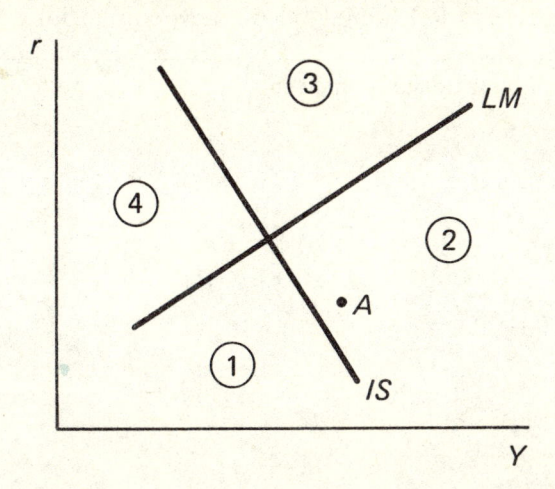

Fig. 2

Q25 Referring to the numbering of segments in Fig. 2, complete the following:

		Segment number	Y rises/ falls	r rises/ falls
(a)	When $M_d > M_s$ and $E > Y$, we are in			
(b)	When $M_d < M_s$ and $E > Y$, we are in			
(c)	When $M_d > M_s$ and $E < Y$, we are in			
(d)	When $M_d < M_s$ and $E < Y$, we are in			

Q26 You are given the following information about an economy:
autonomous consumption is £10m and autonomous investment £125m; the marginal propensity to consume is 0.8; $b = -10$, $d = 0.3$ and $3 = -15$. M^*/P = £90m.

(a) Find the equation of the IS curve. _____
(b) What is the equation of the LM curve? _____
(c) What is autonomous expenditure, A^*? _____
(d) What is the equilibrium level of income and rate of interest? _____

Q27 Using the information from the previous question:

(a) Find the interest-constant multiplier. _____
(b) What is the value of the interest-variable multiplier? _____
(c) If there is an increase of £10m in the autonomous component of investment, what will be the new equilibrium levels of income and interest rate? _____ What are consumption and investment? _____

(d) Suppose that the interest rate had been fixed at 3.75 instead of rising. Find consumption, investment and aggregate expenditure. _____

Did you use the multipliers to find the answers to (c) and (d)? Draw (overleaf) an IS-LM diagram to illustrate your answers, showing the crowding-out. Be sure to label the axes.

Q 28 Using the information from Question 26:

    (a)   If the money supply were to rise to £112.5m, find the new equilibrium.

    (b)   Draw an *IS–LM* diagram to illustrate your answer.

Q 29 What would be the effect of the following on the equilibrium levels of income and rate of interest?

    (a)   The marginal propensity to save rises.

    (b)   The demand for transactions balances rises.

    (c)   Businessmen's pessimism about the recession deepens.

    (d)   Demand for speculative balances falls.

If you found it difficult to answer these questions by examining the equations for the *IS* and *LM* curves, try deriving the *IS* and *LM* curves by the geometric method explained in the Appendix to Chapter 32. The quadrant diagrams will permit you to examine each of the above changes, but you will need some graph paper to do it properly.

QUESTIONS FOR DISCUSSION

1 If you purchase shares in the stock market, are you investing?

2 What is the importance of interest rates in the theory of investment? What do the theories discussed in this chapter predict about how interest rates behave in response to changes in investment?

3 What will be the effect of changes in interest rates on housing investments and the demand for housing?

4 In his Budget speech on 11 April 1978 the Chancellor of the Exchequer said, 'A major purpose of this Budget is to adjust taxation so as to help and improve our industrial performance ... I have therefore decided again to make no major changes this year in the rate of Corporation Tax or in the levels of investment incentives.' What theory of investment do you think lies behind this statement?

5 Is a university education a good investment? Is it possible to calculate the rate of return?

6 This is an extract from an article by Roger Elgin printed in *The Observer* (7.3.71). Sadly, many of the points he makes still apply today.

   'Squirrels that don't stock up on nuts in the autumn are dead by spring. Nations that don't invest in extra capacity and all the other tools of a modern, competitive industrial society don't actually die, they go into a painful decline.

   '"The long, slow sapping of our strength by under-investment" as Sir Fred Catherwood, director-general of Neddy, calls it, is what is happening in Britain at the moment.

   'Faced with inflating costs and tight purse strings, three major companies, BP, Shell and Alcoa, have cut back or curtailed major investment projects.

   'Over the past few years, another disturbing element has crept into the equation. Until 1965, it was broadly true that the income going to companies represented roughly 15.2 per cent of the gross national product. Since this date, profits as a percentage of GNP have dropped by a quarter to what looks like being 10 per cent last year. The share of GNP going to wages has gone from 67.8 per cent to comfortably over 70 per cent.

   'Diverting British industry from this inexorable march to the knacker's yard is not going to be easy. Industry has not only lost the confidence to invest, but has also run out of cash.

   'Wage bills and material costs are rocketing. The stock market is so depressed that the chances of raising money through it at anything but penal terms are impossible at the moment. To keep afloat many have resorted to increasing their bank overdrafts. But any industrialist who uses casual bank finance to pay for investment deserves to follow Rolls-Royce.'

   What theories of the determination of investment are contained in this article? Why does a 'depressed stock market' mean that to raise money through the stock market would be very expensive?

7 If the government wished to lower interest rates, how could it achieve this?

8 What is 'crowding-out'?

9 If the government wishes to raise the level of income and, at the same time, avoid crowding-out, can you suggest how it might do this?

10 What might be adjustment paths towards equilibrium starting from points A, B and C in the diagram overleaf?

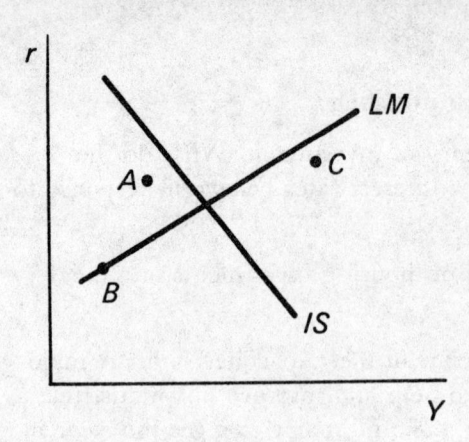

Fig. 3

11 As reported in the *Financial Times* (15.3.79) the *Bank of England Quarterly Bulletin* for March 1979 noted that 'the ratio of stock to sales of finished goods remains historically high, though survey evidence suggests that managements do not regard the present level of stocks as excessive. The apparent change in the relationship between desired stocks and the level of activity may reflect only partial adjustment by companies to the recession of the last few years ... Some of the increase in stocks during 1978 probably arose from expectation of continuing buoyancy in demand.' The *Bulletin* then went on to say that it thought the recent rise in interest rates might result in a reduction in stockbuilding, or even some destocking, as a response to future growth of demand.

(a) The *Bulletin* is suggesting that there seems to have been a change in managements' view of the desirable level of stock relative to sales. What factors might be responsible for such a shift?
(b) Why should changes in interest rates affect stock levels?
(c) If stocks only partially adjust in recession, will this strengthen or weaken any relationship between inventory levels and fluctuations in national income?

CHAPTER 33

The Aggregate Demand, Aggregate Supply Model

Q1 The *IS–LM* model is not 'closed' because it does not have an equation to determine income/prices/interest rates.

Q2 Closure in the aggregate demand, aggregate supply model is obtained by bringing in the price level as an exogenous/endogenous/fixed variable.

THE AGGREGATE DEMAND CURVE

Q3 The aggregate demand curve shows all combinations of _____ _____ which ensure equilibrium in the _____ and the _____ markets.

Q4 A fall in the price level

  (a) means that the real money supply rises/falls and raises/lowers the nominal demand for money;

  (b) creates excess demand for/excess supply of money, which will cause interest rates to rise/fall and the level of real national income to rise/fall.

  (c) This change in the rate of interest means that the aggregate expenditure function shifts up/is unchanged/shifts down, the *IS* curve shifts up/is unchanged/shifts down, the *LM* curve shifts up/is unchanged/shifts down and the aggregate demand curve shifts to right/is unchanged/shifts to left.

Q5 The aggregate demand curve slopes downwards.

  (a) What behavioural parameters determine the slope? _____

  (b) A low interest responsiveness of demand for money will make the slope of the *AD* curve steeper/flatter? Why? _____

  (c) A high interest responsiveness of aggregate expenditure makes the slope of the *AD* curve steeper/flatter, as _____

  (d) Given both a low interest responsiveness of demand for money and a high interest responsiveness of expenditure, a small increase in the price level will bring about a small/large _____ in the income level.

  (e) When parameters b, d and e are constant but the marginal propensity to consume falls, this will make the *AD* curve steeper/flatter.

Q6 What variables are held constant
  (a) for a given *IS* curve? _____
  (b) for a given *LM* curve? _____
  (c) for a given aggregate demand curve? _____

Q7 The monetary transmission mechanism describes the adjustment of equilibrium national income to given changes in
  (a) wages.
  (b) the money supply and price level.
  (c) autonomous investment.

Q8 The intermediate (endogenous) variables through which this adjustment process occurs include the demand for money, the interest rate, bond prices, and desired expenditure (aggregate demand). Consider a one-off rise in the real money supply, which could be the result of a rise in the nominal money supply and/or of a fall in the price level. ($\frac{M^*}{P}$ rises if M^* rises and/or if P falls.) In which direction would each of the following move as the monetary transmission mechanism brings the economy back to equilibrium?
  (a) demand for money holdings would rise/fall.
  (b) interest rate would rise/fall.
  (c) bond prices would rise/fall.
  (d) aggregate demand would rise/fall.
  (e) equilibrium real national income would rise/fall.

This example is the case of an expansionary monetary shock (Fig. 32.9 in the text).

Q9 What effect would each of the following have on the location of the aggregate demand curve?
  (a) a rise in autonomous consumption expenditure due to an advertising campaign would cause a shift left/shift right.
  (b) a fall in the demand for money due to a change in expectations would cause a shift left/shift right.
  (c) a rise in the nominal money supply would cause a shift left/shift right.

Q10 When the aggregate demand curve is drawn in the standard (Marshallian) way, *Y/P/r* goes on the vertical axis and *Y/P/r* goes on the horizontal axis.

Q11 What parameters determine the slope of the *AD* curve?

  (in words) _____

  (in symbols) _____

Q12 Increasing the nominal money supply means that, at the current price level, the *IS/LM* curve will shift up/down resulting in higher/lower income level and higher/lower rate of interest, and the *AD* curve shifts to right/is unchanged/shifts to left.

Q13 If the nominal money supply increases by 10% and prices increase by a similar amount, the *AD* curve shifts to right/is unchanged/shifts to left and income rises/remains the same/falls.

THE SHORT-RUN AGGREGATE SUPPLY CURVE

Q14 The *SRAS* curve assumes that wages are rising/fixed/high.

Q15 When national output is below its potential level Y_F, which of the aggregate supply curve(s) in Fig. 1 would be appropriate? $AS_0/AS_1/AS_2$

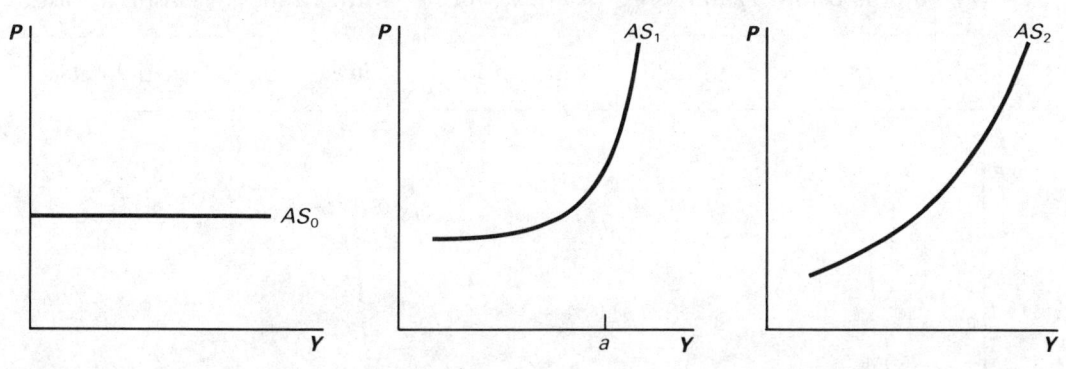

Fig. 1

Q16 When national output is above its potential level Y_F, which *AS* curve(s) would be appropriate? $AS_0/AS_1/AS_2$

Q17 Given that national income tends to fluctuate above and below its potential level during the course of the business cycle (i.e. booms and recessions), which short-run *AS* curve seems most generally appropriate? $AS_0/AS_1/AS_2$

Q18 How would you label the point *a* on the graph of AS_1?

Q19 Name four changes that would cause shifts in the *SRAS* curve.

EQUILIBRIUM OF AGGREGATE DEMAND AND AGGREGATE SUPPLY

Q20 Which of the aggregate supply curves in Fig. 2 is more suitable for a short-run analysis? AS_0/AS_1

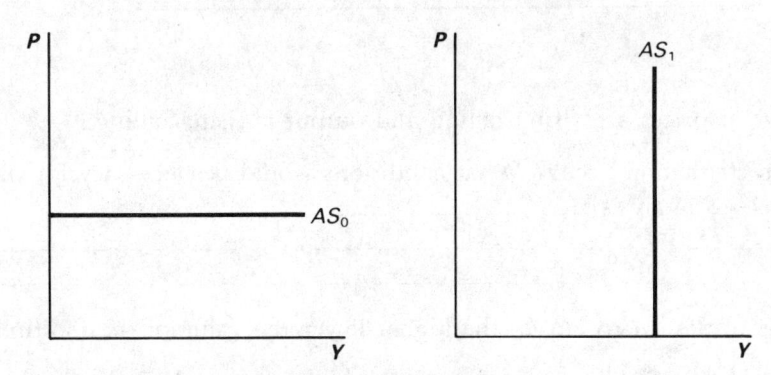

Fig. 2

Q21 Which one is perfectly inelastic? AS_0/AS_1

Q22 Label one curve *SRAS* and the other *LRAS*. Which one corresponds more closely to the Keynesian aggregate supply curve?

Q23 Points on the aggregate demand, aggregate supply graph that lie off both the *AS* and *AD* curves reflect equilibrium/disequilibrium in the market for goods/money/both.

Q 24 Use Fig. 3 to analyse the short-run effects on the price level and national income of a one-off rise in autonomous expenditure. Use your graph to fill in the following table:

	P rises:	Y rises:	AS is relatively:
(a) if Y is below Y_F initially	a little/a lot	a little/a lot	elastic/inelastic
(b) if Y is above Y_F initially	a little/a lot	a little/a lot	elastic/inelastic

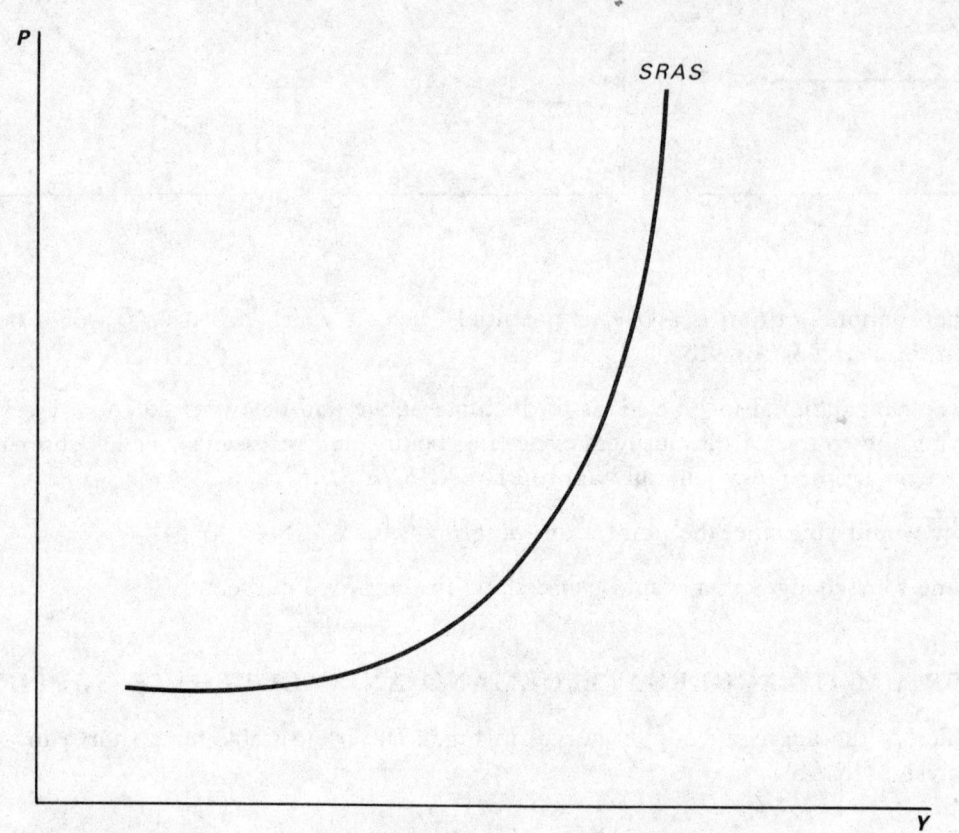

Fig. 3

Q 25 Stagflation occurs when prices are rising/falling and output is rising/falling.

Q 26 In the long run, can stagflation occur? What conditions would be necessary for this to happen, using *AD–AS* analysis? _____

Q 27 The higher the slope of the *SRAS* curve, the higher/lower the value of the multiplier.

Q 28 The higher the level of autonomous expenditure, the higher/lower the value of the multiplier.

Q 29 Use Fig. 4 to illustrate the last two answers.

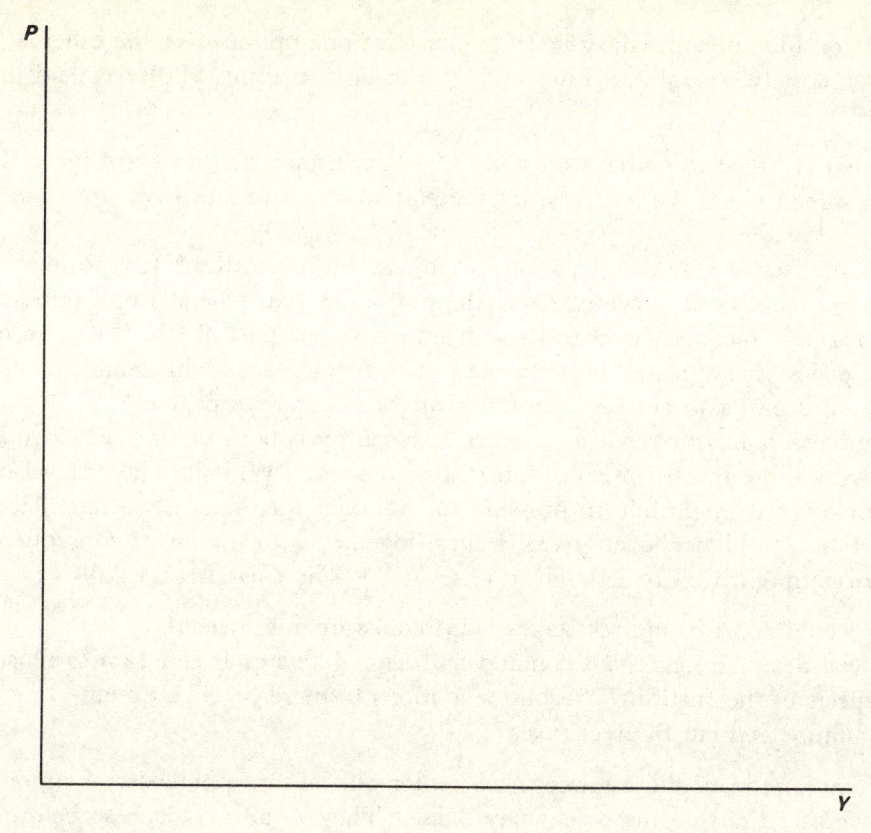

Fig. 4

QUESTIONS FOR DISCUSSION

1 Why does the aggregate demand curve slope downwards?

2 What determines the shape and the position of the aggregate supply curve?

3 When aggregate demand exceeds aggregate supply what happens to the price level and to income?

4 Do you think the assumption that each factor market (e.g. labour, rental, etc.) is in equilibrium can be justified?

5 In a letter to the *Financial Times* (28.2.83) C.A. Williams argued that 'the trouble with the [Government's] strategy has been that while it set a path for public expenditure no target was set for the composition of that expenditure. It is clear that the consequences of cutting public expenditure will be very different if this is done by slashing the road programme than if the savings are made in the social security programme, or if the borrowing target is met by sale of assets.'

Do changes in the composition of government expenditure affect the position of the aggregate demand curve?

6 As reported in Hansard, Mr Baker asked the following question on 8 February 1979:

'Does the Prime Minister appreciate that if there is a choice between a policy of high money interest rates and reducing government expenditure, for the government always to choose to increase money interest rates means that they are sacrificing future growth prospects of the economy?'

(a) What circumstances might make high interest rates or reduced government expenditure appropriate policy options?

(b) What considerations might guide the choice of one option over the other?
(c) What link between interest rates and growth do you think Mr Baker had in mind?

7 'The Government is urged to embark on a gradual but sustained reflation of the UK economy to be spread over several years, by the National Institute of Economic and Social Research.

'The most cost-effective way of increasing output, according to the NI, is to increase public spending on goods and services. Over the past eight years the share of public investment in national income has been halved, only a minor part of which was an object of government policy. It happened because the public sector, faced with financial constraints, found it easier to cut back capital projects rather than people.

'The Institute also points out that a recovery induced by cuts in indirect taxes could be achieved with very little upward pressure on prices. It says: "Whilst a higher level of output and employment might add to pressure for nominal wage increases, the effect in the other direction of a higher level of real wages (together with the direct consequence of tax cuts for prices) might well be enough to offset it."' (The *Guardian*, 24.2.83.)

(a) How would a cut in indirect taxes help reduce unemployment?
(b) Can you draw an aggregate demand and aggregate supply diagram to illustrate the effects of the Institute's recommendations to increase government expenditure and cut indirect taxes?

8 '"Why can't they just print more money?" a senior official in a public-sector union is reported to have asked during the recent pay talks. "They've always done so before." Perhaps he was joking. Certainly the one thing which the Chancellor has made repeatedly and quite courageously clear is that the Government will not yield to the old temptation to finance big settlements in the public sector by ditching its targets for monetary growth and public sector borrowing.' (Leader in the *Guardian*, 20.2.79.)

What would be the effect on the economy of printing more money?

CHAPTER 34
Inflation

Q1 Name the three factors that affect the rate of increase of unit wage costs:

(a) _____
(b) _____
(c) _____

INFLATIONARY SHOCKS

Q2 When unit wage costs go up suddenly, the short-run aggregate supply (*SRAS*) curve shifts up/shifts down/becomes steeper.

Q3 If other input costs (such as imported computer chip prices) go up, what happens to the *SRAS* curve? _____

Q4 Rising costs of production correspond to an *SRAS* curve that moves up/down and to the left/right over time.

Q5 A supply shock shifts the _____ curve, whereas a demand shock shifts the _____ curve.

Q6 A supply shock shifts the long-run aggregate supply (*LRAS*) curve. T/F

Q7 Monetary accommodation of an upward supply shock shifts the _____ curve to the left/right and up/down.

Q8 When Lipsey discusses the business cycle in Chapter 34, he refers to the 'recessionary gap' created by an upward supply shock and the 'inflationary gap' created by an upward shift in aggregate demand. These gaps refer to the horizontal distance between actual output, Y, and potential (or full-employment) output, Y_F, on the *AD–AS* diagrams in Chapter 34. To remove either of these gaps, which of the following curves must shift? *SRAS/LRAS/AD/* Phillips Curve?

_____

Q9 In Figure 34.1, the horizontal distance Y_1-Y_F is the recessionary gap. What does the vertical distance P_1-P_0 represent? _____

Q10 Monetary accommodation to offset a one-off, upward supply shock will cause a rise in the price level/inflation rate. (Be careful in distinguishing the price level from the inflation rate. They are two different things.)

Q11 Draw a diagram to illustrate how the above response (monetary accommodation) can be used to bring the economy back to full employment. Label your figure carefully.

Q12 Monetary accommodation refers to the central bank's response to a short-run shift in supply/demand. Monetary validation refers to the central bank's response to a _____ shift in supply/demand.

THE PHILLIPS CURVE

Q13 Asymmetry in the Phillips curve results in it having a falling/constant/changing/rising slope.

Q14 When drawn in its original form, the Phillips curve shows that the rate of growth of wages rises/falls as unemployment rises. However, at very low levels of unemployment wages rise very slowly/quickly.

Q15 The shift downward in the Phillips curve as we change the vertical axis variable from '% change in wages' to '% change in unit costs' results from changes in inflation/productivity/capital stock.

Q16 The higher productivity growth, the lower/higher the Phillips curve in $(U,\dot{c})$ space compared to the original Phillips curve in $(U,\dot{w})$ space.

Q17 The standard Phillips curve is drawn in $(Y,\dot{c})$ space instead of $(U,\dot{c})$ or $(U,\dot{w})$ space. What assumption is necessary to make this transformation?

Q18 In other words, the higher national income is, the lower/higher unemployment is.

EXPECTATIONAL FORCES

Q19 Which of the following methods of forming expectations about prices are backward-looking, and which are forward-looking?

(a) extrapolative expectations _____
(b) adaptive expectations _____
(c) rational expectations _____

Q20 If the short-run Phillips curve is given by the curve H_1 in Fig. 1 below, and $Y = Y_1$.

(a) at what rate are unit costs rising? _____
(b) what is the expected rate of inflation? _____

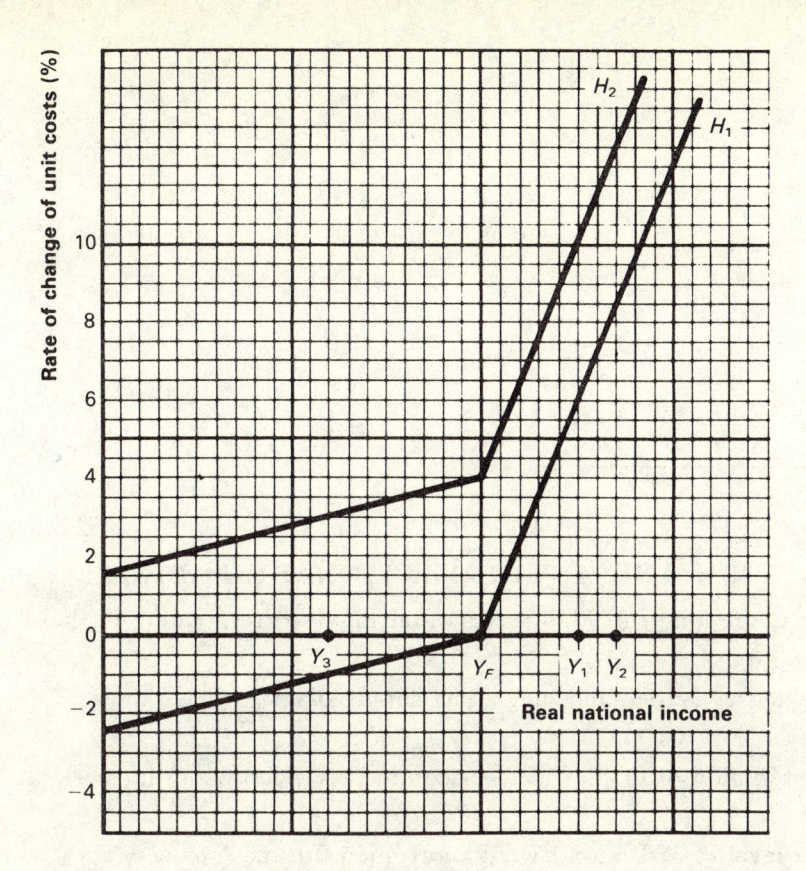

Fig. 1

Q21 If the SRPC is given by the curve H_2 in Fig. 1,

(a) at what rate are unit costs rising? _____
(b) what is the expected rate of inflation? _____

Q22 If the SRPC is the curve H_2 but the level of real national income falls to Y_3,

(a) at what rate are unit costs rising? _____
(b) what is the expected rate of inflation? _____

Q23 In the case just described, are people likely to reduce their expectations of inflation if they form

(a) extrapolative expectations? _____
(b) adaptive expectations? _____
(c) rational expectations? _____

Q24 Which of the following statements are consistent with Lipsey's discussion of the expectations-augmented Phillips curve?

(a) The short-run Phillips curve shows a positive relationship between income and price levels.
(b) A validated inflation can continue indefinitely when the economy is at full employment.
(c) Fiscal policy expanding at a constant rate will result in a constant rate of inflation.
(d) The short-run Phillips curve shows that the lower the unemployment rate, the more rapid the rate of inflation.
(e) Any validated stable inflation rate is compatible with potential output.

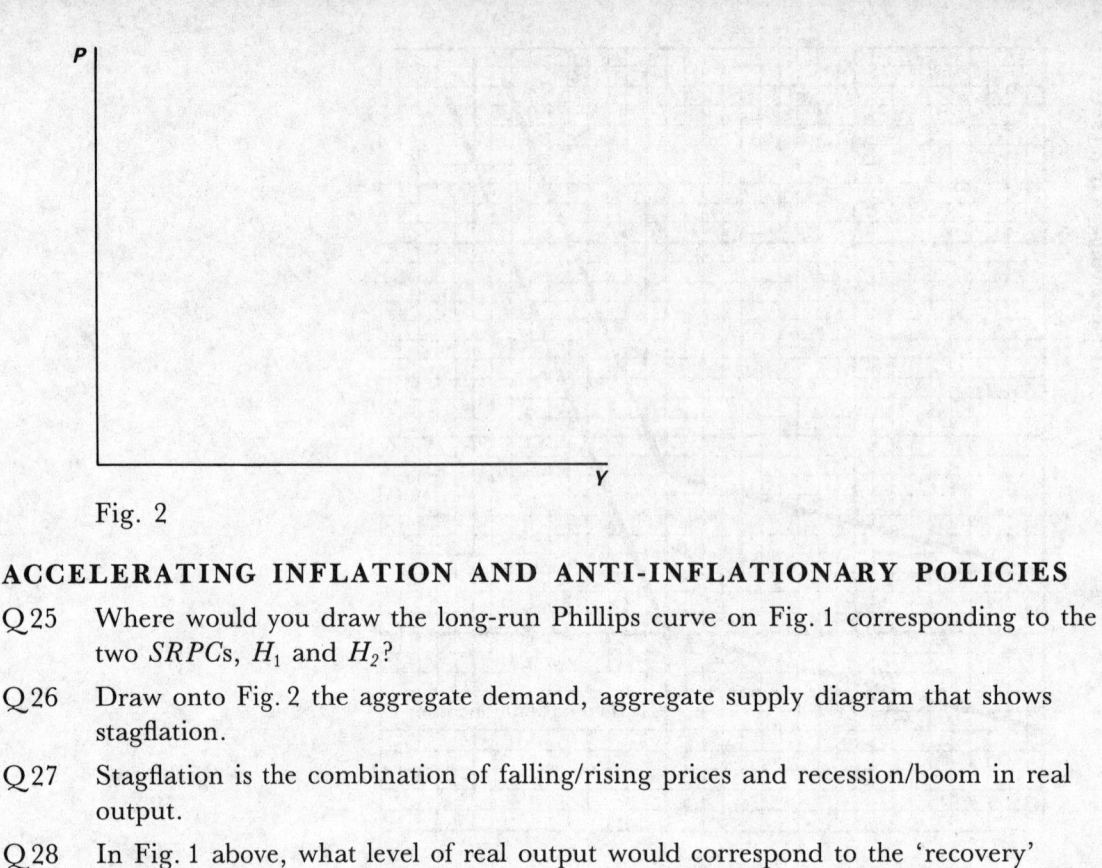

Fig. 2

ACCELERATING INFLATION AND ANTI-INFLATIONARY POLICIES

Q 25 Where would you draw the long-run Phillips curve on Fig. 1 corresponding to the two *SRPC*s, H_1 and H_2?

Q 26 Draw onto Fig. 2 the aggregate demand, aggregate supply diagram that shows stagflation.

Q 27 Stagflation is the combination of falling/rising prices and recession/boom in real output.

Q 28 In Fig. 1 above, what level of real output would correspond to the 'recovery' (Phase 3) discussed by Lipsey in Chapter 34?
   (a) (in words) _____
   (b) (in symbols) _____

Q 29 One could argue that the UK economy had a large recessionary gap until the mid-1980s, as it recovered from the recession of 1982. However, by 1988 inflation had reappeared and reached 8% in 1989. Draw on to Fig. 3 (on p. 201) a diagram analogue to Fig. 34.11, to show this process. The three stages in your model of the business cycle should be: (i) recession of the early 1980s; (ii) inflation of the late 1980s; and (iii) recovery. In stage (ii), show how an inflationary gap can be created by a combination of falling input prices (especially oil) and rising productivity; both factors that affect the SRAS curve.

Q 30 In the problem above, name two policies that could cause the fall in aggregate demand necessary for a return to full employment and low inflation (recovery).

_____
_____

QUESTIONS FOR DISCUSSION

1 Why is the short-run Phillips curve steep above and flat below potential output? What difference would it make if it were linear?

2 Under what circumstances will the Phillips curve shift up or down?

3 Explain carefully the difference between a theory of inflation based on an independent wage push and a theory where wage changes are endogenous.

4 Suppose there is a tendency for more women to join the labour force over time. In these circumstances, can the Phillips curve of Fig. 34.5(i) still be changed into the transformed Phillips curve of Fig. 34.5(iii)? Explain how the transformation would have to be altered.

P

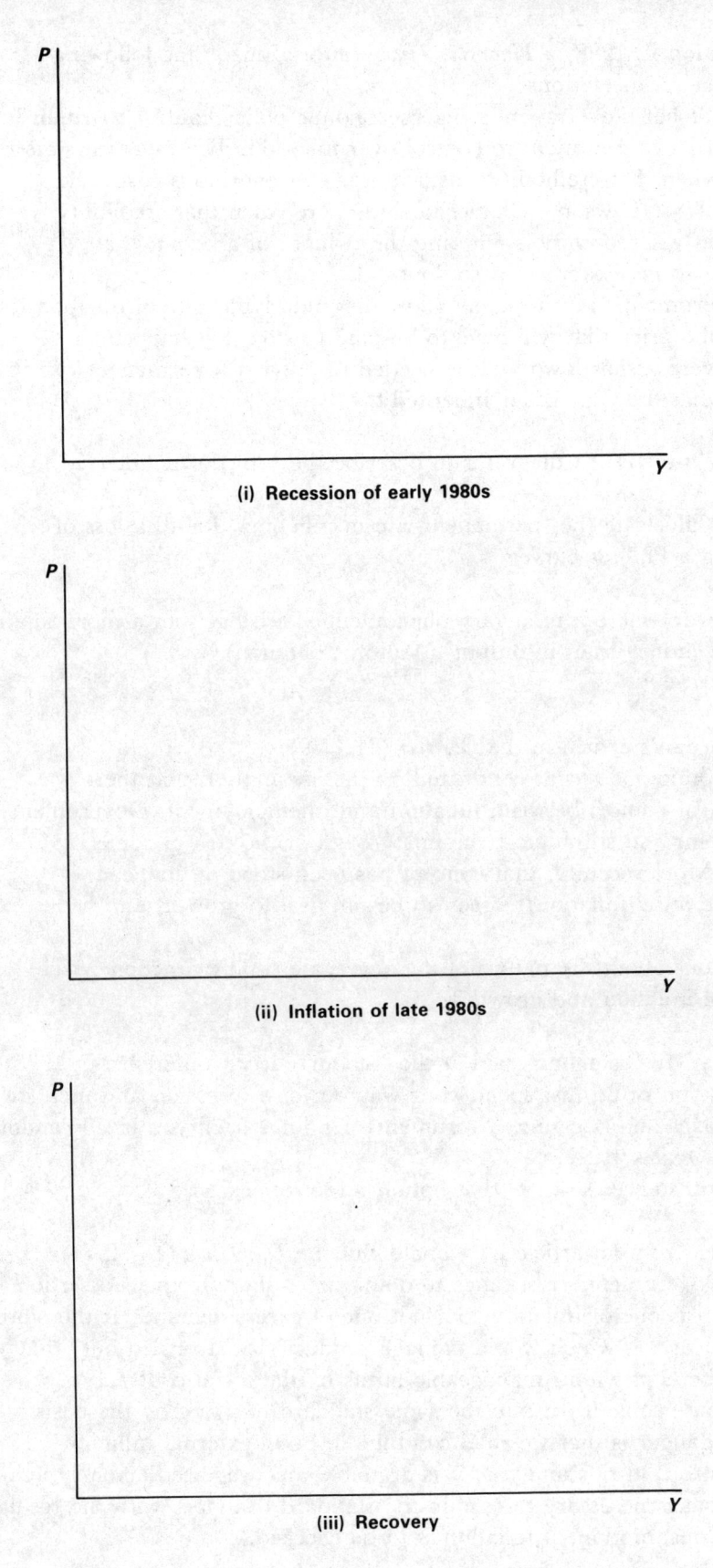

(i) Recession of early 1980s

P

(ii) Inflation of late 1980s

P

(iii) Recovery

Fig. 3

5   In the face of rising inflation in 1988, a *Financial Times* editorial made the following comments about inflationary expectations:

'The history of the Thatcher Government's macroeconomic policy could be written in terms of the credibility of its commitment to control over inflation. The four years after its election in 1979 was when that credibility was acquired – at enormous cost. The subsequent years, those of Mr Lawson's Chancellorship, were when that credibility was exploited. Now, when the UK economy is entering the twilight of a boom, that credibility has never been so necessary – and so doubtful....

'It is not that the Government can ultimately allow the underlying rate of inflation to rise. The issue is rather the price that will have to be paid to stop that happening....

'More bluntly, how severe a slowdown will be needed to prevent a permanent rise in inflation above the level that the Chancellor inherited?'

(a) How would you use *AD-AS* diagrams to describe the 'slowdown' referred to here?
(b) How would you illustrate the 'permanent rise in inflation' due to a loss of credibility, using a Phillips curve?

6   'Inflation is always and everywhere a monetary phenomenon, arising from a more rapid growth in the quantity of money than in output' (Milton Friedman).

Do you agree?

7   Extract from William Keegan's article in the *Observer* (21.1.79):

'For many years, economic policy was conducted on the assumption that there was some sort of "trade off" (or choice) between inflation and unemployment. Governments could reduce unemployment and stimulate economic growth at the cost of some acceleration of inflation. More recently, that concept has been stood on its head. Inflation, especially accelerating inflation, is seen to be inimical to growth, and hence to employment.'

What are the assumptions about the nature of the aggregate supply function which underlie this discussion of inflation and growth?

8   The then Prime Minister, Mr Callaghan, said at the Labour Party Conference in 1976:

'We used to think that you could just spend your way out of a recession and increase employment by cutting taxes and boosting government spending. I tell you in all candour that that option no longer exists....'

What must be the circumstances so that 'that option no longer exists'?

9   The following is an extract from an article by Ronald Butt in *The Times* (18.12.74):

'The rationale of the Government's resistance to doing more starts from its assertion that our domestic problem is one of inflation, but not one of excess demand. It therefore insists that deflationary measures which would damage productivity are ruled out; that the wage increases must be kept within manageable limits by the social contract...

'If wage increases enable people to sustain the same standard of living on the basis of rising import prices, the danger is that we shall continue to build external inflation into our own economic structure. On this analysis, it is arguable that wage settlements ought to be marginally *below* what is necessary to sustain the standard of living, with the result that people reduce their consumption, if inflation is to be checked.'

(a) Can inflation occur without excess demand?
(b) Evaluate the argument that wage settlements should not keep up with the cost of living in order to check inflation.

10   Two ways of fighting inflation are:

   (i)   to reduce the government's fiscal deficit $(G - T)$.
   (ii) to raise interest rates and/or slow the rate of growth of money supply.

   In late 1988, the British Chancellor of the Exchequer, Mr Nigel Lawson, told the Confederation of British Industry that the Government would keep interest rates '"as high as we need, for as long as we need' to control inflation... He stressed that the Government would not modify its tight monetary and fiscal policies to accommodate inflationary pressures caused by high wage increases.' (*Financial Times*, 24.11.88.) What effect could this policy of tight money be expected to have:

   (a) on the aggregate supply curve?
   (b) on output?
   (c) on prices?

11   The Director-General of the Confederation of British Industry (CBI), Mr J. Banham, complained that to combat the inflation of 1988/89 the British government should concentrate more on (i) above and less on (ii). He was reported as saying that 'wage increases in the manufacturing sector were not causing inflationary pressure... He defended the right of employers to give increases that were matched by improvements in productivity' (*Financial Times*, 18.10.88).

   (a) Can you explain why the CBI would be against using high interest rates to fight inflation?
   (b) If wage rises are due to productivity increases alone, then will high interest rates have the desired effect of reducing inflationary pressure? Explain.

CHAPTER 35
Employment and Unemployment

So far we have examined how the government can eliminate unemployment when actual income falls short of potential income, but we have not examined the different kinds of unemployment which can occur.

Q1   At potential output, Y_F, is there any unemployment? _____

Q2   If unemployment can be eradicated by expansionary fiscal and monetary policy, what sort of unemployment are we talking about? _____

Q3   What other categories of unemployment does Lipsey discuss? _____

Q4   'Full employment' means only that there is no frictional/structural/demand-deficient unemployment.

Q5   At the natural rate of unemployment, frictional/real-wage/demand-deficient unemployment may still exist.

Q6   In 1942, while in the Treasury, Keynes wrote a Memorandum in which he classified unemployment as follows:[1]

(a)   the hard core of the virtually unemployable;
(b)   seasonal factors;
(c)   men moving between jobs;
(d)   misfits of trade or locality due to lack of mobility;
(e)   a deficiency in the aggregate effective demand for labour.

Are these categories the same as the ones used by Lipsey?
_____
_____

Q7   If labour were homogeneous, perfectly informed and mobile, would there be any structural and frictional unemployment? _____

Q8   Why is the u–v curve in Lipsey's Fig. 35.3 hyperbolic and not a straight line? _____

Q9   The u–v curve in Fig. 1 below shows the combinations of vacancies v, and unemployment, u, consistent with a given level of structural and frictional unemployment. What is the level of structural and frictional unemployment assumed here?

[1] See R. Kahn, 'Unemployment as seen by the Keynesians' in G.D.N.Worswick (ed.), *The Concept and Measurement of Involuntary Unemployment* (George Allen & Unwin, 1976).

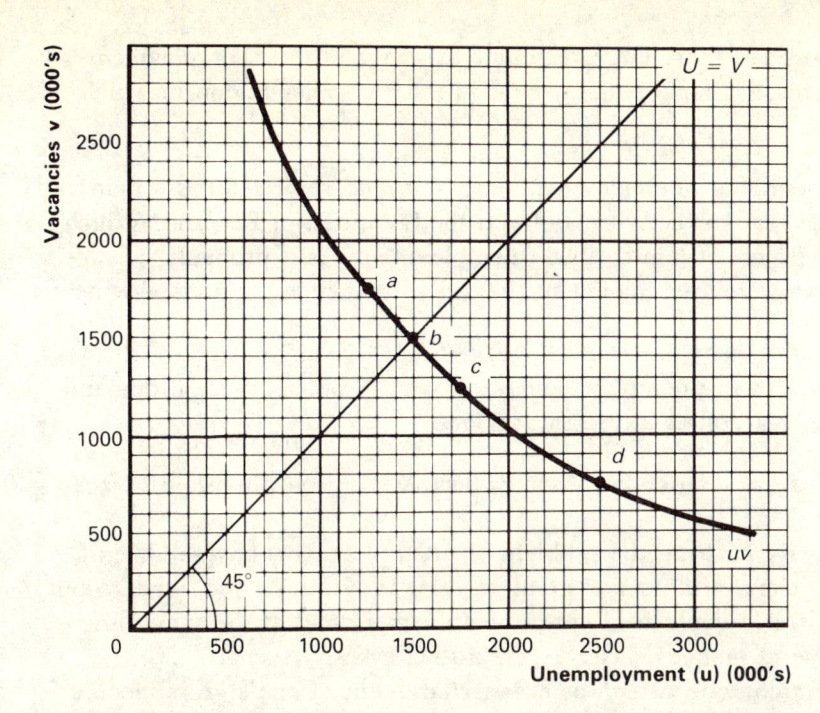

Fig. 1

Q 10 If the economy is at point *a* in Fig. 1, at one point in the business cycle, is the economy in a recession or a boom? _____

Q 11 If structural unemployment increases, how would Fig. 1 change? _____

Q 12 What effect on the curve would a rise in unemployment benefit have? _____

Q 13 Over the late 1970s and early 1980s, structural unemployment was rising/falling in Britain.

Q 14 If the real product wage is too high throughout the economy, and real-wage unemployment results, at what point in Fig. 1 is the economy likely to be? _____

Q 15 If the number of persons seeking jobs exceeds the number of unfilled vacancies, demand-deficient unemployment necessarily exists. T/F

QUESTIONS FOR DISCUSSION

TABLE 1. Unemployment Rates for Selected Regions of the UK

	1983	1988
Northern Ireland	20%	16%
Southeast	10%	5%
North	17%	12%
Wales	17%	10%
West Midlands	18%	9%
UK overall	14%	8%

1 Look at Table 1 above. Why are there large regional variations in the unemployment figures? Outline the main reasons for unemployment in the particular region in which you live.

2 From 1983 to 1988 all the regional unemployment rates fell, and some fell more than others. Compare the figures for Northern Ireland and the Southeast of England. Which area seems to have a higher level of non-cyclical unemployment? Is it probably structural, frictional, or real-wage unemployment that keeps that region's unemployment rate high? Explain.

3 Given these regional differences in unemployment rates, what problems arise if demand-management policies are used to offset a recessionary gap?

4 The following is an extract from a letter from Mr Robert A. Paterson published in *The Times* (9.9.78):

'The traditional methods (of clearing the problem of unemployment) have all been tried by most modern politicians without any great success. Would it be too naive to put forward a simple solution which would help cure unemployment and at the same time help to solve the other curse of modern society – the no-tax cash payment?

'If one was allowed to employ one person as a first charge out of one's gross income this would help. At the same time if the tax bands were lowered at the lower end, the incentive to work would be given and a new group of future employers would emerge.

'The new executive class would then be able to afford gardeners, chauffeurs, etc. and the relevant "moonlighting" would be left within the tax structure thus giving work and extra net income to those who want to work but who would have been put off by the higher rate bands of taxation.'

What do you think of Mr Paterson's proposal?

5 Blake Leslie wrote to the *Birmingham Post* on 2.3.83 as follows:

'During the water workers' dispute the phrase "the earnings league" was used *ad nauseam*.

'Whoever first coined this expression as a justification for another wage increase has surely done incalculable harm over the years to British industry by encouraging competitive demands for no other reason than to be one up on one's fellows.

'But the field of comparison, football, is indeed ironic, for it is in almost as parlous a condition as is, alas, so much industry.

'Constant rivalry for rises will neither score goals nor achieve promotion only relegation, and in the end put more firms out of business. There will be no point in being top of the league then.'

Is Mr Leslie's letter about relative wages or about the average real wage?

6 In the House of Commons on 18.3.83, Mr Arthur Bottomley said that 'low pay caused great sacrifice and was a nationwide problem. The Government's philosophy was job creation through low pay, but this did not work.

'Low wages, as well as being a cause of poverty, hardship and injustice, were also the cause of gross economic inefficiency. Whole industries had come to rely on low wages as a way of life. As a result there was high staff turn-over, low productivity, and little incentive to invest in training.

'The main cause of unemployment in Britain today, as most people now recognized, was the low level of demand. A minimum wage would raise the living standards and therefore spending power of the poorest workers and provide a stimulus for jobs.' (*The Times*, 19.3.83)

Evaluate Mr Bottomley's argument.

7   'There are many areas, from gardening to retailing, where the labour to capital ratio changes quickly in response to labour and capital costs. But there is much long-lived equipment that cannot easily shift to new production methods.

   'The moral is that the main influences of real wages on employment are long term.' (Samuel Brittan, *Financial Times*, 16.9.82.)

   Explain why the effects of changes in real wages are experienced in the long, rather than short, term.

8   '... this year's Budget [will] raise tax thresholds and child allowances, aiming to disarm the poverty traps which subject people on low incomes to high marginal tax rates (thought to deter them from seeking work).

   'But the high and still rising unemployment level shows that encouraging people to enter the labour market should scarcely be the top priority; the main problem of that market just now is a deficiency of demand. In this context it is not surprising that industrial lobbyists have been clamouring for abolition of the National Insurance Surcharge, which is a flat-rate tax on the hiring of additional workers.

   'Arguments against the abolition (or even reduction) of the NIS have hinged on the idea that an income-tax cut would be more effective as an instrument of reflation.' (Jeremy Stone, *Financial Times*, 14.3.83.)

   Evaluate the argument for abolition of the National Insurance Surcharge against the case for an income-tax cut. Are both tax cuts examples of demand management?

9   The British Labour Party's policy review of 1988 mentioned that 'Britain's labour force is becoming more divided. For example, there is a "core" of relatively secure workers and a "periphery" of less secure workers employed by small firms and sub-contractors. Individual employment rights are being eroded under the Tories and low pay condemns an increasing number of people to poverty, compounded by little or no job security.' (The Labour Party, *A Productive and Competitive Economy*, July, 1988.)

   What types of unemployment are these 'insecure', 'peripheral' workers likely to experience? How likely is real-wage unemployment to be a problem as the periphery gets larger relative to the core of permanently employed workers? Give examples of job categories that you would classify as relatively insecure.

10 In 1988 Mr Michael Meacher, Labour MP for Oldham, described the changes made in the reporting conventions for unemployment figures. He wrote,

   'For the first time ever, all (350,000) young people on Youth Training Schemes are suddenly being counted as "employed" ... In addition last month, the Government abruptly stopped counting the number of unemployed school leavers at all. Last year these youngsters totalled 100,000 to 130,000 over the three summer months. On top of that, a further 106,000 under-18 unemployed people will be unceremoniously offloaded from the jobless figures from October because they are no longer allowed to claim unemployment benefit. Then next September everyone on the new Employment Training scheme, for which 600,000 places are targeted, will suddenly be classified as "employed". The unemployment rate will again be reduced artificially by another 500,000 supposedly in work.

   '... Since 1979 there have been at least 16 other changes in the methods for counting the unemployed, all but one of which have had the effect of reducing the total ...

   'If all the Government's 19 statistical fiddles listed here were discounted, the real level of unemployment would be revealed to be still almost exactly 3m.' (*Financial Times*, 14.9.88.)

Do you think trainees should be included in the unemployed figures? Do you think unemployed school-leavers should be included? If so, what type of unemployment do these two categories represent?

11 Evaluate the claim that 'when there is classical unemployment, real wages are too high', from (i) a positive and (ii) a normative point of view.

CHAPTER 36

Fluctuations and Growth

On pp. 634–635 Lipsey describes four stages in a cycle and he then goes on to examine attempts to explain why national income fluctuates in the short term. In the first part of this chapter of the Workbook we concentrate on changes in investment expenditure: in particular we examine in more detail the accelerator and multiplier-accelerator theories discussed by Lipsey on pp. 638–640.

Investment is also important in determining potential output. So far (and in Fig. 36.1), we have considered the level of potential output to be fixed, but in the long run the aggregate supply schedule will shift to the right if the economy grows. Investment in capital, together with changes in both the quantity and quality of labour, will affect the growth rate, and the second part of this chapter will turn to an examination of the factors determining the level of potential income in the long term.

THEORIES OF THE CYCLE

Q1   At the peak of the trade cycle there is no unemployment. T/F

Q2   During a recovery unemployment falls. T/F

Q3   Aggregate demand shocks can be illustrated using the *IS/LM* model. T/F

Q4   A downward shift in the aggregate supply function could cause a boom. T/F

Q5   A trough always follows a recession. T/F

THE ACCELERATOR AND MULTIPLIER-ACCELERATOR THEORIES

The rate of change of national income is usually a reasonable approximation to the rate of change of output. So a change in income usually means a change in output, and so long as entrepreneurs have some desired ratio of capital equipment to output (a ratio based on profit maximization, convention, or anything else), they will have sought to change the level of their capital to produce this different output. If they were successful, therefore, investment (positive or negative) will have taken place.

Q6   Can you represent the simple accelerator theory symbolically? _____

Q7   Is the accelerator coefficient likely to be smaller or greater than 1? Greater/Smaller. Explain why. _____

Q8   Suppose a manufacturer is currently producing £200,000 worth of goods. He has 20 machines, each costing £15,000 and each capable of producing £10,000 worth of goods in a year.

(a) How many £s worth of capital does he need to produce £1 of output p.a.?

_____

(b) If demand increases so that the manufacturer could sell an additional £50,000 of goods next year, how many additional machines would he have to purchase?

_____

Q 9 Complete the following table:

(a) What assumption are we making about delivery times for new capital?

_____

(b) What is happening to the capital stock in period 8?

_____

(c) This example is an instance of capital-deepening rather than capital-widening. T/F

TABLE 1

Year	Sales (£000)	Change in sales (£000)	Required stock of capital assuming capital-output ratio of 4/1 (£000)	Net investment (£000)
1	15	0		0
2	20			
3	24			
4	25			
5	26			
6	27			
7	27			
8	25			

Three causes of cumulative movements are described in Lipsey on pp. 639–640.

(1) the multiplier;

(2) the accelerator;

(3) self-realizing expectations.

Q 10 Which of these do the following exemplify? (They may exemplify more than one, or none.)

(a) A factory's installation of new plant to meet rising demand for its product.

_____

(b) New expenditure of the owners of the factory on holidays in Spain.

_____

(c) Expenditure of the owners on Jaguar cars. _____

(d) If speculators expect the rate of interest to fall, they will demand more bonds and less money. The rate of interest falls as a result. _____

Q 11 There is a ceiling beyond which income cannot rise in the short run. What is it?

_____

Q 12 What sort of investment generally continues, even in the worst slumps? _____

Q 13 If gross investment did fall to zero, what would still prevent national income from falling to zero? _____

The multiplier-accelerator process explains why turning points need not necessarily be at the floors and ceilings mentioned above. The multiplier is, of course, straightforward. Think about what additional assumption is involved in the multiplier-accelerator theory.

Illustrating the multiplier-accelerator cycle. Consider a very simple economy with no foreign trade in which consumption is a function of the previous year's income. Symbolically we can write this as $C_t = f(Y_{t-1})$, where t means the current year and $t-1$ stands for last year.

Q 14 Thus, $t-2$ would mean _____
We are given the following information:

$C_t = 100 + 0.5Y_{t-1}$
$I_n = 1.2(Y_{t-1} - Y_{t-2})$, where I_n represents net investment.

Replacement investment amounts to £20m a year and government expenditure is £80m in period t and rises to £90m in period $t+1$. Now fill in the columns of Table 2 below (all amounts in £ million).

Q 15 Between period $t+1$ and period $t+3$:

(a) output increased by approximately _____ %;
(b) total investment increased by _____ %.

Q 16 In period $t+7$, output has fallen and replacement investment is _____
Explain your answer.

Q 17 The increase in government spending starts an upswing which lasts until period _____. Output rises at an increasing rate up to period $t+2$ but then slows down as the rate of induced investment declines. Output falls from period _____ until period _____ when it begins to rise again. Unless the system receives any further 'shocks', it will eventually reach an equilibrium income of £ _____

TABLE 2

Period	C_c	I_r	I_n	Total investment	G	Y	Change in Y
t	300	20	0	20	80	400	0
$t+1$		20			90		
$t+2$							
$t+3$							
$t+4$							
$t+5$							
$t+6$							
$t+7$							
$t+8$							
$t+9$							
$t+10$							
...							

Q 18 Stop-go policies can eliminate the business cycle. T/F

Q 19 With a fixed capital-output ratio, net investment occurs only when it is necessary to raise the rate of employment/stock of capital/rate of sales.

Q 20 In Chapter 32 we saw the Keynesian investment function $I = a_1 + br$, where b is negative. Is the accelerator theory of investment complementary to, or incompatible with, the earlier approach? _____

Q 21 According to the hypotheses of this chapter, net investment would be likely to occur

(a) when profits are falling, in order to raise them.
(b) in the recovery rather than the recession stage of the cycle.
(c) when prices are falling, because capital is cheap then.

ECONOMIC GROWTH

In this section we consider what factors affect or determine the rate of growth of goods and services. Much of the chapter in Lipsey is taken up with discussing the economic and social implications of growth for any society and with weighing the benefits against the costs. This is an area in which opinions are divided and there are no easy, clear-cut answers – you will have to form your own opinion. In this part of the Workbook, we will concentrate on extending our understanding of the concepts and of their usefulness in analysing the process of growth.

In Fig. 1 the production-possibility curve for a very simple economy is drawn, in which only two goods, vegetables and clothing, are produced.

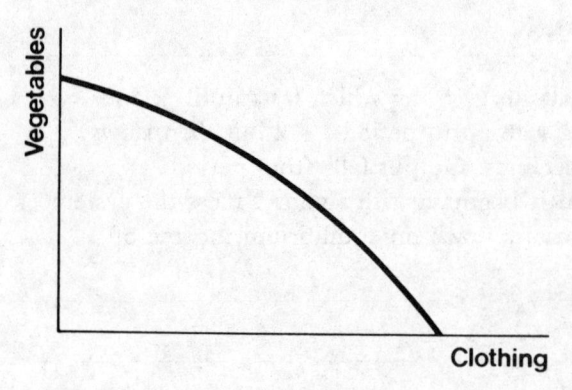

Fig. 1

Q 22 Potential national income is represented by _____

Q 23 If productive capacity is not being fully utilized, this will be represented by _____

Q 24 What will change in Fig. 1 if

(a) new varieties of vegetable seed are discovered which yield larger crops?
(b) the minimum school-leaving age is *lowered* by one year? _____
(c) the country receives some looms under a UN aid programme? _____

Q25 Suppose now that the country starts to produce investment goods such as tractors, knitting machines, etc. As we have seen from Q24, growth is represented by a movement outwards of the production-possibility curve. From Fig. 2, would you expect the rate of growth to be greater if current output is represented by point A or point B?

Q26 Summarize the main sources of economic growth: _____
_____

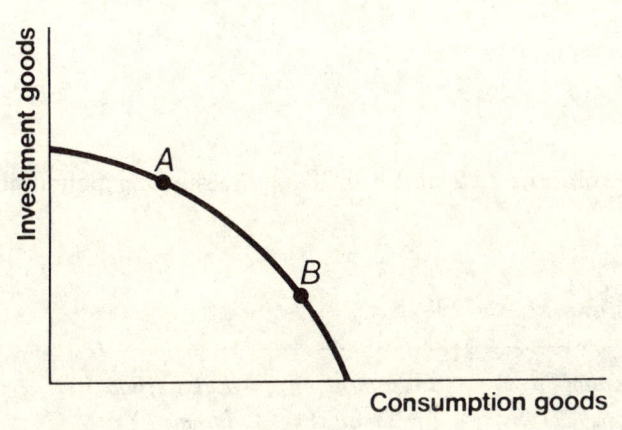

Fig. 2

If we put a larger proportion of our resources into investment goods, we do so in the hope that the consumption we sacrifice today will be compensated by higher consumption levels, i.e. standards of living, in the future. Problems facing any economy therefore include what proportion of national income to invest and how to ensure that the desired level of investment does occur. To extend our understanding of these and other problems, we will work through a very simple model of growth.

Output depends both on the amount of available resources and on their productivity, and potential output (Y_F) is that output which is achieved when this productive capacity is operating at its fullest extent. We will start by assuming that the relationship between potential output (Y_F) and the capital stock (K) takes the following form:

$$Y_F = \frac{1}{\alpha} K$$

Re-arranging this, we get $$\frac{K}{Y_F} = \alpha$$

Now K/Y_F is the capital-output ratio, but what is α? Well, α represents the amount of capital which is needed to produce one unit of total output – or, in other words, $1/\alpha$ is the productivity of capital. To take an example, if the marginal efficiency of capital is known to be 0.20, then

$$Y_F = 0.2K$$

and *five* units of capital will be needed to produce *one* unit of output.

Q27 If the marginal efficiency of capital is constant and equal to 0.25, what is the equilibrium capital-output ratio? _____

Q 28 Assume that in 1985 a country's capital stock is £160,000m, and that the marginal efficiency of capital is the same as in Q 27. What is the value of potential output? _____

(Note that by assuming the marginal efficiency of capital is constant, the capital-output ratio is also constant. This is of course unrealistic – see Lipsey, Fig. 36.5.)

Q 29 Now suppose that in 1985 investment amounted to £8,000m and that it is increasing at a rate of 2% per annum. (To keep matters simple, we will assume that all capital has an infinite life so that we can ignore depreciation.) This means that capital stock amounted to:

(a) In 1986 _____
(b) In 1987 _____

You should now be able to complete columns 1, 2 and 3 in Table 3, showing potential income, capital stock and investment.

TABLE 3 (INVESTMENT INCREASING AT 2% P.A.)

	Potential income (Y_F) 1	Capital stock (K) 2	Investment (= savings) 3	Equilibrium income (Y) 4
	(£m)	(£m)	(£m)	(£m)
1985	_____	160,000	8,000	_____
1986	_____	_____	_____	_____
1987	_____	_____	_____	_____
1988	_____	_____	_____	_____

Q 30 What is the annual rate of growth of potential output? _____

We now need to explore whether the actual equilibrium level of output achieved by the economy will be the same as the potential output – in other words, will we be on the production-possibility frontier as it moves outwards, or inside it?

Q 31 For simplicity, we will assume that in this economy there is no government sector and no foreign trade. If consumption $(C) = 0.8Y$, the multiplier is _____.

Q 32 Assuming the country is producing at full capacity in 1985, consumption will be _____ and savings will amount to _____.
Now complete the remaining column in Table 3 showing the equilibrium levels of income.

Q 33 Does the country continue to produce at full capacity? Yes/No
What is the actual growth rate achieved? _____

Q 34 Why does the economy run at less than full capacity? _____

Complete Table 4 on the assumption that investment is now increasing *at 5% per annum.*

TABLE 4 (INVESTMENT INCREASING AT 5% P.A.)

	Potential income (Y_F) (£m)	Capital stock (K) (£m)	Investment (= savings) (£m)	Equilibrium income (Y) (£m)
1985	_____	160,000	8,000	_____
1986	_____	_____	_____	_____
1987	_____	_____	_____	_____
1988	_____	_____	_____	_____

Q 35 What is now the actual growth rate? _____

Q 36 What is the rate of growth of potential output? _____

Q 37 If population is 50 million in 1985 and is growing at an annual rate of 3%, find income *per capita* in:

  (a) 1985 _____
  (b) 1988, when income reaches the level shown in Table 3: _____
  (c) 1988, when income reaches the level shown in Table 4: _____

MACRO THEORIES OF GROWTH

Q 38 The downward slope of the marginal efficiency of capital (*MEC*) curve means that there are diminishing/constant/increasing returns to capital.

Q 39 A single *MEC* curve assumes profits/capital stock/labour force to be held constant.

Q 40 Population growth could be represented by a movement along/shift up in the *MEC* curve.

Q 41 Define the following symbols in words:

  (a) K/Y. _____
  (b) Y/K. _____
  (c) ΔK. _____
  (d) *MEC*. _____
   which in theory equals the rate of _____ for a given stock of capital.

Q 42 A rising rate of return to capital over time (see Fig. 36.5) suggests that:

  (a) the *MEC* curve is upward-sloping.
  (b) the capital stock is shrinking.
  (c) the rate of investment exceeds the rate at which new investment opportunities are created.
  (d) the rate at which new investment opportunities are created exceeds the rate of investment.

Q 43 Which of the following policies would be put forward by the supply-side economists?

  (a) reduce the income-tax rate for high-income earners;
  (b) increase taxation of business profits;
  (c) remove taxes on interest received from bonds and deposit accounts;
  (d) remove the value-added tax.

QUESTIONS FOR DISCUSSION

1 'The only thing we have to fear is fear itself – nameless, unreasoning, unjustified terror which paralyses needed efforts to convert retreat into advance...' So said Franklin D. Roosevelt in his Inaugural Address in 1933 at the height of the most serious depression ever recorded in American history. Is this statement consistent with the theory of the business cycle we have developed? What theory of the cycle was Roosevelt propounding?

2 A great deal of talk in the Great Depression was of 'priming the pump'. How might a small amount of government expenditure do this? What might happen if business confidence is very, very low?

3 Why do we ever level off, once we get into the downward spiral of a depression?

4 Should the UK Government be encouraged by the headline, 'End of US recession in sight'?

5 The following are extracts from a letter to *The Times* (5.2.75) from Professor Nicholson of the London Graduate School of Business Studies:

'Once again, with a reported fall in industrial investment intentions, it is presumed that the United Kingdom economy must decline further. But what do we mean by investment and how much is necessary anyway?

'We tend to think of investment in industry as the purchase and installation of new shiny machinery. In fact, investment consists of any change in the production system which contributes to the better capability of a company to meet market needs.

'...why do we want all this investment in machinery? The most detailed surveys of industry so far undertaken (excluding oil and chemicals) have shown that machine utilization averages 40 per cent; that work-in-progress in the United Kingdom is twice the level of the United States; that despite the high stocks we have hopeless shortages; that only 5 per cent of deliveries are made on or before their due date; that what you get is in all probability a part delivery; and that for every hour a job spends being worked on it (there are about 20 hours spent waiting around).'

Is Professor Nicholson arguing that investment is not a prerequisite of growth?

6 What is the basic notion of the accelerator theory? Is investment endogenous or exogenous in this theory? Why, when we assume investment to be determined by an accelerator, can we not illustrate the investment function by drawing a graph showing investment expenditure and the level of income?

7 It might take some time to complete an investment project. Can you give examples of lags in connection with government expenditure? Do you think the time-lags will be the same whether the change in expenditure is an increase or a decrease?

8 Ian Richardson writing in the *Birmingham Post* (23.1.79) said '...the four indicators (share prices, short-term interest rates, companies' net acquisition of assets, housing starts) which traditionally give twelve months' warning of changes in the course of an economy were pointing to a recession ahead from October 1977'.

Can you provide an explanation why these 'leading indicators' might suggest changes in national income?

9 In mid-1988 as Britain's inflation rate rose and consumer spending reached a new peak, the *Economist* magazine made the following remarks in its editorial pages:

'Britain's chancellor of the exchequer, Mr Nigel Lawson, cherishes his reputation for unflappability. Accordingly, he was "relaxed" this week about trade figures which came as a nasty surprise to everybody else. The widening trade gap is only one sign among many that the British economy is over-heating. The writing on the wall outside

11 Downing Street now reads "danger: excessive demand". If Mr Lawson isn't worried, he should be.' (*The Economist*, 2.7.88, p. 11.)

What could be done to curb aggregate demand? Would your remedy cure the trade gap (current account deficit)?

10 Opponents of growth stress the costs of economic growth, many of which are difficult (if not impossible) to measure. Are there any *benefits* that go unmeasured by conventional measures of economic growth?

11 On which side would you line up in the growth/anti-growth argument? State your reasons carefully.

12 Which groups in a capitalist society gain the most from growth in the short run? In the long run? Which groups bear most of the costs of recession?

CHAPTER 37

Demand Management 1: Fiscal Policy

Now that we have some understanding of what determines the level of national income and hence employment, we can begin our study of *demand management*. In this chapter we concentrate on fiscal policy, that is, the management of aggregate demand through tax and (government) expenditure changes, and we explore how the government can use the multiplier effect to stabilize the economy. An alternative way of managing aggregate demand is through monetary policy, which we will examine in the next chapter. For the moment we concentrate on shifts in the *IS* curve and assume that the government keeps the nominal money supply constant.

Q1 Shifts in the *IS/AS/LM* curves can be expressed as corresponding shifts in the aggregate demand (*AD*) curve. (Choose two of the three.) _____ and _____

Q2 Stabilization policy refers to changing the *AD/LRAS/SRAS* curve (choose one) in order to achieve potential output and full employment.

Q3 Supply-side economics refers to theories that predict shifts in the *IS/LM/AD/SRAS/LRAS* curves. (Choose two.) _____ and _____

THE THEORY OF FISCAL POLICY

In Chapter 29 we looked at equilibrium ($Y = E$) in a three-sector economy, and in Chapter 32 we derived the *IS* curve for a simple two-sector economy. We can now combine these analyses by finding a new equation for the *IS* curve incorporating the third sector, government. Before doing so, check that you know a few terms.

Q4 When the Confederation of British Industry (CBI) argues against high interest rates as a way of combating inflation, it is using a supply-side/Keynesian/monetarist argument. Why?
_____
_____

Q5 Name the three 'private expenditure functions' referred to by Lipsey in Chapter 37.

(a) _____
(b) _____
(c) _____

Q6 What would the 'public expenditure function' be?

(a) (in words) _____
(b) (in symbols) _____

Q7 A balanced budget occurs when the PSBR is rising/zero/constant, the national debt is rising/zero/constant, and government spending

  (a) (in words) equals _____
  (b) (in symbols) $G =$ _____

Q8 What is the equilibrium condition underlying the *IS* curve?

  (a) (in words) _____
  (b) (in symbols) _____

Q9 Given the following functions, derive the *IS* curve. Find the equation first in terms of r and then in terms of Y.

  $C = a_0 + cY_d$ $0 < c < 1, \quad 0 < a_0$
  $I = a_1 + br$ $b < 0 < a_1$
  $T = tY$ $0 < t < 1$
  $G = G^*$
  $Q = Q^*$

  (a) $r =$ _____
  (b) $Y =$ _____
  (c) What is the intercept with the r axis? _____
  (d) What is the intercept with the Y axis? _____
  (e) What is the slope of the *IS* curve? _____

  (f) What is the (interest-constant) multiplier? _____

Q10 You are given the following information: $c = 0.8$, $t = 0.25$, $b = -20$, $a_0 = 0$, $a_1 =$ £140m, $G =$ £200m, $Q =$ £50m.

  (a) When $r = 6\%$, find the level of income at which there is equilibrium in the goods market. _____
  (b) What is the value of the (interest-constant) multiplier? _____

Now suppose that the current level of income means that there is substantial unemployment and the government decides to raise aggregate demand by fiscal policy. We start by examining the effect on the *IS* curve and we *assume that the interest rate is held at 6%*.

Q11 In order to raise the level of income, the government can increase _____ and/or decrease _____

Q12 Using the information in Question 10, and taking each option in turn, find the effect on income of the following:

  (a) Government expenditure on goods and services is increased by £10m. _____

  (b) Transfers are increased by £54m. _____
  (c) The tax rate is cut by 2%. _____
  (d) When the government increases spending on transfers or on goods and services, the *IS* curve shifts to the right and its slope is steeper/unchanged/less steep; a cut in the tax rate pivots the *IS* in a clockwise/anti-clockwise direction and the slope becomes more/less steep.

THE PARADOX OF THRIFT

Refer to Lipsey's Box 27.1 on p. 484 to review the concept of the paradox of thrift.

Q 13 What does the paradox of thrift predict will be the effect on the level of income and employment if households save more? _____

Q 14 We can use the information in Question 9 to illustrate this.

(a) Suppose that people wish to save more and the marginal propensity to save becomes 0.3. If r remains at 6% and all other figures remain the same, what will happen to the level of income? _____

(b) What is the size of the budget deficit? _____

(c) Suppose that the government decides to increase expenditure on goods and services in order to return income to its previous level of £650m. By how much will it have to increase government expenditure? (Use the multiplier.) _____

(d) As a result of increasing government expenditure, has the budget deficit changed? _____

(e) Suppose that, instead of changing government expenditure, the government cut the tax rate to 0.13. Would this return income to its previous level? _____ . What would happen to the budget deficit?

Q 15 During the post First World War crisis in Britain in the early 1920s unemployment rose to alarming heights and a large deficit appeared in the government's budget. Why do you think this deficit appeared?

(a) _____

In order to deal with this crisis, cuts were made in the programme of building houses for servicemen and in pension payments to widows, orphans and disabled servicemen. What items in the national income of the brave new world for which the servicemen had fought were affected by the cuts?

(b) Building-programme cuts which formed part of injections/withdrawals/transfer payments, and
(c) Pension cuts which formed part of injections/withdrawals/transfer payments.

What does the theory predict would have been the effect on the volume of unemployment of each of these cuts?

(d) Building programmes. _____
(e) Pensions. _____

Q 16 In 1930 Sir Oswald Mosley, then a member of the Labour Government, proposed that the government should step up the road-building programme. Would this have reduced or increased employment? _____

Q 17 'Saving always causes investment.' Is this consistent with the paradox-of-thrift theory, as presented here? Yes/No

Q 18 Work through the following 'Keynesian sequence':

(a) There is an autonomous increase in the desire to save.

(b) The *IS* curve shifts inwards/outwards.
(c) As a result, the level of income will rise/fall.
(d) When the income level changes, this raises/lowers the demand for transactions balances.
(e) Consequently wealth-holders will purchase/sell bonds and the interest rate will rise/fall.
(f) The asset market will return to equilibrium when an interest rate emerges such that _____

The paradox of thrift appears paradoxical because at the individual level relationships are ignored which are crucial at the aggregate level. At the individual level saving is done for many reasons but most of them can be reduced to the desire to have command over *future* rather than *present* goods. But the only way in which this can be achieved at the aggregate level is by physical investment – otherwise when the goods are demanded in the future there will be no capital equipment to produce them. *But our theory rules out any direct link between saving and investment*, so there is *no* assumption which states that aggregate saving now will enable more goods to be produced in the future.

FISCAL POLICY WHEN PRIVATE EXPENDITURE FUNCTIONS DO NOT SHIFT

Throughout this section we shall assume that the aggregate supply curve is perfectly elastic up to potential output and perfectly inelastic at the full-employment level of income.

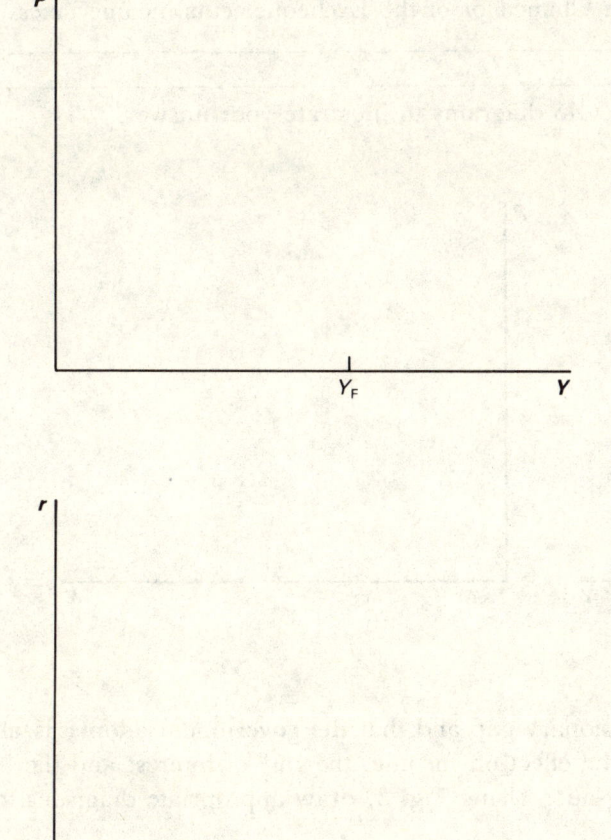

Fig. 1

Q19   Draw on the top diagram of Fig. 1, an aggregate supply curve with those characteristics. On the lower diagram, draw an *IS-LM* diagram showing full-employment income Y_F at the same point on the horizontal axis as in the *AD-AS* diagram.

Q20   Based on your reading of the whole of Chapter 37, fill in the table below with the expected effects of a debt-financed rise in government expenditure. Write 'no', 'some', or 'yes' as appropriate.

	Case 1 Y below Y_F and nominal money supply raised to cover ΔG	Case 2 Y below Y_F and no rise in nominal money supply	Case 3 Y equal to Y_F
Will crowding-out occur?			
Will prices rise?			
Will the interest rate rise?			

Now you are ready to work through some particular examples of these Keynesian cases.

Q21   If aggregate demand is equal to aggregate supply at the full-employment level of income, what would happen if the Chancellor of the Exchequer cuts income taxes? Is there any crowding-out? _____

Using Fig. 2, draw *IS-LM* and *AD-AS* diagrams to illustrate your answer.

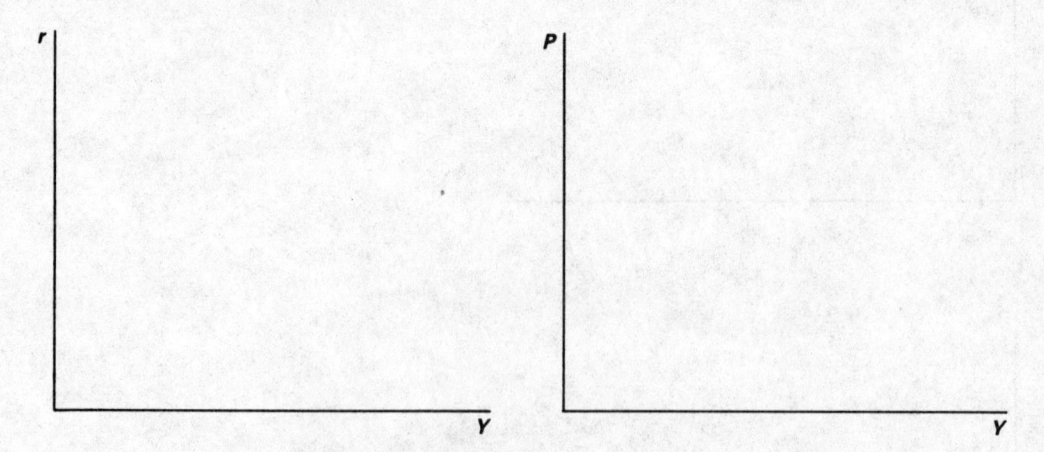

Fig. 2

Q22   Suppose now that there is a recessionary gap and that the government adopts fiscal policy to eliminate this. What is the effect on income, the rate of interest and the price level? Is there any crowding-out? Using Fig. 3, draw appropriate diagrams to illustrate your answer.

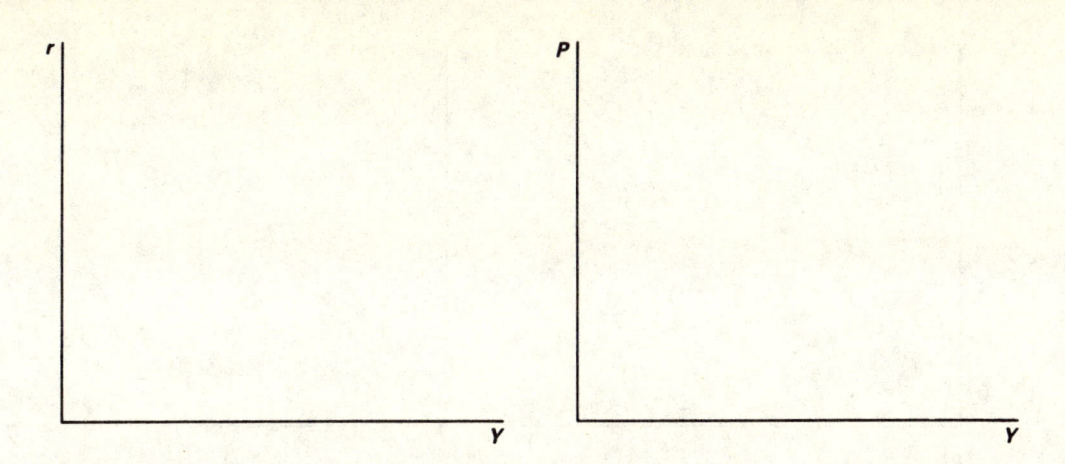

Fig. 3

Q23 You are given the following information about the economy:

$C = 0.8Y_d$
$I = 140 - 20r$
$T = 0.25Y$
$G = £200m$
$Q = £50m$
$M_d = 0.3Y - 12r$
$\dfrac{M^*}{P} = £150m.$

(a) Find the equilibrium levels of income and rate of interest. Does the budget balance? _____

(b) The government decides to increase expenditure on goods and services by £54m. What effect will this have? _____

(c) If the interest rate had been held at the original level, by how much would income have risen? _____ What is the crowding-out effect when the interest rate is allowed to vary? _____

(d) From your answer to (b), find the (interest-variable) multiplier. _____

(e) Now suppose that instead of increasing expenditure on goods and services, the government had increased transfers by £54m. What effect will this have? _____

(f) The remaining option is to cut the tax rate. If G and Q are left at their original levels but the tax rate is cut to 0.15, what will be the effect? _____

(g) Suppose that the government knows that $Y_F = £780m$, and decides to increase expenditure on goods and services so that the recessionary gap is eliminated. By what amount should the government increase G? _____

(h) When the government increases government expenditure or cuts taxes, the IS curve shifts inwards/outwards and the AD curve shifts to the left/right. At the new equilibrium, the level of income and the rate of interest will be lower/higher.

(i) If we wish to increase national income to a given level, this will require a larger/smaller increase in expenditure on goods and services than on transfers.

r

(j)
                                                                    Y

P

                                                                    Y

r

(b) and (c)
                                                                    Y

P

                                                                    Y

Fig. 4

(j) In your answers to (b), (e) and (f) you saw that the use of an expansionary fiscal policy raised income but also raised the interest rate so that crowding-out occurred. Suppose that the government increases the money supply by £40.5m at the same time as it raises government expenditure on goods and services by £54m. Find the equilibrium level of income and rate of interest, together with the crowding-out effect. _____
_____ Using Fig. 4, draw *IS-LM* and *AD-AS* diagrams to illustrate your answers to this question and to (b) and (c) above.

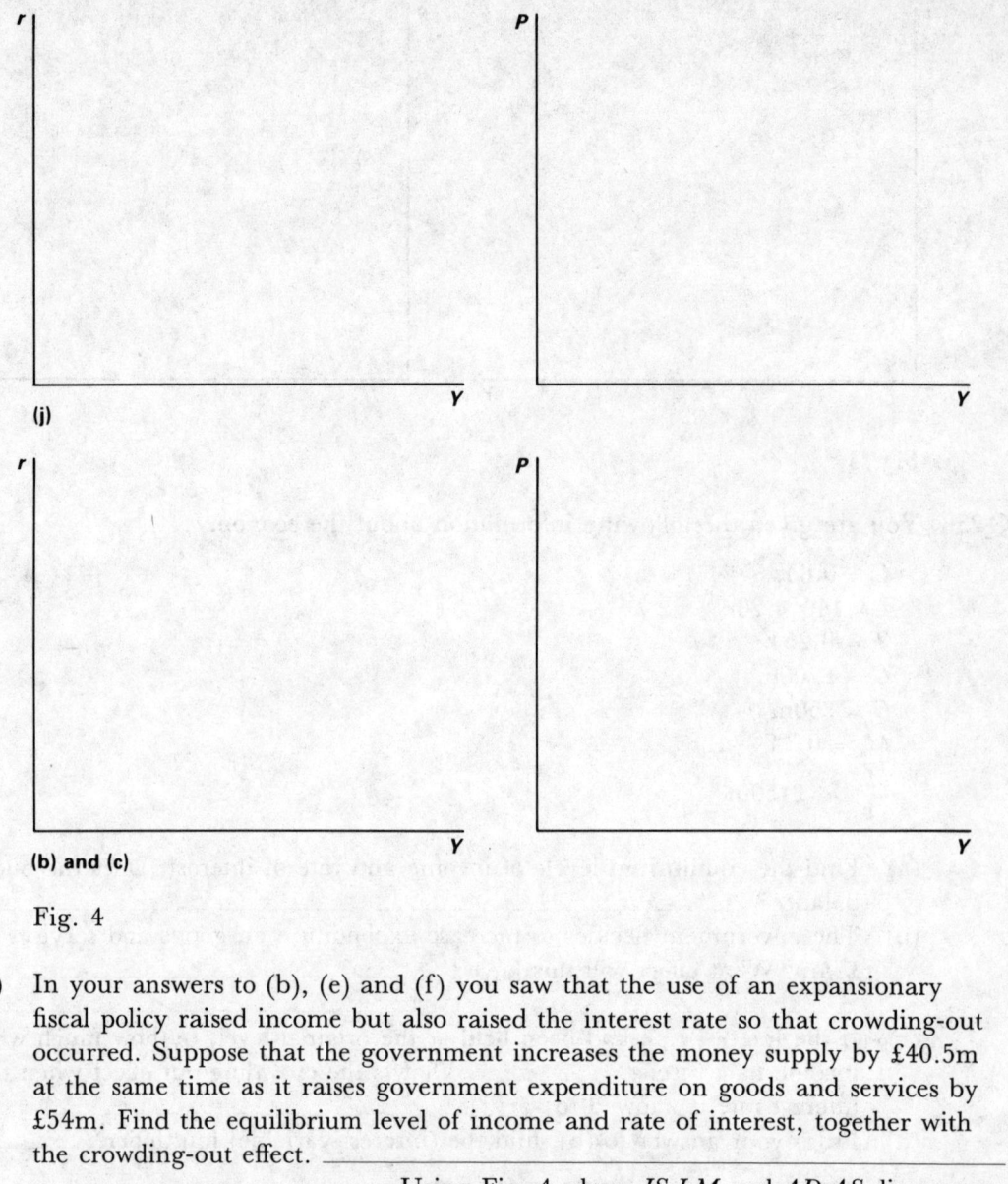

Q 24 Using the information given in Question 23, find the effect of a simultaneous increase in government expenditure of £54m and an increase in the tax rate to 0.32. What has happened to income, the rate of interest and the budget deficit? _____

Q 25 Find the balanced-budget multiplier and compare it with your answer to Question (d) above. _____

When we injected more government expenditure into the economy, we saw that, *if the tax rate had been held constant*, income would have risen through the multiplier process by £68m (see Question 23(b) above). A balanced-budget increase in expenditure means, however, that we do not keep the tax rate constant but we raise it and this reduces consumer spending by $c\Delta t$ (i.e. the marginal propensity to consume multiplied by the change in the tax rate). The injection of £54m raises income in the first round of the multiplier chain by £54m but, at the same time, £54m has been taken out in tax revenue so that increasing the tax rate means that in the first round there was no increase in disposable income. The increase in national income results from the subsequent rounds in the multiplier chain and, of course, the final change in income (once equilibrium has been re-established) must be much less than it would have been when the tax rate was unchanged.

If the interest rate were constant, then the balanced-budget multiplier would have had a value of 1. However, when the interest rate varies as the level of income changes, the value of the balanced-budget multiplier will be less than 1.

Any government endeavouring to eliminate a recessionary gap by a balanced-budget increase in expenditure faces a difficult control problem in establishing the appropriate changes in G and t.

Q26 Why will an increase in the level of government activity in an economy have an expansionary effect even when increased tax revenues pay for all the extra government expenditure? _____
_____
_____

Q27 When government expenditure is decreased by £10m, income will rise/fall by _____ _____ times £10m. When taxes are cut by £10m, consumption will rise/fall by more/less than this amount because _____ _____. If 70% would have been spent on domestically produced goods, the remaining 30% would have been _____ _____. If the government had not cut its expenditure by £10m, _____% of this sum would have been injected into/withdrawn from the circular flow. The government's propensity to spend is greater/smaller than that of the private sector. If the government balances its cut in expenditure by an equal cut in tax revenue, this will have a contractionary/ expansionary effect on national income.

Q28 What is the equation of the budget deficit function? _____
_____

(a) If the government's fiscal policy is unchanged, as income rises the budget balance moves from deficit to surplus/surplus to deficit.
(b) An expansionary fiscal policy will shift the budget deficit function up/down.
(c) An increase in the tax rate will pivot the function in a clockwise/anti-clockwise direction.

Q29 In practice, unlike our simple examples of Q23(f) and Q24, a change in the income-tax rate will not only shift the IS curve but also _____

FISCAL POLICY WHEN PRIVATE EXPENDITURE FUNCTIONS ARE SHIFTING

Up to this point we have assumed that the government knew the consumption and investment functions and that these functions were constant. All shifts in the *IS* and *AD* curves have been the result of fiscal policy. If, however, these curves shift for reasons other than government intervention, then the level of income may rise and fall, and we need to consider whether the government can intervene in order to offset such undesirable fluctuations and thus stabilize income and employment. Before you go on with this chapter you might like to stop and think of reasons why private expenditure functions could shift.

In his discussion of the tools of fiscal policy, Lipsey discusses built-in stabilizers.

Q 30 Define a built-in stabilizer. _____

_____

_____

Two of the built-in stabilizers mentioned by Lipsey are transfer payments (i.e. National Insurance and welfare services) and government expenditure. So far we have taken transfer payments (Q) as exogenous to our model, but now we shall explore whether it makes a difference if transfer payments are endogenous. In particular, we wish to examine whether such transfers will tend to stabilize income, i.e. reduce fluctuations caused by shifts in consumption and investment functions.

This time try using the algebraic method without graphing the functions.

Q 31 Given the following information about an economy, examine firstly the case where transfers are exogenous.

$C = 0.8Y_d$
$t = 0.25$
$I = 250 - 20r$
$Q = 125$
$G = 300$
$M_d = 0.3Y - 12r$
$\dfrac{M^*}{P} = 312$

(a) Find equilibrium income. _____
(b) Suppose that the autonomous component of investment falls by £50m, what will be the change in income? _____
(c) What is the value of the interest-variable multiplier? _____
(d) What is the value of the interest-constant multiplier? _____

Q 32 Now let $Q = 125 - 0.15Y$.

(a) Find equilibrium income. _____
(b) Find the change in income following a fall in autonomous investment of £50m.

_____

(c) What is the value of the interest-variable multiplier? _____
(d) What is the value of the interest-constant multiplier? _____
(e) When transfers are endogenous, do they stabilize or destabilize income?

_____

Q 33 Now examine government expenditure on goods and services (G). Up to now we have taken this to be exogenous, but now assume that $G = 0.2Y$. We will consider transfers to be exogenous at £125m (so that we can concentrate on G) and the rest of the information is as set out in Question 31.

(a) Find equilibrium income. _____
(b) Find the change in income following a fall in autonomous investment amounting to £50m. _____
(c) What is the value of the interest-variable multiplier? _____
(d) What is the value of the interest-constant multiplier? _____
(e) Compare your answers with those to Question 31. When government expenditure is positively related to income, does this stabilize or destabilize income?

_____

_____

FISCAL POLICY IN PRACTICE

Q 34 List two sources of government revenue which will neither increase the money supply nor cause crowding-out:

(a) _____

(b) _____

Q 35 List two sources of revenue which can be used by government and which may cause crowding-out and/or an increase in the money supply:

(a) _____

(b) _____

Q 36 If the government sells bonds to private households, or banks (this means, of course, that it borrows money from them), the money would otherwise have been _____ or _____. If it had been saved, it could either have been taken up for private investment, or kept as liquid reserves. In all, therefore, it could have been either

(a) consumed, or
(b) saved, and taken up for investment, or
(c) saved, and not taken up for investment.

In which one of these circumstances will there be no extra net withdrawal?

_____

The cost of government expenditure (remember, to an economist, cost means opportunity cost) is incurred by members of the community at the time of expenditure. The government will strive to make this cost as small as possible by utilizing factors with the lowest opportunity cost.

Q 37 The choice of method of finance will affect the _____ of the burden.

If the government expenditure is financed by taxes, the cost is borne by the taxpayer.

Q 38 If government expenditure is financed by borrowing, the cost is borne *in the first period* by _____ and in subsequent periods by those who finance the interest and redemption payments.

Q 39 If a war is financed by borrowing money from abroad, the current burden on the home population can be completely avoided. T/F

Q 40 'As government borrowing for expenditure fluctuates, national income must fluctuate by a factor of K times the fluctuation in borrowing.' T/F

Q 41 The opportunity cost of a given government expenditure is the same regardless of/varies according to how it is financed. If government expenditures take resources away from consumer goods production, the opportunity cost is borne in the present/future. If government expenditures take resources from the production of capital goods, the opportunity costs will be borne by the _____ generation, in the form of fewer/more consumer goods produced than otherwise. If government expenditures use unemployed resources, opportunity cost is _____.

227

QUESTIONS FOR DISCUSSION

1. The following letter from Mr Graham Presland was published in *The Times* (13.10.78):

   'It is sad to find Lord Keynes misrepresented yet again. Sir Frederick Catherwood writes, "Keynesian economics... have shifted resources out of the market sector into the public sector and high and progressive personal taxes have discouraged the investment sources on which industry has been built up."'

   'The Keynesian position is surely that action is needed to ensure sufficient spending to buy what can be produced with resources fully employed. Whilst this can indeed be achieved by raising public sector spending, cuts in income tax and in corporation tax are equally effective. The choice is the politicians' and not dictated by Keynesian economics.'

   (a) What do you think Sir Frederick means when he talks about resources being shifted from the market to the public sector? What sort of resources might he be referring to?
   (b) Why might 'high and progressive personal taxes' discourage investment sources?
   (c) Would you agree with Mr Presland that changes in tax rates or in government expenditure are 'equally effective'?

2. What is the balanced-budget multiplier? How can national income increase if exactly the same amount is put back into the system through spending as is removed from it through taxes?

3. If there is inflation, tax revenue will increase even though tax rates are constant. How can this be?

4. If a single individual is thrifty, we normally expect him to be better off than if he is a spendthrift. The theory developed in Box 27.1 and Box 37.3 predicts that the thriftier people are in the aggregate (the more they try to save at each level), the lower total income will be, while the more spendthrift they are (the less they try to save at each level of income), the higher their total income will be! The theory also predicts that the actual amount of savings that they make will be the same in equilibrium whether they are thrifty or spendthrift. Derive these predictions, which are often referred to as the paradox of thrift, graphically.

5. Consider Fig. 5 below, which shows personal savings in the UK from 1985 to mid-1988 (*Financial Times*, 6.1.89).

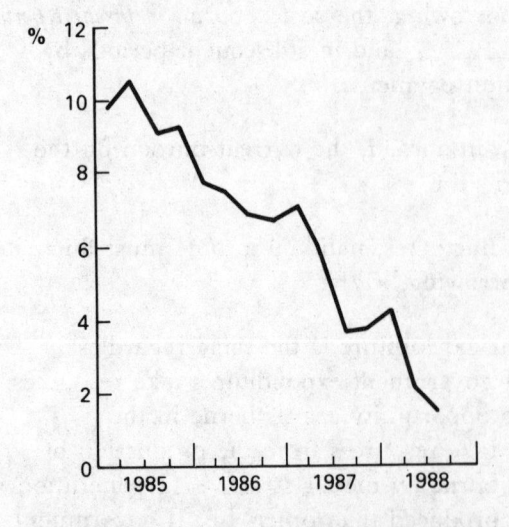

Fig. 5. Personal Saving as % of Personal Disposable Income

Over this period, consumer expenditure was rising and inflation developed. Is this consistent with the paradox of thrift?

An alternative explanation of the fall in personal savings is that over the same period UK interest rates were falling. Do low interest rates discourage saving? Is this argument consistent with, or incompatible with, the paradox of thrift?

Finally, if savings react to interest rates then does our model of savings need to be altered? (At present, consumption is a function of income, and savings is just the 'residual', $Y - C = S$.)

6 During the 1980s, changes in the UK tax rates and welfare system led to a net redistribution of wealth toward the rich. By one estimate, the best-off 10% of families gained £37 per week while the worst-off 40% of families lost £8–14 (see Fig. 6 below).

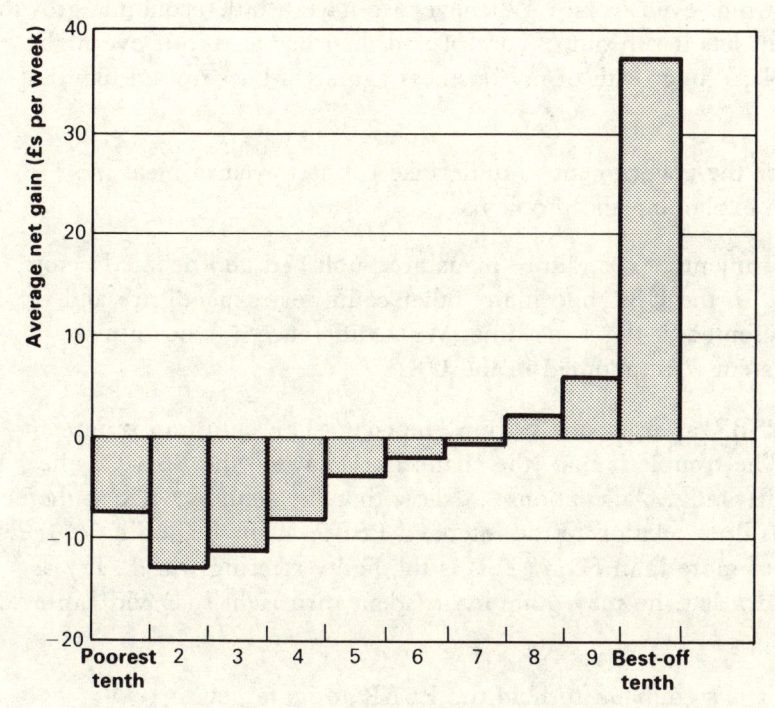

Fig. 6. The Effect of Direct Tax and Benefit Changes since 1978–79 (*Average Net Gain By Income Group*) (*Source:* Changing Tax; Child Poverty Action Group).

What effect would you expect these changes to have on aggregate personal saving in Britain, and why? What effect would this change have on the multiplier? I.e., would this change tend to cause government expenditure to have a stronger or weaker effect on national income?

7 In 1988 the UK budget cut the basic income-tax rate by 2% to 25%, lowered the top income-tax rate to 40%, and used the sale of assets (newly privatized industries) as a major source of government revenue. One commentator on that year's budget said:

'Whatever else may be said about Mr Nigel Lawson's Budget, boring it was not. In one fell swoop the Chancellor has instituted the lowest top marginal rate of income tax in the leading developed countries.

'He has announced £1bn more in tax cuts than the City expected, while forecasting a Public Sector Debt Repayment (PSDR) – a positive version of the old Public Sector Borrowing Requirement – of £3bn both this year and next...

'On one thing even the politicians are all agreed: in neutral terminology, the well-off have emerged better off from the whole proceeding.' (John Plender, *Financial Times*, 19.3.88.)

Mr Plender added that the UK government was 'still a long way from fiscal neutrality'. Is that true? Is fiscal neutrality an objective governments should seek? What would justify the UK budget surpluses of 1988 and 1989?

8 Extract from an article by Sir John Clark, Chairman of Plessey, the giant electronics company:

'... Four times in the last 15 years we have had periods of strong economic growth, periods of real optimism. In each case our hopes have been cruelly dashed by a return to stagnation. Nobody would claim that it is easy to avoid these cycles. But why is Government so powerless to prolong the good times and smooth out the dips? Why is it always caught unawares? Why does it never correct its course in good time? Why have so many economists concluded that the main effect of Government's so-called "fine tuning" is to make the swings even worse? Whenever we have a little economic growth in Britain the Government lets it run out of control and then has to stop it overnight. How am I supposed to plan the growth of my business against a background like that?' (*The Observer*, 29.9.74.)

Why is it so difficult for the government to undertake counter-cyclical measures? Write a reply to Sir John explaining the problems.

9 In this country, the government's expenditure plans are published and debated before the Budget is announced. In the USA and many other countries, expenditure and revenue proposals are presented at the same time. What difference do you think it might make if the US system were adopted in the UK?

10 '[The 1982] Budget set PSBR a target of £8½bn. The chancellor's autumn statement revised this to £8bn... The trouble is that [the chancellor] may set the PSBR as he likes; it will come out differently. Calculations... show that the actual PSBR at the end of the year bears precious little relation to the intended PSBR at the beginning of the year, out by an average of more than £2bn. This is the faulty steering wheel. Try as [the chancellor] may to turn left, he may quite by accident turn right.' (David Lipsey, *Sunday Times*, 6.3.83.)

Can you suggest why it is so difficult to hold the PSBR to its target?

11 President Ronald Reagan was elected on a platform of supply-side economics, including cuts in government spending and taxes. Many economists have pointed out that in practice his administration (1980–88) reflated the US economy through huge annual budget deficits. The deficit peaked at $220 billion in 1986. America's current account deficit (exports minus imports) also grew from zero in 1980 to $160 billion in 1987. Before the election of the new Republican President, George Bush, the economist Mr Fred Bergsten gave a warning in the pages of the *Economist* magazine:

'The new American administration will have to act decisively on the budget in early 1989, to restore confidence. The private markets and foreign central banks will foresee four more years of large twin deficits and probably stop financing the United States in the absence of such action. The dollar would then crash, driving up inflation and interest rates. The economy would turn down sharply. Financial disturbances would follow. A world recession could result, bringing with it a final eruption of the debt crisis of the third world and much greater protectionism.' (*The Economist*, 2.7.88.)

(a) Whose confidence needed to be restored and why?
(b) Should the US government reduce its budget deficit or is there an economic justification for the deficit?

12 We saw above that the large US budget deficit was seen as a problem by some economists. Consider the case of Italy as a contrasting situation:

'Italy's public-sector debt reached 93% of GDP at the end of 1987, up from 58% in 1980. This makes America, with its public-debt-to-GDP ratio of about 30%, seem a model of fiscal rectitude...

'The snag is that Italy, the big industrial country with the highest debt-to-GDP ratio, seems to be thriving on it. In the past decade it has had the fastest growth rate of the four big European economies; its share of private investment in GDP is higher than the EEC average (so much for crowding-out); and its inflation rate, though still higher than the European average, has fallen to less than 5% from more than 20% in 1980. What is Italy's secret?' (*The Economist*, 2.7.88, p. 69.)

Try to answer the *Economist*'s question.
What is crowding-out and why could it be a problem in the USA but not in Italy?

13 On p. 659, Lipsey states that 'In the long run, when all markets are fully adjusted, there will be neither inflationary, nor recessionary gaps.' Fig. 7 below, which appeared in the *Economist*'s 'Survey of the World Economy' (24.9.88, p. 29), shows that even during boom periods such as 1972, 1978, and 1987, the US economy still never reached 90% capacity utilization in manufacturing.

Does this fact suggest that there is a problem with our theory of inflationary gaps, or is our measurement of 100% capacity utilization different from full-employment potential output? (Note: This is a question on which many economists disagree.)

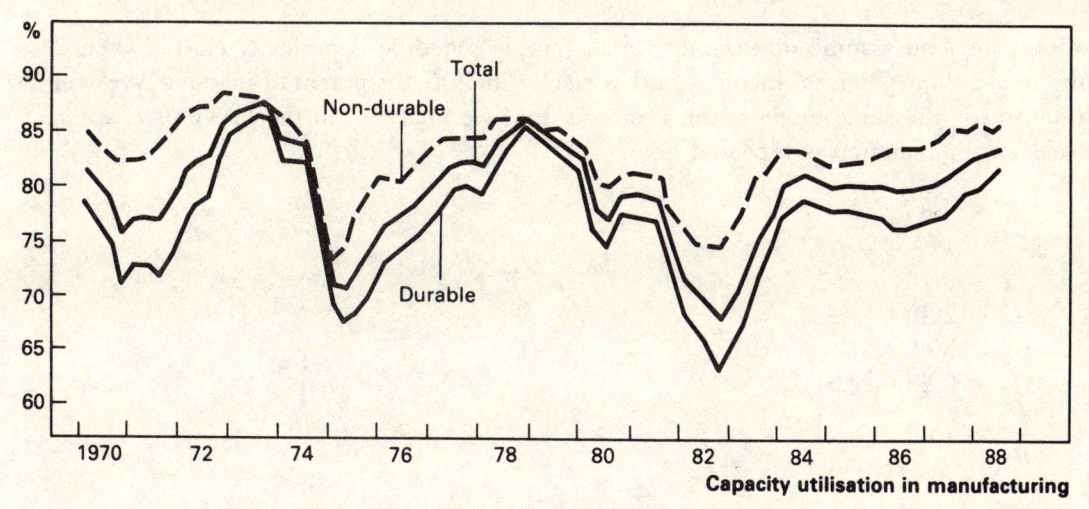

Fig. 7. Capacity Utilization in US Manufacturing, 1970–88

CHAPTER 38

Demand Management 2: Monetary Policy

Monetary policy is an alternative way of managing aggregate demand. In the previous chapter we saw that the government could use fiscal policy to shift the aggregate demand curve, and we now see that changes in the money supply can also change aggregate demand. We start by examining the use of monetary policy when there is either a recessionary or an inflationary gap. Once we understand the effect of changing the money supply, we shall be able to compare monetary and fiscal policy.

THE TRADITIONAL THEORY OF MONETARY POLICY

As before, we shall assume that the aggregate supply schedule is perfectly elastic when income is less than potential income, and perfectly inelastic at potential income. We will also continue to use the same model of an economy that we analysed in the previous chapter. The relevant information is repeated here.

$$C = 0.8Y_d$$
$$I = 140 - 20r$$
$$t = 0.25$$
$$G = 200$$
$$Q = 50$$
$$M_d = 0.3Y - 12r$$
$$\frac{M^*}{P} = 150$$

As you will remember, we found the equilibrium level of income to be £700m and the equilibrium rate of interest 5%. Assume that potential income is £780m.

Q1 If the government increases the money supply by £33m, what will be the change in the level of income and the interest rate? _____

Q2 What would be the effect of a cut of £33m in the money supply? _____

Q3 By how much would the money supply have to be increased in order to eliminate the recessionary gap? (This may seem a difficult question but have another look at your answer to Question 1. Can you find the 'money multiplier'?) _____

Assume that aggregate demand is equal to aggregate supply at potential output.

Q4 Suppose there is an increase in autonomous investment.

(a) This shifts the *IS* schedule inwards/outwards and the aggregate demand curve to the left/right.

(b) Draw *IS-LM* and *AD-AS* diagrams to show what happens to income, the rate of interest and the price level if the money supply (M^*) is constant.

(b)

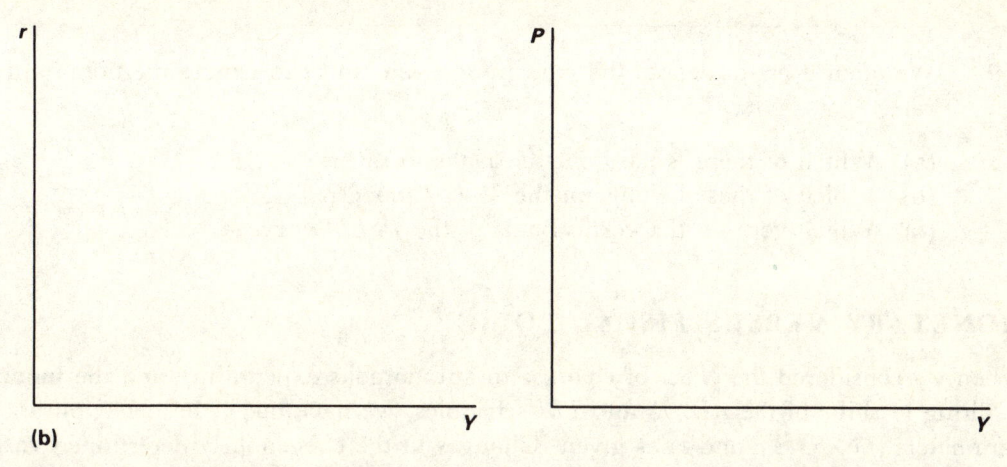

Fig. 1

(c) Draw *IS-LM* and *AD-AS* diagrams to show what happens to Y, r and P if the central bank keeps the real money supply constant.

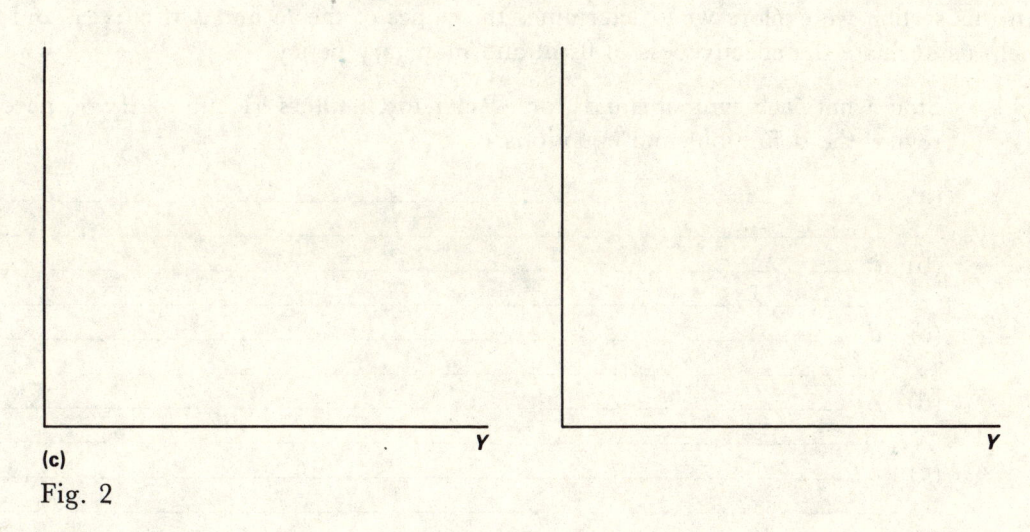

(c)

Fig. 2

(d) Now suppose, however, that the government anticipated the increase in aggregate demand. Can you think of any policies it could adopt in order to maintain $Y = Y_F$ with rising prices? Explain how such policies would work.

_____
_____
_____
_____
_____
_____

Q5 If nominal money supply is held constant when prices are rising, inflation is validated by monetary policy. T/F

Q6 What causes the *AD* function to shift but leaves the slope unchanged? _____

Q7 If the interest rate is 13% and inflation is running at 8%, what is the real interest rate? _____

Q8 Nominal interest rates are always positive. Are real interest rates always positive? _____

Q9 We often use r to denote the real interest rate and i to denote the nominal interest rate.

   (a) Which of these is paid out by banks to savers? _____
   (b) Which of these belongs in the *IS-LM* model? _____
   (c) Which goes on the vertical axis of the *IS-LM* curve? _____

MONETARY VERSUS FISCAL POLICY

When we considered the effect of changes in autonomous expenditure and the money supply, resulting in shifts of the *AD*, *IS* and *LM* schedules, we have taken the behavioural parameters (i.e. b, c, d and e) as given. Changes in the exogenously determined variables shifted the *AD*, *IS* and *LM* schedules to right or to left but left the slopes of the curves unchanged. However, when we varied the tax rate (t), this did change the slope of the *IS* and *AD* curves. Now the effect of shifts in the *IS* and *LM* curves on the level of national income and the rate of interest is greater or smaller depending on the *slope* of these curves. In this section we explore what determines the slopes of the *IS* and *LM* curves, and this will help us evaluate the effectiveness of fiscal and monetary policy.

Q10 State what each symbol stands for. (Refer to Chapters 31 and 32 if you need to review the definitions and equations.)

   (a) b. _____
   (b) c. _____
   (c) d. _____
   (d) e. _____
   (e) r. _____
   (f) n. _____

Q11 Explain why n drops out of the *LM* curve in the example at the beginning of this chapter.

   (a) (in words) _____
   (b) (in symbols, referring to the money demand equation) _____

Q12 Write the equation for the *IS* function. _____

   (a) Which parameters affect the slope? _____

(b) When $b = -20$, what is the effect of a 1% fall in the rate of interest when the investment function is given by $I = a_1 + br$? _____

(c) The larger b is, the greater/smaller the increase in investment following a fall in r, and the greater/smaller the upward/downward shift of the aggregate expenditure function. Therefore, the larger b is, the steeper/flatter is the *IS* curve.

You should be able to work out the answer to the next question:

(d) The larger the *MPC*, the steeper/flatter the *IS* curve.

Q13 Write the equation of the *LM* function. _____

(a) Which parameters affect the slope? _____
(b) When income rises by £10, what is the effect on the demand for money, assuming that r is unchanged? _____
(c) The larger d is (r held constant), the steeper/flatter is the *LM* curve.
(d) The larger e is (Y held constant), the steeper/flatter is the *LM* curve.
(e) We conclude that the *LM* curve will be flatter, the larger/smaller is d and the larger/smaller is e. The flatter the *LM* curve, the greater/smaller is the effect of a change in income on the rate of interest.

We are, of course, particularly interested in the effect of a change in the rate of interest on the level of income.

Q14 When we use fiscal policy to eliminate a recessionary gap, an injection of G raises/lowers income and raises/lowers the rate of interest. When we use monetary policy, increasing the money supply will raise/lower income and raise/lower the rate of interest. The change in the rate of interest following *the increase in G* means that government expenditure has _____ private expenditure.

Q15 When the *LM* curve is perfectly elastic (i.e. flat), the crowding-out effect will be 100%/positive but less than 100%/zero; and when the *LM* curve is perfectly inelastic, it will be 100%/positive but less than 100%/zero. The less elastic the *LM* curve, the greater/smaller the crowding-out effect of any expansionary fiscal policy.

We will now use the model set out at the beginning of the chapter to evaluate the effects of fiscal and monetary policy by making different assumptions about the values of the parameters b and e. We start by examining the effect of a given expansion through fiscal policy when we *vary the slope of the LM schedule*.

Q16 We know from earlier exercises that when $c = 0.8$, $t = 0.25$, $b = -20$, $d = 0.3$, autonomous expenditure = 380 and the real money supply = 150, the equilibrium level of income is £700m and the rate of interest is 5%, when $e = -12$.

(a) Following an increase in G of £45m, find:
(i) ΔY. _____
(ii) Δr. _____
(iii) ΔI. _____
(iv) Crowding-out. _____

(b) Now suppose that the value of e is -15. Would you expect an injection of $G = £45m$ to result in a larger or smaller increase in income than when e was -12?

_____

(c) Taking $e = -15$, find the equilibrium levels of Y and r for the initial situation when autonomous expenditure is £380m. _____

(d) Now check your prediction in (b) above and find ΔY, Δr, ΔI and crowding-out following an injection of $G = £45m$.

(i) ΔY. _____
(ii) Δr. _____
(iii) ΔI. _____
(iv) Crowding-out. _____

Now take the case of a given increase in the money supply, *varying the slope of the IS curve.*

Q17 When c, t, d, autonomous expenditure and M^*/P are as in Question 16, and $e = -12$ and $b = -20$, we know equilibrium $Y = £700m$ and equilibrium $r = 5\%$.

(a) When we increased the money supply by £33m in Question 1, we found the change in income to be £61m and the change in the rate of interest to be -1.22%. Find the change in the level of investment. _____

(b) Now let b equal -10. Would you expect a similar increase in the money supply to result in a larger or smaller change in income than before? _____

(c) With $b = -10$, find the equilibrium levels of Y and r. _____

(d) Now, once again, increase the money supply by £33m and check your prediction.
(i) ΔY. _____
(ii) Δr. _____
(iii) ΔI. _____

Q18 Assuming the *LM* curve to be neither perfectly *interest-inelastic* nor perfectly *interest-elastic*, and the *IS* curve to be perfectly *interest-elastic*,

(a) Increasing the money supply would raise/lower/leave unchanged income and raise/lower/leave unchanged the rate of interest;

(b) Increasing autonomous expenditure would raise/lower income and raise/lower the rate of interest.

Q19 If the *LM* curve is perfectly *interest-elastic* and the *IS* curve slopes downwards to the right, increasing autonomous expenditure will raise/lower/leave unchanged income, and raise/lower/leave unchanged the rate of interest. If the *LM* curve were perfectly *interest-inelastic*, an increase in autonomous expenditure would raise/lower/leave unchanged income and raise/lower/leave unchanged the rate of interest.

Q20 Fiscal policy is more effective the more/less interest-elastic is the *LM* curve, whereas monetary policy is more effective the more/less elastic is the *IS* curve.

HOW CENTRAL BANKS WORK

Q21 How does the central bank alter the money supply? _____

Q22 What is the main difference between Treasury Bills and government bonds? _____

Q23 'When the government borrows from the central bank, which does not undertake commercial transactions, it is equivalent to printing money.' T/F

Q24 Assume that the Bank of England wishes to contract the money supply by £10m but the commercial banks do not wish to take up government bonds. How will the Bank achieve its purpose on the open market? (The cash ratio is 10%.) _____

Q25 In what circumstances will this not work? _____

Q26 When the Bank undertakes open-market operations and buys bonds, does it pay for these by creating new notes and coins? _____

Q27 (a) If the government wishes short-term interest rates to rise, how might it achieve this by open-market operations? _____

(b) As a result of these open-market operations, the cash reserves of commercial banks will rise/fall and the money supply will expand/contract.

Q28 The customer of a commercial bank in a many-bank system draws out £100 in cash and hoards it. By how much will *this* bank contract its lending? _____

Q29 (a) Suppose the cash-reserve ratio is 10% and banks currently have cash reserves of £12,500m. Complete the balance sheet below (assuming that all banks expand deposits to the legal limit and that there is no cash drain to the public).

Liabilities £m		Assets £m
Deposits _____	Cash	12,500
	Other	_____

(b) Now suppose the government raises the cash-reserve ratio to 12.5%. By how much must deposits contract in order to comply with the new ratio?

Liabilities £m		Assets £m
Deposits _____	Cash	12,500
	Other	_____

(c) Suppose that instead of contracting deposit money, banks had been able to increase their reserves (as might be possible if the reserve assets do not comprise cash only). By how much would reserve assets have had to rise in order to comply with a reserve-asset ratio of 12.5%? _____

Q30 Why did the change from a cash-reserve ratio to a reserve-asset ratio, as was the case in Britain from 1971 to 1981, mean that the Bank had less tight control over the money supply? _____

NON-MONETARY TARGETS

On p. 702 Lipsey discusses measures introduced in 1981, for the control of the money supply. Make quite sure you understand the implications of setting a target (band) rate of interest, compared with a target money supply.

Q31 Suppose that the current level of income is £700m, the money supply is £150m, and the demand-for-money function is given as $M_d = 0.3Y - 12r$.

(a) At what rate of interest will the money market be in equilibrium? _____
(b) Suppose that the Bank's target money supply is £120m. By how much must it increase the rate of interest in order to achieve this? _____
(c) How would it manage this? _____

In the previous chapter we noted that some components of expenditure may fluctuate, causing stabilization problems.

Q32 What might cause the demand for money function to fluctuate? _____

Q33 Suppose that the Bank adopts a *target money supply* of £150m. The money market is currently in equilibrium as national income is £700m and the money-demand function is given by $M_d = 0.3Y - 12r$. Given this target money supply, find the effect on the rate of interest of the following:

(a) Income rises by £50m. _____
(b) d changes to 0.35. _____
(c) e changes to -10. _____

Q34 Now suppose that the Bank adopts a *target rate of interest* of 5%. How would it achieve this target when faced with a fluctuating demand-for-money function as a result of the changes listed in (a), (b) and (c) of the previous question?

(a) _____
(b) _____
(c) _____

Q35 When the Bank of England sets a target rate of interest, this will mean increasing/decreasing the money supply when income is rising and increasing/decreasing the money supply when income is falling, with the result that income fluctuations will be greater/smaller than would be the case if the money supply were fixed. In these circumstances the money supply is endogenous/exogenous.

Q36 What money-market considerations might make commercial banks unwilling to lend to the maximum possible extent? _____

Q37 If there are unemployed resources, then an increase in the supply of money will result in output increasing/decreasing/remaining constant. If, however, all resources are fully employed, an increase in the money supply will result in output increasing/decreasing/remaining constant, and national income in current prices will rise/fall/be unchanged while national income in constant prices will rise/fall/be unchanged.

Q38 Suppose that the economy is in equilibrium at full-employment level.

(a) This means that in the money market, _____ = _____, and in the commodities market, _____ = _____. Now suppose that, for some reason, people decide to save less.
(b) As the economy is at full employment, real output cannot meet the higher demand and consequently _____.
(c) The demand for nominal/real money balances will decrease/increase/remain constant.

238

(d) The nominal money supply is unchanged, so the real money supply has risen/fallen/remained constant.
(e) The nominal demand for money is greater/less than the nominal supply of money.
(f) The excess demand for/supply of money means that people will buy/sell bonds, with the result that _____
(g) This will encourage/check interest-sensitive expenditure, so that aggregate expenditure will rise/fall and the inflationary gap will be enlarged/removed.
(h) If instead of holding the nominal supply of money constant (as assumed in (d) above), it were increased at the same rate as prices increased, then the real demand for money would exceed/fall short of/equal the real supply of money. As a result, interest rates would rise/fall/be unchanged, so that aggregate demand adjusts/is unchanged and the inflationary gap is eliminated/persists.

If you answered either (or both) of the last two questions wrongly you should re-read Lipsey, pp. 682–684, again.

QUESTIONS FOR DISCUSSION

1 What is the object of the following actions of a central bank?

    (a) Selling bonds in the open market
    (b) Lowering the required reserve ratio
    (c) Specifying that down-payments on instalment-plan buying may not be less than one-third of the item bought
    (d) Exhorting commercial banks to give preference in lending to exporters.

    How is each supposed to work?

2 What options are open to a government for financing a budget deficit? Is there any link between budget finance and inflation?

3 Will expansionary monetary policy always lower interest rates?

4 On 11.11.78, *The Times* leader noted 'The growth in the size of the [building society] movement, so that collectively it now accounts for more deposits than the clearing banks, has posed the question whether it is right that building societies should continue in effect to be left outside the normal controls exercised by the authorities over the rest of the financial system.'

    (a) What were the 'normal controls' referred to in the leader and why might it suggest that building societies should be subject to them?
    (b) Do you think there is any relationship between the rates of interest charged by commercial banks and building society rates?
    (c) If, instead of using a cheque book, you were to open a building society deposit account, put your income in it and withdraw cash to pay your bills, and if all other bank users were to do likewise, what would be the total effect?
    (d) According to Mr Robert G. Alexander, President of the Scottish Building Societies Association, building societies are 'safer than a bank' (quoted in *Glasgow Herald*, 19.3.71). What are building societies' assets? What are banks'? How liquid is each? Comment on Mr Alexander's assertion.

5 The following is an extract from a report by Clifford German, published in the *Daily Telegraph*, 23.2.79:

    'Pandemonium broke out in the new issue office of the Bank of England yesterday morning as hundreds of messengers struggled to get last minute applications for the two new Government stocks across the counter before the deadline at one minute past ten.

'Between 30 and 40 applicants with orders for up to £1,000 million worth of stock were turned away when bank officials closed the counter.

'The two new stocks – £500 million worth of Exchequer 13¼ p.c. 1987 and £800 million worth of Treasury 13¾ p.c. 2,000 to 2,003 – were oversubscribed almost 10 times.'

On 11.3.79, John Davis in the *Observer* reported that the stocks were selling at premiums of £10⅝ and £13⅝ respectively and he commented:

'The premiums are unprecedented in the history of gilt-edged issues. It means that the Government, assisted by the Bank of England, has effectively given away £164 million.'

(a) Explain what went wrong and what Davis means when he says that the government has given away £164 million. Who were the beneficiaries of this gift and who pays for it?

(b) Can you suggest how such a situation might be prevented from recurring? (*Hint*: can a seller set both price and quantity?)

6 In April 1965, the Bank of England told the commercial banks that they would have to pay in to their accounts 'special deposits' which have the effect of increasing their reserves by £90 million. The next day, the headline in the *Guardian* read, 'Banks' ability to make loans cut by £90 million'. What do you think of this? Suppose the banks raised all the money for their special deposits by restricting loans? Suppose, on the other hand, all they did was to sell government bonds in their possession, the price of which the Treasury was committed to keep fairly steady?

7 The following is an extract from Peter Riddell's report in the *Financial Times* (30.3.79). The Governor of the Bank of England, giving evidence to the Wilson Committee, said that the 'corset scheme was devised because the Bank thought "rather than restrict lending directly it was better to go for the point where the expansion was taking place fastest. We thought also it would be less constricting in the management of portfolios than would a direct control on lending."

'He admitted that the corset inhibited competition and diverted business into possibly less efficient channels. "It is probably true of this and any other direct control that with time it becomes less effective in achieving its purpose, as ways round it develop – in a fairly sophisticated financial system this is inevitable – and at the same time its costs in terms of distortions of the system increases".'

(a) What do you think the Governor meant by 'direct control on lending'? Why should the corset 'go to the point where the expansion was taking place fastest'?

(b) What sort of competition might be inhibited by the corset and what business might be diverted?

8 '[The Chancellor's] first difficulty is to decide which money supply he is trying to control. Official policy – set out in last March's financial statement, is to consider a "range of indicators". Broad money (M3) and narrow (M1) both convey useful information on the tightness of policy, as does the exchange rate, the financial statement said.

'[The Chancellor's] problem is that all three of these measures are now sending out disrupted signals. M1, notes and coin plus bank sight deposits, is increasingly meaningless as the non-bank sector starts its own sight deposits. (One such is the Abbey National's new interest-bearing current account.) New banking techniques will increasingly distort M1, until – as has happened in the US – it is abandoned.

'As for M3, the wider measure which includes bank deposit accounts, the monetarists themselves are now having grave doubts as to whether it should be screwed down. Tim Congden, monetarist high priest of Messel's the stockbrokers... [said] "Money, as measured by M3 may increase by more than the underlying growth of productive capacity without generating inflationary pressures." (David Lipsey, *Sunday Times*, 6.3.83.)

(a) Explain why new developments in the bank and non-bank sectors may result in M1 becoming useless as a measure of the money supply.

(b) How would you explain Tim Congden's statement about the M3 measure?

9 Extract from an article by Malcolm Crawford in the *Sunday Times* (15.10.78):

'... depending on how the banking figures for this month turn out... a continuation of the present M3 targets – 8% to 12% growth through the year – could be shown as a tightening. The money supply figures out next week will show an annual rate of increase in the first five months (since April) of about 5%. The figures for October could well show the rise over six months at the bottom end of the target range (8½% per annum since April), or even a shade below.

'Equally, however, the money supply for the first six months could be about 10% per annum up on April. Despite the small increase in money to last month, this could easily happen, for gilt sales are not going well, so the Government is presumably borrowing from the banking system... In that event I expect the target figures for the year ahead to be lowered.

'A further tightening in the money supply... would be bad news for business generally. Profits are already being squeezed... With the wage bill in the private sector rising at about 14% per annum, even a 10% growth of M3 (the middle of the present target range) looks pretty tight.'

(a) If the money supply is growing at 8 to 12%, how can this be a tightening of the supply?

(b) If the government is borrowing from the banking system, as Crawford suggests, what effect would this have on the money supply?

(c) If gilt sales had been going well, would the implications for the money supply have been different?

10 Letter from Professor D. Wood to the *Financial Times* (3.3.83):

'... the medium-term economic strategy cash limits, control of public-sector borrowing requirements and money supply control were justified not for their own sake but for their claimed effectiveness in improving the performance of the UK's real economy.

'The evidence for this transmission process was extremely patchy, but the experiment was undertaken.'

What is the 'transmission process' to which Professor Wood refers?

11 Consider the following two extracts concerning the money supply and the velocity of circulation (but first review Chapter 30 on the quantity theory of money):

'... an increase of about 10½ per cent [in nominal national income] was anticipated for last year, with real output going up to about 1½ per cent and the remainder being dissipated in inflation. In the event, prices rose less but so, unfortunately, did output which increased by only ½ per cent. Thus the rise in expenditure was not on quite the expected scale, but the money stock, as measured by £M3, did rise by about 10½ per cent which was within its target range. The inference is, of course, that the money supply is being used less actively. This is not a new development. The velocity of circulation of £M3 – that is to say, the ratio of nominal GNP to £M3 – had already fallen from 3.80 in the second quarter of 1980 to 3.17 in the last quarter of 1981 and must now be still closer to 3.0.' (Letter from Professor T. Wilson to the *Financial Times*, 9.3.83.)

'The monetary growth targets of 7 to 11 per cent for three different aggregates accord with the predicted 8 per cent growth in the nominal national income (Money GDP) provided that velocity continues to fall slightly. This would be likely if interest rates and inflation were to fall, but at least a temporary upward surge is officially expected in inflation and the possible effects of the oil market on sterling, together with the effects of the huge US budget deficit on world interest rates, should make one very cautious on the interest-rate front. Velocity is as likely to rise as to fall further.' (S. Brittan, *Financial Times*, 17.3.83.)

(a) What is 'nominal national income'?
(b) Why does the velocity of circulation vary?
(c) If velocity varies, what problems does this pose for the government in its monetary policy?

12 Extracts from an article by David Lipsey, *Sunday Times* (23.1.82):

'... the markets are still in the grip of an inflationary psychology. Whatever Mrs Thatcher may think and hope, they do not expect the 5.4% inflation rate announced on Friday to stick.

'This is bad news for Mrs Thatcher ... But for those concerned with the real world of output and jobs it is very good news indeed. For the plain fact is that if inflationary expectations came down much further, the prospect of economic recovery would be substantially reduced.

'The reason lies in what lower inflationary expectations would do to real interest rates. If you are a businessman thinking of borrowing to invest, you consider first what the funds to do so might cost you – at present, at least 12% from a bank. But you have to consider also what, over the years, you will get for the products that the investment enables you to produce. The faster you expect prices to go up, the more you will expect to get back, and thus, the more attractive the investment becomes.'

(a) What were the real and nominal interest rates faced by businessmen in 1982?
(b) For any given nominal interest rate, what is the relationship between the real rate and the inflation rate?
(c) What are the nominal and real interest rates for borrowers today?

13 An *Economist* editorial in March 1989 said:

'The present inflation threat seems trivial beside the two big inflations of the 1970s. But the correct historical parallel for 1989 is the late 1960s, not the oil-shocked decade that followed. In 1968–69, as now, America saw an inching up of inflation, not a sudden leap. Then, as now, the main cause was an excessive growth of domestic demand, left unchecked for too long. A spiral of wage and price increases caused interest rates to rise, and the recession of 1970 followed. It was a shallow slump by later standards – but a slump all the same. It happened because tight money was used to squash inflation.' (*The Economist*, 4.3.89, p. 16.)

Is there any alternative?

CHAPTER 39
Exchange rates

Q1 A small open economy can/cannot influence its own terms of trade.

Q2 The terms of trade show how many units of _____ _____ have to be exported to pay for each unit of imported goods.

THE INFLUENCE OF EXCHANGE RATES

Q3 Is foreign exchange a single currency or many currencies? _____

Q4 An exchange rate is the price of a particular _____

Exchange rates can often be reported in either of two forms:

(i) units of domestic currency per unit of foreign currency; or
(ii) the opposite ratio, i.e. units of foreign currency per unit of domestic currency.

Forms (i) and (ii) are simply the reciprocal of each other. You should always specify which form you are using by writing the two currencies' symbols in the right order (e.g. $s per £), unless it is obvious from the context.

For example, in November 1988 one pound sterling (£1) cost 4,200 Mexican Pesos. This exchange rate is reported as 4,200 Pesos per £ because the other form would be too cumbersome: 1/4,200 = £0.0002381 per Peso!

Q5 When there are three German Deutschmarks per pound sterling, what is the cost of a Mark in Britain? _____

Q6 Suppose the US dollar exchanges for 50p in Britain, as it did in the early 1980s. State this exchange rate in its two forms:

(i) _____
(ii) _____

The standard form used in British newspaper reports of this particular bilateral exchange rate is the latter of these, e.g. $2 per £.

Q7 By 1985 the dollar exchange rate in the UK reached the level of $1.05 per £. The dollar had depreciated/appreciated from its earlier level. The pound had depreciated/appreciated over the same period. The price of dollars in Britain had gone up/down. (To see why, recall that form (i) gives the price of the foreign currency. This form of the exchange rate had *risen* from 1/$2 = £0.50 to 1/$1.05 = £0.95, i.e. from 50p to 95p per dollar.)

Note here that we always say that *the currency appreciates* or *depreciates*, *not* that *the exchange rate appreciates* or *depreciates* – because for every exchange-rate movement, one currency appreciates while the other depreciates.

Q 8 The trend in the US dollar's movement changed in 1985. During 1985–88, the dollar depreciated relative to many currencies, while the pound sterling held steady. The exchange rate in terms of dollars per pound goes up/down as the dollar depreciates.

Q 9 By November 1988, the rate had reached $1.85 per £.

(a) Relative to the 1985 rate of $1.05 per £, the dollar had depreciated/appreciated.
(b) Relative to the original rate quoted for the early 1980s ($2 per £), the dollar had depreciated/appreciated.

The above example shows how much exchange rates can fluctuate under the system of flexible exchange rates. Many countries, even today, fix their exchange rate relative to another currency and only adjust it when necessary. Table 1 below shows Mexico's experience with the Peso/US$ exchange rate.

TABLE 1. *Mexican Exchange Rate (pesos per US$)*

Year	Rate
1950–53	8.65
1954–74	12.50
1975	15.44
1980	29.66
1985	231.27
November 1988	4198.48
April 1989	4039.20

Q 10 Mexico's exchange rate was fixed at _____ during 1950–53 and at _____ during 1954–74. Between 1953 and 1954 the currency depreciated/appreciated by _____ %.

This kind of one-off adjustment of an otherwise fixed exchange rate to a new level is also called a *devaluation* of the currency. Since 1975, Mexico has had a more flexible exchange rate. The figures given for 1975, 1980, 1988 and 1989 are just four snapshots of a moving picture.

Q 11 Over the whole period shown in Table 1, the Mexican Peso has depreciated/appreciated a lot. However, between November 1988 and April 1989 the currency depreciated/appreciated by about 4%.

Q 12 As the Peso depreciated, foreign imports got more/less expensive inside Mexico.

THE DETERMINATION OF EXCHANGE RATES

Q 13 The demand for dollars in Britain comes mainly from _____ of foreign goods, and the supply of dollars from the _____ of British goods.

Q 14 The demand and supply curves for foreign exchange are drawn on a graph with _____ on the vertical axis (i.e. the price of _____), and _____ on the horizontal axis.

Q 15   Thus an upward shift in the demand curve for foreign currency would (all else being equal) cause a rise/fall in the price of foreign currency. Such a change corresponds to a depreciation/appreciation of the domestic currency.

Q 16   Inflation in the home country can, as shown in Fig. 39.6 in the text, cause a depreciation/appreciation of the currency relative to foreign currencies.

Multiple exchange rates

Q 17   Instead of looking at all the various bilateral exchange rates for a country, it is often better to work out a weighted average of these. Two examples of such multilateral exchange rates are the _____ and the _____

Q 18   These rates cannot be expressed as a ratio of currencies, as in our old example of 50p per $. How would you express them? _____

Long-run exchange rates

Q 19   Suppose that the current exchange rate is DM4.00 = £1.00. British cars are priced at £10,000 for export while German cars are sold at DM40,000. Find the relative price ratio in pounds sterling.

Q 20   Now suppose that inflation is running at 5% per year in both countries and that this is fully reflected in export prices.

  (a) UK car prices will rise to £_____, while German car prices will rise to DM_____.
  (b) What is the relative price ratio in pounds sterling? _____
  (c) Has the purchasing-power-parity exchange rate changed? _____

Q 21   What if inflation had been 12% in the UK and 4% in Germany, instead of 5%?

  (a) UK car prices rise to £_____.
  (b) German car prices rise to DM_____.
  (c) What is the relative price ratio now? _____
  (d) By how much must the exchange rate change in order to maintain purchasing-power-parity? _____
  (e) As usual when the domestic inflation rate exceeds the foreign exchange rate, the British currency needs to _____ to maintain purchasing-power-parity.

Q 22   Purchasing-power-parity can be defined as: _____
_____
_____

Q 23   If the exchange rate is held constant, but the local inflation rate is much lower than the inflation rates of trading partners, the exchange rate will stay at/deviate from the PPP rate.

BALANCE-OF-PAYMENTS RECORDS

Q 24   The balance of payments is an account of all flows of banknotes/money/goods across national boundaries.

Q 25   The three broad types of flows recorded in the balance of payments are _____,
_____ , and
_____ .

Q 26   If the current account has a negative balance (a deficit) and the capital account has a zero balance, then by the equation C + K + F = 0, the official financing account must have a negative/zero/positive balance.

Q 27   Give three examples of positive items on the official financing account of the balance of payments.

(a) _____
(b) _____
(c) _____

Q 28   State whether each of the following count as a credit (plus) or debit (minus) on the British balance of payments:

(a) purchase of Japanese televisions.
(b) sale of coal to France.
(c) interest paid by borrowers to a German bank.
(d) wages earned in Saudi Arabia by an electrician and sent back to the electrician's family in London.
(e) Chinese purchase of a shop and warehouse in London from which the Chinese government will sell its exports for the next 10 years.
(f) a British company's purchase of 50 acres of land in Brazil on which a factory will later be built.

Credits: _____   Debits: _____

QUESTIONS FOR DISCUSSION

1 Looking again at the table of Mexican exchange rates, which of the following figures is closest to the average annual rate of depreciation of the Peso over the period 1975–1988: 5%, 25%, or 55% per year? _____ (See below for a hint.)

Initial Rate:	15	15	15	Pesos/$
Annual Rate of Change:	5%	25%	55%	per year
Rate 13 Years Later:	28	273	4,471	Pesos/$

What does your answer tell you about Mexico's and the USA's inflation rates over that period? Discuss.

2 The discovery of mineral or fuel reserves such as North Sea oil in Britain is an example of a 'structural change' which can cause the exchange rate to move away from its old PPP rate. Explain the series of changes which might cause the currency to appreciate in such a situation. (*Hint:* assume a fixed, equilibrium exchange rate initially, and think about changes in the demand for and/or supply of foreign exchange. Use a foreign exchange supply/demand graph to work out and illustrate your answer.)

CHAPTER 40
Macro Policy in an Open Economy

ALTERNATIVE EXCHANGE-RATE REGIMES

Q1 What was the Bretton Woods system? _____
_____
_____
_____

Q2 Under Bretton Woods, countries fixed the number of dollars which were equivalent to a unit of their currency. This meant that the USA could/could not independently fix the value of dollars in terms of other currencies.

Q3 How did the IMF intend to achieve one of its objectives, that of preventing competitive devaluations? _____
_____
_____

Q4 Two of the three major problems of the Bretton Woods system were:

(a) Handling speculative crises.
(b) Providing sufficient reserves to iron out short-term fluctuations in receipts and payments.

What was the third?

(c) _____
_____

Q5 What does SDR stand for, and what are SDRs? _____
_____
_____

Q6 If aggregate world demand is insufficient for worldwide full employment, what will be the effect on other countries if one country manages to increase its exports and employment?
_____
_____

Q7 The adjustable peg system involves no/periodic/continuous changes to an initially fixed exchange rate.

Q8 An exchange-rate system where no fixed rate is announced, but the government uses its official reserves to influence the exchange rate, is called a _____
or _____.

247

MACROECONOMIC POLICY AND THE CURRENT ACCOUNT

Q 9   Internal balance means achieving _____
_____
_____

Q 10   External balance means achieving _____
_____

Q 11   Domestic absorption is defined as:

     (a)   (in words) _____
_____

     (b)   (in symbols) _____

Q 12   Expenditure-switching policies, such as a devaluation of the currency, transfer spending from _____ to _____ goods.

Q 13   Which of the following items of desired expenditure would be reduced by the expenditure-reducing policy of a rise in personal and corporate tax rates?

     (a) C
     (b) I
     (c) G
     (d) X
     (e) M

     Answer: _____

Q 14   Using Fig. 1, draw a graph to show the position of simultaneous internal and external balance in the long run.

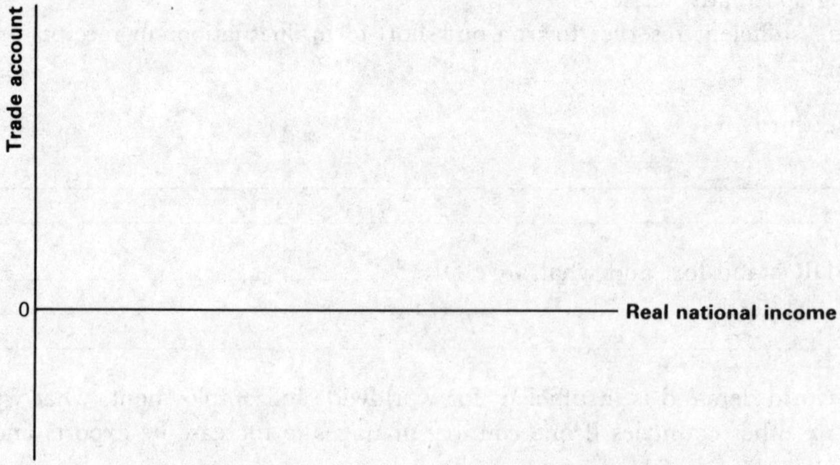

Fig. 1

Q 15   In your graph, the NX function represents:

     (a)   (in words) _____
     (b)   (in symbols) _____

Q 16   In Fig. 2, will the trade account be in deficit or in surplus in the long run?

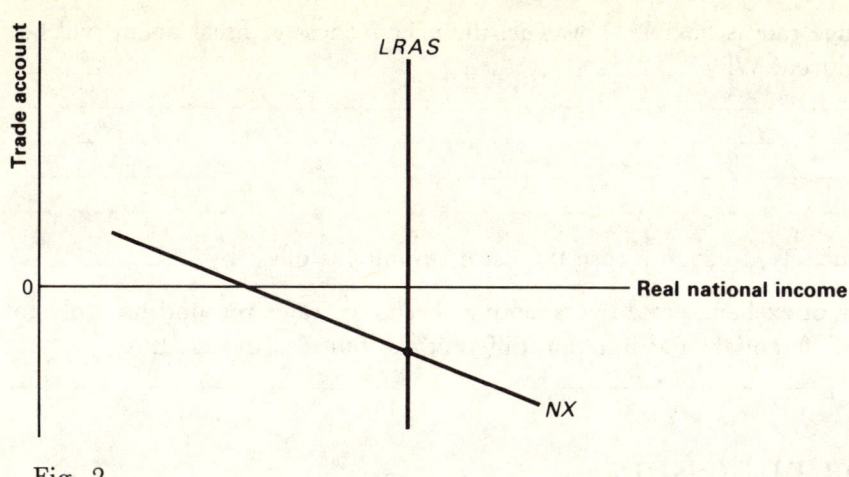

Fig. 2

MACROECONOMIC POLICY AND THE CAPITAL ACCOUNT

So far the trade with foreign countries which we have been considering has been limited to goods and services. But we must now also take into account that there is trade in assets – that is to say, that there are international, as well as national, financial markets. The international capital market is remarkably closely integrated, especially among the more industrialized countries. Capital moves rapidly from one country to another, following a change in the rate of interest or the exchange rate.

Q 17 When capital flows are substantial, external balance may be usefully re-defined as _____

instead of simply as a balanced trade account.

Q 18 Expansionary fiscal policies in an open economy can cause:

(a) the interest rate to rise/fall.
(b) capital to flow in/out of the country.
(c) the capital account to go into deficit/surplus.

Q 19 A contractionary monetary policy in an open economy can cause:

(a) the interest rate to rise/fall.
(b) capital to flow in/out of the country.
(c) the capital account to go into deficit/surplus.

Q 20 A balance-of-payments deficit can cause a rise/fall in the domestic money supply. To offset this, _____ may be necessary. That is, the government would have to raise/lower bank reserves by selling/buying bonds.

Q 21 With a fixed exchange rate, the rate of flow of capital into a country depends on two factors: _____

_____ ;

and _____

_____

Q 22 In the long run with a fixed exchange rate, the domestic interest rate will tend to be stabilized/destabilized by international capital flows. As a result, fiscal policy will have an enhanced/reduced effect.

Q 23   If the exchange rate is flexible, however, the effectiveness of fiscal policy will be enhanced/reduced. Why? _____
_____
_____
_____

Q 24   To put it concisely, in such a case the fiscal stimulus is offset by _____.

Q 25   In the theory of exchange-rate overshooting, exchange rates respond not only to interest-rate differentials and inflation differentials, but also to _____
_____.

QUESTIONS FOR DISCUSSION

1   Consider two countries, active in international trade. The economy of the first contains many independent firms, producing a wide range of different exports, from raw materials to complex manufactures. The second contains a few large firms, linked together and with the government, producing a very small range of tradeable products. The first, under a fixed-exchange-rate system, will, *ceteris paribus*, require less foreign exchange than the second. Why?

2   In March 1983, after lengthy discussions, members of the European Monetary System realigned their currencies – some revaluing their currencies and others devaluing. On 24.3.83, S. Brittan wrote in the *Financial Times* as follows:

'Under the latest currency realignments, the European Monetary System becomes in effect a crawling peg. There has been no harmonisation of underlying inflation rates or of economic policy inside the Community. Thus exchange-rate changes are inevitable. The EMS is simply a way by which the parity changes are made in a series of steps by governments, instead of continuously in the market place.

'The pros and cons of making exchange-rate changes this way are much less important than many people think. But if there is to be a European crawling peg, it might be less disruptive to the foreign-exchange market if the changes were smaller and more frequent.'

(a)   Why are there exchange-rate changes if there is 'no harmonisation of inflation rates'?
(b)   Why does Brittan argue that the EMS has become a 'crawling peg'?
(c)   What are the pros and cons of 'crawling peg' versus flexible exchange rates?

3   What is the difference between expenditure-changing and expenditure-switching policies?

4   Speculation in the stock market is not always destabilizing. Why is this speculation different, in respect of risks borne, from currency speculation under a regime of fixed exchange rates? (*Hint*: in the stock market, prices of stocks can easily go up or down. In a fixed-exchange-rate regime, how often is there this sort of uncertainty about the likely direction of changes?)

5   'Sweden's Scandinavian neighbours reacted bitterly yesterday to the decision by the new Stockholm Government to devalue the Krona by 16 per cent. Finland was forced to follow suit by devaluing the Markka for the second time in less than a week, this time by 6 per cent.

'Norway said it would not devalue but it expected to decide today on other measures to protect the competitiveness of its industry. Sweden was exporting its problems, Norwegian ministers said.' (Reports in the *Financial Times*, 11.10.82.)

(a) What did the Norwegian ministers mean when they said that 'Sweden was exporting its problems'?

(b) Why was Finland forced to devalue again in such a short time when Norway did not? Can you suggest any reasons?

6 A British trade union policy paper of February 1975 read:

'A reasonable objective would be to cut our current trade deficit by £1,000m. Some growth in exports is likely and 3% more in real terms (a very modest goal) would provide an extra £500m. So we would need to reduce imports by £500m (at 1974 prices) to reduce the deficit by £1,000m.

'Until North Sea oil comes on stream, fuel imports cannot be affected more than marginally. Nor is there much to be gained in the short-term by cutting back on food, raw materials or semi-manufactured goods. In general these are essential for consumption or industry.

'The burden must fall chiefly on manufactured goods, which provide about one quarter of all imports. This is also the sector in which unemployment is most prone to occur domestically.

'It makes eminent political and industrial sense to protect British jobs in such industries as motors, electrical consumer durables and telecommunications. In 1974, car imports from West Germany, France and Japan alone contributed £240m to our trade deficit, while textiles and yarns from the EEC contributed £256m.'

Retaliation was not expected: 'After all, the alternative to controls is deflation, which hits the rest of the world as much.'

The *Sunday Times* (9.2.75) reported, however, that the 'second permanent secretary at the Department of Industry warned that import controls would be against the rules of GATT, and could lead to trouble with our EEC partners'.

Discuss this; are there no alternatives to protection or deflation?

7 '... if you run an import-prone economy, like Britain's, you simply dare not get out of line on competitiveness. When you have done whatever can be done by increasing efficiency and moderating wage settlements, there is no other option but to allow the exchange rate to decline to absorb any residual loss of competitiveness.' (David Lipsey, *Sunday Times*, 19.12.82.)

'How far devaluation helps to maintain employment and how far it is just frittered away depends crucially on the wage response. A successful devaluation is a way of reducing real wages below what they would otherwise be, just as putting the clock forward is a convenient way of making us all get up a little earlier.' (Samuel Brittan, *Financial Times*, 24.3.83.)

Why do both writers stress wage settlements when talking about devaluation? How does devaluation reduce real wages?

8 According to the *Guardian* (29.3.79), Malaysia 'is fast becoming one of the richest [countries] in South-East Asia', '... Malaysia is the world's leading producer of rubber, palm oil, hardwood, cocoa, and pepper, with large resources of petroleum and natural gas.'. '... Malaysia last year registered its third trade surplus in excess of $3 billion [despite] the fact that for the greater part of the year, surplus showed an alarming downward trend. This situation is a reflection of the vulnerability of Malaysia's open economy, which is heavily dependent on exports. About 75 per cent of the exports are made up of primary raw materials .... This means that in times of recession export earnings are drastically trimmed by the sharp drop in demand by Malaysia's main trading partners, particularly Japan, United States, and the EEC countries.'

Trace out the effect on the Malaysian economy of:

(a) recession in the US and EEC economies;
(b) decline of the US dollar;
(c) appreciation of foreign currencies against the ringgit (Malaysian currency).

What policies would you recommend to the Malaysian Government in order to make the economy less vulnerable to recession in other parts of the world?

9 Mr Peter Walker, a Conservative MP and president of the Tory Reform Group, commented that 'the challenges of the 1990s would not be solved by any single 'simplistic economic dogma'.

'Mr Walker singled out two main problems. These were "inflation due to a consumer credit boom and our worst ever non-oil balance of payments provoked again by consumer credit sucking in imports of consumer goods from overseas."' (*Financial Times*, 11.4.89.)

(a) Discuss how (i) monetary policy and/or (ii) exchange-rate policy could be used to stop the excessive *import* of consumer goods. Consider the effect your policy may have on *export* production and sales.

(b) What could have caused the 'consumer credit boom' in the first place? Is private consumption of domestic goods (i.e. absorption) determined by interest rates or (as in our model of the consumption function in Chapter 28) by income levels alone? If interest rates determine consumption, perhaps they should be made endogenous to the consumption function (and hence implicitly the savings function). Keeping these points in mind, discuss whether each of the policies discussed in (a) above would solve the problem of a consumer credit boom.

CHAPTER 41
Growth in Less Developed Countries

QUESTIONS FOR DISCUSSION

1 Up to the time of the oil price rise, many industrialized countries were happy to receive migrant workers, but as unemployment rates rose in later years, these countries tried to check the inflow. Nevertheless, in many countries migrant workers are still a significant proportion of the total workforce. 'In 1977 foreign manpower accounted for nearly 10% of West Germany's, and over 7% of France's economically active population. But between 1974 and 1977, the number of foreign workers in West Germany had fallen by 19%, and that in France by 16%' (*Economist*, 24.2.79, p. 33). Some of the migrant labour had moved to the oil-rich countries. For example, the *Financial Times* estimated that 700,000 Pakistanis were working abroad and that about half of these were working in Middle East oil-producing countries in 1979 (P. Bowring, 23.3.79).

What are the benefits and costs of such labour (a) to labour-importing countries; and (b) to labour-exporting countries?

2 In November 1974, at the opening of the UN World Food Conference, Kurt Waldheim, UN Secretary-General, said: 'If enough food is to be produced to keep up with the world population growth, if some improvement in living standards is to be achieved for the most underprivileged, and if adequate security stocks are to be established and maintained, then we must begin immediately to work for an expansion of food production in magnitudes never before undertaken or even achieved.' (Reported in *The Times*, 6.11.74.) At about the same time, the EC, having disposed of a butter mountain, was facing a beef surplus.

Is there really a food problem? Is the problem to be found not in production but in distribution?

3 Mexico is one of the heavily indebted yet industrializing countries of the Third World. In October 1988 the US government announced a $3.5 *billion* loan to help Mexico meet its existing debt-repayment obligations. The new loan prevented an impending crisis, but did not reduce Mexico's overall level of debt.

Is this kind of borrowing a good response to the debt crisis? Answer first from the US government's point of view, then from the Mexican government's point of view. What are the alternatives?

4 Mexico is also a country with a rapid population growth rate. The rate was 3.4% per year during the 1970s, but it fell to 2.6% per year over 1980–85 and is predicted to fall to 2.2% per year in the 1990s. What factors could have caused this fall in the population growth rate?

5 In Kenya, the population growth rate rose from 3.9% in the 1970s to 4.1% in the period 1980–85. In other words the Kenyans have found it difficult to limit the growth of their population. Looking at the table below, can you give some reasons why there may be such a difference between Kenya's and Mexico's experience?

	Mexico	Kenya
% of GDP in agriculture	11%	31%
% of GDP in industry	35%	20%
% of population in the rural areas	31%	80%
Average life expectancy	67	54
Estimated average daily calorie supply	3177	2151

6 'Debt reduction' is the phrase used when international banks write off a portion (e.g. 20%) of the outstanding loans of a heavily indebted country. Instead of forcing a complete default, banks have decided in some cases to allow non-payment of *part* of each loan but to require payment of the remaining debts as usual. In 1989 the US government proposed a plan of limited 'official support' for such write-offs, seeing this as a way to avoid a further debt crisis. 'Official support' refers to the World Bank and International Monetary Fund providing funds for commercial banks to use to partially cover themselves for losses incurred on bad LDC debts. The *Financial Times* leader at that time commented:

'Debt reduction is perilous. Moral hazard is the greatest risk, with the largest rewards going to the worst-managed countries. Debt reduction will also inevitably militate against the provision of new money from commercial lenders. Finally, debt reduction could well prove contagious across countries and progressive within each.

'It is important, therefore, to minimise official support for debt reduction as a general principle . . .' (*Financial Times*, 13.3.89.).

(a) Why is default so undesirable for banks?
(b) Do you agree that 'debt reduction is perilous'? Explain.
(c) Explain why the commercial banks might be *against* official support for debt reduction.
(d) How can the debt crisis be resolved in the long run?

7 Many LDCs depend on just one or two export commodities for a large proportion of their export earnings: Ivory Coast exports a lot of coffee; Mauritius depends on sugar exports; etc; Zambia depends on copper exports for over 80% of its export earnings. Yet the world price of these commodities can rise or fall drastically overnight, leaving the country with severe balance-of-payments problems. What can a country like Zambia do to reduce its dependence on a single major export?

CHAPTER 42
Macroeconomic Controversies

QUESTIONS FOR DISCUSSION

1 'Differences between Monetarists and Keynesians over the control of inflation arise because of different views about the aggregate supply function.'
   Do you agree?

2 Analyse carefully the reasons why Keynesians believe that changes in the money supply are caused by fluctuations in business activity, rather than the other way round.

3 Are expectations about the value of economic variables as important in influencing behaviour as actual observations of the values of these variables?

4 Is there agreement amongst economists as to the usefulness of systematic stabilization policy?

5 Extract from a speech by Lord Kaldor in the House of Lords on 16.4.80, published in *The Economic Consequences of Mrs Thatcher*, Fabian Tract 486, Jan. 1983, p. 9:
   'When Lord Cockfield told the House the other day that the "money supply was the critical factor in the level of inflation" he was saying in effect no more than a doctor who says "body temperature is a critical factor in health". You cannot cure disease by bringing down the temperature, even though your temperature will necessarily come down if and when the disease is cured.
   'The true instrumental variables are fiscal policy and interest rate policy. These influence the level of expenditure of consumers and businesses and, through them, the public's demand to hold liquid assets, cash and bank deposits.'
   Is Lord Kaldor arguing that monetary policy is ineffective?

6 Extracts from an article by Alan Budd, *Financial Times* (6.10.82):
   '[The Conservative Government] has, however, shown itself exceptionally determined to concentrate on inflation. That leaves it open to two types of criticism. The first is that the gains in reducing inflation have not been worth the cost in terms of lost output and high unemployment. The second is that the gains could have been achieved at much lower cost.
   'If the government continues to concentrate on reducing inflation, it must believe that the economy will eventually recover of its own accord.'

   (a) Prepare two brief statements: (i) defending the government's policy against the criticisms made above; (ii) elaborating the criticisms.
   (b) What is the monetary adjustment path which will cause the economy to recover?

7 In *Economic Recovery: What Labour Must Do*, Fabian Tract 485, published in December 1982, the following proposals were put forward:

(a) Increases in government capital expenditure;
(b) Abolition of the National Insurance Surcharge, and cuts in employees' National Insurance contributions;
(c) Raise income tax thresholds by 10%;
(d) Reduce interest rates to 6% (long-term) and 4% (short-term);
(e) Subsidize food by £3 billion;
(f) Maintain real value of social security payments.

The authors of the pamphlet argue that 'a package on these lines would boost real income and reduce prices. It would change inflationary expectations and make it worthwhile for all sections of the community to cooperate in helping to achieve price stabilization in conditions of rapid expansion ....

'Our problems are entirely due to a combination of an overvalued exchange rate, combined with excessive saving and they will only be solved by giving people the opportunity to spend more and, as a necessary corollary, allowing a more flexible monetary policy to bring down the exchange rate. We must not be afraid of increasing the quantity of money by whatever amount is required to achieve this objective. We must likewise ignore pressure from the City to fund the borrowing requirement, because funding takes out of circulation money which would be better spent on goods and services.' (pp. 5–8)

Evaluate these proposals.

Answers

CHAPTER 1

1   The production obtainable from using all available resources is insufficient to satisfy all the wants that people have.

2   Opportunity cost

3   (1) Land, Labour, Capital.
       (2) Entrepreneurship
       (3) Factors of production

4   (2) By what methods are these commodities produced?
       (3) How is society's output of goods and services divided among its members?

5   (1) Are the country's resources being fully utilized, or are some of them lying idle?
       (2) Its resources, though fully utilized, may be used inefficiently in production.

6   If all resources are being utilized efficiently, then producing more of one commodity requires shifting resources away from producing some other commodity.

7   (1) 7,200 kg
       (2) None (the economy would operate inside the production possibility boundary).
       (3) 30 36
       (4) 2,400 kg of butter

8   (a), (c), (d), (e)

9   (a), (c), (f), (h)

10   (b), (d), down, up.

11   (1) An increase in demand for tennis racquets is followed by a rise in price.
      (2) A rise in the cost of producing bats causes their price to rise and some people then substitute tennis for cricket.
      (3) The reverse of (2).
      (4) The reasoning is incorrect.

12   (b)

CHAPTER 2

1   (1) P   (3) A
       (2) N   (4) P

Answers to Chapters 2-3

    (5) P + N   (8) P
    (6) P   (9) P + N
    (7) N

2   (1) stock   (4) flow
      (2) flow   (5) stock
      (3) flow   (6) flow

3   (1) exogenous
      (2) endogenous
      (3) exogenous

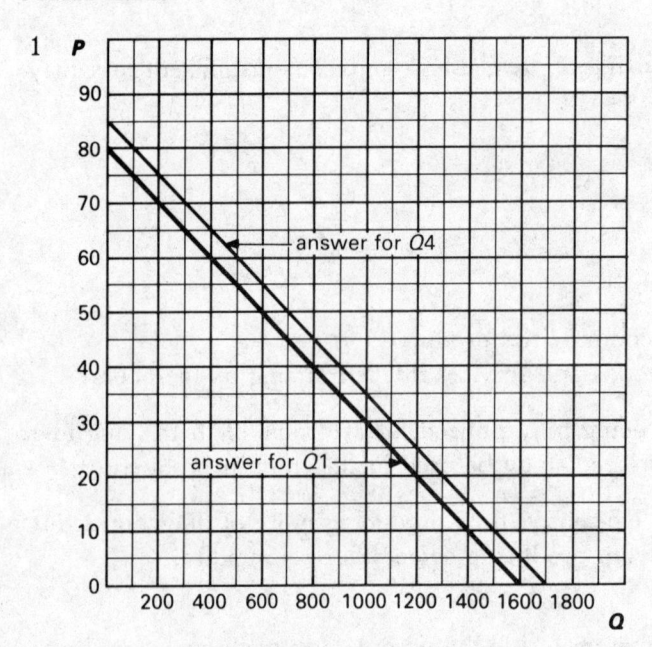

CHAPTER 3

1

2   1,600

3     $a = 1,600;\ b = 20$

5     $1,700 - 20P$

6   (a) and (b)

7   No

8   No

9   Because people with a telephone listing will naturally have more communication with other people than those without telephones. Our sample will be *biased*.

10   Consider, for example, individuals B and C – same size of estate but different number of acquaintances.

11

—	—	47	—
—	38.5	37	55
17	28	33.5	—
—	—	17	—

258

Answers to Chapters 3–5

12 People whose gardens join three other gardens know, on average, less people the larger the estate on which they live.

13 People who live on an estate of 81–120 houses know, on average, less people the fewer is the number of gardens adjoining their own.

APPENDIX TO CHAPTER 3

2   $+780$; $MR = 80 - 1/10q$

CHAPTER 4

1   Household

2   One

3   Firm

4   Yes

5   Utility; profit

6   Factors of production; firms

7   (b), (d), (e).

8   An area over which buyers and sellers negotiate the exchange of a well-defined commodity.

9   Lancashire

10 The world

11 All wine-drinking countries

12 Products perceived as not of equivalent quality; transport costs; tariffs and other import restrictions.

13 Firms; households, firms or central authorities; households; firms or central authorities.

14 Competitive

15 Free-market

16 Private

17 Market

18 Public; non-market; market

19 Macroeconomics; microeconomics

20 Factors of production; goods and services

21 Leakage from

CHAPTER 5

1   The prices of other commodities

2   (1)

Answers to Chapter 5

3   Horizontal

4   Holding constant every other variable (except price) that influences demand.

5   Per year and per cwt (or some similar expressions)

6   Approximately £2.90

7   £2

8   3

9   17

11   (d) and (f)

12   False

13   A good of which households wish to buy less as their incomes are increased.

14   Households would reduce their purchase of all goods and therefore spend less in total.

15
- (1) Left
- (2) Right
- (3) Left
- (4) Right
- (5) Indeterminate
- (6) Right
- (7) Left
- (8) Right

16   (6)

17
- (1) Movement along
- (2) Shift
- (3) Movement along
- (4) Shift

18   The prices of factors of production

19   3,700

20   250

21
- (1) Left
- (2) Not at all
- (3) Not at all

22   (d)

23   The price at which quantity demanded equals quantity supplied.

24   £3.50 per ton

25   4 tons per year

26   Yes

27   Upward

28   Downward

29
- (1) 5.5 tons per year
- (2) 1.75 tons per year
- (3) −1.4 tons per year
- (4) −6.25 tons per year

30   2 tons per year

31   Approximately £4.20

32   Approximately 5.1 tons per year

33 Right

34 Left

35 Impossible

36 Approximately 5.75 tons per year

37 + 1.75 tons per year

38 Price rises to induce extra supply and this chokes off some of the extra demand.

39 (1) supply; left; demand; higher; lower
    (2) demand; right; supply; higher; higher
    (3) demand; left; supply; lower; lower
    (4) rise; indeterminate change

40 25

CHAPTER 6

1 $\dfrac{\text{the percentage change in quantity demanded}}{\text{the percentage change in income}}$

2 $\dfrac{\text{the percentage change in quantity supplied}}{\text{the percentage change in price}}$

3 (1) insufficient information   (3) insufficient information
   (2) 5   (4) 0.5

4 (1) No   (2) 1½

5 (1) ⅔   (2) 4

6 Below price x, none will be supplied; at or above price x, as many units will be supplied as the market will take.

7 No. No seller will supply at a price below £5; no buyer will be willing to pay more than £4.

8 45 pence

9 Rises

10 Rises

11 Greater

12 Negative

13 $\dfrac{\text{the percentage change in quantity demanded of good } X}{\text{the percentage change in price of good } Y}$

14 Positive

15 False

16 True

17 False

18 False

19   (a)

20   (b)

21   (e)

22   It is zero.

23   (1) £12
     (2) £15

24   Zero

25   (c)

APPENDIX TO CHAPTER 6

1   − 35   0.7
     − 16   0.8
     − 9   0.9
     + 11   1.1
     + 25   1.2
     + 85   1.7

2   £0–£5

3   £5–£10

4   Not changed.

5   False

6   Yes; one.

CHAPTER 7

1   (d)

2   £20 and over

3   approximately 35 units

4   approximately £25.50 per unit

5   £50 and below

6   Rise

7   Fall

8   Approximately 80

9   Falls; greater than one

10   If demand were inelastic

11   (2) You should shift the demand curve to the right
     (3) Elastic
     (4) q_2
     (5) q_1

(6) $q_4 - q_1$
(7) queueing, landlords choosing by race or age preference, entrance fees or deposits, etc.

12   £6

13   40,000

14   2,000

15   12,000

16   £84,000

17   38,000

18   Greater; inelastic

APPENDIX TO CHAPTER 7

1   (1) £4   (6) £2.70
     (2) $t + 2$ (7) 28
     (3) $t + 4$ (8) £2.05
     (4) £1.55   (9) 24
     (5) 20.5

2   Stable

3   Stable

4   2; never

5   Stable

6   True

CHAPTER 8

1   The household

2   (1) Below the line   (5) No
     (2) Both   (6) Yes
     (3) 2; down by £2.50   (7) Yes
     (4) No

3   p

4    $2.5x$

5   (1) (a)   (2) (c)

6   (1) 0   (3) 2
     (2) 2   (4) 2

7   (a)

Answers to Chapter 8

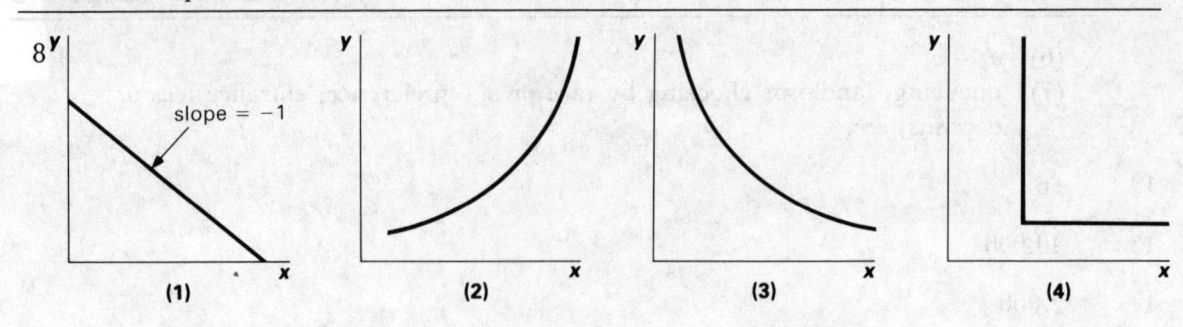

8 [Four graphs labeled (1), (2), (3), (4): (1) downward-sloping straight line with slope = −1; (2) upward-curving convex increasing curve; (3) decreasing convex curve (hyperbola-like); (4) L-shaped right-angle curve]

9   (2) Yes; approximately 1.6
    (3) Yes; yes; yes; 13
    (4) (a) No
        (b) No
        (c) Yes
        (d) Between approximately 13 and 25 units of clothes

10 (2) Right
    (3) 2.3 times
    (4) (a) No (b) No
        (c) Yes (d) between approximately 13 and 25 units of clothes

11 True

12 False

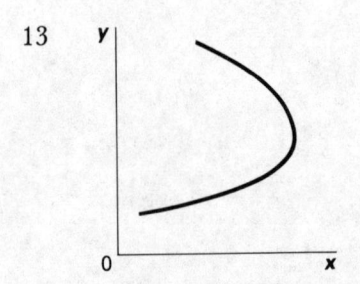

13 [Graph showing a curve on x-y axes that opens to the left, forming a sideways parabola-like shape]

14 (1) approximately 1,175
    (2) approximately 800

15 (c)

16 (1) approximately 110 loaves
    (2) approximately − 35
    (3) approximately − 15
    (4) approximately + 25
    (5) approximately − 30

17 True

18 True

19 False

20 False

APPENDIX TO CHAPTER 8

1   The consumption of all other commodities is held constant.

Answers to Chapters 8–10

2   False

3   (1) Approximately 0.4
    (2) Approximately 0.4
    (3) Oppose

4   (1) Smaller   (3) (c) and sometimes (b)
    (2) (b)   (4) (b)

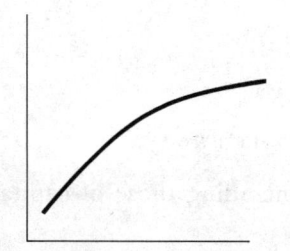

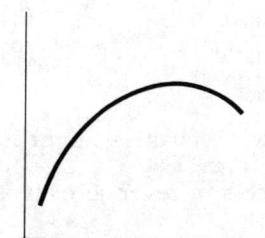

5   (1) [graph: increasing concave curve]   (2) [graph: inverted-U curve]

6   $$\frac{\text{MU of good } x}{\text{price of good } x} = \frac{\text{MU of good } y}{\text{price of good } y}$$

7   (1) 5
    (2) 5

8   (1) 50
    (2) 8

CHAPTER 9

1   £560

2   (b)

3   Diminishing

4   False

5   Inelastic

6   Greater

7   False

8   (c)

CHAPTER 10

1   (a) Single proprietorship
    (b) Partnership
    (c) Joint-stock company
    (d) Public corporation

2   Undistributed

3   To maximize profits

Answers to Chapters 10–11

4 False. A firm with spare cash could lend it elsewhere and secure interest receipts which would be forgone if the cash were used for its own investments.

5 True. The opportunity cost would be lower if the firm used its own funds. The interest rate which its funds could attract elsewhere is lower than the interest rate it would have to pay if it used borrowed funds.

6 (1) £500 (6) Zero
   (2) £500 (7) It halves
   (3) Zero (8) True
   (4) £1,000 (9) Yes. £250.
   (5) £500

7 Otherwise, farmers might have to pay to have it taken away.

8 An excess of revenue over all opportunity costs including those of capital.

CHAPTER 11

1 The relation between inputs and outputs.

2 Neither

3 The period of time over which at least one factor is fixed.

4 (1) Short-run
   (2)
AP	MP
10	10
14	17
16	22
18	24
19	23
19	16
17	7
15	2
14	1

   (4) Yes
   (5) 73
   (6) 96

5 True

6 (1)
1	10	500	20	520	50	2	52	2
2	27	500	40	540	18.5	1.5	20	1.18
3	49	500	60	560	10.2	1.22	11.4	0.9
4	73	500	80	580	6.9	1.10	7.9	0.8
5	96	500	100	600	5.2	1.04	6.3	0.9
6	112	500	120	620	4.5	1.07	5.5	1.2
7	119	500	140	640	4.2	1.18	5.4	2.9
8	121	500	160	660	4.1	1.5	5.5	10
9	122	500	180	680	4.1	1.5	5.6	20

   (3) 73
   (4) 119
   (5) 96
   (6) Never
   (7) Lowest

7   119

8   True. Maximizing profits always involves minimizing the cost of producing the given output level, but it is also necessary to choose correctly which level of output gives the highest excess of revenue over cost.

9 & 10 $\dfrac{MP_K}{P_K} = \dfrac{MP_L}{P_L}$ and $\dfrac{MP_K}{MP_L} = \dfrac{P_K}{P_L}$

11 (1) Less; more
    (2) Rise by 100

12 Yes; more

13 (c)

14 (1) *LRATC*
    (2) One
    (3) Because the capital usage of the *SRATC* curve is inappropriate to the output of Q^1.

15 (1) Isoquants   (6) 20
    (2) Right   (7) £380
    (3) Capital   (8) Capital up 2; labour down 2½
    (4) £265   (9) Substitution
    (5) £340

16 (1) £6   (2) 75 units

17 False

18 True

19 True

20 (d)

21 (d)

22 (d)

CHAPTER 12

1   Price-taker
    Freedom of entry and exit

2   Same horizontal straight line

3   It is a horizontal straight line at a price of 50p

4   (1) No   (2) £250

5   Cost; revenue; marginal cost

6   It is not a profit-maximizer.

7   (1) 23   (3) £4.25
    (2) £15   (4) £5.25; 20; £60

8   (1) £1; 6,000   (2) 10 per week   (3) 12½ per week

9   Yes; 15

Answers to Chapters 12-13

10   (1)   £350
       (2)   £150
       (3)   £300

11   The industry has freedom of entry and exit.

12   (1)   Yes
       (2)   Out of; rise

13   (e)

14   (f)

15   (e)

16   (b)

17   True

18   False

19   True

20   False

21   True

CHAPTER 13

1   (1)   The quantity of a good demanded at each price.
      (2)   The change in revenue resulting from a change in sales of one unit.
      (3)   The total cost of producing a given output (with the existing amount of the fixed factors of production) divided by that output.
      (4)   The total cost of producing a given output (with the optimal factor proportions) divided by that output.
      (5)   The cost of all the variable factors of production used to produce a given output divided by that output.
      (6)   The change in total cost arising from a change in the rate of output of one unit per period.
      (7)   The excess of revenue over all costs.

2   No. $MR \neq (AR = P)$

3   (1)   £136.50   (5)   £148.50
      (2)   £144   (6)   −£1.50
      (3)   £7.50   (7)   greater than
      (4)   £150   (8)   less than

4   (1)   less than   (6) $\dfrac{\Delta Q}{\Delta P} \cdot \dfrac{P}{Q}$
      (2)   increase
      (3)   £10   (7)   ⅔
      (4)   falls   (8)   1½
      (5)   halfway down   (9)   +£60

5   £3.50

6   Both

Answers to Chapters 13–14

7   (1)   100   (5)   £16
     (2)   £700   (6)   Zero
     (3)   £15   (7)   need not
     (4)   Until the fixed equipment wears out.

8   (1)   12.50   (3)   13
     (2)   One   (4)   Elastic

9   They can all be barriers to entry.

10   No. Price discrimination describes situations where different customers are charged different prices for reasons not associated with different costs of supplying them.

11   Yes. It costs the same to supply a student as anyone else.

12   Resale of the product

13   False

APPENDIX TO CHAPTER 13

1   (1)   5,000
     (2)   5.50
     (3)   20,000
     (4)   15
     (5)   Although more tickets would be sold, price would have to be cut so much that revenue would fall – one would be moving along inelastic parts of these two demand curves.

2   (1)   £11   (3)   5¼
     (2)   £13.75   (4)   3¼

CHAPTER 14

1   By shifting it

2   (2)   £0.70
     (3)   1.475m
     (4)   £0.35 profit per unit, a total of £516,250 per month

3   They will wish to enter the industry.

4   (1)   Left
     (2)   Yes
     (3)   Leave the industry

5   £0.40

6   (1)   £5 ; 12
     (2)   £10 ; 22
     (3)   £15 ; 12

7   Yes. There is no incentive to leave or enter the industry.

8   (1)   Excess capacity
     (2)   Attract
     (3)   Fall

Answers to Chapters 14-15

  (4) Left
  (5) *LRAC*
  (6) The demand curve falls more sharply than the SRAC curve so to sell the extra output price would have to drop by more than average cost.

9 (1) Normal capacity
  (2) Full capacity

10 (2) Because you cannot shut down part of a main-frame computer.

11 (1) Kinked

12 Will remain at its current output

13 (1) 30 (7) 45
  (2) 20 (8) 15
  (3) 10 (9) True
  (6) 20, 20, 40

14 (1) £30 (2) True

15 (a)

16 (1) £160,000
  (2) £80,000
  (3) £52,000

17 Less

18 (d)

19 (g)

20 (d)

21 True

22 False

23 True

24 False

CHAPTER 15

1 $p^0 \times q^0$

2 No (it is possible that demand elasticity is one at equilibrium).

3 Yes (at a lower output).

4 (1) Demand elasticity > 1 between old and new equilibrium quantities
  (2) Shallower
  (3) Less
  (4) Costs fall by more

5 Price was above marginal cost – and, as *individual* farmers, they would not drive down price by adding to output.

6 (2) £1 per pig
  (3) £280 per month
  (4) About £580 per month

Answers to Chapters 15-16

7   (2) $P = 2$; $Q = 3,000$
      (3) $32 - \dfrac{Q}{200}$
      (4)   + £2.20 (approximately)
      (5)   About £17

8   New firms will be drawn into the industry raising total output.

9   The long-run supply curve is a horizontal straight line.

10   There are more firms in the industry.

11   No change; number of firms

12   True

13   True

14   True

15   Variable

16   Rise

17   Fall

19   (1)   + about £1.20; − about 18
      (2)   + about £0.80; − about 10
      (3)   competition

20   False

21   Neither

22   All passed on

23   A lump-sum tax raises the *LRAC* curve: at the initial price, there would be exit from the industry and this will continue until profits return to zero.

24   A 'profits' tax is usually levied even on items treated by the economist as costs, most importantly on the return to capital.

25   (c)

26   (1)   True   (3)   False
      (2)   True   (4)   False

27   (c)

28   False

29   True

30   True

31   False

32   False

33   True

CHAPTER 16

1   The principal-agent problem

2   (b)

Answers to Chapters 16–17

3   higher

4   (1)   900
         (2)   The firm would make losses beyond $Q = 2,100$ and would go out of business – managers would lose their jobs.

5   Stay the same

6   Fall

7   Yes

8   No, if this alibi is used whenever a firm is observed not to be maximizing short-run profits.

9   No

10   £218.75

CHAPTER 17

1   The relative incomes received by each factor of production.

2   The society would have exact equality of income.

3   Greater

4   (1)   Decreased
         (2)   Increased
         (3)   Decreased

5   £1,250

6   Left; £850

7   It will fall

8   The demand for the products it helps to produce.

9   Marginal revenue product

10   (1)   £40   (4)   £4
         (2)   £18   (5)   −£1
         (3)   £9   (6)   24

11   (1)   −12   (3)   11
         (2)   −8   (4)   20

12   (1)   14   (3)   41
         (2)   22   (4)   7

13   Marginal cost; price of the variable factor; all

14   diminishing returns

15   not at all

16   Correct

17   150

18   125

19   100

Answers to Chapter 17

20	£0.10
21	550
22	£0.10
23	(550, £0.10)
24	75
25	£0.13
26	625
27	(625, £0.13)
28	(675, £0.20)
29	(700, £0.40)
30	£0.10
31	£5
32	£0.15
33	(2.7, £20) (2.7 is a feasible employment level as 2 units can be hired for the whole working day and the 0.7 extra made up by a part-time worker).
34	Steeper
35	right; fall; left.
36	(1) More (2) False (3) True
37	more
38	False
39	easily
40	False
41	(1) £40 (3) 10; 25 (2) 8 (4) risen; income
42	measure
43	Differences in non-monetary advantages between different factor uses are stable.
44	(1) shift to left (2) shift to right (3) shift to left (4) no shift – the equilibrium will be further up their supply curve (5) shift to left (6) shift to right
45	transfer earnings
46	Zero
47	£1,000 per year

Answers to Chapters 17–19

48 Yes – if you are paid less than your transfer earnings (though you would presumably remedy this at the first opportunity).

49 Intra industry: TE £100,000   rent zero
Inter industry: TE £193,760   rent £6,240

50 (1) £40 per week
(2) £80 per week

51 Quasi-rent

52 A factor payment which is an economic rent in the short run and transfer earnings in the long run.

53 No; some would be transfer earnings since lower 'rents' would lead to some rooms being put to other uses (e.g. landlord's own use).

CHAPTER 18

1 forgone earnings from not taking a job immediately; higher wage receipts in future years.

2 The imparting of skills which have value in the labour market beyond just one particular firm.

3 False. Workers will accept less because they are obtaining skills which will enhance their incomes in future years.

4 (1) W_2
(2) L_1
(3) W_1; L_1
(4) False; some wage increase is possible that would raise employment – the firm would be forced to become a price-taker in the labour market and no longer would it have an incentive to restrict employment to avoid driving up the wage rate against itself.
(5) W_2
(6) W_3
(7) L_4 minus L_1

5 True

6 True

7 (1) 3   (4) 2
(2) £20   (5) 4; £25.50
(3) 4

8 True

9 True

10 equal to

CHAPTER 19

1 depreciation

2 zero

3 contract

Answers to Chapters 19-20

4   signal the need to reallocate resources

5   1.05

6   1.05

7     $Y \times 1.05$

8     $Z = (£100 \times 1.05^2) \times 1.05 = £100 \times 1.05^3$

9     $Z = K(1 + i)^t$

10    $K = \dfrac{Z}{(1 + i)^t}$

11   (1) £90.90   (3) £55.89
       (2) £97.63   (4) £244.42

12   £24.44

13   0.469

14   (b)

15   (1) 11.25%   (3) £5,500
       (2) £9,500   (4) No; yes

16   False

17   rise

18   raising

19   minus 3%

20   True

21   a loss of £667

22   £500

23   Higher

24   Higher risk

25   Lower

26   You get your money back more quickly if you want it

27   risk; expected inflation

28   (b)

29   (b)

30   (1) rate of interest
       (2) fallen

CHAPTER 20

1   False

2   True

3   Greater than

Answers to Chapters 20–21

4   raise; rise; will; Yes

5   No. The wage rate must fall but, since the number of workers rises, labour's share in national income could go up or down.

6   No. The price of land is predicted to rise. The total income of land-owners therefore rises but their share of a growing national income could go either way.

7   Yes. The rise in the marginal productivity of capital will raise its price. Since the number of units of capital is constant, the absolute income of capital must rise.

CHAPTER 21

1   (1) coffee beans; Land-Rovers; Land-Rovers; coffee beans
    (2) 50; Land-Rovers; 250; coffee beans; 5,000; coffee beans; 5; Land-Rovers
    (3) 4,750; 45

2   absolute

3   reciprocal absolute advantage

4   No

5   False

6   comparative

7   amplifiers; speakers

8   10,000; amplifiers; 5,000; speakers; 4,000; speakers; 3,000; amplifiers

9   1,000 fewer; 7,000 more

10 4,000; 3,000

11 3,000 more; 4,000 more

12 200,000 litres; 20,000 litres

13 (1) 1,000 bushels of coffee beans   0.2 Land-Rovers

    (2) 0.75 amplifiers   1.33 speakers
        2 amplifiers   0.5 speakers

    (3) 0.4 litres of olive oil   2.5 litres of wine
        0.2 litres of olive oil   5 litres of wine

14 lower

15 Terms of trade

16 below 1.33

17 (1) No
    (2) No
    (3) Yes

18 0.5; 1.33

19 (1) 350   (3) 300; 30
    (2) 400   (4) 50

20 (1) 16,000
    (2) 800
    (3) 4,000

CHAPTER 22

1.
   (1) £19.67
   (2) 40
   (3) 12 million
   (4) 28 million
   (5) £18
   (6) 28 million
   (7) 18 million
   (8) 10 million
   (9) £102m
   (10) £30m
   (11) £45m
   (12) £102m; £30m; £45m; £27m

2. 10 million

3. £57m; £30m of the consumer surplus loss accrues to the government as tariff revenue in the one case, but is transferred away to foreign producers in the other.

4. 50

5. The canning industry can have up to 50% higher costs in Northland than in Southland and still be viable.

6. True

7. False

CHAPTER 23

1. It would be impossible to make one person better off without making someone else worse off.

2. productive

3. allocative

4. All firms face the same price. Each firm maximizes profits with $P = MC$. Therefore MC must be the same everywhere.

5. True

6.
   (1) 40
   (2) £120
   (3) 80
   (4) £4,800
   (5) £3,200
   (6) £1,600

7.
   (1) a
   (2) $c; k$
   (3) $abgc$
   (4) $abdc$
   (5) fgh
   (6) bfg

8. The number of extra units of Y that can be produced if the production of X is reduced by one unit.

9. The number of extra units of Y that a consumer must be given to be prepared to give up one unit of X.

10. Every consumer faces the same prices.

11. Price equals marginal cost.

12. too high

13. False

14. True

15. A tendency towards a high rate of innovation.

Answers to Chapters 24-26

CHAPTER 24

1 A potential participant would only consider the benefits and costs to himself. In fact, accepting innoculation benefits all the non-innoculated population because there is one less potential carrier from whom they could be infected.

2 (1) 1,800
   (2) 1,600
   (3) Drivers only take into account costs borne by themselves and not costs imposed on other road users.
   (4) £0.12
   (5) £12

3 (1) £200; 100   (5) £1,900
   (2) £210   (6) £2,700
   (3) £20   (7) £150
   (4) £950

4 False

5 regressive

6 £50

7 £90

8 False. The substitution effect will tend to reduce hours of work but the income effect operates in the opposite direction.

CHAPTER 25

1 True

2 False

3 externality

4 less; True

5 True; internalizing the externality

6 True

7 higher; over-invested

8 False

9 It shows the relationship between the tax rate and the amount of tax revenue raised.

CHAPTER 26

1 False

2 (c)

3 True

4 current

Answers to Chapter 26

5
	GDP Deflator
1978	54
1979	61
1980	72
1981	80
1982	85
1983	90
1984	95
1985	100
1986	103
1987	108

6 1985

7 (a) 1%;   (b) 11%;   (c) 7%

8 Yes, from approximately £5,161 to £5,813 in 1985 prices.

9 £260 billion

10 False

11 inventories

12 cost of materials purchased

13 (1) *Fishermen*

Output		Factor incomes	
Sales of goods	£12,000	Wages	£8,000
less goods purchased from		Rent	100
other firms	− 900	Interest	500
		Profits	2,500
Total	£11,100	Total	£11,100

(2) *Factory*

Output		Factor incomes	
Sales of goods	£60,000	Wages	£15,000
less goods purchased from		Rent	7,000
other firms	− 11,000	Interest	6,000
		Profits	21,000
Total	£49,000	Total	£49,000

(3) *Fishmonger*

Output		Factor incomes	
Sales of goods	£10,000	Wages	£2,000
less goods purchased from		Rent	1,000
other firms	− 7,000	Interest	100
		Profit	− 100
Total	£3,000	Total	£3,000

(a) Value-added: fishermen £11,100, factory £49,000, fishmonger £3,000.
(b) Total value-added: £63,100.
(c) Profits: fishermen £2,500, factory £21,000, fishmonger − £100.

14 $C + I + G + (X - M)$

15 No – we define investment as the act of *producing* goods that are not for immediate consumption.

16 Inventories, capital goods and residential housing

Answers to Chapter 26

17 unsold; rising; intentional

18 False

19 True

20 True

21 less

22 False

23 False

24 False

25

National Product		National Expenditure		National Income	
Value-added in:		Consumers' expenditure	450	Wages and salaries	430
Agriculture	100			Self-employed	60
Manufacturing	700	Government expenditure	130	Company profits:	
Construction	120			Dividends 500	610
Distribution	180	Gross fixed investment	150	Retained profits 100	
Other sectors	290	Change in stocks	10	Public corporations	20
Less Imports	−220	Exports	210	Rent	50
		less Imports	−220		
Gross national product	1,170	Gross national expenditure	1,170	Gross national income	1,170
less depreciation	−70	*less* depreciation	−70	*less* depreciation	−70
Net national product	1,100	Net national expenditure	1,100	Net national income	1,100

26 There is the necessary information to calculate gross national income. As gross national income is, by definition, equal to gross national product at factor prices, and we are given amounts for gross and net fixed investment, we can find net national product.

(a)
Wages and salaries	1,850
Incomes of self-employed	780
Gross trading profits of companies	170
Gross trading surplus of public corporations	40
Rent	60
GNI = GNP at factor prices	2,900
less depreciation	−40
NNP at factor prices	2,860

(b)
GNP at factor prices	2,900
plus indirect taxes on expenditure	120
GNP at market prices	3,020

(c)
GNP	2,900
less Retained profits of companies	−130
Gross trading surplus of public corporations	−40
Income tax	−600
plus Transfers	30
Disposable Income	2,160

CHAPTER 27

1. (c)

2. False

3. decreased

4. (a) False   (b) False

5. True

6. True

7. $E = C + I$

8. (a) $Y = C + I$ (b) $S = I$

9. (a) 7. Unplanned fixed investment:
      Canoes   40
   8. Unplanned inventory investment:
      Yams   20
   (b) £410,000
   (c) £350,000
   (d) £90,000
   (e) £60,000
   (f) less than

10. falling, since aggregate demand excludes unplanned investment.

11. True

12. £410,000

13. $S = Y - C = £150,000$

14. greater than; equal to

15. zero; positive or zero or negative

16.
	Saving	Investment
Changes in business inventories		−10
Expenditure on plant and equipment (net)		100
Personal saving	90	
Total volume of transactions on the Stock Exchange	—	—
Expenditure on residential construction (net)		50
Undistributed business profits	60	
Value of individuals' building society deposits	120	
	270	140

17. False

18.
National Income (Y)	Consumption (C)	Saving (S)
0	0	0
20	12	8
40	24	16
60	36	24
70	42	28
100	60	40
120	72	48
125	75	50

Answers to Chapter 27

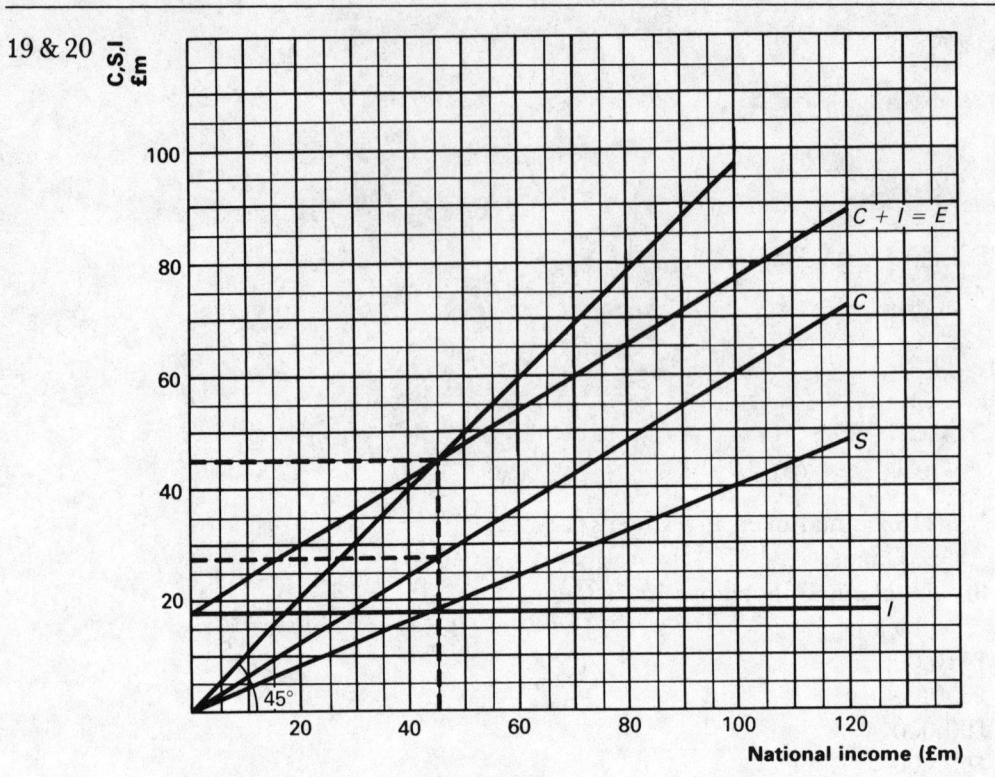

19 & 20

21 Add consumption and investment

22 investment; the aggregate expenditure function

23 $S = Y - C$, therefore $S = Y - \frac{3}{5}Y = \frac{2}{5}Y$

24 £48m

25 £20m

26 $E = 18 + \frac{3}{5}Y$

27 £45m

28 $S = I$, i.e. $\frac{2}{5}Y = 18$ and $Y = £45m$

29 (a) $Y = 0.75Y + 100$ $Y = 400$
   (b) $0.25Y = 100$ $Y = 400$

30 (a) False   (c) False
   (b) False   (d) True

31 less than

32 (a) Total consumption expenditure divided by total income, or the proportion of income spent on consumption.
   (b) $\dfrac{C}{Y}$

33 (a) The change in consumption divided by the change in income that brought it about.
   (b) $\dfrac{\Delta C}{\Delta Y}$

34 £100m

Answers to Chapters 27-28

35	£116; £4; £24; £24; contract output
36	£72; £18; £20; £92; £2; £18; £18; £2; £20; £20
37	£100
38	Rises to £110m
39	£94; £72; expand output; rise; £22
40	£75m; £60; £15; £25
41	£80; £60
42	changes the slope of; changes the slope of
43	shifts down; shifts down
44	0.9; £20
45	the change in national income; change in expenditure
46	£25
47	(a) $S = 0.2Y$ (b) The MPS
48	$Y = cY + I^*$; c is MPC and s the MPS
49	False
50	(a) 4 (b) Income rises by £4m (c) £24m

CHAPTER 28

1. (a) A is total autonomous expenditure, whereas a is autonomous consumption only. They differ by the amount of autonomous investment.
   (b) $A - a = I^*$, since $A = a + I^*$.

2. may

3. (a) APC 1.3; 1.05; 0.97; 0.93; 0.9
      MPC 0.8
   (b) falls; constant
   (c) £8
   (d) £24

4. (a) Total saving divided by total income, or the proportion of total income devoted to saving.
   (b) $\dfrac{S}{Y}$

5. (a) The change in saving divided by the change in income that brought it about.
   (b) $\dfrac{\Delta S}{\Delta Y}$

6. APS −0.3; 0.05; 0.03; 0.075; 0.11
   MPS 0.2

7. (a) 0.25   (b) 1/3   (c) 0.72

Answers to Chapter 28

8   (a) *OM*; *SM/OM*; *OS*
    (b) *RL/OL*; *OR*; greater
    (c) *UP/OP*; *OU* (not drawn); less
    (d) *UW/NP* (or *UW/TW*); *AC* (or *TU*)
    (e) *SV/LM* (or *SV/VR*); *AC* (or *RS*)
    (f) constant; less than; falling
    (g) equal to; greater than; less than

9   (a) *OA*   (b) −*OA*   (c) *AC*

10 (a) £10m (b) 3/5

11 (a) zero (b) 0.75 (c) 0.75 (d) 0.25 (e) 0.25

12 remains constant

13 (a) C_2 (c) Neither
    (b) Neither   (d) C_1

14 part; 0; 1

15 £150; 0.8; £30; shifts down

16 5

17 clockwise; decreases

18 anti-clockwise; increases

19 up; down; increases

20 less than; the *MPC* is positive but less than unity

21 (a) 4
    (b) Income rises by £4m
    (c) £24m

22 Region A − *MPC*: 0.85, 0.8, 0.75, 0.70
    Region B − *MPC*: 0.8
    (a) (1) £15,600 (2) £15,400 (3) £14,800
    (b) (1) £14,800 (2) £14,800 (3) £14,800

23 (a) £12,250
    (b) Increase by £500
    (c) (i) £50; £450   (ii) £50; £400
    (d) £12,750 plus approx. £3,111

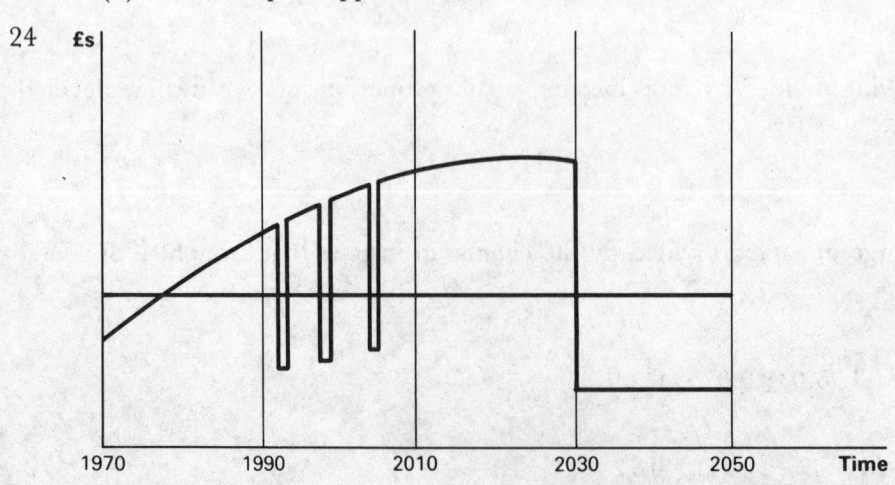

24

CHAPTER 29

1. £1,500

2. less than; government expenditure on goods and services and government transfer payments

3. income received by households after taxes have been deducted and transfers have been added

4. $Y_d = Y(1 - t) + Q$

5. (a) $C = c(1 - t)Y + cQ$
   (b) $S = s(1 - t)Y + sQ$ or $S = (1 - c)Y(1 - t) + (1 - c)Q$

6. (a) $C = 0.8(1 - 0.30)Y + 0.8(10) = 0.56Y + 8$
   (b) £36m
   (c) Tax revenue = 0.3(50m) = £15m and is therefore sufficient to cover transfers
   (d) $S = £9m$
   (e) $Y_d = £45m$

7. $C + I + G$

8. $W + J$, where $W = s(1 - t)Y + sQ + tY$ and $J = I + G + Q$
   or $s(1 - t)Y + tY = I + G + cQ$

9.

Level of national income (£m)	Disposable income (£m)	Consumption (£m)	Investment (£m)	Government expenditure (£m)	Tax revenue (£m)	Aggregate expenditure (£m)
0	40.0	32	78	70	0	180
150	152.5	122	78	70	37.5	270
250	227.5	182	78	70	62.5	330
350	302.5	242	78	70	87.5	390
450	377.5	302	78	70	112.5	450
550	452.5	362	78	70	137.5	510
650	527.5	422	78	70	162.5	570

   (a) $E = C + I + G = 180 + 0.6Y$
   (b) Slope is 0.6 and intercept is £180m
   (c) £450m
   (d) $C = £302m$, $S = £75.5m$, $Y_d = £377.5m$
   (e) Surplus of £2.5m
   (f) (See graph on p. 286)
   (g) $W = 0.15Y + 0.25Y = 0.4Y$. $J = 78 + 70 + 32 = 180$.
       When $W = J$, $Y = £180m$.
   (h) £80m
   (i) £60m

10. (a) It will be lowered or, in other words, it will pivot in a clockwise direction.
    (b) The slope will be less steep as the function pivots from the same intercept in a clockwise direction.
    (c) It will fall.

11. (a) 0.56
    (b) 0.56 and £180m
    (c) It will fall to approx. £409m.
    (d) greater than
    (e) £122.7m

12. (a) The slope will be unchanged but the intercept will be lower by the amount of the decrease in G, shifting the function downwards
    (b) It will fall

Answers to Chapter 29

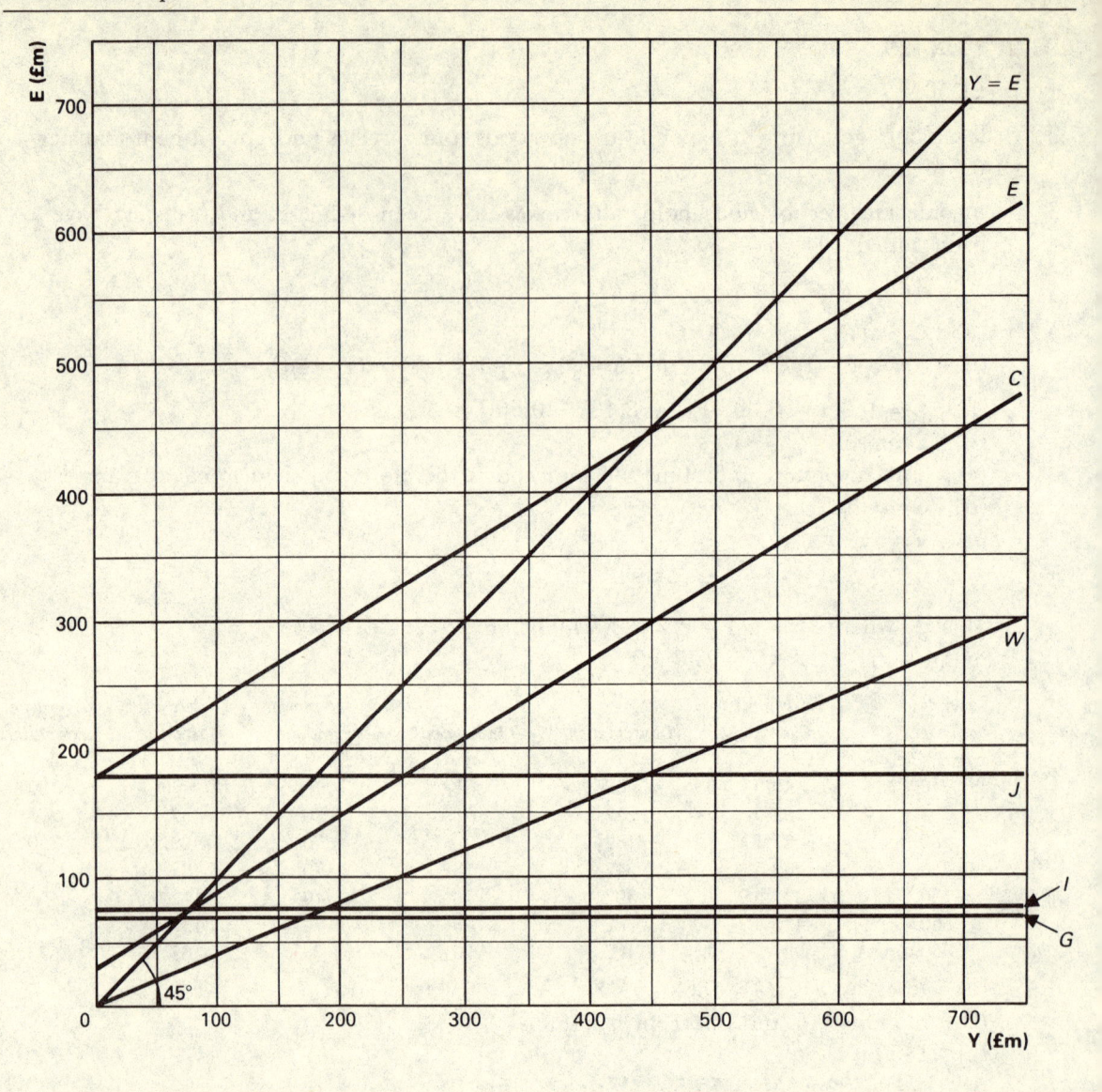

13   (a)   £436.4m approx.
         (b)   The surplus will fall to approx. £0.9m.
         (c)   The tax increase resulted in income falling by approx. £41m, but the increased government expenditure has offset this to some extent by raising income from £409m (see Question 11(c)) by approx. £27.4m.

14   (a)   £430.9m approx.
         (b)   Moves to a deficit of approx. £0.7m.
         (c)   Both shift the aggregate expenditure function upwards but injection through transfers will shift it by a smaller amount, $c(\Delta Q)$, rather than ΔG. The transfer payments' multiplier is smaller than the government expenditure multiplier as only a proportion ($c = 0.8$) enters the income stream.

15   The new equilibrium would have been the same at approx. £430.9m; however the government budget would have been in surplus.

16   remain unchanged; rise; rise; rise

17   remain unchanged; fall; fall; fall

Answers to Chapter 29

18   The marginal propensity to withdraw is the proportion of income not passed on through consumption spending, i.e. $s = 1 - c$.

19    $1/s$

20   (a) savings and tax payments
       (b) investment and government expenditure
       (c) $S = s(1 - t)Y$
       (d) $W = s(1 - t)Y + tY$
       (e) $J = I^* + G^*$
       (f) $Y = \dfrac{I^*}{s(1 - t) + t} + \dfrac{G^*}{s(1 - t) + t}$
       (g) $\dfrac{1}{s(1 - t) + t}$
       (h) $\dfrac{1}{s(1 - t) + t}$

21   (a) $S = s(1 - t) + sQ$
       (b) $W = s(1 - t)Y + sQ + tY$
       (c) $J = I^* + G^* + Q^*$
       (d) $Y = \dfrac{I^*}{s(1 - t) + t} + \dfrac{G^*}{s(1 - t) + t} + \dfrac{cQ^*}{s(1 - t) + t}$
       (e) $\dfrac{c}{s(1 - t) + t}$

22   (a) 2.5   (b) 2

23   5

24   (a) £10m   (b) £8m   (c) £25m

25   rise

26   fall; fall

27   (a) fallen   (b) fallen

28   An injection is an addition to the income of domestic firms that does not arise from the expenditure of domestic households, or an addition to the income of domestic households that does not arise from the spending of domestic firms. Investment is controlled by firms; government spending is controlled by the state.

29   (a) Withdrawal   (e) Injection
       (b) Withdrawal   (f) Neither
       (c) Injection   (g) Neither
       (d) Withdrawal   (h) Injection

30   saving; investment

31   contractionary; expansionary

32   fall

33    $K = \dfrac{1}{1 - c(1 - t)}$

       $= \dfrac{1}{1 - c + ct} = \dfrac{1}{1 - (1 - s) + (1 - s)t}$ by substitution

       $= \dfrac{1}{1 - 1 + s + t - st} = \dfrac{1}{s + t - st} = \dfrac{1}{s(1 - t) + t}$

Answers to Chapters 29-30

34	Households, firms, government and foreign trade
35	Savings, taxes and imports; none
36	Investment, government expenditure and exports; exogenous
37	Aggregate desired expenditure = national income; withdrawals = injections
38	$E = C + I + G + (X - M) = Y$ $W = J$
39	True

40 (a) $X; J$ (e) $I; J$
    (b) $F; W$ (f) $N; W$
    (c) $I; J$ (g) $M; W$
    (d) $C; N$ (h) $G; J$

41 (a) The marginal propensity to import.
    (b) $E = 0.5Y + 230$
    (c) £460m
    (d) $X - M = £4m$
    (e) $\dfrac{1}{1 - c(1 - t) + m}$ or $\dfrac{1}{s(1 - t) + t + m} = 2$
    (f) £20m
    (g) (i) Fall to approx. £383m
        (ii) £26.6m approx.

42	reduces; leakage from
43	rise; less than
44	firms (and government, if nationalized industries export)
45	all three
46	negatively
47	All else being equal

CHAPTER 30

1 medium of exchange, store of value, and unit of account

2 unit of account and standard of deferred payment

3 Paper money may be convertible into gold or another metal; fiat money is not.

4 Yes, cigarettes may serve all three functions, if there is confidence in the cigarette's future exchange value.

5 In order to repay a claim in gold, if it did happen to be demanded.

6 The fact that they would be required to redeem the paper claims on themselves in gold to the value of one-third of their outstanding debt.

7 The fact that the cowrie shell is generally acceptable is sufficient to give it the attributes of money – so the missionary does not understand the nature of money.

8 False

Answers to Chapter 30

9   A fiat currency ('fiat' is Latin for 'let it become').

10 Commercial banks, discount houses and the central bank (i.e. Bank of England).

11 Banker to commercial banks; banker to the government; controller and regulator of the money supply; manager of the public debt; lender of last resort and supporter of money markets.

12 Borrow from the central bank (in Britain the commercial banks would call in their loans to the discount houses which in turn borrow from the central bank).

13 £450

14 (1) 50 cash; 50 deposits
         450 loans; 450 extra deposits
    (2) expand its loans immediately to the maximum.

15
	A		B		C		D		E	
	A	L	A	L	A	L	A	L	A	L
	100	100	90	90	81	81	72.9	72.9	65.61	65.61
cash:	10	100	9	90	8.1	81	7.29	72.9	6.561	65.61
loans:	90		81		72.9		65.61		59.049	

16 (a) (1)   Bank I
               L   A
            + 300   + 300
          (deposit)   (cash)
    (2)   Bank I
               L   A
            + 329.66   + 32.94 cash
           (deposits)   + 296.73 loans
    (3) True

    (b) (1)   Bank I   Banks II-X
               L   A   L   A
            + 300   + 30 cash   + 2,700   + 270 cash
           deposits   + 270 loans   deposits   + 2,430 loans
    (2) True

17 (a) Zero   (b) £50m

18 Reduce it by £2,000.

19 That the public does not wish to hold any of its money in cash.

20 (a) £2,000   (b) £1,148.94   (c) £918.92

21 smaller

22 Near money

23 Near money is an asset which fulfils the store-of-value function but, while transferable, cannot be transformed into a medium of exchange at a moment's notice and thus has not achieved the monetary status of notes and coins. Money substitutes fulfil the medium-of-exchange function but are not themselves money.

Answers to Chapters 30–31

24

	Store of value	Medium of exchange
Building society deposits	√	X
Company securities:		
– ordinary shares	√	X
– debenture & preference shares	√	X
Local authority bonds held by the private sector	√	X
Notes and coins	√	√
New domestic share issues	√	X
Deposits in current accounts at commercial banks	√	√
UK government bonds	√	X
Money held in deposit accounts at commercial banks	√	X

25   (a) £13,440m   (b) £32,339m

26

	Real value of output
1985	4,000
1986	4,200
1987	4,200
1988	4,200
1989	4,200
1990	4,200

The value of output rose by 5% in real terms in 1985–86 but was not rising after that.

27   is not

28   Yes; no

29   kPY

30   Exogenous

31   The average number of times a unit of money turns over in transactions.

32   V is the reciprocal of k

33   (a) £25m   (c) £140m
       (b) Price rises to 1.4   (d) £100m

34   money; the price level; real; the level of income

CHAPTER 31

1   That the size of the money supply is determined by forces outside the model of the economy, i.e. by the central bank.

2   Because that money could have earned interest if it had been held in, say, a deposit account at a bank.

3   Transactions, precautionary and speculative.

4   The level of income.

Answers to Chapter 31

5   transactions and precautionary; rise; precautionary and speculative; rise

6   Wealth held in money form rather than in interest-earning assets.

7   fall

8   buy. If they can buy bonds at one price and subsequently sell them at a higher price, they will make a capital gain.

9   directly; directly; inversely

10   (a) Transactions   (c) None
        (b) Precautionary   (d) Precautionary

11   (a) Raise precautionary   (e) Raise precautionary
        (b) Raise transactions   (f) Lower transactions
        (c) Raise speculative   (g) Raise precautionary
        (d) Raise all

12   False

13     $M_d = L(Y, r, W)$

14   Real demand is measured in purchasing-power units. In order to obtain the nominal demand we have to multiply the real demand by the price level, P.

15   rises by 10%; is unchanged

16   (a) rising   (b) rising

17   (a) £50m   (c) £80m
        (b) £70m   (d) £40m

18   (a) rises; transactions and precautionary; risen
        (b) (iii)

19   (a) Curve shifts to right.
        (b) Curve shifts to left.
        (c) This is already represented by the curve.

20   the demand for bonds is equal to the supply of bonds.

21   (a) $M_d = £40m < M^*/P$
        (b) $M_d = £80m = M^*/P$
        (c) $M_d = £100m > M^*/P$

22   buy; fall; rise; the demand for money is equal to the supply

23   (a) remains the same
        (b) more
        (c) fall; buy; fall

24   (a) rise   (c) rise
        (b) greater than   (d) raising

25   (a) £90m   (b) 8½%   (c) £10m

26   income and interest-rate

27   Set $M_d = M^*/P$ and solve for r.

28     $r = \dfrac{M^*}{P}\dfrac{1}{e} - \dfrac{d}{e}Y = 0.02Y - 4$

Answers to Chapter 31

29 Slope is 0.02 and intercept is −4.

30 (a) Shifts *LM* curve upwards.
    (b) No change – this reflects movement along the *LM* curve.
    (c) The *LM* curve shifts upwards in an anti-clockwise direction.
    (d) Pivots *LM* in clockwise direction, only the slope changing.

31 10%

32 rise to 10.5%; fall to £675m

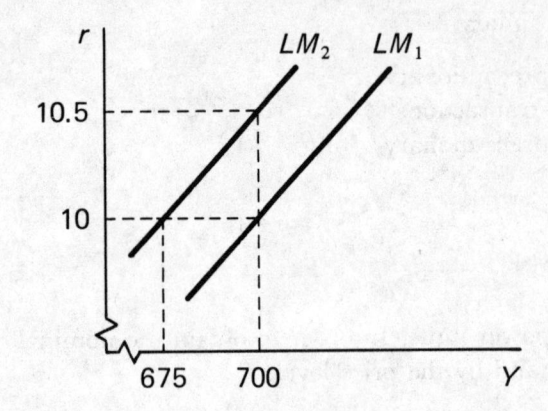

33 rise to 20%; fall to £450m

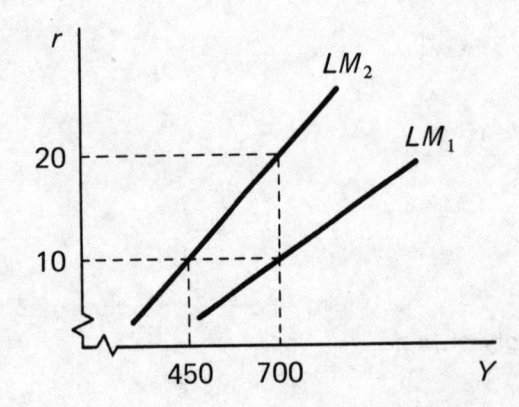

34 8.25%; rise to £800m

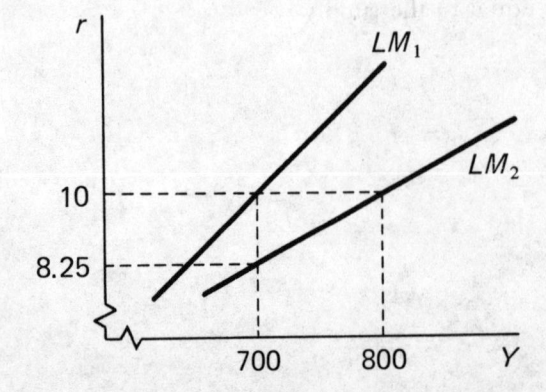

35 (a) greater than; rise
    (b) less than; fall

CHAPTER 32

1. False

2. smaller

3. False

4.
   (a) Increase; raise revenue
   (b) Decrease; raise costs
   (c) Increase; raise revenue
   (d) Decrease; raise costs
   (e) Increase; raise revenue
   (f) Decrease; raise costs
   (g) Decrease; lower revenue

5. False

6. True

7.
   (a) 12%
   (b) K_2
   (c) $K_3 - K_2$
   (d) less than
   (e) By not replacing plant and machinery as it wears out.

8. The capacity of capital-goods producing industry may be unable to meet all orders immediately and subsequent variation in the interest rate may cause firms to revise their orders.

9. Current savings of firms; current savings of households; newly created money.

10. The sale of bonds to the public.

11.
    (a) The lending of money by the public to financial institutions;
    (b) The sale of bonds by firms to financial institutions.

12.
    (a) $E = 184 + 0.8Y - 10r$
    (b) £420m

13. income and interest rates

14.
    (a) Set desired aggregate expenditure equal to national income and solve for r.
    (b) $r = 18.4 - 0.02Y$
    (c) -0.02
    (d) The marginal propensity to save divided by the behavioural parameter b which denotes the change in investment brought about by a 1% change in the rate of interest.

15.
    (a) $C = £360m$, $I = £80m$ and $E = £440m$
    (b) less than
    (c) fall; increase
    (d) 9½%
    (e) £85m

16. As income rises, consumption also increases but by an amount less than the change in income (as the *MPC* is less than one). If aggregate expenditure is to equal the higher level of income, the interest rate must fall so that the other component of expenditure (i.e. investment) rises and raises aggregate expenditure to match income.

Answers to Chapter 32

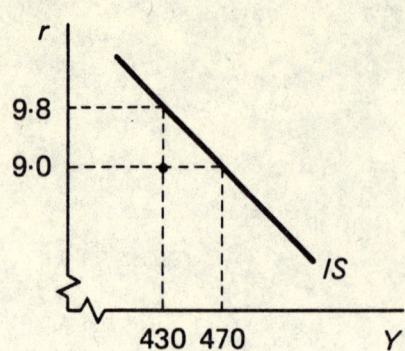

17   (a)   £8m
      (b)   9.8%
      (c)   £470m
      (d)

[Graph: IS curve with r on vertical axis showing 9.0 and 9.8; Y on horizontal axis showing 430 and 470]

18   (a) $0 < a_0$, c and $c < 1$; $b < 0 < a_1$
      (b) $r = \dfrac{(1-c)}{b} Y - \dfrac{A^*}{b}$, where $A^* = a_0 + a_1$
      (c)   Aggregate expenditure function shifts down and *IS* curve shifts inwards.
      (d)   Aggregate expenditure pivots anti-clockwise and *IS* shifts outwards and is flatter.
      (e)   Aggregate expenditure shifts down, *IS* shifts inwards and is steeper.

19   goods; asset

20   (a)   Desired aggregate expenditure = real national income
      (b)   The demand for money = the supply
      (c)   An income level and an interest rate that satisfy the equilibrium conditions for both markets. Put another way, that Y and r at which the *IS* and *LM* schedules intersect.

21   (a) $r = \dfrac{(1-c)}{b} Y - \dfrac{A^*}{b}$
      (b) $r = \dfrac{M^*}{P} \dfrac{1}{e} - \dfrac{d}{e} Y$
      (c) $Y = \dfrac{1}{(1-c) + bd/e} A^* + \dfrac{1}{e(1-c)/b + d} \cdot \dfrac{M^*}{P}$
      If you looked this up in Lipsey, you ought not to have done! You must be sure you can work this out for yourself – what would you do if you didn't have Lipsey handy?
      (d) $\dfrac{1}{(1-c)}$
      (e) $\dfrac{1}{(1-c) + bd/e}$

22   (a)   greater than   (d)   exceed   (f)   curb
      (b)   raises; outwards   (e)   fall; rise   (g)   higher; high
      (c)   rises

23   (a)   upwards
      (b)   greater than
      (c)   sell; raising
      (d)   lower; shift in; fall
      (e)   fall; fall; decreases; transaction
      (f)   higher; lower

Answers to Chapter 32

24   (a) greater than; less than
     (b) It will rise.
     (c) As E is less than Y, unplanned inventory investment is rising; this will lead producers to cut back on output and income will begin to fall.
     (d) fall; rise

25

	Segment number	Y rises/falls	r rises/falls
(a)	1	rises	rises
(b)	4	rises	falls
(c)	2	falls	rises
(d)	3	falls	falls

26   (a) $r = 13.5 - 0.02Y$ (or $Y = 675 - 50r$)
     (b) $r = 0.02Y - 6$ (or $Y = 300 + 50r$)
     (c) £135m
     (d) $Y = £487.5$m and $r = £3.75\%$

27   (a) $1/(1 - c) = 5$
     (b) $1/0.4 = 2.5$
     (c) $Y = £512.5$m and $r = 4.25\%$; $C = £420$m, $I = £92.5$m
     (d) $C = £440$m, $I = £97.5$m and $E = £537.5$m

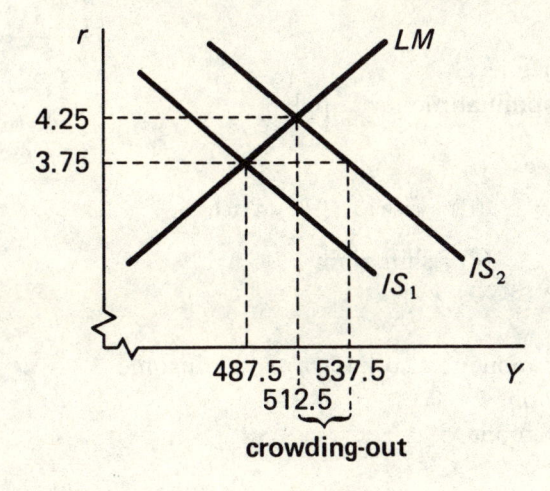

[Graph: IS-LM diagram showing LM curve intersecting IS_1 at $r = 3.75$, $Y = 487.5$ and IS_2 at $r = 4.25$, $Y = 512.5$; $Y = 537.5$ marked on IS_2; "crowding-out" indicated between 512.5 and 537.5]

28   (a) $Y = £525$m and $r = 3\%$
     (b)

[Graph: IS-LM diagram showing LM_1 and LM_2 curves; IS intersects LM_1 at $r = 3.75$, $Y = 487.5$ and LM_2 at $r = 3.0$, $Y = 525$]

29   (a) Shifts IS downwards, lowering income and rate of interest.
     (b) Shifts LM upwards, raising r and lowering Y.
     (c) Shifts IS inwards, lowering Y and r.
     (d) Shifts LM downwards, increasing Y and reducing r.

CHAPTER 33

1. prices

2. endogenous

3. the aggregate price level and national income level; goods; asset

4. (a) rises; lowers
   (b) excess supply of; fall; rise
   (c) shifts up; is unchanged; is unchanged; is unchanged

5. (a) c, the marginal propensity to consume; b and e, measuring the interest responsiveness of investment expenditure and demand for money, respectively; d, measuring the responsiveness of demand for money to changes in the level of national income.
   (b) flatter. A low responsiveness means that for any given change in real (speculative) balances, there will be a larger change in the rate of interest.
   (c) flatter; a fall in the interest rate results in a large increase in investment expenditure
   (d) large fall
   (e) steeper

6. (a) Autonomous expenditure
   (b) Nominal money supply, the price level
   (c) Autonomous expenditure and nominal money supply

7. (b)

8. (a) fall; (b) fall; (c) rise; (d) rise; (e) rise

9. (a) shift right; (b) shift right; (c) shift right

10. P; Y

11. (a) income-elasticity of demand for money, also known as the income responsiveness of demand for money;
    interest-elasticity of demand for money;
    marginal propensity to leak;
    interest-elasticity of investment; and
    the nominal money supply
    (b) d, e, z, b, and M^* (see equation (3) on p. 578 of Lipsey; see also equation A2 on p. 591 of Lipsey)

12. LM; down; higher; lower; shifts to right

13. is unchanged; remains the same

14. fixed

15. AS_0 or AS_1

16. AS_1 or AS_2

17. AS_1

18. Y_F

19. wage rise; productivity increase; change in profit margins; fall in cost of production, e.g. cheaper purchased inputs from abroad.

20. AS_0

Answers to Chapters 33–34

21   AS_1

22   AS_0 is $SRAS$ and AS_1 is $LRAS$; AS_0 is like a Keynesian aggregate supply curve

23   disequilibrium; both

24   (a) P rises little; Y rises a lot; AS is relatively elastic
       (b) P rises a lot; Y rises a little; AS is relatively inelastic

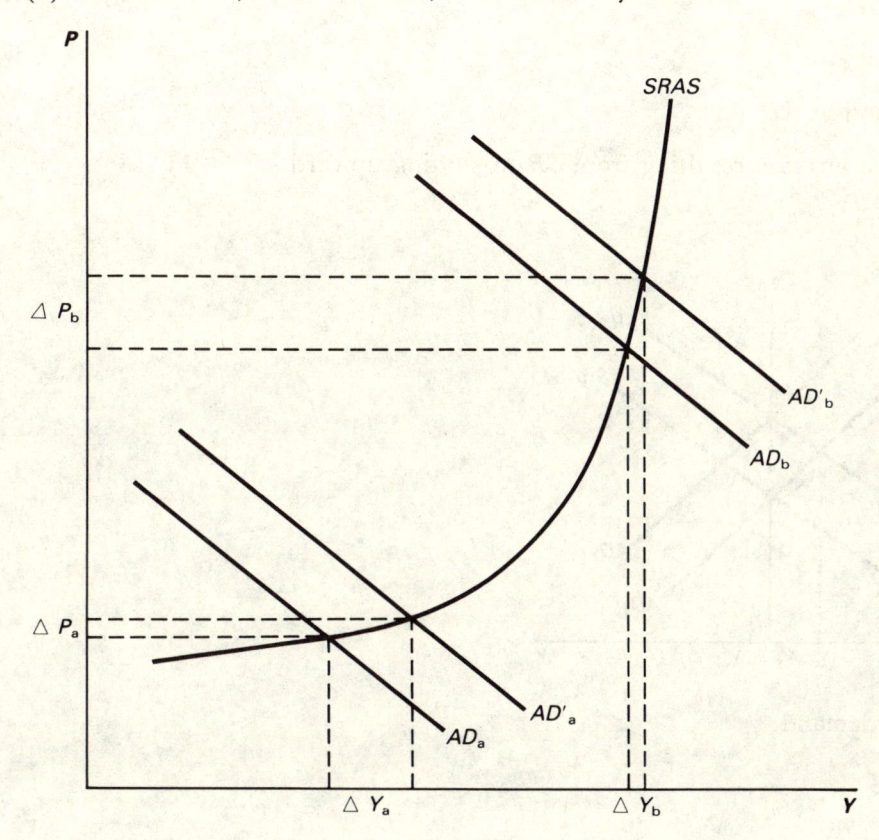

25   rising; falling

26   Yes, e.g. if the $LRAS$ curve were vertical and shifted backward over time (potential output Y_F falling over time, as during war). Otherwise according to our theory stagflation is a short-run phenomenon.

27   lower

28   lower

29   The graph for Question 24 above applies here as well. Note that $\Delta Y = K \cdot \Delta A^*$, where K is the multiplier and A^* is autonomous expenditure and Δ means 'change in'. By looking at ΔY compared with ΔA^* you can estimate the multiplier, since $K = \dfrac{\Delta Y}{\Delta A^*}$. As A^* rises, K gets smaller.

CHAPTER 34

1   (a)   demand effect
      (b)   expectational effect
      (c)   shock effect

Answers to Chapter 34

2. shifts up
3. shifts up
4. up and left
5. *SRAS*: *AD*
6. False
7. *AD*; right; up
8. SRAS and/or *AD*
9. The price increase resulting from *SRAS* shifting upward.
10. price level
11.

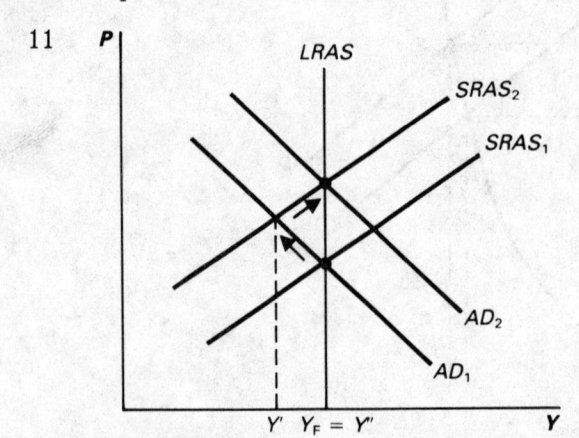

(Diagram showing P on vertical axis and Y on horizontal axis, with LRAS vertical line, SRAS₁ and SRAS₂ curves, AD₁ and AD₂ curves. Points marked Y' and $Y_F = Y''$ on the horizontal axis.)

12. supply; demand
13. changing
14. falls; quickly
15. productivity
16. lower
17. No change in the size of labour force
18. lower
19. (a) backward-looking
    (b) backward-looking
    (c) forward-looking
20. (a) 6%; (b) 4%
22. (a) 3%; (b) 4%
23. (a) yes; (b) probably; (c) cannot say; it depends on what they know about the economy. They might have a correct expectation of a 4% rate of unit-cost increase but have been unexpectedly wrong this year when $Y = Y_3$ because of a random shock.
24. (b), assuming no shock inflation; (d); and (e)
25. A vertical line at Y_F

26

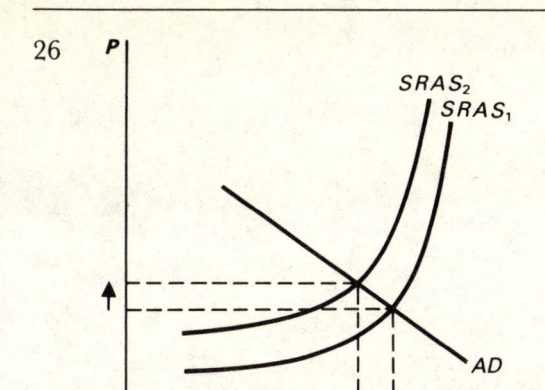

[Graph: P on vertical axis, Y on horizontal axis, showing SRAS₂ shifted left of SRAS₁, and AD curve; arrows indicate price rises and output falls]

27 rising prices and recession

28 (a) full-employment output (also called potential output)
    (b) Y_F

29 (*See graphs on next page*)

30 budget surplus (fall in G or rise in T or both); rise in interest rates, causing a fall in I.

CHAPTER 35

1   Yes – frictional

2   Demand-deficient

3   Structural and real-wage

4   demand-deficient

5   frictional

6   (a) structural
    (b) demand-deficient
    (c) frictional
    (d) structural
    (e) demand-deficient
    These categories are consistent with Lipsey's. Some unemployment within categories, except (c), may be real-wage unemployment.

7   No locational structural unemployment; lower level of frictional unemployment.

8   The observed relationship is that way. It shows a falling ratio $\Delta v : \Delta u$ as u increases. Neither u nor v can go below zero.

9   1,500

10 boom

11 The u-v curve would shift outward.

12 Shift outward since v rises and u rises.

13 rising

14 point c and d

Answers to Chapters 35–36

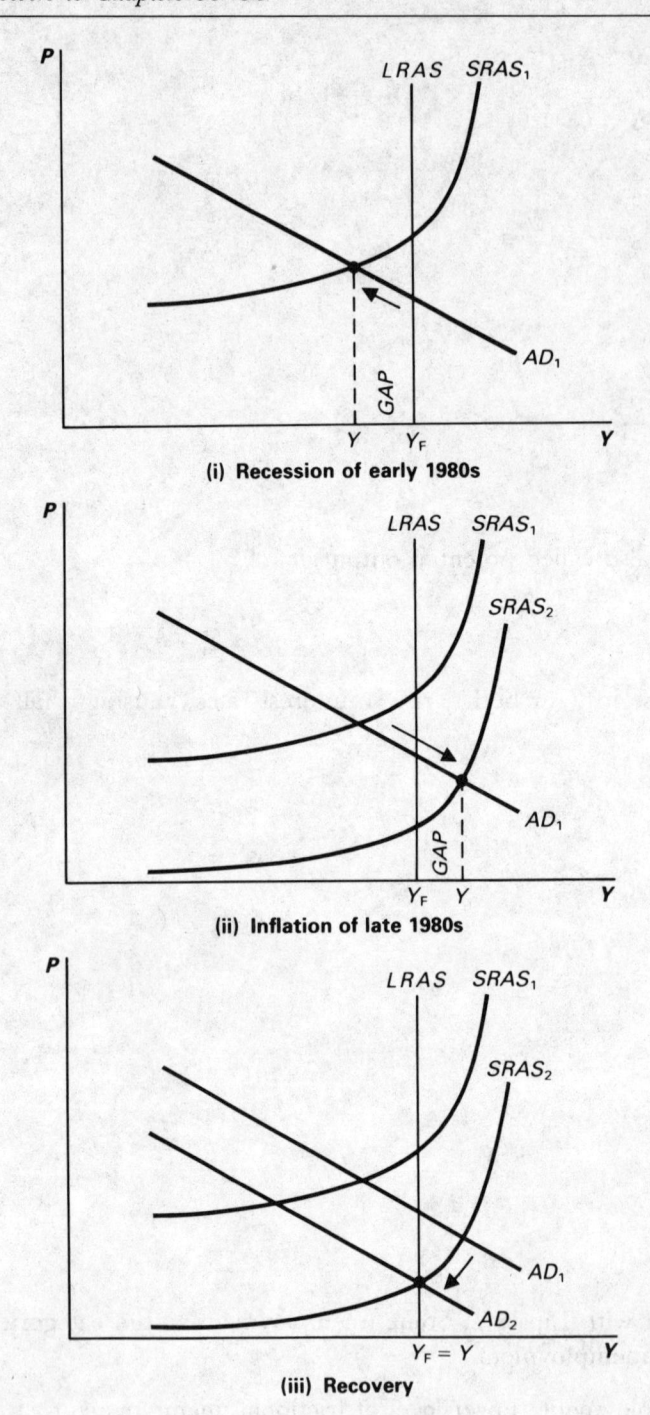

(i) Recession of early 1980s

(ii) Inflation of late 1980s

(iii) Recovery

15 False (see Lipsey, p. 621, where two measures of demand-deficient unemployment is explained).

CHAPTER 36

1 False

2 True

3   True; *IS* curve shifts right

4   True; it could result from temporarily lower imported-input prices.

5   True (in history), although a depression may intervene.

6   $I = I(\Delta y)$

7   Greater. The value of a machine is usually more than its annual production.

8   (a) 1.5   (b) 5 machines

9

Year	Change in sales (£000)	Required stock of capital assuming capital-output ratio of 4/1 (£000)	Net investment (£000)
1	0	60	0
2	5	80	20
3	4	96	16
4	1	100	4
5	1	104	4
6	1	108	4
7	0	108	0
8	−2	100	0

(a) That immediate delivery is possible.
(b) £8,000 of capital stock is idle as it is now surplus to requirements.
(c) False

10 (a) Accelerator   (c) Multiplier
    (b) None   (d) Self-realizing expectations

11 The income produced when there is full employment.

12 Replacement investment.

13 The 'subsistence' level of income, where consumption equals income.

14 the year before last.

Period	C_c	I_r	I_n	Total investment	G	Y	Change in Y
t	300	20	0	20	80	400	0
t + 1	300	20	0	20	90	410	10
t + 2	305	20	12	32	90	427	17
t + 3	313.5	20	20.4	40.4	90	443.9	16.9
t + 4	322	20	20.3	40.3	90	452.3	8.4
t + 5	326.2	20	10.1	30.1	90	446.3	−6
t + 6	323.2	12.8	(−7.2)	12.8	90	426	−20.3
t + 7	313	0	(−24.4)	0	90	403	−23
t + 8	301.5	0	(−27.6)	0	90	391.5	−11.5
t + 9	295.8	6.2	(−13.8)	6.2	90	392	0.5
t + 10	296	20	0.6	20.6	90	406.6	14.6

15 (a) 8%   (b) 100%

16 zero. There would be no point in replacing a machine when there is already more capacity than is needed to meet demand.

Answers to Chapter 36

17 $t + 4$; $t + 5$, $t + 9$; £420m

18 False

19 stock of capital

20 complementary to

21 (b)

22 points on the production-possibility frontier.

23 points inside the frontier.

24 (a) The production-possibility curve will move out along the vegetable axis but the intercept with the clothing axis will remain the same.
    (b) To the extent that the loss of one year's education lowers the quality of human capital and labour productivity, the frontier will move inwards. Offsetting this, however, will be the increase in the labour supply if people choose to leave school as soon as it is legal. If growing vegetables and making clothing requires relatively unskilled labour, it is probable the curve will shift outwards.
    (c) The curve will move out along the clothing axis but the intercept on the vegetable axis will be unchanged. Alternatively if labour must shift from vegetable into clothing production, the new PPC will start at a lower point on the vegetable axis, then cross the old PPC.

25 Point A, as this represents a greater proportion of resources being used for investment good production than does point B.

26 (a) Increases in the availability of resources, (b) changes in the productivity of these resources as a result of changes in technology, increased efficiency in the use of existing resources, changes in the composition of the output of consumption and investment goods.

27 4

28 £40,000m

29 (a) £168,000m   (b) £176,160m

TABLE 3

	Potential income	Capital stock	Investment (= savings)	Equilibrium income
	£m	£m	£m	£m
1975	40,000	160,000	8,000	40,000
1976	42,000	168,000	8,160	40,800
1977	44,040	176,160	8,323.2	41,616
1978	46,120.8	184,483.2	8,489.7	42,448

30 Approx. 5%

31 5

32 C = £32,000m and S = £8,000m

33 No; 2%

34   Aggregate demand is not increasing fast enough to keep up with the increase in productive capacity.

TABLE 4

	Potential income	Capital stock	Investment (= savings)	Equilibrium income
	£m	£m	£m	£m
1975	40,000	160,000	8,000	40,000
1976	42,000	168,000	8,400	42,000
1977	44,100	176,400	8,820	44,100
1978	46,304	185,220	9,261	46,305

35   5%

36   5%

37   (a) £800   (b) approx. £777   (c) approx. £848

38   diminishing

39   labour force

40   shift up

41   (a) capital-output ratio
      (b) average efficiency of capital
      (c) change in (or increase in) the capital stock
      (d) marginal efficiency of capital; rate of return

42   (d)

43   (a) and (c)

CHAPTER 37

1   *IS* and *LM*

2   *AD*

3   *SRAS* and *LRAS*

4   A supply-side argument, because high interest rates can push up the costs of production and of investment and hence affect the aggregate supply curves *SRAS* and *LRAS*.

5   (a) consumption function
     (b) investment function
     (c) net exports (or imports)

6   (a) government spending, including transfer payments
     (b) G, including Q

7   zero; constant
     (a) government spending equals tax revenue
     (b) $G = T$

8   (a) $E = Y$
     (b) Desired aggregate expenditure equals real national income.

Answers to Chapter 37

9 (a) $r = \dfrac{1 - c(1 - t)Y}{b} - \dfrac{(A^* + G^* + cQ^*)}{b}$

   (b) $Y = \dfrac{(A^* + G^* + cQ^*)}{1 - c(1 - t)} + \dfrac{br}{1 - c(1 - t)}$

   (c) $(A^* + G^* + cQ)/b$
   (d) $(A^* + G^* + cQ^*)/[1 - c(1 - t)]$
   (e) $[1 - c(1 - t)]/b$ or $b/[1 - c(1 - t)]$
   (f) $1/[1 - c(1 - t)]$ for A^* and G^*; $c/[1 - c(1 - t)]$ for Q^*

10 (a) £650m   (b) 2.5

11 expenditure on goods and services and/or transfers; taxes

12 (a) Income rises by £25m to £675m.
    (b) Income rises by £20m.
    (c) Income rises by £27.1m.
    (d) unchanged; anti-clockwise; less

13 The more thrifty households are, the lower will be the level of national income and the lower will be employment.

14 (a) The marginal propensity to consume is now 0.7, the IS curve pivots in a clockwise direction and income falls to approx. £536.8m.
    (b) $G + Q = £250$, $T = 0.25(536.8) = £134.2m$. Deficit = £115.8m.
    (c) Increase G by £53.6m. (Did you remember that the value of the multiplier changed?)
    (d) Increased to £141.5m.
    (e) Income would rise to £652.2m. approx. Deficit rises to £165.2m.

15 (a) Because taxes are a function of income.
    (b) injections
    (c) transfer payments
    (d) Raise unemployment
    (e) Raise unemployment

16 Increased

17 No

18 (b) inwards
    (c) fall
    (d) lowers
    (e) purchase; fall
    (f) the demand for bonds is equal to the supply of bonds, and the demand for money is equal to the supply of money.

Answers to Chapter 37

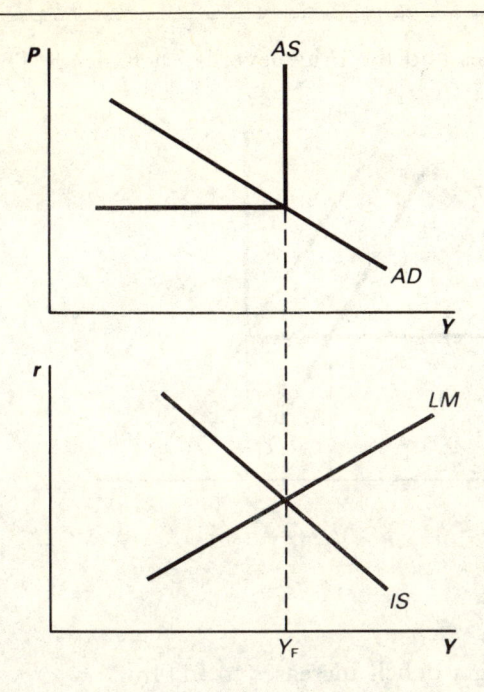

19

20

	Case 1	Case 2	Case 3
crowding-out	no	some	yes
prices rise	some	no*	yes
interest-rate rise	no	yes	yes

* or some, if interest rates enter into production costs.

21   AD shifts to right raising prices, but output and employment would be unchanged. Crowding-out is 100%.

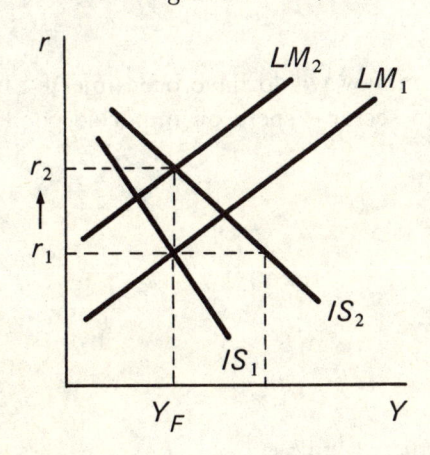

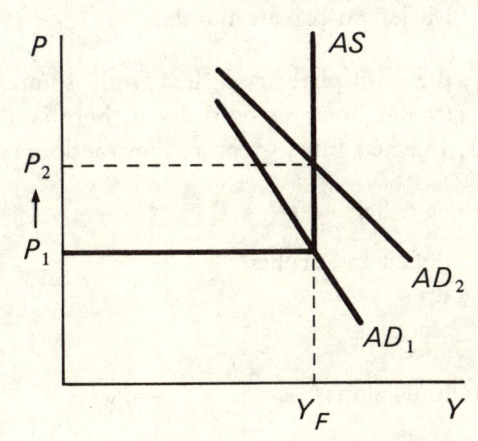

(I hope you did not forget that the higher price level shifts the LM curve upwards – the nominal money supply being unchanged.)

Answers to Chapter 37

22. Income rises to Y_F, the rate of interest rises and the price level is unchanged. There is crowding-out equal to $Y_2 - Y_F$.

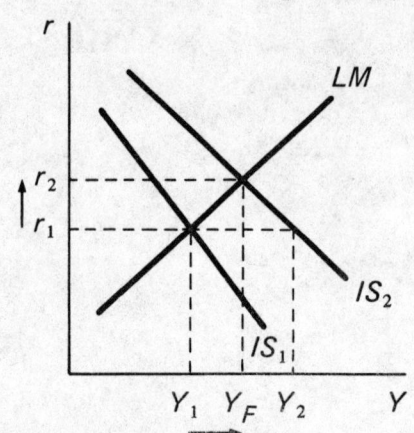

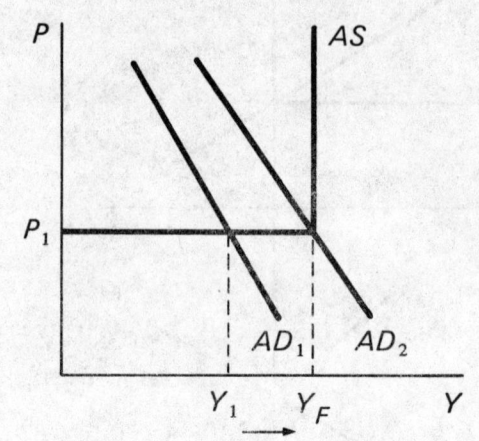

23. (a) $Y = £700m$, $r = 5\%$. Deficit of £75m.
    (b) Y rises by £60m, $r = 6½\%$ and budget deficit increases to £114m.
    (c) £135m. Crowding-out £75m.
    (d) $\dfrac{\Delta Y}{\Delta G} = \dfrac{60}{54} = 1.1$
    (e) Income rises by £48m, $r = 6.2\%$ and deficit is £117m.
    (f) $Y = £768.3m$, $r = 6.7\%$ and deficit is £135m.
    (g) £72.7m. Did you remember to make use of your answer to (d)?
    (h) outwards; right; higher
    (i) smaller
    (j) $Y = £835m$, $r = 5\%$ and crowding-out is zero.
    (See Figures on next page)

24. Income rises by £15.5m, r rises by 0.4% and deficit remains at £75m.

25. The balanced-budget multiplier is 0.29 and is therefore lower than the multiplier when the change in income is brought about by an increase in G with *tax rates constant*.

26. Because the government spends all its income, whereas some of it would have been saved if left in private hands.

27. fall; the multiplier; rise; less; only some of the money would have been injected into the circular flow; saved (or – if there is a foreign sector – spent on imported goods); 100; injected into; greater; contractionary

28. Budget deficit = $G^* + Q^* - tY$
    (a) deficit to surplus
    (b) up
    (c) clockwise

29. change its slope

30. Anything that causes government expenditure to be positively related, and government tax receipts to be negatively related, to national income, without the government's having to make policy decisions to bring about these changes.

Answers to Chapter 37

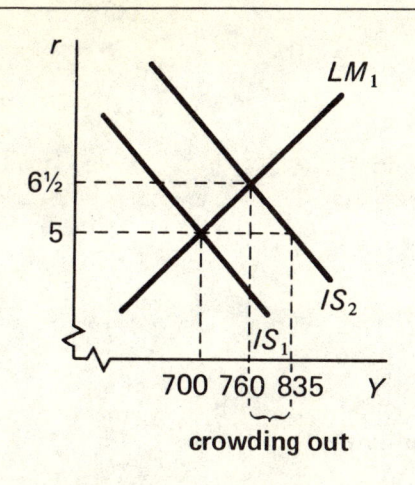

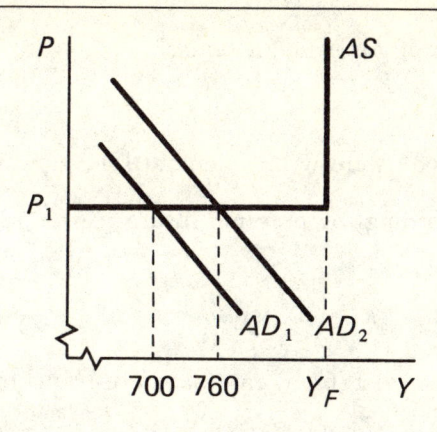

(b) and (c)

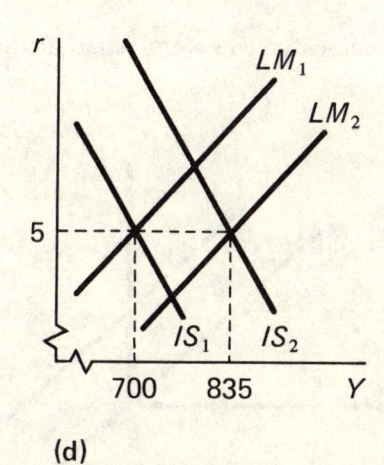

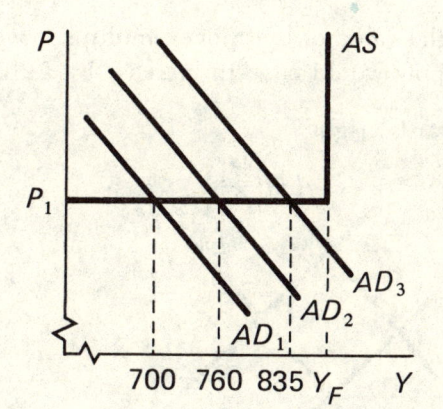

(d)

31	(a) $Y = £1,300$m	(c) 1.1	
	(b) Falls by £55.6m	(d) 2.5	

32 (a) $Y = £1,147$m
    (b) Falls by £49m
    (c) 0.98
    (d) 1.923
    (e) Stabilize, as they reduce the value of the multiplier.

33 (a) $Y = £1,175.7$m
    (b) Falls by £67.7m
    (c) 1.354
    (d) 4.16
    (e) Destabilize, as this increases the value of the multiplier. Only when G is stable will it act as a built-in stabilizer.

34 (a) raise taxes t or T
    (b) sell off assets

35 (a) print money (usually by selling bonds)
    (b) borrow from commercial banks

36 spent or saved; (c)

37 distribution

Answers to Chapters 37–38

38   purchasers of government bonds

39   True

40   False. (If you were wrong, look at Question 36 again.)

41   varies according to; present; future; fewer; zero

CHAPTER 38

1   Income rises to £761m, rate of interest falls to 3.78%.

2     $Y = £639m$, $r = 6.22\%$ (I hope you saw this straightaway!)

3     $\dfrac{\Delta Y}{\Delta M_s}$ is the money multiplier. You know ΔY and ΔM_s from Question 1, so you can now find the value of the money multiplier which enables you to work out that the money supply would have to increase by £43.2m.

4   (a)   outwards; right

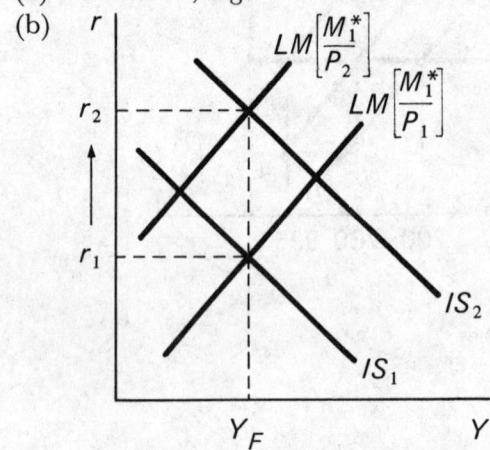

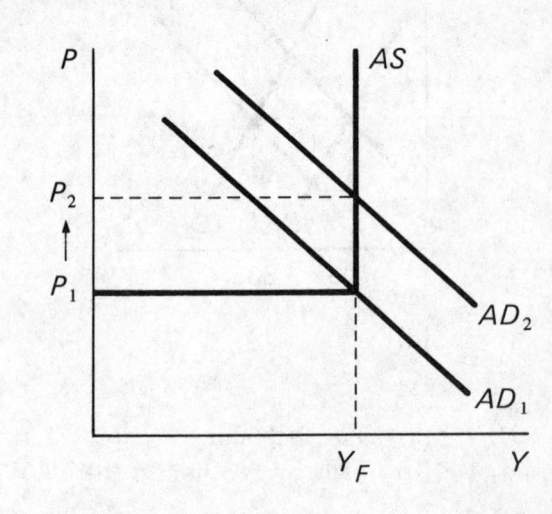

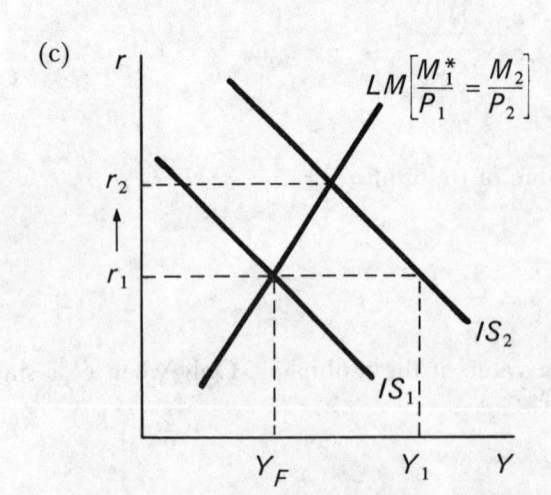

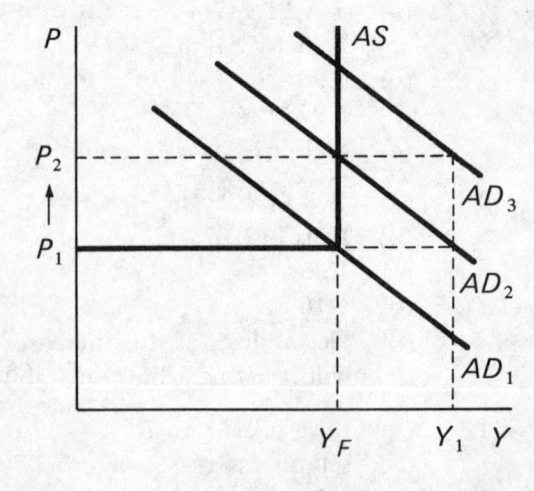

        (b)

        (c)

        (d)   Contractionary fiscal policy, which offsets the injection to the circular flow (from the additional autonomous investment). This would shift the *IS* curve back to its original position. Alternatively, contractionary monetary policy, i.e. lowering the money supply, which would shift the *LM* to the left and would leave the economy at a higher rate of interest than before.

Answers to Chapter 38

5   False

6   Changes in autonomous expenditure and changes in money supply.

7   5%

8   No, they are negative whenever $\dot{P} > i$.

9   (a) i
    (b) r
    (c) r

10 (a) b measures the responsiveness of investment to a one-point change in the rate of interest.
    (b) c is the marginal propensity to consume.
    (c) d measures how the demand for money (for transactions and precautionary balances) responds to a one-point change in the level of income.
    (d) e measures the responsiveness of the demand for money (for speculative balances) to a one-point change in the rate of interest.
    (e) r is the real interest rate $i - \dot{P}$.
    (f) n is the autonomous demand for money (as in the equation $M_d = n + dY + er$).

11 (a) Because there is no autonomous demand for money (unrelated to Y or r) in the example.
    (b) Because the equation, $M_d = 0.3Y - 12r$, is of the form $M = dY + er$, $n = 0$ in equation (2) of Lipsey's Chapter 31.

12 $r = \left(\dfrac{1-z}{b}\right) Y - \dfrac{A}{b}$

    or, in more detail,

    $r = \dfrac{[1 - c(1-t)]Y}{b} - \dfrac{A^* + G^* + cQ^*}{b}$

    (a) b and c. t is an instrumental variable (i.e. a policy tool), not a parameter.
    (b) I rises by £20m
    (c) greater; greater; upward; flatter
    (d) flatter

13 $r = \left(\dfrac{M^*}{P} - n\right)\dfrac{1}{e} + \left(\dfrac{d}{e}\right) Y$

    (a) d and e
    (b) rises by £3m
    (c) steeper
    (d) flatter
    (e) smaller; larger; smaller

14 raises; raises; raise; lower; crowded out

15 zero; 100%; greater

16 (a) (i) + £50m; (ii) + 1.25%; (iii) − £25m; (iv) £62.5m
    (b) Larger, as LM now more interest-elastic.
    (c) $Y = £725m$, $r = 4.5\%$
    (d) (i) + £56.25m; (ii) + 1.126%; (iii) − £22.5m; (iv) £56.25m

Answers to Chapter 38

17   (a) + £24.4m
       (b) Smaller, the *IS* curve is steeper.
       (c) $Y = £777m$, $r = 6.9\%$
       (d) (i) + £42m; (ii) − 1.7%; (iii) + £17.2m

18   (a) leave unchanged; lower
       (b) raise; raise

19   raise; leave unchanged; leave unchanged; raise

20   more; more

21   By open-market operations or by varying the reserve-asset ratio.

22   Treasury bills are instruments for *short-term* borrowing, whereas government bonds are *long-term*, fixed-interest securities.

23   True

24   By selling £1m in bonds to the public.

25   If the public buy bonds with funds not within the money-creating system − e.g. cash, or deposits held in foreign countries − instead of from bank accounts.

26   Only to the extent that credit expansion results in some cash drain to the public.

27   (a) By sale of bills. This will drive down the price of bills with the result that short-term interest rates will rise.
       (b) fall; contract

28   £90

29   (a)

Liabilities £m		Assets £m	
Deposits	125,000	Cash	12,500
		Other	112,500
	125,000		125,000

       (b)

Liabilities £m		Assets £m	
Deposits	100,000	Cash	12,500
		Other	87,500
	100,000		100,000

    Therefore deposits contract by £25,000m.

       (c) £3,125m.

30   Because it is less easy for the Bank to control the quantity of such reserve assets − as compared with cash − since changes in the relative prices of these assets and other assets which are close substitutes (but not included in the reserve base) can enable the commercial banks to purchase appropriate assets and thus adjust their reserves.

31   (a) 5%   (c) By open-market operations.
       (b) 1.5%

32   Changes in the level of income, changes in the parameters *d* and *e*. For example, the demand for transactions balances may vary at different times of the year.

33   (a) r rises by 1.25%   (c) r rises by 1%
       (b) r rises by 2.9%

34 (a) Raise money supply by £15m
    (b) Raise money supply by £35m
    (c) Raise money supply by £10m

35 increasing; decreasing; greater; endogenous

36 They expect the rate of interest to rise.

37 increasing; remaining constant; rise; be unchanged

38 (a) Demand for money equal to money supply; aggregate demand equal to aggregate supply
    (b) prices will rise.
    (c) nominal; increase
    (d) fallen
    (e) greater
    (f) demand for; sell; the rate of interest rises
    (g) check; fall; removed
    (h) equal; be unchanged; is unchanged; persists

CHAPTER 39

1   cannot

2   domestically produced goods

3   many currencies

4   foreign currency

5   33p

6   (i) £0.50 per $1
    (ii) $2 per £1

7   dollars had appreciated; pound had depreciated; price of dollars had gone up

8   goes up

9   (a) depreciated
    (b) appreciated

10 8.65 Pesos/$, 12.5 Pesos/$, depreciated by 44.5%. Since 12.5 ÷ 8.65 = 1.445, the rate rose by 44.5%.

11 depreciated, appreciated

12 more

13 importers, exporters

14 the exchange rate; the price of foreign currency; the quantity of foreign currency

15 rise, depreciation

16 depreciation

17 trade-weighted exchange rate, effective exchange rate

18 as index number series

19 £10,000 ÷ [DM 40,000 ÷ (DM 4/£1)] = 1.0, i.e. 1:1 ratio.

Answers to Chapters 39–40

20   (a) £10,500, DM 42,000
      (b) 1 : 1
      (c) no

21   (a) £11,200
      (b) DM 41,600
      (c) 1.077 : 1
      (d) fall to DM 3.7143 = £1, i.e. a fall of just over 7%
      (e) depreciate

22   that level of the exchange rate which gives both currencies equal purchasing power over traded goods in the two countries.

23   deviate from

24   money

25   payments for traded goods and services; payments for capital goods and investments; and official financing

26   positive

27   (a) a loan from the IMF
      (b) a loan from a foreign central bank
      (c) a fall in the central bank's official reserves of foreign exchange

28   Credits: (b), (d), and (e).
      Debits: (a), (c), and (f)

CHAPTER 40

1   An adjustable-peg, gold exchange standard with countries holding their exchange reserves either in US dollars or pounds sterling.

2   could not

3   By consultations with countries wishing to alter their exchange rates.

4   (c) Making adjustments to long-term trends in the balance of payments.

5   Special Drawing Rights; credits which are an addition to the capacity of the IMF to supply foreign exchange to member countries.

6   reduce employment

7   periodic

8   managed float or dirty float

9   a target level for real national income (and hence related targets for inflation and employment).

10   a target for the current account, or for the trade account.

11   (a) desired spending on domestic goods by domestic residents (i.e. excluding exports and imports)
       (b) $C + I + G$

12   foreign, domestically-produced goods

13   C, I and M. Reducing G also reduces absorption directly.

14

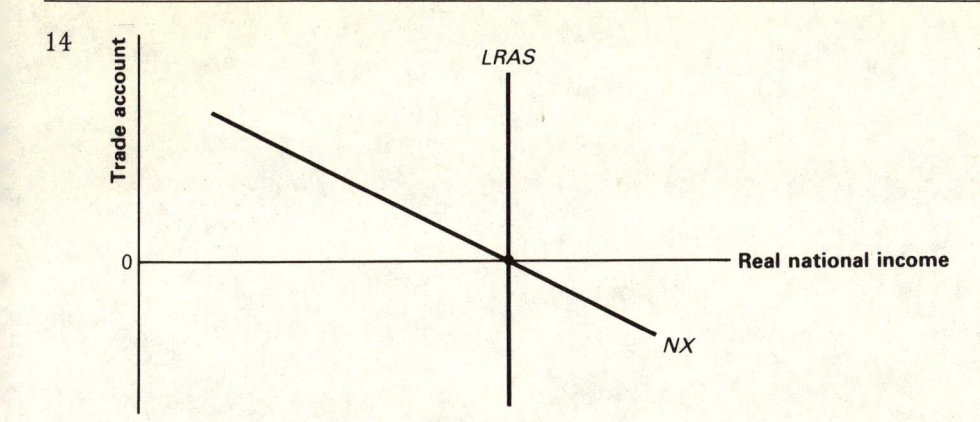

[Figure: Graph with "Trade account" on vertical axis and "Real national income" on horizontal axis. A vertical line labeled LRAS crosses the horizontal axis, and a downward-sloping line labeled NX crosses zero at the LRAS intersection.]

15   (a)   net exports (exports minus imports)
      (b) $X - M$

16   deficit

17   achieving a target for the balance of payments as a whole.

18   (a)   rise
      (b)   in
      (c)   surplus

19   (a)   rise
      (b)   in
      (c)   surplus

20   fall; sterilization; raise; buying

21   the difference between its interest rate and foreign interest rates; and the sensitivity of capital flows to interest rates

22   stabilized, enhanced

23   reduced, because fiscal policy which causes interest rates to rise will cause a capital inflow *and* an appreciation of the currency. This will depress aggregate demand. Imports are cheaper after the appreciation.

24   expenditure-switching

25   *expected* exchange-rate movements